Content and Language Integrated Learning in Spanish and Japanese Contexts

T0393447

Keiko Tsuchiya • María Dolores
Pérez Murillo
Editors

Content and Language Integrated Learning in Spanish and Japanese Contexts

Policy, Practice and Pedagogy

palgrave
macmillan

Editors
Keiko Tsuchiya
International College of Arts & Sciences
Yokohama City University
Yokohama, Kanagawa, Japan

María Dolores Pérez Murillo
Faculty of Education
Complutense University of Madrid
Madrid, Madrid, Spain

ISBN 978-3-030-27445-0   ISBN 978-3-030-27443-6   (eBook)
https://doi.org/10.1007/978-3-030-27443-6

This Palgrave Macmillan imprint is published by the registered company Springer Nature Switzerland AG.
The registered company address is: Gewerbestrasse 11, 6330 Cham, Switzerland

Foreword: CLIL as Transgressive Policy and Practice

Content and Language Integrated Learning (CLIL), while drawing inspiration from earlier bilingual education programmes such as French immersion in Canada, has generally been seen as a European phenomenon. It is a European solution to a range of European practical problems and wider societal issues such as the presumed failings of conventional foreign language teaching and the need for a more multilingual Europe driven by the European Union's integration agenda. More recently, CLIL has been attracting attention beyond Europe, especially in Asian contexts such as Japan, Hong Kong, Taiwan and Malaysia. However, although the label "CLIL" is used, what is actually happening on the ground can enormously vary across contexts. Thus, for example, "CLIL" in Hong Kong is seen as an approach to content and language integration in the teaching of academic subjects, such as science, while, in Japan, as will be seen in this book, it has mainly been seen as a "soft" approach consisting in introducing content in language lessons.

This book is extremely timely in that it examines how CLIL has been and is being conceptualised in two very different contexts—Spain and Japan. In many ways, Spain can be considered as the paradigm European CLIL case, as it is the country that has most enthusiastically adopted this approach to bilingual education. In Spain, it is a national and regional policy issue, as state schools from pre-primary to upper secondary have introduced bilingual streams. As can be seen in some of the Spanish chapters, this has brought its own problems. In Japan, on the other hand, CLIL is in an experimental phase and has not been a large-scale national policy issue. This raises questions, which the book admirably responds to, about the mobility of the "CLIL" concept and the extent to which a European "solution" might address an Asian "problem".

A key over-riding theme of this volume is that of boundary crossings, or of concepts and practices on the move. In the conclusion to the volume, Tsuchiya and Pérez Murillo refer to this as "transgressing" borders. The idea of transgressing is one of going beyond limits, perhaps beyond what is acceptable. In that sense, perhaps, CLIL could be a "dangerous" idea exported from Europe to a non-European context like Japan. What is more, the "transgression" goes beyond national or world regional boundaries. CLIL calls into question other formerly rigidly patrolled borders, such as those between academic disciplines, educational levels (pre-primary, primary, secondary, tertiary), approaches to (English) language in education English as a Foreign Language (EFL), English for Academic Purposes (EAP), English for Specific Purposes (ESP), English Medium Instruction (EMI), languages (lingua francas, translanguaging) and, most importantly, among educators. All of these topics, and the possible associated transgressions, are covered in the volume. As such, it is a unique contribution to the growing literature on CLIL and bilingual education.

The volume is organised around a three-part framework for conceptualising and describing CLIL as a social phenomenon and providing for comparison across sites and settings. The three areas are policy, practice and pedagogy. The editors argue that, while many studies have focused on practices in CLIL classrooms, fewer have explored issues of CLIL policy and pedagogy. Here, pedagogy is seen as referring to the methodological principles underpinning CLIL practice, especially as they are packaged and transmitted to current or prospective CLIL practitioners (i.e., in teacher education programmes). The first section of the book looks at the policy dimension, while the area of practices is divided into two sections (case studies of specific CLIL programmes and studies of interaction in CLIL classrooms). The fourth section focuses on pedagogy and teacher education. Organising the book in this way allows for, as the authors claim, a more holistic view of CLIL as it is enacted in the two very different national, cultural and social contexts.

Overall, the chapters focusing on the Japanese context exhibit a note of caution towards the adoption of CLIL as an educational policy, with a "soft-CLIL" approach mainly favoured at the primary and secondary levels. This would appear to be a wise strategy for a number of reasons. One is the pragmatic reason that if CLIL is rolled out on a large scale, there will simply not be enough teachers with the linguistic and methodological training to cope with the demand. Even in the Spanish context, where a "hard" version of CLIL is quite well established, teacher training has not caught up with the demand (as seen in Custodio Espinar's chapter). A tentative approach is also advisable in order to avoid the possible downsides of overenthusiastic and rapid implementation. This could lead to a political backlash, as has occurred in some sectors of public opinion in Spain. What has happened in Spain is that some parents and sections of the media have used anecdotal evidence and unfounded assertions to cast doubt on the bilingual education programmes. For example, they accuse these programmes of not covering the curriculum adequately and in sufficient depth, and often call into question the language skills (in English) of the teachers.

Public and media criticism of bilingual education in Spain is more well founded when it focuses on issues related to poor implementation and organisation, such as rushing to add new bilingual programmes without the guarantee of a supply of adequately trained teachers. The criticisms do not damage CLIL's inherent credentials as a powerful approach to improving education, as it is rightly identified by Tsuchiya and Pérez Murillo in the book's conclusion. However, when it is poorly or haphazardly implemented, it unnecessarily exposes the approach itself to often unjustified criticism, which can then hinder bilingual education from making its important contribution to improving education in general. In this sense, it is probably right that the take-up of CLIL in Japan should be cautious and tentative and wait until a "soft-CLIL" approach is firmly established before considering taking further steps towards a "hard CLIL" or more genuinely bilingual approach.

The two chapters in Part I on CLIL and language policy provide a rich historical overview of how the introduction of CLIL has been seen as a policy response to a perceived need to improve the foreign language proficiency of citizens in the two contexts. The chapter by Daniel Madrid,

Jóse Luis Ortega-Martín and Stephen P. Hughes highlights how CLIL appears to be a natural progression from the communicative and task-based approaches to foreign language teaching which have driven policy initiatives in Spain in the last two decades. It paints a picture of an enthusiastic roll-out of this bilingual approach and a favourable overall reception, however with some darker spots relating to issues like teacher preparation and the need to ensure that content learning is not negatively affected. The second chapter in this section, by Keiko Tsuchiya, reviews the history of language education in Japan, from successive reforms in which English became the dominant foreign language, through the introduction of CLIL first in universities and then in primary and secondary education. By highlighting such issues as translanguaging and English as a Lingua Franca, the chapter suggests ways forward in which CLIL practitioners in Japan may avoid some of the problems that have bedevilled CLIL implementation elsewhere.

If one problem in transgressing boundaries is that the "import" may not be that well understood, it is important to come down from the abstract level and to provide concrete evidence of what CLIL looks like in practice, in both contexts. This is ably done in Part II, in the chapters by Fleta, Yamano, del Pozo, Yamazaki, and Uemura, Gilmour and Costa. The chapters from the Japanese context provide rich examples of the "soft-CLIL" approach at primary, secondary and tertiary levels. Although this means that CLIL is "confined" to language lessons, the approach is still quite transgressive as it calls into question many well-established methodological precepts about language teaching in Japan. Even soft CLIL is a highly communicative approach to language teaching and is a radical departure from a strongly forms-focused (grammar and vocabulary) pedagogy. In the Spanish context, del Pozo's chapter is a clear example of a "hard CLIL" setting where the emphasis is on teaching history through the second language (L2), not teaching the L2 through history. Although Fleta's chapter focuses clearly on supporting very young learners' language learning, it does so in a "hard CLIL" context, the bilingual education system in Spain where children will have to cope with learning content in English from grade 1 primary.

Within CLIL practices, the three chapters that focus on classroom interaction provide fine-grained analyses of how CLIL "gets done" at primary, secondary and tertiary levels in both contexts. Again, we can see transgressions of borders, this time disciplinary ones, as a range of theoretical and methodological frameworks are drawn on to explicate knowledge construction and performance of identities in CLIL classrooms. Both Pastrana's and Evnitskaya's chapters (as well as Chap. 6 by del Pozo) draw on Dalton-Puffer's (2013) construct of Cognitive Discourse Functions (CDFs). CDFs form a bridge between the kinds of cognitive operations often identified as learning outcomes (e.g., classify, define, explore, explain) and their verbal representations. Pastrana's chapter combines CDFs with systemic functional linguistics and sociocultural theory and uses a corpus-based methodology to show how primary CLIL students engage in discourse and construct knowledge in group work. Evnitskaya focuses on the CDF of "classify" and uses a multimodal conversation analysis methodology to analyse how a secondary science teacher in Spain guides the students in establishing taxonomies and categories relevant to empirical phenomena observed in science lessons.

Tsuchiya's chapter shifts the focus to the tertiary level in Japan, and it draws on the theoretical perspectives of translanguaging and English as a Lingua Franca (ELF). Her analysis shows how Japanese- and Arabic-speaking students create a translanguaging space in a university classroom by using the linguistic resources of Japanese and ELF to perform a range of interactional functions and to present themselves as bi/multilingual speakers. These three studies illustrate how a transdisciplinary perspective is necessary if researchers are to do justice to the concept of "integration" in CLIL. That is, we need to go beyond the use of parallel frameworks from general education and second language acquisition but to integrate the different models in an interdisciplinary or even transdisciplinary way.

The third component of the book's conceptual framework is that of pedagogy. Pedagogy here is taken to be how the knowledge and practices of CLIL are packaged and transmitted to prospective teachers. Again, the notion of transgressing appears, as CLIL is seen in Custodio Espinar's chapter as a "paradigm shift" in education. However, as she argues, this transgression has not been fully reflected in the content of CLIL teacher education courses in Spain, even though there is more formal provision than in Japan. The key idea is that CLIL raises issues in education that go beyond a simple focus on methodology. This is argued by Sasajima, whose chapter provides an account of how teacher development for CLIL teachers in Japan has been promoted through ground-up initiatives culminating in a national teachers' association. The chapter clearly shows that it is not just a question of applying an imported methodology, which has already "transgressed" borders. CLIL requires a pedagogy which can adapt to local conditions and constraints, and in the Japanese context, it appears that a "soft-CLIL" approach is the best fit.

The context of Pérez Murillo's chapter is the European Union's drive for a plurilingual citizenry and the internationalisation of the European Higher Education area in line with the Bologna process and its effects on pre-service teacher education for primary CLIL in Spain. Strangely, as a result of the implementation of the Bologna process, the curricular space for pre-service primary teacher education for bilingual programmes has been reduced. The chapter describes an innovation project for the pre-service education of primary teachers in bilingual programmes in a large state university in Madrid. The project focuses on interdisciplinarity in response to the increasing provision of CLIL in schools and the growth in English-taught modules and programmes in universities. As seen throughout the volume, CLIL calls for a transgressing of boundaries in which language and other content specialists in universities need to work with teachers in schools, also across subject boundaries. The project described in Pérez Murillo's chapter very clearly shows how an interdisciplinary perspective needs to be an essential component of pre-service teacher education for CLIL/bilingual education programmes.

The chapter by Tsuchiya and Pérez Murillo compares how pre-service teachers in Spain and Japan perceive EMI/CLIL. Drawing on the theoretical framework of transnational and translingual social transformations, they show how prospective teachers in the two settings differently perceive the benefits of CLIL/EMI and position themselves in relation to imagined local and transnational communities. Again, we see how CLIL can transmute as it travels across contexts. The Spanish students appear to be more open to translingual transformation in the sociocultural domain, perhaps due to the experience of bilingual education at primary and secondary school levels, and the presence of international (Erasmus) students in their university classrooms. For the Japanese students, EMI/CLIL is more linked to the economic policy domain as a means to equip the workforce with language skills to boost the country's economic prospects. The foreign language, English, is much less likely to be seen as relevant in the students' local imagined communities. This may be because English is not so present in schools (there are relatively few CLIL/bilingual programmes) and there are fewer international students in Japanese universities.

Together, the chapters in this collection highlight tensions which need to be resolved if CLIL is going to be successfully able to move across national, regional, global, social and cultural frontiers. Perhaps the most important tension is that between top-down imposition as a (supra)national policy and small-scale ground-up experimentation. As several chapters, especially in the Spanish contexts, point out, CLIL has been identified by the European Union as a promising instrument in furthering its goals for societal multilingualism and individual plurilingualism. The Spanish state and regional governments have been very sensitive to this policy and have mandated large-scale state-funded implementation. This has generally been of the "hard CLIL" variety, as (usually) English is adopted as a medium of instruction for up to 40% of the curriculum. In Japan, CLIL seems to be more of a bottom-up affair and has been left to practitioners at the local level to find their own ways to implement it.

There is real tension here, as given the lack of agreement of what CLIL is, even in contexts where it is more well established, there is a need for small-scale tinkering and risk-free experimentation. However, there is also growing impatience for clear models or even a "theory" of CLIL, which will facilitate its wider implementation as a policy solution. As the chapters in the Japanese context show, there is a sharp awareness that CLIL is indeed a European import and that it needs adaptation to the rather different social, political, linguistic and education conditions. As Baetens Beardsmore noted in 1993, "Comparisons between different models reveal how different paths can lead to high levels of proficiency, that such proficiency is tempered by contextual variables more so than by programme variables, and that the former plays a considerable role in determining ultimate achievement" (p. 117). This means, as Baetens Beardsmore also points out, that there needs to be a very careful and realistic appraisal of what any bilingual programme can be expected to achieve. The danger is that if CLIL is seized upon by policy-makers at national or supranational levels, it may lead to unrealistic expectations about what can be achieved. If these expectations are not met, this may lead to a backlash, which will ultimately damage aspirations for a more multilingual society and the creation of more opportunities for more citizens. This important book serves both as a rich and detailed introduction to what has already been achieved in CLIL in both contexts and as a warning of the possible pitfalls of taking (or not taking) certain routes towards wider implementation.

Autonomous University of Madrid, Spain   Tom Morton

Reference

Baetens Beardsmore, H. (1993). European models of bilingual education: Practice, theory and development. *Journal of Multilingual & Multicultural Development, 14*(1–2), 103–120.

Acknowledgements

This volume is the fruit of several collaborative CLIL research projects which we first started in 2012 (JSPS Grant-in-Aid for Young Scientists B No. 26870599; Support from the University Complutense of Madrid: PIMCD 2014/166; PIMCD 2015/124; Innova Docencia No. 10 [2016–2017], Innova Docencia No. 13 [2017–2018], Innova Docencia No. 32 [2018–2019]). Since then, our colleagues and friends both in Spain and in Japan have helped us in many ways. We are deeply indebted to Tom Morton and Ana Llinares, who always inspire us through their work and our conversations with them. Tom kindly wrote the Foreword for this volume and gave valuable feedback on every single chapter in a detailed manner, without which we could not have got this volume into shape for publication. Ana also provided the Afterword and her continuous encouragement from the beginning of this book project. Our thanks to Do Coyle, Rachel Whittaker and Linda Taylor, without whom we would not have met each other. We would like to thank our colleagues in the Education Department at the University Complutense of Madrid (UCM) and the members of the innovation projects at UCM for their kind contribution and warm support for our research project. We have also benefited greatly from the discussions with our colleagues in the Japan CLIL Pedagogy Association (J-CLIL). We are grateful to Cathy Scott, Beth Farrow, Alice Green and Mahalakshmi Mariappan of Palgrave Macmillan for their great support and patience through the process of publishing and to the reviewers for their insightful comments. Acknowledgements are also made to the following publishers and institutions for their generous permission for the reproduction and adaptation of copyright material: Chap. 5 is based on the published article, Yamano (2013): "Utilizing the CLIL Approach in a Japanese Primary School: A Comparative Study of CLIL and EFL Lessons" in *Asian EFL Journal, 15*(4), 70–92. The lessons reported in Chap. 7 were conducted as a part of the project, *Learning for Paving the Way to the Future* (in Japanese, 未来を拓く「学び」プロジェクト), led by Saitama Prefectural Board of Education and the Consortium for Renovating Education of the Future (CoREF) at the University of Tokyo in collaboration with Google Education. The teaching materials in Chap. 8 were extracted from two textbooks: Anthony Hoysted and Luis Fernando Costa (2015) *Advanced Technical Communication* (Yamaguchi University) and Takashi Uemura (2014–2015) *Technical Communication (Basic): Workplace English for Global Engineers Book I* (Yamaguchi University). Chapter 11 is based on the published article, Tsuchiya (2017): Co-constructing a Translanguaging Space: Analysing a Japanese/ELF Group Discussion in a CLIL Classroom at University. *Translation and Translanguaging in Multilingual Contexts, 3*(2), 229–253, which was published by John Benjamins Publishing Company, Amsterdam/Philadelphia (https://benjamins.com/catalog/ttmc). We would like to thank Mami Kosemura, a Japanese artist, for her work on the book cover, which chimes with the theme of our volume.

Contents

Part IV   CLIL Pedagogy and Teacher Education   285

12   Teacher Development: J-CLIL   287
Shigeru Sasajima

13   CLIL Teacher Education in Spain   313
Magdalena Custodio Espinar

**14   The Internationalization of Spanish Higher Education:
An Interdisciplinary Approach to Initial Teacher
Education for CLIL**   339
María Dolores Pérez Murillo

**15   Prospective Teachers' Perceptions of CLIL in Spain and
Japan: Translingual Social Formation through EMI-CLIL
Lectures**   373
Keiko Tsuchiya and María Dolores Pérez Murillo

16   Conclusion: CLIL—Reflection and Transmission   403
Keiko Tsuchiya and María Dolores Pérez Murillo

**Afterword: CLIL in Spain and Japan: Synergies, Specificities
and New Horizons**   409

Index   415

Notes on Contributors

Luis Fernando Costa is an associate professor in the Faculty of Engineering at Yamaguchi University. He studied Computer Science and Engineering at Instituto Superior Técnico in Portugal. Costa worked in industrial and research positions in Portugal and Norway, where he contributed to national and international projects. These projects covered the areas of natural language processing, semantic web and cloud computing. His research is documented in over 30 publications, and he presented his work in about 20 conferences and invited lectures. Costa has been teaching English Technical Communication and promoting international academic collaborations at Yamaguchi University since 2013. He created the textbook that has been used in the Advanced Technical Communication classes.

Magdalena Custodio Espinar is an English teacher. She graduated with honours in Education from Complutense University in Madrid, Spain, and holds two master's degree in Management and Leadership of Schools from Universidad Internacional de la Rioja (UNIR) and Teaching Spanish as a Second Language from Universidad Camilo Jose Cela (UCJC). She also holds a PhD in Education in the area of teacher training for bilingual education from Complutense University. She was Technical Advisory Teacher for the Consejeria de Educacion in Madrid and has been collaborating as a consultant and author with Pearson since 2010. After 20 years teaching English as a foreign language (EFL) and Content and Language Integrated Learning (CLIL) in Primary, she is a lecturer and researcher at Universidad Pontificia Comillas. Her research interests include teacher training, didactic programming, CLIL, Foreign Language Teaching (FLT), English Language Teaching (ELT) and Information and Communication Technologies (ICT).

Elena del Pozo is a History and Geography teacher in a secondary school in Madrid. She has degrees in English Language, Geography and History (Universidad Complutense de Madrid) and holds a master's degree in International Education (Endicott College, Massachusetts). She is a PhD researcher at the Universidad Autónoma de Madrid. Her interests include research on bilingual programmes evaluation and CLIL teaching. She writes articles and does teacher training based on her teaching experience and co-operates with some publishers engaged in bilingual education.

Natalia Evnitskaya is a lecturer at the Institute for Multilingualism at the Universitat Internacional de Catalunya, Spain, where she is actively involved in EFL teacher education at the undergraduate and postgraduate levels. She holds MA and PhD in Language Teaching from the Universitat Autónoma de Barcelona (Spain). Her main research interests are CLIL (Content and Language Integrated Learning), classroom interaction, multimodality, EFL/CLIL teacher education, conversation analysis and systemic functional linguistics. She is studying small group interaction and the development of students' academic language in the L2 and L1 in CLIL primary and secondary classrooms.

María Teresa Fleta Guillén has experience in ELT as a teacher, teacher trainer and researcher. She holds an MA in Linguistics from Westminster University and a PhD in English Philology in the area of Child Language Acquisition from the Complutense University of Madrid. She has been a master's professor at the University of Alcalá de Henares and at the International University of La Rioja. She is Honorary Collaborator at the School of Education of Complutense University of Madrid. She has published extensively in the field of teaching English to young learners and child second language acquisition of English. Her main research areas are early years language education, teaching English to young learners, illustrated children's literature and picturebooks, classroom-based research, discourse analysis and teacher education development.

Graeme J. Gilmour is an associate professor in the Faculty of Engineering at Yamaguchi University. He holds a BA Hons and an MEd (Applied Linguistics). He has taught English at a variety of levels in Japan from in-house language training for corporate clients to undergraduate students at university level. During his time with Yamaguchi University, he has developed and published an English language textbook *Technical Communication II: Authentic Written & Spoken Communication Skills* specifically designed for undergraduate Engineering students.

Stephen Pearse Hughes is a full-time lecturer at the University of Granada, Spain, specialising in Foreign Language Teacher Education and postgraduate training in Content and Language Integrated Learning (CLIL). In addition to this teaching role, Hughes has been involved in research into quality indicators in language teaching and learning, bilingual education and in good practices in CLIL. This research has included participation in initiatives such as the ECML QualiTraining Project as well as national R&D, Ministry of Education and British Council projects in the teaching of content areas through the medium of another language.

Daniel Madrid Fernández is a full-time professor of TEFL at the Faculty of Education of the University of Granada, giving pre-service and in-service EFL methodology courses for Primary and Secondary teachers. He has also given a large number of courses and seminars on TEFL. He has promoted and coordinated several student exchange programmes with European universities and has published a considerable number of articles, chapters and books on TEFL and CLIL. He has also produced a wide variety of teaching materials for primary, secondary education and university students, and has directed and carried out several research projects on a variety of topics.

José Luis Ortega-Martín is an associate professor at the University of Granada. His experience includes his role as principal in a secondary school, Director of University Teacher Training at the Vice-chancellor's Office of Quality at the University of Granada and Director of the Masters on Teaching of Spanish as a Foreign Language. At present, Ortega- Martín is a lecturer and researcher at the Faculty of Education at the University of Granada, belongs to the working group for foreign language teaching and learning of the Spanish Ministry of Education and coordinates a national research on bilingual education sponsored by the Spanish Ministry of Education and the British Council.

Amanda Pastrana has been an EFL and CLIL teacher at a private Bilingual school (Liceo Europeo) and Teacher Educator at a subsidized school (Colegio Estudiantes las Tablas), Madrid, for more than 10 years and is working as a Spanish Immersion teacher in Minnesota (USA). She has a PhD degree in Applied Linguistics from the Universidad Autónoma of Madrid, which she obtained in 2017, and holds an MA in Applied Linguistics in Pedagogy from the Universidad Autónoma de Madrid. She has been involved in research activities and projects in the areas of CLIL, second language learning and classroom interaction in the Autónoma University of Madrid (UAM)-CLIL research group led by Dr Ana Llinares Garcia and Dr Rachel Whittaker in the Department of Applied Linguistics at the Autónoma University of Madrid (UAM).

María Dolores Pérez Murillo is an associate professor at the School of Education, Complutense University in Madrid (Spain), where she is involved in undergraduate and postgraduate courses of training for prospective teachers. She holds an MA in Applied Linguistics and a PhD in Linguistics in the area of Bilingual Education from Lancaster University, UK. She has been a visiting scholar at the School of Education, University of Wales, Aberystwyth, and at the Institute of Educational Research and Service, at ICU (Tokyo), since April 1, 2011. Her research interests include the Spanish Diaspora in European and Asian contexts, bi/multilingual classroom interaction, bi/multilingual teacher development and Content and Language Integrated Learning (CLIL).

Shigeru Sasajima is Professor of ELT and teacher education at Toyo Eiwa University and a president of Japan CLIL Pedagogy Association (J-CLIL), which has started as a leading organization of CLIL in Japan since 2017. He holds a PhD from the University of Stirling in Scotland. He has worked as an English teacher, a teacher educator and a teacher researcher for some 40 years. He is interested in CLIL, English for Specific Purposes (ESP), The Common European Framework of Reference for Languages (CEFR), Intercultural Communicative Competence (ICC), learner autonomy, language teacher cognition and qualitative teacher research. He has so far published several books, articles and textbooks about CLIL, such as *CLIL-New Classroom Ideas and CLIL Human Biology.*

Keiko Tsuchiya is an associate professor at the International College of Arts and Sciences, Yokohama City University (Japan), where she teaches graduate/undergraduate modules of English Philology, Linguistics and English Language Teaching, and supervises postgraduate students. She received an MA in English Language Teaching from Nottingham Trent University (UK) and a PhD in Applied Linguistics from Nottingham University (UK). Her research involves CLIL, multimodal corpus analysis, health care communication, and ELF (English as a Lingua Franca) in institutional and academic settings.

Takashi Uemura is an associate professor in the Faculty of Engineering at Yamaguchi University in Japan. Prior to his English teaching career, he worked as an auditor at an international audit firm and also in the finance and banking field for approximately ten years. He is the author of *Technical Communication Basic: Workplace English for Global Engineers*, with which he teaches business English to engineering students using a CLIL approach. His research interests include CLIL and neuroscience in English Language Teaching (neuroELT), an emergent interdisciplinary field in applied linguistics. He holds an MA in TESL/TEFL from the University of Birmingham, UK.

Yuki Yamano is an associate professor in the Faculty of Education at Utsunomiya University (Japan), where she teaches CLIL in graduate/

undergraduate courses of English Language Teaching. She received an MA in Teaching English to Speakers of Other Languages (TESOL) from the Graduate School of Languages and Linguistics, Sophia University. She is a proactive researcher whose main areas of interest are providing multi-sensory foreign language learning with rich authentic contents to match the cognitive development of learners, facilitating cooperative learning as well as intercultural communication in order to realise inclusive education in English language classroom in Japan with the use of CLIL.

Masaru Yamazaki is an experienced English teacher who teaches in Wako Kokusai High School in Saitama, Japan. He has been actively involved in in-service teacher education programmes of Saitama Prefectural Board of Education for more than seven years. His interest includes CLIL and collaborative learning in secondary education. He is a co-author of a textbook, *CLIL Global Issues* (2014).

List of Figures

List of Tables

1

Introduction: CLIL in Spain and Japan

Keiko Tsuchiya and María Dolores Pérez Murillo

1 CLIL as a Social Phenomenon

Globalisation affects every aspect of our lives (Vertovec, 2009), and education is one of the social structures which have been in the process of transformation to meet the demand of the globalised and multilingual society. Maher (2017) defines multilingualism as "language crossing the boundaries of nations, continents, and cultures" (p. 1), and as Duff (2015) describes, "multilingualism and transnationalism are intimately tied to globalization, which affects policies related to citizenship, education, language assessment, and many other areas of 21st-century applied linguistics and society" (p. 61). To realise the multilingual policy in the

K. Tsuchiya (✉)
International College of Arts and Sciences, Yokohama City University, Yokohama, Japan
e-mail: ktsuchiy@yokohama-cu.ac.jp

M. D. Pérez Murillo
School of Education, Complutense University of Madrid, Madrid, Spain
e-mail: perezmur@edu.ucm.es

1
K. Tsuchiya, M. D. Pérez Murillo (eds.), *Content and Language Integrated Learning in Spanish and Japanese Contexts*, https://doi.org/10.1007/978-3-030-27443-6_1

European Union, Content and Language Integrated Learning (CLIL) has been widely implemented in the education system in Europe since the mid-1990s. CLIL with English as the target language has now been introduced in non-European countries in Asia and Latin America (Morton, 2016), and Japan is no exception (Ikeda, 2013). Thus, CLIL has caused ripples in the education system beyond European countries.

On the basis of the concept of *reproduction* in Bourdieu and Passeron (1977), Martin-Jones (2015) characterises bi/multilingual education as "education-based processes of social and cultural (re)production", which involves "uses of multilinguistic and semiotic resources", "different social actors" and "language-in-education practice and policies" (p. 446) (also see Canagarajah, 1999 and Lin, 2001). CLIL is one such practice. To capture the current state of CLIL, this book aims to explore practices in CLIL at two sites: Spain and Japan. We chose these two countries since Spain is "rapidly becoming one of the European leaders in CLIL practice and research" (Coyle, 2010, p. viii), and in Japan, CLIL has been gaining momentum now (e.g. the foundation of the Japan CLIL Pedagogy Association in 2017, see Chap. 12 in this volume).

2   CLIL and CLIL Research

CLIL is "an umbrella term" (Coyle, 2007, p. 545), which refers to "any dual-focussed educational context in which an additional language, thus not usually the first foreign language of the learners involved, is used as a medium in the teaching and learning of non-language content'" (Marsh, 2002, p. 15). Furthermore, in CLIL pedagogy, *the 4Cs framework* (content, communication, cognition and culture), as coined by Coyle (1999), has a major role to play. As she puts it, "it is through progression in the knowledge, skills and understanding of the content, by engagement in associated cognitive processing, interaction in the communicative context, and a deepening awareness and positioning of cultural self and otherness, that learning takes place" (p. 53). Another key concept in the CLIL approach is the language triptych: language *of* learning (language learners need to understand concepts in the subject), language *for* learning (language learners use to process learning) and language *through* learning (language learners capture in the process of learning) (Coyle, Hood, & Marsh, 2010).

The emergence of CLIL has invoked significant discussions on similarities and differences with other closely related approaches, such as content-based instruction and immersion (Lasagabaster & Sierra, 2009; Lyster & Ballinger, 2011), as is also seen in the debate on the definition of CLIL between Cenoz, Genesee, and Gorter (2014) and Dalton-Puffer, Llinares, Lorenzo, and Nikula (2014) in the journal, *Applied Linguistics*. We are also aware of the terminological argument around English medium instruction (EMI) and CLIL, especially in tertiary education (Brown & Bradford, 2017; Smit & Dafouz, 2012). It is not our intention to take part in the debate, but what is meant by CLIL in this book should be explained. We basically adapt the definition of Coyle (2007) and Marsh (2002), but we narrow down the context of CLIL practices discussed in this book to formal education at both sites from primary to tertiary levels, including CLIL practices in subject classes, particularly in Spanish contexts, and in language courses in Japanese contexts.

Dalton-Puffer and Smit (2013, p. 545) identified three areas of CLIL research: *political issues, classroom discourse* and *classroom pedagogy* (p. 545) (see also the introductory chapter of Nikula, Dalton-Puffer, Llinares, & Lorenzo, 2016). For the second category, classroom discourse, Nikula, Dalton-Puffer, and Llinares (2013, p. 74) visualised three focus areas in CLIL classroom discourse research: (1) "CLIL classroom discourse and language use", (2) "CLIL classroom discourse and knowledge construction in the L2" and (3) "CLIL classroom discourse and language learning" (p. 74). Applying the approaches of systemic functional linguistics (Halliday, 2004) and conversation and discourse analysis (Sacks, Schegloff, & Jefferson, 1974; Sinclair & Coulthard, 1975), a good body of research has been conducted to investigate students' and teachers' language and their interaction in CLIL classrooms (Dalton-Puffer, 2007; Llinares & Morton, 2017; Llinares, Morton, & Whittaker, 2012; Nikula et al., 2013). However, the other two areas, political issues and pedagogy of CLIL, do not seem to be fully explored yet. To fill this gap, this book attempts to capture a holistic view of CLIL, describing the policy (who are the stakeholders and the agency of CLIL?), practice (what is happening in CLIL classrooms?) and pedagogy of CLIL (how has CLIL been disseminated to practitioners and prospective teachers?) at the respective sites and comparing them to gain a better understanding of CLIL as a social phenomenon.

3 Preview of the Chapters

This volume is divided into four main parts: Part I provides an overview of language education policies in Japan and Spain. The second part describes practices in CLIL classrooms at all educational levels. The third part looks at CLIL classroom interaction from primary to tertiary levels. Finally, Part IV discusses CLIL pedagogical considerations and the role of teacher education in a CLIL approach.

Part I, *Language Policy*, includes two chapters which represent CLIL and language policy in Spain and Japan. Chapter 2 by Daniel Madrid, José Luis Ortega-Martín and Stephen P. Hughes provides a concise overview of the history of the language policies and methodologies for language teaching and learning in the Spanish education system, describing the introduction of CLIL in the 1990s and its outcomes. Chapter 3 by Keiko Tsuchiya reviews the history of foreign language education and related policies in Japan since the Meiji era. The chapter also describes the current education system with the recent change in the guidelines (*the Course of Study*) for foreign language education in secondary schools, depicting the status of CLIL in formal education.

Part II, *Practices in CLIL Classrooms*, consists of five chapters which address practices in CLIL classrooms at the two sites through a collection of case studies at different educational levels from each context. Chapter 4, by Teresa Fleta, reports the key components (i.e., lessons, teaching staff and evaluations) for primary bilingual education identified through CLIL practices in the Madrid region. In Chap. 5, Yuki Yamano presents a comparative study between CLIL and non-CLIL practices in a primary school in Utsunomiya, focusing on pupils' classroom interaction and experiential learning. Elena del Pozo's chapter (Chap. 6) offers a detailed description of the CLIL project for learning history in a secondary bilingual school in Madrid, applying Dalton-Puffer's cognitive discourse functions (CDFs) for conceptualising content and language (Dalton-Puffer, 2013). Chapter 7 is a case study of CLIL in Japanese secondary education, in which Masaru Yamazaki describes a CLIL lesson plan and practice at the Wako Kokusai High School in Saitama prefecture, where a Japanese version of *collaborative learning* is integrated with the CLIL approach (Miyake, CoREF, & Kawai-juku, 2016). The last chapter of Part II (Chap. 8) by Takashi Uemura, Graeme Gilmour and Luis Costa reports a CLIL project for engineering students, which is situated in Yamaguchi University in Japan.

Part III, *Interactions in CLIL Classrooms*, focuses on interactions in CLIL classrooms as another aspect of CLIL practice. Amanda Pastrana in Chap. 9 investigates speech functions students produce for the co-construction of knowledge in a primary CLIL classroom, adapting Halliday's systemic functional linguistics and Dalton-Puffer's CDF. In Chap. 10, Natalia Evnitskaya examines multimodal interactions between a teacher and students for comparison in secondary science CLIL classrooms. Chapter 11 by Keiko Tsuchiya explores students' use of *translanguaging* (García & Li Wei, 2014) in a CLIL classroom at a Japanese University. Part IV concerns issues in CLIL pedagogy and teacher education. Shigeru Sasajima (Chap. 12) reviews the current teacher education programme in Japan and offers a framework for CLIL teacher development, referring to activities of the *Japan CLIL Pedagogy Association* which he founded. Magdalena Custodio Espinar in Chap. 13 provides a detailed diagnosis of pre-service and in-service teacher training for CLIL in Spain, highlighting Spanish CLIL teachers' needs for CLIL teacher training. Chapter 14 by María D. Pérez Murillo reports on a collaborative teacher education project across academic disciplines, suggesting an interdisciplinary approach to initial teacher education for CLIL in the Primary Education degree. The last chapter (Chap. 15), co-authored by Keiko Tsuchiya and María D. Pérez Murillo, describes a three-year research project at universities at the two sites, Madrid, Spain, and Kanagawa, Japan, which investigates students' and teachers' perceptions of CLIL and social transformation through CLIL.

We hope that this book is accessible and beneficial not only for CLIL practitioners and researchers in Spain and Japan but also for those who are doing CLIL or are interested in CLIL in European and non-European contexts. This volume covers a range of CLIL-related topics, from CLIL and language policies and CLIL practices in different levels, to CLIL pedagogy and teacher education in both settings, which enables readers to see different rationales and realisations of CLIL, helping them (re) consider and reflect on their own CLIL practices from multidimensional perspectives.

References

Bourdieu, P., & Passeron, J. C. (1977). *Reproduction in Education, Society and Culture*. London: Sage.

Brown, H., & Bradford, A. (2017). EMI, CLIL, & CBI: Differing approaches and goals. *JALT2016—Transformation in Language Education: Postconference Publication, 2016*, 328–334.

Canagarajah, S. A. (1999). *Resisting Linguistic Imperialism in English Teaching*. Oxford: Oxford University Press.

Cenoz, J., Genesee, F., & Gorter, D. (2014). Critical analysis of CLIL: Taking stock and looking forward. *Applied Linguistics, 35*(3), 243–262.

Coyle, D. (1999). Supporting students in content and language integrated learning contexts: planning for effective classrooms. In J. Masih (Ed.), *Learning through a Foreign Language: Models, Methods and Outcomes* (pp. 53–69). London: CILT Publications.

Coyle, D. (2007). Content and language integrated learning: Towards a connected research agenda for CLIL pedagogies. *International Journal of Bilingual Education and Bilingualism, 10*(5), 543–562.

Coyle, D. (2010). Foreword. In D. Lasagabaster & Y. R. de Zarobe (Eds.), *CLIL in Spain: Implementation, Results and Teacher Training* (pp. vii–viii). Cambridge: Cambridge Scholars Publishing.

Coyle, D., Hood, P., & Marsh, D. (2010). *Content and Language Integrated Learning*. Cambridge: Cambridge University Press.

Dalton-Puffer, C. (2007). *Discourse in Content and Language Integrated Learning (CLIL) Classrooms*. Amsterdam: John Benjamins Publishing Company.

Dalton-Puffer, C. (2013). A construct of cognitive discourse functions for conceptualising content-language integration in CLIL and multilingual education. *European Journal of Applied Linguistics, 1*(2), 216–253.

Dalton-Puffer, C., Llinares, A., Lorenzo, F., & Nikula, T. (2014). "You can stand under my umbrella": Immersion, CLIL and bilingual education. A response to Cenoz, Genesee & Gorter (2013). *Applied Linguistics, 35*(2), 213–218.

Dalton-Puffer, C., & Smit, U. (2013). Content and language integrated learning: A research agenda. *Language Teaching, 46*(4), 545–559.

Duff, P. A. (2015). Transnationalism, multilingualism, and identity. *Annual Review of Applied Linguistics, 35*, 57–80.

García, O., & Li Wei (2014). *Translanguaging*. London: Palgrave Macmillan.

Halliday, M. A. K. (2004). *An Introduction to Functional Grammar* (3rd ed.). London: Arnold.

Ikeda, M. (2013). Does CLIL work for Japanese secondary school students?: Potential for the 'weak' version of CLIL. *International CLIL Research Journal, 2*(1), 31–43.

Lasagabaster, D., & Sierra, J. M. (2009). Immersion and CLIL in English: More differences than similarities. *ELT Journal, 64*(4), 367–375.

Lin, A. M. Y. (2001). Doing-English-lessons in the reproduction or transformation of social worlds? In C. N. Candlin & N. Mercer (Eds.), *English Language Teaching in its Social Context* (pp. 271–286). London: Routledge.

Llinares, A., & Morton, T. (2017). *Applied Linguistics Perspectives on CLIL*. Amsterdam: John Benjamins Publications.

Llinares, A., Morton, T., & Whittaker, R. (2012). *The Role of Language in CLIL*. Cambridge: Cambridge University Press.

Lyster, R., & Ballinger, S. (2011). Content-based language teaching: Convergent concerns across divergent contexts. *Language Teaching Research, 15*(3), 279–288.

Maher, J. C. (2017). *Multilingualism: A Very Short Introduction*. Oxford: Oxford University Press.

Marsh, D. (2002). *CLIL/EMILE-The European Dimension: Actions, Trends and Foresight Potential*. Brussels: European Commission.

Martin-Jones, M. (2015). Multilingual classroom discourse as a window on wider social, political and ideological processes. In N. Markee (Ed.), *The Handbook of Classroom Discourse and Interaction* (pp. 446–460). Chichester: Wiley Blackwell.

Miyake, N., CoREF, & Kawai-juku (Eds.). (2016). *Collaborative Learning— Active Learning Lessons to Deepen the Understanding through Dialogues [in Japanese, 協調学習とは—対話を通して理解を深めるアクティブラーニング型授業]*. Kyoto: Kitaoji Shobo [北大路書房].

Morton, T. (2016). Content and language integrated learning. In G. Hall (Ed.), *The Routledge Handbook of English Language Teaching* (pp. 252–264). London: Routledge.

Nikula, T., Dalton-Puffer, C., & Llinares, A. (2013). CLIL classroom discourse: Research from Europe. *Journal of Immersion and Content-Based Language Education, 1*(1), 70–100.

Nikula, T., Dalton-Puffer, C., Llinares, A., & Lorenzo, F. (2016). More than content and language: The complexity of integration in CLIL and bilingual education. In T. Nikula, E. Dafouz, P. Moore, & U. Smit (Eds.), *Conceptualising Integration in CLIL and Multilingual Education* (pp. 1–28). Bristol: Multilingual Matters.

Sacks, H., Schegloff, E. A., & Jefferson, G. (1974). A simplest systematics for the organization of turn-taking for conversation. *Language, 50*(4), 696–735.

Sinclair, J. M., & Coulthard, M. (1975). *Towards an Analysis of Discourse: The English Used by Teachers and Pupils*. Oxford: Oxford University Press.

Smit, U., & Dafouz, E. (2012). Integrating content and language in higher education: An introduction to English-medium policies, conceptual issues and research practices across Europe. *AILA Review, 25*, 1–12.

Vertovec, S. (2009). *Transnationalism*. London: Routledge.

Part I

CLIL and Language Policy

2

CLIL and Language Education in Spain

Daniel Madrid Fernández, José Luis Ortega-Martín, and Stephen Pearse Hughes

1 Language Education Policy and CLIL

Before the introduction of formalised legislation which included language training, language learning was essentially reserved for the elite and generally took place among the nobles and people of great social influence and high economic status. It was not until the end of the nineteenth century that Spanish educational laws began to include the teaching of foreign languages as a curricular subject in the public school curricula.

The first regulation that established the obligatory nature of languages in the school curriculum was *the Law of Public Instruction* promoted by Claudio Moyano in 1857, when he was the Minister of Development. This law established that general studies in education were to include the study of living languages from the age of 10 to 11.

In the twentieth century, the 1926 education *Royal Decree* divided secondary education in two periods, *elementary baccalaureate*, with three

D. Madrid Fernández (✉) • J. L. Ortega-Martín • S. P. Hughes
Faculty of Education, University of Granada, Granada, Spain
e-mail: dmadrid@ugr.es; ortegam@ugr.es

© The Author(s) 2019
K. Tsuchiya, M. D. Pérez Murillo (eds.), *Content and Language Integrated Learning in Spanish and Japanese Contexts*, https://doi.org/10.1007/978-3-030-27443-6_2

grades (age 12–14), and *upper baccalaureate*, including two academic years (age 15–16); the latter was divided into two itineraries: sciences and arts. In the three years of the elementary baccalaureate, French was studied, and in the two years of the upper stage, the students could choose between English, German or Italian.

Thanks to the reforms of 1926, important innovations in the development of language teaching in Spain were incorporated and some schools and institutes of languages were created (Morales, 2009). A few years later, the 1938 *Reform Act of Secondary Education* continued to include the teaching of foreign languages for three hours per week, throughout the seven years of the baccalaureate.

With the arrival of *the Spanish Second Republic* (1931–1936), education in Spain improved considerably, and so did the teaching of foreign languages, due to the fact that two languages were studied: French during the first four years of secondary education and a second language (English or German) in the last two (out of a total of seven grades). Regarding the teaching methodology, there were also notable advances: more practical objectives were established, cultural aspects were included, the direct method was given a certain emphasis and audio devices, such as the use of the gramophone, were recommended for the learning of oral language (Fernández Fraile, 1996; Morales, 2009). Nevertheless, the study of literary texts, translation, written expression and the grammar were still predominant.

Later, the law of 1945 for primary education did not include the study of foreign languages in the compulsory education school curriculum. Legislation did, however, provide training for foreign learners as well as for Spanish migrant students in Spanish schools abroad. With the legislative reforms carried out in 1965, schooling was divided into eight grades, from ages five to six up to 13–14 years old. In the eighth grade (ages 13–14), the introduction of the foreign language was established to provide students with the knowledge and habits that allowed them to speak, understand, read and write the language. Yet it was in the secondary education stage (from ages 11 to 16) where the foreign language was studied in a systematic way and where specialised language teachers became the norm (Madrid, 2017).

1.1 The Consolidation of Modern Languages in the Spanish Education System

During the 1960s, modern languages experienced an extraordinary boom in Spain, which was associated with rapid economic growth, especially with tourism, and new scientific and technological advances. Europe was moving towards its unification and expansion, and in this process, it was considered that the study and promotion of European languages was fundamental. In 1954, the member states of the Council of Europe signed the *European Cultural Convention* by which the signatory countries committed themselves to the promotion of foreign languages in order to enhance better understanding among Europeans and to consolidate European unity.

The national curriculum in the 1960s established that the objective of teaching a foreign language was to develop the student's oral and written communication, although this legislation recommended that the teaching method should be active and that oral expression was to be developed in conversations and dialogues and with the help of recordings; in practice, however, the didactic techniques of the grammar-translation method prevailed (Fernández Fraile, 1996). In fact, in external examinations, students were asked to translate a text from a second language (L2) to their first language (L1) without the use of the dictionary.

In order to reinforce the training of language teachers, the Ministry of Education and Science created the English departments at the Spanish universities in the 1960s, and the 1967 study plan was designed at primary school teacher training colleges (Madrid, 2000). At that time, school pre-service teachers could study French or English throughout their training period, but the vast majority would normally choose English, given that at the end of the 1960s, the interest and demand for the English language had far surpassed that of French, which had predominated in the previous years.

1.2   From the Audiolingual Method to the Communicative Approach

With the *General Education Law*, passed in 1970, the teaching of foreign languages was strongly influenced by audiolingual methodology (Brooks, 1966; Rivers, 1964) and behaviourism (Skinner, 1957). This influence was clearly reflected in the pedagogical orientations offered by the Spanish Ministry of Education (*New Orientations for the Basic and General Education*) published in 1970. According to these official guidelines, the learning of the foreign language was to reinforce the general objectives of education and those specific to the language area. The introduction of the L2 started during the second stage of basic education, in grade six (age 12). This legislation recommended the acquisition of a foreign language as a communication tool, which could also favour familiarity with other cultures and help encourage future commercial, technical and cultural exchanges with other countries.

1.3   The Early Teaching and Learning of Foreign Languages

One of the most important innovations in foreign language teaching in Spain during the 1970s was the early introduction of L2 training in the first years of schooling (Madrid, 1980). At the time, legislation took into account the extraordinary plasticity of children's brains (Lenneberg, 1967); their excellent imitation capacity and adaptability; their ease to distinguish, imitate and articulate sounds and to acquire a good level of phonological control (Oyama, 1976); as well as their spontaneity and lack of inhibitions. For all these reasons, the *General Law of Education*, for the first time in the Spanish education history, recommended the need to start the study of foreign languages at an earlier age and provided several methodological considerations to be taken into account in those cases where schools decided to start from grade three, at the age of eight. Since then, the early teaching of foreign languages has been developed in almost all schools, and at present, most early learning educational institutions begin with the teaching of English from infant education (ages three to five) (Cortina-Pérez & Andújar, 2018).

1.4 The Integration of Contents and the Foreign Language

In the 1980s, the Spanish Ministry of Education published the reformed programmes of basic education in which the influence of the notional and functional curriculum (Wilkins, 1976) and communicative language teaching methodology was decisive (Brumfit & Johnson, 1979; Johnson & Morrow, 1981; Widdowson, 1972, 1978). The structural paradigm employed previously was highly criticised and replaced by the principles of speech act theory (Searle, 1969) and the pragmatics paradigm (Leech, 1983) in foreign language teaching (van Ek & Alexander, 1975). It is in this decade when the integration of curricular contents and the foreign language emerged, denominated in origin *content-based instruction* (CBI) (Brinton, Snow, & Wesche, 1989; Snow & Brinton, 1997). This approach introduced the use of an L2 as a medium of instruction for imparting certain school curricular subjects, although it was not until the early twenty-first century that mass adoption of Content and Language Integrated Learning (CLIL) would take place (see Ortega-Martín & Trujillo, 2018). In those schools where CLIL has been adopted, generally two or three curricular subjects are taught in an L2 (normally English) at all educational levels, from early childhood education to university.

1.5 Examples of the Integration of Contents and the L2 in Spanish Textbooks

In the 1980s, a number of English textbooks published in Spain included activities that integrated the study of content and the L2. For example, McLaren and Madrid, in their English textbook *Let's Write*, published by Miñón (Valladolid) in 1983 for grade seven students of primary education (age 13), introduced a teaching unit on *Our Nature* and the different types of lands: farms, the wood, mountainous areas and the desert.

Another lesson dealt with the *Water Cycle*, where children studied the formation of clouds from sea water and how rain and snow are produced. In *Use Your English*, for grade eight (age 14), they studied *Oil-Petroleum*: its formation from the decomposition of animals and plants buried below ground, its extraction in oil wells, refineries, distribution and use as fuel. Another example included a teaching unit on *Pollution*: contamination caused by factories, aerosols and motorised transport vehicles. The presentation of these contents was accompanied by linguistic activities whereby students studied and revised certain grammatical, lexical, phonetic and pragmatic aspects of the English language. At university level, Madrid, Muros, Pérez and Cordovilla also published *Education Through English, Physical Education Through English* and *Music Through English* for the Spanish Faculties of Education students (Cordovilla, Madrid, Muros, & Pérez, 1999; Madrid, Pérez, Muros, & Cordovilla, 1998; Muros, Pérez, Madrid, & Cordovilla, 1998).

1.6   Implementation and Development of CLIL in Spain

Despite the advances of bilingual instruction in other international contexts, the *General Organic Law of the Educational System (LOGSE)* passed in 1990 did not mention this modality of learning. Thanks to the focus on the communicative approach, however, teachers frequently introduced topics and contents in class which favoured authentic communication, and an important emphasis was placed not only on grammatical aspects of texts but also on content. In this sense, classes were message oriented and activities often included authentic language, relevant topics and problem-solving tasks, all of which are aspects which were to later form an integral part of CLIL training.

In addition to the influence of *communicative language teaching* in the development of CLIL, other approaches that shared several characteristics also contributed to its consolidation (Madrid & García-Sánchez, 2001). These approaches included language for specific purposes (Strevens, 1977), cognitive academic language learning approach (CALLA) (Chamot & O'Malley, 1994) and the task-based approach

(Estaire & Zanón, 1994; Willis, 1996). In spite of the impetus of all these developments, it was necessary to wait until the first years of the twenty-first century for CLIL programmes to be regulated and implemented in the Spanish autonomous communities (Ortega-Martín & Trujillo, 2018).

In the case of Andalusia, one of the pioneering regions in the creation of bilingual schools, the implementation of CLIL programmes started with the *Plan for the Promotion of Multilingualism*, approved in March 2005 by the Office of Education of the Andalusian Local Authorities (CEJA, 2005). Subsequent publications have provided useful information for the functioning and management of bilingual schools in the Spanish autonomous communities. These publiations include the informative guide for bilingual schools (CEJA, 2011), where valuable information is provided on bilingual schools, bilingual coordination, the roles of language and non-language teachers, language assistants, students and families, materials and resources, and certain European projects of interest for the stakeholders professional development.

In the last two decades, Spain has made efforts to address its historic deficit in the teaching and learning of foreign languages by assuming a leading position in the European context in relation to the implementation of CLIL programmes (Ruiz de Zarobe & Lasagabaster, 2010), as acknowledged by Coyle (2010, p. viii):

> Spain is rapidly becoming one of the European leaders in CLIL practice and research. The richness of its cultural and linguistic diversity has led to a wide variety of CLIL policies and practices which provide us with many examples of CLIL in different stages of development that are applicable to contexts both within and beyond Spain. (Coyle, 2010, p. viii)

In this sense, Pérez-Cañado (2011, 2012) has recognised the value of Spain as a language education laboratory and as a country where the many possibilities offered by CLIL can be appreciated: "Spain could well serve as a model for the multiple possibilities offered by the broader CLIL spectrum and thus for other countries seeking to implement it" (2011, p. 327).

Subsequent laws, such as *the Organic Law for Quality Improvement of Education* (LOMCE), published in 2013, also support plurilingualism and, indeed, contemplate the establishment of CLIL programmes in autonomous communities. As Pérez-Cañado (2012) has pointed out, then, bolstered by the previous political and social factors, CLIL has had an exponential uptake in Spain and across Europe over the past two decades, and it seems to be for the foreseeable future the most popular approach for the teaching and learning of foreign languages.

2   CLIL in School Curricula

In Spain, early childhood education starts at the age of zero and finishes by age five and is divided into two stages. At age six, children attend primary education for six years. This stage is divided into three "cycles" of two years each; this is followed by compulsory secondary education (CSE) for another four years, and after that, there are two years of pre-university preparation (*Bachillerato*). Alternatively, students can opt for further education (vocational training) or enter the job market at 16 years of age. Nevertheless, it is not an easy task to consider the implementation of CLIL across all of Spain, since there is no single unifying legislative document for the whole country, but instead, different laws, orders and instructions that should be followed in each of the 17 different autonomous governments. Additionally, the design of the current regulations is, in some cases, far removed from the everyday realities present in certain of schools.

Thus, we can speak of resources that are, on occasion, not available or are insufficient, or we may theorise in excess, and we often lack recommendations of a practical, organisational or methodological nature. In this section, then, we will consider the four essential pillars in the implementation of bilingual education in schools: the management of the schools, the coordination of the programmes, the teaching staff and the students involved.

2.1   Importance of School Management

Ortega-Martín, Hughes, and Madrid (2018) carried out an exhaustive study reviewing the schools' operations in Spain in terms of quality, scrutinising the factors that can more decisively influence the implementation of bilingual teaching in this country: management, coordination, teachers and students. In the first case, the school management is considered to be the essential element for the proper development of bilingual plans because it is the knowledge that the leadership team has of the said programme, the elements included, the difficulties entailed and the additional efforts involved for the teaching staff, students and families that will determine the success of the development of the bilingual education curriculum.

Indeed, the leadership exercised by the management team (first pillar) often translates into a constant and positive supervision of the teaching and learning processes; this is reflected in the systematic support for the task carried out by the team members, who ensure the correct use and availability of the materials and maintain a fluid and constant relationship with the educational administration. Leadership involvement also ensures compliance with published regulations and instructions, as well as the correct provision of material and human resources. The educational administrations, in turn, oversee adequate training of the management teams and facilitate information in terms of managerial and methodological practices.

The role of the bilingual coordinator (second pillar) involves having not only the necessary theoretical and legislative knowledge but also methodological experience that enables them to provide solutions for those diverse and potentially problematic situations which may arise at the school. It is expected that those with the responsibility for the coordination of bilingual programmes will be able to solve doubts, propose possible methodological adjustments, offer teaching resources and address issues such as diversity and differentiation in the classrooms. Yet the figure of the bilingual coordinator does not have the same role nationwide. Ortega-Martín and Trujillo (2018), for example, indicate significant differences between the different autonomous communities when establishing criteria for the selection of coordinators, the benefits they can have by assuming such tasks or their expected roles in the school.

The task of developing the curriculum in the bilingual classroom rests primarily with the teaching staff, which often requires levels of training that may not have been accessed. With regard to the requisites for providing bilingual teaching, the tendency is for all autonomous communities to demand a C1 level established by the *Common European Framework of Reference for Languages* (CEFR, 2001).

The state and regional education administrations, however, do provide teachers with different resources for continuing education, as well as stays abroad and courses for methodological renewal. Additionally, there are a growing number of networks for bilingual education across the country. This cooperative work between schools may be seen at the Community of Castilla and León with the *Observation-Action Innovation Project* for the 2017–2018 academic year (http://www.educa.jcyl.es/educacyl/cm), which gives greater visibility to the good practice of the schools and serves as a training tool for others. The objective of this particular project is to promote, through observation and exchange, teacher training and professional development in scientific, didactic and communicative competence in foreign languages, as well as ICT skills, competence in innovation and improvement and competence in teamwork. It also aims to provide the necessary support for the development of innovation projects and methodological changes in the classroom.

2.2   Teachers and Students

One of the great challenges for teachers (third pillar) is the use of information and communication technologies. This is particularly true for bilingual education, which often relies heavily on online resources. According to the *General Activity Plan 2013–2014, Detection of good ICT practices* (2014) of the Regional Government of Andalucía, good use of ICT increases motivation, improves the classroom environment, favours autonomous production, reinforces communication with families and serves as support for attention to diversity. This same report detects weaknesses, including the lack of well-maintained equipment, the incorrect application of these resources in schools, a lack of attention to diversity when using ICTs or insufficient use of the resources provided by the administration.

The fourth pillar mentioned would be the students themselves since they are the ones who stand to benefit from the result of the appropriate implementation of the curriculum in the classroom, from a methodology that adapts to their current level of foreign language competence and from the learning of contents in an effective and accessible way. The concern of educational administrations in Spain is that bilingual education should not be elitist or classist, and this requires that schools must strive to have web pages, blogs and free platforms (e.g., Edmodo, SeeSaw) that offer adequate resources and make bilingual education an element of social balance that offers the same possibilities to all students.

The fifth factor to consider in bilingual schools is the conversation assistant. By virtue of bilateral agreements with countries from (mostly) European and some non-EU countries, the Ministry of Education and Vocational Training annually hires a relatively large number of teaching assistants, who spend a maximum of 12 hours per week in the school in a non-supervisory, auxiliary role. In the Autonomous Community of Madrid, for example, the maximum number of assistants for 2018 was 2618, with a total expenditure of 22 million euros.

2.3 Hours of Instruction in the Second Language

Madrid has a longer tradition than the rest of the other autonomous communities in the implementation of bilingual education. After Madrid, the second most long-running programme is that of the regional government of Andalusia which introduced CLIL training on a large scale under the *Plan for the Promotion of Multilingualism* (CEJA, 2005; Jáimez & López Morillas, 2011). In this plan, the bases of bilingual education in Andalusia were established and subsequently updated by the educational administration. This plan also meant that students in the second cycle of early childhood education (three to six years) should receive one and a half hours of foreign language instruction per week each year (spread over three sessions a week). Students in the first cycle of primary education (ages seven and eight) were to receive two hours a week divided into three days, if deemed appropriate by the school. For students in the second and third cycles (ages nine to ten and 11–12), the subjects to be taught in a foreign language were specified and included social sciences, education for citizenship, natural sciences, physical education and arts and crafts. Legislation also stipulated that the subjects taught under the bilingual modality should employ the L2 for at least 50% of the total teaching time. In the case of Andalusia, for example, a second foreign language was also included in the bilingual schools.

For secondary education, it was originally stipulated (CEJA, 2005) that the students in the first three years (ages 13, 14 and 15) were to have four hours per week of teaching in a foreign language. In the fourth and final year of CSE, the hours would be increased to five per week. At present, and according to the *Instructions of the Junta de Andalucía* for the 2018–2019 academic year, the distribution of hours per week is as follows in Table 2.1.

The curriculum to be taught in a foreign language is left to the choice of the school, taking into consideration the training and preparation of the teaching staff involved.

Table 2.1 Example of distribution of hours per week in the Andalusian bilingual schools (CEJA, 2018)

	1st CSE	2nd CSE	3rd CSE	4th CSE
Geography and History	3	3	3	3
Biology and Geology	3		2	
Physics and Chemistry		3	2	
Mathematics	4	3		
Academic Mathematics or Applied Mathematics			4	4
Physical Education	2	2	2	2
Visual, Audiovisual and Manual Arts	2	2		
Music	2	2		

2.4   Methodology

With respect to methodology, administrations suggest certain actions but do not impose a concrete style of teaching. Thus, the Andalusian government published the *Informative Guide for Schools with Bilingual Teaching* (CEJA, 2011) in which there is no mention of specific methodological recommendations; details are provided, however, of the characteristics of the CLIL approach, which includes the following:

- Flexible work by tasks or projects
- Meaningful learning, focused on the students and integration of L2 as a vehicle for other areas or professional training courses
- Classes contextualised around a theme that creates synergies between different departments
- Collaborative and cooperative work of teacher groups
- Use of multiple resources, especially ICT
- Promotion of teamwork among teachers, contributing to sharing and creating common methods and activities

It is also noted that the teaching of a subject in a foreign language does not imply the same effort on the part of the learner as the same process in the mother tongue. Hence, there is a need to use different tools when considering the learning situation and to include multiple situations in which the contents are repeated to consolidate learning.

Of all the recommendations made by the Andalusian government, the need for teamwork is emphasised, as it combines criteria, defines common goals and distributes tasks among teachers. Guidelines also recommend the use of tasks or projects rather than more passive approaches, and promote the presentation of final projects as a culmination of the work that is done in a didactic unit.

At the classroom level, one of the most widely used tools is the Integrated Unit of Work. With this type of planning strategy, the concept of classroom as four walls that separate teachers from the rest of the staff or from the reality external to the school disappears, and work is encouraged among the teaching professionals from different areas or subjects with a series of common objectives.

The three steps that are established for the correct development of an integrated didactic unit are the selection of objectives by the teachers involved, the didactic transposition, in other words, the development of a task in the subjects involved and, finally, assessment, for which the use of rubrics that detail the degree of acquisition of the proposed competences is recommended.

In the latest methodological guidelines published by the Andalusian Government, emphasis is placed on the use of the CLIL approach as well as on the use of the European Language Portfolio, both in its paper version and in the electronic format (ePEL). In these recent guidelines published for the academic year 2018–2019, it is detailed that the curriculum to be taught in the foreign language will be between 50% and 100% of the non-language subject areas that make use of English, French or German as the vehicular language. It is also advised that greater use should be made of the foreign language, and, if possible, 100% of class time should be in the L2.

Finally, with regard to assessment, the foreign language teachers are the ones who assess the linguistic competence of the students taking into account the basic receptive, productive and interactive skills and the levels established by CEFR. In the content class, the assessment of linguistic production, if substandard, cannot negatively influence the final assessment of the area (CEJA, 2018). Additionally, the percentage of time assigned to the use of the L2 in the subjects taught in a foreign language is to be made public for the educational community.

3   The Current State of CLIL and Its Challenges

After more than a decade of experiences in CLIL in Spain, we are now in a position to tentatively examine the effects and consequences of this type of instruction. Focusing primarily on this particular national context, in this section, we will examine how CLIL has affected performance, both in terms of L2 development and content acquisition. Additionally, we will provide information obtained from those professionals involved at school level, including L2 and subject teachers as well as school management and bilingual coordinators.

3.1 Effects on L2 Development and General Satisfaction with CLIL

The positive effects of CLIL or bilingual training on L2 development have been detected in a variety of international contexts (see Dallinger, Jonkmann, Holm, & Fiege, 2016). This trend is also reflected in Spain in several studies at different educational levels.

One example can be seen in Ruiz de Zarobe's (2008) longitudinal study, with a sample of 161 students from Secondary Education in the Basque Country in Northern Spain, which compared performance in oral production based on the related subcategories of: (a) pronunciation, (b) vocabulary, (c) grammar, (d) fluency and (e) content. In this study, CLIL groups significantly outperformed non-CLIL groups in all subcategories, leading the authors to conclude that higher levels of exposure to L2 in content-based subjects led to positive outcomes in oral performance.

Lasagabaster and Sierra (2009), on the other hand, examined attitudes (e.g. perceived usefulness, importance, necessity and interest) towards the foreign language and mother tongue(s) in a study with a sample of 287 secondary students from four Basque schools. The authors found significant differences between non-CLIL and CLIL students, with the latter holding more favourable attitudes towards English, and they suggest that among the reasons for these differences, CLIL seems to provide higher levels of L2 exposure and affords more meaningful opportunities to employ the target language.

Another study by Lasagabaster (2008) in the Basque country with 198 secondary students found statistically significant differences in speaking, writing, grammar and listening in favour of CLIL groups. Additionally, one of the participating CLIL groups, comprised of students who had received only one year of CLIL instruction, also outperformed the non-CLIL groups in all of the above areas with the exception of listening comprehension.

In Barcelona, Pérez-Vidal and Roquet (2015) examined the performance of 100 lower secondary school students over the course of an academic year in listening, reading and writing. In this study, while significant differences were not found in listening, CLIL learners did significantly outperform non-CLIL students in reading and writing, and within the latter case, students showed better results in grammar and vocabulary. Similarly, Lahuerta's (2017) study, with a sample of 400 secondary school students in Asturias, northern Spain, found significant differences in global writing scores and individual writing components in favour of CLIL.

The study of Villoria, Hughes, and Madrid (2001) in primary and secondary education in public, semi-private and private schools in Granada, southern Spain, also found statistically significant differences in performance between CLIL and non-CLIL students. In this particular study, in which a total of 196 state school students participated, CLIL students in public primary and secondary education outperformed public non-CLIL students in receptive (listening and reading) and productive (speaking and writing) skills.

To examine satisfaction regarding CLIL programmes, Rodríguez-Sabiote, Madrid, Ortega-Martín, and Hughes (2018) carried out a study involving 1983 participants (headteachers, bilingual coordinators, language and non-language teachers, and students) across different provinces in Spain, and the results indicate relatively high levels of satisfaction among all stakeholders. This study shows some statistically significant differences, however, between certain groups of participants depending on the region researched. Additionally, participating students showed higher levels of satisfaction with language instruction than with bilingual content classes.

3.2 Effects of CLIL on L1 Competence and Content Acquisition

For the most part, studies on CLIL in Spain deal with the effects of this instructional modality on L2 development and relatively little is to be found in terms of how CLIL influences performance in other subject areas. Moreover, as discussed below, the few studies that do exist do not always use comparable testing instruments, nor do they tend to focus on learners who have had a substantial number of hours of L2 training.

When looking at mother tongue (Spanish) and content subjects, the question of comparable testing is more of an issue for bilingual content classes, since unlike the L1 classes, they are conducted in more than one language, and this plurilingual reality makes the use of identical instruments near impossible. While the case of content subjects is discussed below, it would appear useful to at least briefly touch upon the possible effects CLIL may have on mother tongue development. Here, in the subject of L1 (Spanish), a frequently expressed concern is whether or not the increased time spent learning through the L2 in other classes is detrimental to the students' own language. Several studies conducted in Spain, however, indicate that there are no significantly negative effects (see Anghel, Cabrales, & Carro, 2016; González Gándara, 2015; Ramos, Ortega-Martín, & Madrid, 2011).

In terms of the effects of CLIL on content acquisition, it would seem reasonable to envisage that, at best, the use of instruction of non-language subjects through L2 would not have a significant negative effect on learner performance; on the other hand, there could be a real risk of students not fully grasping what is being taught. To a large degree, both of these situations are reflected in several studies in Spain.

Madrid's (2011) study, for example, measures performance in social sciences in primary and secondary education in private, semi-private and public schools. Within the sample, those groups which were directly comparable (i.e., public schools) showed no significant differences in scores in this subject area. Fernández-Sanjurjo, Fernández-Costales, and Arias Blanco (2017) conducted a study in primary education and found that non-CLIL students had slightly better performance than CLIL learners, but these differences, again, were not significant.

In contrast, Anghel et al. (2016) examined student performance in standardised tests on mathematics and general knowledge (taught in English) at the final stages of primary education. In this study, no significant differences were found between CLIL and non-CLIL learners in mathematics (taught in L1); however, significant differences were found in the subject of general knowledge (taught in L2).

Further rigorous and comparable investigation is still required in Spain. Additionally, it should be remembered that learners in primary education have had relatively little time to acquire sufficient language skills in order to be able to function in content subjects in a foreign language at relatively similar levels to peers in their mother tongue. Given time, it is possible that higher levels of L2 competence may allow CLIL learners to perform on a more equal footing to their non-CLIL peers and that possible early levels of underperformance might be tolerated if, by the end of compulsory education stages, CLIL learners obtain similar levels in content results with the added benefit of increased communicative competence in L2. This phenomenon of low performance levels in primary and more equal results in secondary education is certainly a possibility and may be seen in other international contexts (e.g., Jäppinen, 2006; Seikkula-Leino, 2007).

In addition to comparisons of scores from performance tests, we also have certain stakeholder information on the functioning of CLIL schools in Spain. In the previously mentioned study by Rodríguez-Sabiote et al. (2018), we found an overall satisfaction score for the CLIL programmes of approximately four points out of a total of five. Here, the highest scores were provided by school management teams (4.51), followed by the English language teachers and subject teachers (4.22) and bilingual coordinators (4.09). All of these scores would suggest acceptable levels of satisfaction with the programme.

In terms of the learners themselves, the mean score for satisfaction was 3.7, although there was a significant level of variability based on their autonomous region, with student scores ranging from 3.3, in areas such as Galicia or the Canary Islands, to 4.2 in Navarre.

This study also pointed out a series of repeated strong points and areas of improvement which could be seen in several learning contexts. Among the strong points, we find areas such as:

- High levels of teacher motivation and involvement in the programme
- Development of language skills and key competences for life-long learning
- Positive students' perception of the usefulness of English
- Increased participation in international projects and student exchanges

- Degree of participation in teacher training courses
- Diversification in learning materials and teaching methods
- Level of student engagement and participation in class

A number of these strong points are corroborated in other national research projects. Pérez-Cañado's (2018) study with 2633 participants in three monolingual regions in Spain found that advances were being made in the application of CLIL methodology and use of materials.

In terms of areas of improvement, Rodríguez-Sabiote et al. (2018) identify the following areas:

- Lack of L2 competence on the part of some teachers
- Need for provision of teacher training
- Need to increase scope of student participation in exchanges
- Availability of ICTs for the programme
- Overdependence in some cases on the textbook
- Insufficient attention paid to cultural aspects
- High numbers of students per class
- Difficulties in catering to diverse levels in class
- Need for greater levels of coordination
- High levels of turnover among content teachers
- Lack of availability of CLIL-specific materials

Again, several of these points, including aspects such as teacher training and attention to diversity, are also mentioned in Pérez-Cañado (2018).

From these results we can extract a number of tentative conclusions. First, in this particular study, there are relatively homogenous levels of satisfaction between those professional groups involved in the bilingual programme. At this point, it might be worth indicating once more that, while recognising the similarity in results, the highest levels of satisfaction came from the school headteachers. This apparent approval is arguably vital for the proper functioning for the programme. At the same time, the support from all sectors of the professionals involved would tend to show that the additional efforts involved are worthwhile.

On the other hand, there is a high degree of variability in student satisfaction scores depending on the region where the programme is implemented. This situation would seem to suggest that CLIL benefits are not equally distributed and that the reality of the difficulties involved are experienced in the content class. However, the fact that some schools have high levels of learner satisfaction points to the possibility that certain approaches, as well as variables related to the availability of qualified personnel and other contextual factors, might provide better learning outcomes.

4   CLIL to Come

Since the introduction of language learning in official school curricula in the mid-1800s, efforts have been made to continuously improve learners' L2 competence. These efforts have not always led to the implementation of recommendations at ground level and it has often been the case that communicative approaches have been resisted by practising teachers. Despite these limitations, with the advent of widespread CLIL implementation and the legislation which encourages language teachers to adopt task-based learning and project work and to employ CEFR type indicators of performance, it would seem that language classroom practices are changing for the better.

While this may seem like good news in terms of the provision of language instruction and the development of learner communicative competence, there is still the question of the usefulness of the CLIL training in relation to content acquisition. It is true that CLIL has, to a large extent, brought a series of important positive methodological changes into the content class; but these changes are also accompanied by a series of limitations, such as the lack of teaching resources or lower levels of L2 competence among teaching professionals, particularly in certain regions.

In Spain, at least, ongoing research is required to ensure that the path taken in adopting CLIL is the most appropriate for students. At the same time, actions are needed to guarantee that high quality CLIL training is in place, not only through the measurement of perceived levels of satisfaction, but also through large-scale objective and reliable performance testing.

In discussing the future of CLIL, Pérez-Cañado (2012) highlights the need for the following avenues of research:

- Empirical research into major recurrent questions, including effects on L1 and L2 development as well as content-related results
- Longitudinal studies which go beyond snapshot testing
- Closer investigation into root causes behind results
- Identification of stakeholder needs
- Study of the methodology employed
- Examination of teacher support and training

These areas of research are still pertinent today, yet there is an emerging trend, stemming, among other areas, from the Council of Europe and the European Centre for Modern Languages (ECML) towards the creation of support instruments for teacher competence. Indeed, one current ECML project at its final stages aims to develop a Common European Framework for Teacher Competence, and related forthcoming publications from this organisation are likely to touch upon the role of the CLIL teacher. It is also expected that an international focus on CLIL systems will, in turn, lead to further improvement and support actions for content teachers across Europe, and this will be of particular interest in Spain, where there has been such an important adoption of this type of instruction. While these initiatives are ongoing, large-scale research into the continued supervision of CLIL results is still needed, particularly in the area of performance in content subjects.

References

Anghel, B., Cabrales, A., & Carro, J. M. (2016). Evaluating a bilingual education program in Spain: The impact beyond foreign language learning. *Economic Inquiry, 54*(2), 1202–1223. https://doi.org/10.1111/ecin.12305

Brinton, D. M., Snow, M. A., & Wesche, M. B. (1989). *Content-based Second Language Instruction*. Boston: Heinle & Heinle Publishers.

Brooks, N. (1966). *Language and Language Learning*. New York: Harcourt Brace & Co.

Brumfit, C. J., & Johnson, K. (Eds.). (1979). *The Communicative Approach to Language Teaching*. Oxford: Oxford University Press.

CEFR (Common European Framework of Reference for Languages). (2001). *A Common European Framework of Reference for Languages. Learning, Teaching Assessment.* Strasbourg: Council of Europe.

CEJA (Consejería de Educación de la Junta de Andalucía). (2005). *Plan de Fomento de Plurilingüismo: Una Política Lingüística para la Sociedad Andaluza.* Retrieved November 28, 2018, from http://cms.ual.es/idc/groups/public/@vic/@vinternacional/documents/documento/jc80302.pdf

CEJA. (2011). *Guía Informativa para Centros de Enseñanza Bilingüe.* Retrieved December 20, 2018, from https://www.juntadeandalucia.es/export/drupaljda/Guia_informativa_centros_ense%C3%B1anza_bilingue_.pdf

CEJA. (2018). Instrucciones sobre la Organización y Funcionamiento de la Enseñanza Bilingüe para el curso 2018–19. Retrieved December 22, 2018, from https://bit.ly/2Sp1jwA

Chamot, A. V., & O'Malley, J. M. (1994). *The CALLA Handbook: Implementing the Cognitive Academic Language Learning Approach.* New York: Addison-Wesley Publishing.

Cordovilla, A., Madrid, D., Muros, J., & Pérez, C. (1999). *Physical Education through English.* Granada: Grupo Editorial Universitario.

Cortina-Pérez, B., & Andújar, A. (2018). *Didáctica de la Lengua Extranjera en Educación Infantil.* Madrid: Pirámide.

Coyle, D. (2010). Preface. In D. Lasagabaster & Y. R. de Zarobe (Eds.), *CLIL in Spain: Implementation Results and Teacher Training* (pp. vii–viii). Newcastle upon Tyne, UK: Cambridge Scholars Publishing.

Dallinger, S., Jonkmann, K., Holm, J., & Fiege, C. (2016). The effect of content and language integrated learning on students' English and history competences—Killing two birds with one stone? *Learning and Instruction, 41*, 23–31.

Estaire, S., & Zanón, J. (1994). *Planning Classwork: A Task-based Approach.* Oxford: Heineman.

Fernández Fraile, M. E. (1996). *La enseñanza-aprendizaje del francés como lengua extranjera en España:1767–1936.* Tesis doctoral. Granada: Universidad de Granada.

Fernández-Sanjurjo, J., Fernández-Costales, A., & Arias Blanco, J. M. (2017). Analysing students' content-learning in science in CLIL vs. Non-CLIL programmes: Empirical evidence from Spain. *International Journal of Bilingual Education and Bilingualism.* https://doi.org/10.1080/13670050.2017.1294142

González Gándara, D. (2015). CLIL in Galicia: Repercussions on academic performance. *Latin American Journal of Content and Language Integrated Learning, 8*(1), 13–24. https://doi.org/10.5294/laclil.2014.8.1.2

Jáimez, S., & López Morillas, A. M. (2011). The Andalusian Plurilingual Programme in primary and secondary education. In D. Madrid & S. Hughes (Eds.), *Studies in Bilingual Education* (pp. 77–106). Bern: Peter Lang.

Jäppinen, A. K. (2006). CLIL and future learning. In S. Björklund, S. K. Mård-Miettinen, M. Bergström, & M. Södergard (Eds.), *Exploring Dual-Focussed Education: Integrating Language and Content for Individual and Societal Needs* (pp. 22–37). Vaasa: Vaasan Yliopiston Julkaisuja.

Johnson, K., & Morrow, K. (Eds.). (1981). *Communication in the Classroom.* Harlow, UK: Longman.

Lahuerta, A. (2017). Analysis of the effect of CLIL programmes on the written competence of secondary education students. *Revista de Filología, 35*, 169–184.

Lasagabaster, D. (2008). Foreign language competence in content and language integrated courses. *The Open Applied Linguistics Journal, 1*, 31–42.

Lasagabaster, D., & Sierra, J. M. (2009). Language attitudes in CLIL and traditional EFL classes. *International CLIL Research Journal, 1*(2), 4–17.

Leech, G. N. (1983). *Principles of Pragmatics.* London: Routledge.

Lenneberg, E. (1967). *Biological Foundations of Language.* New York: Wiley.

Madrid, D. (1980). *Estudio experimental sobre la enseñanza del inglés de 6 a 8 años.* Doctoral dissertation, Department of English Studies, University of Granada, Granada. Retrieved October 20, 2018, from https://www.ugr.es/~dmadrid/Publicaciones/PublicoGEN.htm

Madrid, D. (2000). La didáctica de la lengua extranjera. In L. Rico Romero & D. Madrid (Eds.), *Fundamentos Didácticos de las Áreas Curriculares* (pp. 249–310). Madrid: Síntesis.

Madrid, D. (2011). Monolingual and bilingual students' competence in social sciences. In D. Madrid & S. Hughes (Eds.), *Studies in Bilingual Education* (pp. 195–222). Bern: Peter Lang.

Madrid, D. (2017). La formación de los maestros de inglés a lo largo de la historia. *Greta, 20*(1 & 2), 36–53.

Madrid, D., & García-Sánchez, E. (2001). Content-based second language teaching. In E. G. Sánchez (Ed.), *Present and Future Trends in TEFL* (pp. 101–134). Universidad de Almería: Secretariado de publicaciones.

Madrid, D., Pérez, C., Muros, J., & Cordovilla, A. (1998). *Education through English.* Granada: Grupo Editorial Universitario.

Morales, F. J. (2009). La enseñanza de idiomas en España en la frontera de los años 30 : las ilusiones perdidas. *Documents pour l'Histoire du Français Langue Étrangère ou Seconde, 42*, 231–248. Retrieved September 20, 2018, from https://journals.openedition.org/dhfles/785

Muros, J., Pérez, C., Madrid, D., & Cordovilla, A. (1998). *Music through English*. Granada: Grupo Editorial Universitario.

Ortega-Martín, J. L., Hughes, S. P., & Madrid, D. (2018). *Influencia de la Política Educativa de Centro en la Enseñanza Bilingüe en España*. Madrid: MECD. Retrieved September 10, 2018, from https://sede.educacion.gob.es/publiventa/influencia-de-la-politica-educativa-de-centro-en-la-ensenanza-bilinge-en-espana/ensenanza-lenguas-espana/22358

Ortega-Martín, J. L., & Trujillo, F. (2018). Legislación y normativa para el funcionamiento de los programas AICLE en España. In J. L. Ortega-Martín, S. Hughes, & D. Madrid (Eds.), *Influencia de la Política Educativa en la Enseñanza Bilingüe* (pp. 21–30). Madrid: Ministerio de Educación, Ciencia y Deporte (MECD).

Oyama, S. (1976). A sensitive period in the acquisition of a non-native phonological system. *Journal of Psycholinguistic Research, 5*(3), 261–283.

Pérez-Cañado, M. L. (2011). The effects of CLIL within the APPP: Lessons learned and ways forward. In R. Crespo & M. G. de Sola (Eds.), *Studies in Honour of Ángeles Linde López* (pp. 389–406). Granada: Universidad de Granada.

Pérez-Cañado, M. L. (2012). CLIL research in Europe: Past, present, and future. *International Journal of Bilingual Education and Bilingualism, 15*(3), 315–341.

Pérez-Cañado, M. L. (2018). CLIL and pedagogical innovation: Fact or fiction. *International Journal of Applied Linguistics, 28*(3). https://doi.org/10.1111/ijal.12208

Pérez-Vidal, C., & Roquet, H. (2015). CLIL in context: Profiling language abilities. In M. Juan-Garau & J. Salazar-Noguera (Eds.), *Content-based Language Learning in Multilingual Educational Environments* (pp. 237–255). Berlin: Springer.

Ramos, A. M., Ortega-Martín, J. L., & Madrid, D. (2011). Bilingualism and competence in the mother tongue. In D. Madrid & S. Hughes (Eds.), *Studies in Bilingual Education* (pp. 135–156). Bern: Peter Lang.

Rivers, W. (1964). *The Psychologist and the Foreign Language Teacher*. Chicago: University of Chicago Press.

Rodríguez-Sabiote, C., Madrid, D., Ortega-Martín, J. L., & Hughes, S. P. (2018). Resultados y Conclusiones sobre la Calidad de los Programas AICLE en España. In J. L. Ortega-Martín, S. Hughes, & D. Madrid (Eds.), *Influencia de la política educativa en la enseñanza bilingüe* (pp. 141–159). Madrid: Ministerio de Educación, Ciencia y Deporte (MECD).

Ruiz de Zarobe, Y. (2008). CLIL and foreign language learning: A longitudinal study in the Basque country. *International CLIL Research Journal, 1*, 60–73.

Ruiz de Zarobe, Y., & Lasagabaster, D. (Eds.). (2010). *CLIL in Spain: Implementation, Results and Teacher Training.* Newcastle upon Tyne, UK: Cambridge Scholars Publishing.

Searle, J. R. (1969). *Speech Acts: An Essay in the Philosophy of Language.* Cambridge: Cambridge University Press.

Seikkula-Leino, J. (2007). CLIL learning: Achievement levels and affective factors. *Language and Education, 24*(1), 328–341.

Skinner, B. F. (1957). *Verbal Behaviour.* New York: Appleton-Century-Crofts.

Snow, M. A., & Brinton, D. M. (1997). *The Content-based Classroom: Perspectives on Integrating Language and Content.* New York: Longman.

Strevens, P. D. (1977). *New Orientations in the Teaching of English.* Oxford: Oxford University Press.

van Ek, J. A., & Alexander, L. G. (1975). *Threshold Level English.* Oxford: Pergamon Press.

Villoria, J., Hughes, S., & Madrid, D. (2001). Learning English and learning through English. In D. Madrid & S. Hughes (Eds.), *Studies in Bilingual Education* (pp. 157–194). Bern: Peter Lang.

Widdowson, H. G. (1972). The teaching of English as communication. *English Language Teaching, 27*(1), 15–18.

Widdowson, H. G. (1978). *Teaching Language as Communication.* Oxford: Oxford University Press.

Wilkins, D. (1976). *Notional Syllabuses.* Oxford: Oxford University Press.

Willis, J. (1996). *A Framework for Task-based Learning.* London: Longman.

3

CLIL and Language Education in Japan

Keiko Tsuchiya

1 Language Education Policy

This chapter starts with a brief history of the language policies in modern Japan since the Meiji era (1668–1912), then describes the current school system with recent changes in the *Course of Study* and its relations with Content and Language Integrated Learning (CLIL). This is followed by sections on the implementation of and the prospects for CLIL in the Japanese context. During the isolation of the country in the Edo era (1603–1867) in Japan, educated people learned Japanese and Chinese, and translators in Nagasaki, which was the only harbour for foreign ships, used Dutch (Mozumi, 2004). It was the incursion of a British ship, *HMS Phaeton*, in 1808 that urged Japanese people to learn English, and the first English textbook in Japan was compiled in 1811 under the supervision of a Dutch teacher, Jan Cock Blomhoff (Tanabe, 1987).

K. Tsuchiya (✉)
International College of Arts and Sciences, Yokohama City University, Yokohama, Japan
e-mail: ktsuchiy@yokohama-cu.ac.jp

© The Author(s) 2019
K. Tsuchiya, M. D. Pérez Murillo (eds.), *Content and Language Integrated Learning in Spanish and Japanese Contexts*, https://doi.org/10.1007/978-3-030-27443-6_3

In the process of modernisation of Japan after the Meiji Restoration in 1868, language policies were discussed from various perspectives and were strongly influenced by the discourses of nationalism (Heinrich, 2012). In the early Meiji period, only a limited number of social elites learned foreign languages through native-speaker teachers in order to gain access to advanced science and technology from Western countries, and those subjects were taught in foreign languages at colleges. With the desperate need for modernisation, the first Minister of Education, Mori Arinori,[1] even suggested Japanese language should be replaced by English. However, this sparked as a response a movement for the promotion of Japanese as the national language (ibid.). Tsubouchi Shoyo, a critic and a novelist, led the *Genbun itchi* Movement to unify the spoken and written forms of Japanese in the 1880s (ibid.) and the then prime minister Ito Hirobumi emphasised the importance of education in the national language, Japanese. The grammar translation method was applied to foreign language education, and publications written in foreign languages were translated to Japanese in order to make the knowledge they contained accessible to Japanese people (Ogawa, 2017; Saitoh, 2007). In 1886, the Ministry of Education launched the first school education policy in which the modern school system, that is, primary/secondary school and university, was introduced. The educational reform in 1900 introduced *kokugo* (literally, the national language) as a school subject, where standard Japanese is taught (Fujita-Round & Maher, 2008). *The Elementary School Ordinance* (*Shōgakkō-rei*) was published in the same year (MEXT, 1900) and English was included as an elective module for secondary level students together with French and German in the Secondary School Ordinance (*Chūgakkō Rei*) in 1901 (MEXT, 1901). In the late Meiji era, the effectiveness of the grammar translation method was questioned, and as a response to the criticism, the oral method proposed by a British phonetician, Harold E. Palmer, was introduced to English education in the Taisho period (1912–1926) (Ogawa, 2017; Saitoh, 2007). The method, however, was not fully implemented at that time since teaching and learning English was prohibited during World War II at the beginning of the Showa era (1926–1989) (ibid.).

---

[1] The names of the historical persons are written in the order of a surname and a first name as they are in Japanese.

The education system in modern Japan was installed under American military occupation after the war. *The School Education Act*, which was based on the educational legislation in the US, was established and the first draft of the *Course of Study*, which is a guideline for school education in Japan, was issued in 1947 (Aoki, 1947). The *Course of Study* was promulgated by the education ministers in the reform in 1958, and since then, it has been revised almost every ten years (MEXT, 2011a). As described previously, three foreign languages were listed in the *Course of Study* (English, French and German) until the late 1990s. English then became a compulsory subject in secondary education in the *Revision of the Course of Study* in 1998 (Fujita-Round & Maher, 2008; Heinrich, 2012). The English language teaching method applied to Japanese schools after the war was the oral approach proposed by Charles C. Fries, which was then replaced by the communicative approach derived from Dell Hymes' communicative competence in the 1960s (Ogawa, 2017; Saitoh, 2007). To foster learners' communication skills has been the primary aim of English education in the *Course of Study* till now (Tsuchiya, 2018).

In 2002, the *Strategic Plan to Cultivate Japanese with English Abilities* was issued and the action plan was enacted in the following year (MEXT, 2002b, 2003), where only English is mentioned as a foreign language for communication in the global society.

> 経済・社会等のグローバル化が進展する中、子どもたちが21世紀を生き抜くためには、国際的共通語となっている「英語」のコミュニケーション能力を身に付けることが必要であり、このことは、子どもたちの将来のためにも、我が国の一層の発展のためにも非常に重要となっています。
>
> With the progress of globalization in the economy and in society, it is essential that our children acquire communication skills in English, which has become a common international language, in order for living in the 21st century. This has become an extremely important issue both in terms of the future of our children and the further development of Japan as a nation. (MEXT, 2002a, 2002b)

The English education reforms since the 1990s have been promoted due to the urgent demand of internationalisation (*kokusaika*) of the country and its economy. This in turn has drawn criticism by applied linguists. To provide an overview of the arguments against the English education policies that the Japanese government applied in these two decades, several articles which examined the policy documents were reviewed here (see Table 3.1).

Hashimoto (2000) conducted a text analysis of the *Japanese Government Policies in Education, Science and Culture 1994—New Directions in School Education: Fostering Strength for Life*. This study concluded that the education reform aims to foster "Japaneseness of individual citizens" by "deconstructing English" only to "accept useful parts" of the language but "not in its entirety" (ibid., p. 49). Thus, Hashimoto (2000) perceived the government policy as a strategy to resist the linguistic and cultural domination of English. Kubota (2002) examines the *Course of Study* documents from 1989 and 1998 and criticises them for reinforcing nationalism, "failing to promote linguistic and cultural pluralism" (ibid., p. 19) and ignoring the increasing cultural and ethnic diversity inside Japan. Similarly, Butler-Goto and Iino (2005) highlight the ambiguous aim of international understanding and a lack of the notion of multilingualism in the *Action Plan to Cultivate Japanese with English Abilities* (MEXT, 2003), which was established for "all Japanese nationals" to acquire "practical English" (ibid., p. 33) in response to the economic demand and also

Table 3.1 Criticisms against the English education reforms in Japan

Article	Document	Findings
Hashimoto (2000)	Japanese GovernmentPolicies in Education, Science and Culture 1994 (*Kyoiku Hakusho*)	Japanisation through English education
Kubota (2002)	The 1989 and 1998 Course of Study Documents	"Foreign language" is "English",Anglicisation and Nationalism
Butler-Goto and Iino (2005)	The Action Plan to Cultivate Japanese with English Abilities 2003	The ambiguous relationship between "internationalisation" and "English"
Kobayashi (2013)	Economic Statistics and National "Globalisation" Policies from the 1970s to 2012	Japan's economic growth and poor English education, no references to social inequality

in the opposition to the Hiraizumi's (a member of parliament) proposal to train selected English specialists (ibid., p. 32). The action plan introduced "Foreign Language Activities" as part of "the period of integrated studies"[2] in primary schools (see the next section for the details), but at the same time stipulated that the Japanese language was to be the basis of school education in contrast to the former Prime Minister Obuchi's idea of English as a second official language in Japan (ibid., p. 32).

The English education policies were also analysed from economic perspectives in Kobayashi (2013), who applied critical discourse analysis (CDA) to investigate the arguments in journal articles and newspapers in relation to Japan's economy from the 1970s to 2012. Kobayashi identifies an underlying discourse in relation to English and economic capital, that is, the Japan Exchange and Teaching (JET) Programme, through which the assistant language teachers (ALTs) from English-speaking countries have been recruited to provide English lessons in secondary classrooms (CLAIR, 2015).[3] It was "instigated by policymakers to ease the trade friction" between Japan and the US (ibid., p. 7). She then warns that the *Action Plan to Cultivate Japanese with English Abilities* (MEXT, 2003) could lead to the separation between "lower-class Japanese children" and those who can afford private English lessons and study abroad (ibid., p. 10).

Following the reform of the *Course of Study* in 2008, *Foreign Language Activities* were introduced to the fifth and sixth grades in primary schools in 2011, where English is the recommended foreign language. English is taught by an assistant English teacher in most cases, and students' English proficiency is not assessed since the emphasis is on the intercultural experience in a foreign language rather than acquiring the language. The *Course of Study* also suggests that English classes in upper secondary schools should be taught in English (MEXT, 2008). Furthermore, in the new *Course of Study* for primary and lower secondary education, which

---

[2] The period for integrated studies was introduced to primary and secondary education in the revision of the *Course of Study* in 1998, which aims to improve students' ability to "think in their own way about life through cross-synthetic studies and inquiry studies, while fostering the qualities and abilities needed to find their own tasks, to learn and think on their own, to make proactive decisions, and to solve problems better" (MEXT, 2011b, p. 1).

[3] The JET programme started in 1987 with ALTs from the four inner circle countries at that time, but now they are from 44 countries including countries in the expanding circle in 2017 (CLAIR, 2015).

was issued in March 2017, Foreign Language Activities are now implemented in the third and fourth grades and English as a subject in the fifth and sixth grades in primary schools. The guidelines also suggest that the medium of instruction in English classes in lower secondary schools should be English (MEXT, 2017d). Another major change in the guidelines for English in secondary schools is the encouragement of cross-curricular lessons in English classes as shown below, which is extracted from the guidelines for lower secondary schools.

> 言語活動で扱う題材は、生徒の興味・関心に合ったものとし、国語科や理科、音楽科など、他の教科等で学習したことを活用したり、学校行事で扱う内容と関連付けたりするなどの工夫をすること。
>
> Materials should align with students' interest, activating the knowledge they learned in other content subjects, such as Japanese, Sciences and Music, and relating to the themes of school events. (MEXT, 2017a, p. 150, my translation)

The notion of cross-curricular teaching was also observed in the new guidelines for upper secondary schools, which was issued in March 2018 (MEXT, 2018a).

At the tertiary level, MEXT introduced the framework of the *300,000 International Students Plan* in 2008, which is called the Global 30 Project, setting the longer-term goal of accepting 300,000 international students by 2020 (MEXT, 2012). The subsequent project is called *the Top Global University Project*, which assigned 37 universities to initiate the internationalisation of higher education in Japan (MEXT, 2014a). The *Promotion of Human Resources for Globalization Development* in 2011 also encouraged universities "to offer unique and challenging curricula (e.g., classes taught in English, requiring overseas studies) and class methods (e.g., small-group education)" (Cabinet, 2011). Similarly, the report of Higher Education in Japan states that the promotion of English medium instruction (EMI) lectures at universities is important to improve local students' English skills and attract international students (MEXT, 2012).

As seen in the review above, English is the compulsory foreign language taught in the current Japanese school systems and encouraged to be used as a medium of instruction in university lectures in Japan to be compatible with the globalised society. It is also expected to promote the internationalisation of higher education in Japan. However, it is noticeable that the notion of multilingualism is absent in the policy documents and the economic demands are emphasised in the drive to teach English as an international language (Tsuchiya & Pérez Murillo, 2015).

2   CLIL in School Curricula

CLIL is implemented mainly in English classes at primary, secondary and tertiary levels and also lectures in EMI at universities in the Japanese context. This section first reviews the current Japanese school curricula, focusing on English language classes.

Compulsory education in Japan comprises nine years, starting from grade 1 at the age of 6 to grade 9 at the age 15, the first six years are primary education and the latter three years are lower secondary education, but most students continue studying another three years in upper secondary schools (98.8% in 2018) (MEXT, 2018c). Half of the secondary school graduates go to universities, and the total percentage of the students who receive higher education, which includes various types of colleges, is more than 80% (ibid.). The Ministry of Education, Culture, Sports, Science and Technology (MEXT) set policy at national level, while at local level, policy is implemented by the prefectural and the municipal government in each city. The school curricula and guidelines are decided by MEXT, which public schools in local governments should follow. Public schools should also choose school textbooks which are authorised by a committee at the national government level.

As briefly mentioned in the previous section, the subject class called Foreign Language Activities was introduced in the fifth and sixth grades in primary education in the reform of the *Course of Study* in 2008, where CLIL approaches have been implemented (see the next section for more detail). Students have 35 lesson hours of the class (once a week). After the new *Course of Study* issued in 2017 is implemented, pupils in the fifth and sixth grades have Foreign Language classes, which should be English adhering to the *Course of Study*, for 70 lesson hours in total (twice a week). The third and fourth grade pupils have a Foreign Language Activities class once a week (MEXT, 2017b).

The number of Foreign Language (English) classes in lower secondary schools is 140 lesson hours (four times per week) annually, which was increased by 35 hours in the previous reform of the *Course of Study* in 2008 and remains the same after the implementation of the new *Course of Study* in 2017. In upper secondary schools, students have to earn more than 74 units (1 unit is 35 lesson hours) in total to graduate, and the subjects and units required in each subject are defined in the *Course of Study*. In general courses at upper secondary schools, there are seven subjects (18 units) in the Foreign Language module, which again should be English, although a limited number of schools offer foreign language classes other than English, such as Chinese, Korean, French and German (514 public and 194 private schools in 2014) (MEXT, 2014b).

The *Course of Study* also defines additional subjects for specialised courses, where students need to earn 25 units in the specialised areas. English specialised courses, for instance, can include five additional subjects: Integrated English, English Understanding, English Expressions, Intercultural Understanding and Current English (MEXT, 2008). The Super Global High Schools are another form of English specialised programme implemented in public schools since 2014, through which 126 schools have received funding from the government to develop the English courses with international student exchanges or study abroad programmes, and another 56 schools are recognised as the associated schools of the programme (MEXT, 2018b). CLIL has also been introduced in some of these specialised courses (see Chap. 7 for the practices in the English specialised course in Wako Kokusai High School).

As reviewed in Sect. 1, lectures in EMI have been encouraged at universities in Japan since the 2000s, and 41% of undergraduate courses (305 universities) and 37% of graduate courses (229 universities) have implemented lectures in EMI and more than 50% of universities offered student exchange programmes with a credit transfer system in 2015 (MEXT, 2017c). Moreover, about 70 undergraduate courses (40 universities) and about 250 graduate schools (126 universities) are providing English medium programmes where students can receive degrees without taking any lectures in Japanese. Various types of CLIL approaches have been applied to English classes and EMI lectures at tertiary levels (see the following section and Chap. 8 for the case study of Yamaguchi University).

The following section describes case studies of CLIL practices in different educational levels to depict the current state of CLIL in Japan and the challenges in its implementations.

3   The Current State of CLIL and Its Challenges

CLIL has been introduced to Japanese education since the late 2000s. As Ohmori (2014) reported, two earliest cases of CLIL implementation were found in English education programmes at two universities: Sophia University in Tokyo (Izumi, Ikeda, & Watanabe, 2012; Watanabe, Ikeda, & Izumi, 2011) and Saitama Medical University in Saitama (Sasajima, 2011). To see an overview of CLIL practices in Japan, journal articles which report case studies of CLIL were extracted from the online database of academic articles issued in Japan (CiNii, 2018), from 2009, when the first article of a CLIL case study appeared, to 2017. The total number of these articles is 151, out of which 95 articles report CLIL practices in higher education (77 articles in universities, 9 in colleges and another 9 in CLIL in foreign languages other than English at universities) and 35 articles in primary education. The first case study in secondary education was found in 2013, and the total number is 21, which is fewer than those in primary education.[4] Thus, as shown in Fig. 3.1, CLIL in Japan has first launched at tertiary level, then began to be applied to primary education, and more recently in secondary schools.

The largest increases in the number of the articles were observed in 2014, when CLIL was chosen as the theme of the summer seminar of JACET (Japan Association of College Teachers), and in 2016, which is the time just before the launch of Japan CLIL Pedagogy Association (J-CLIL) in April 2017 (see Chap. 12 for the detail of J-CLIL).

---

[4] The articles which include the term "CLIL" in the title were extracted from the database. The articles about the CLIL approach, reports about CLIL practices in other countries and reviews on CLIL books or articles were excluded from the list.

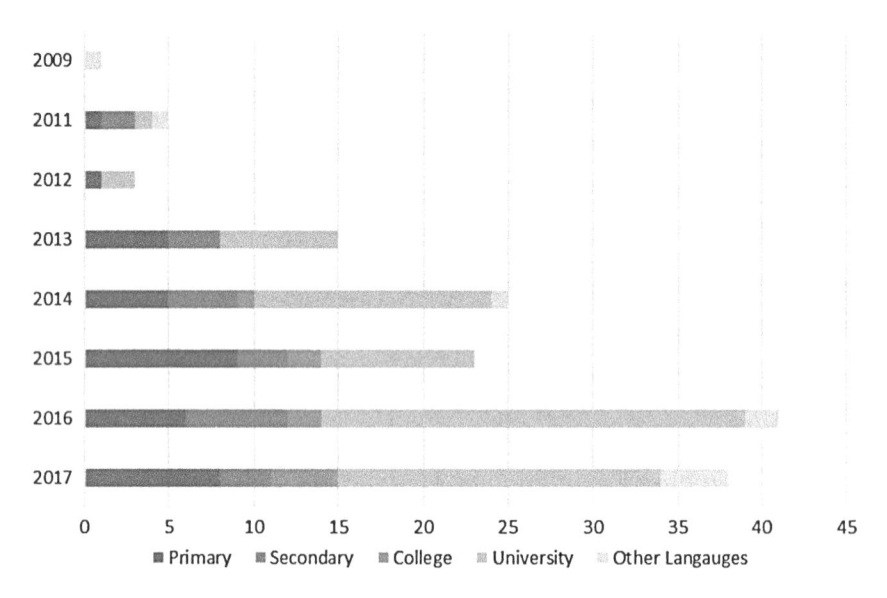

Fig. 3.1 Number of articles about case studies of CLIL

Table 3.2 CLIL practices in primary schools in Japan

Grade	Content	Hours	Resource
Grade 6	International understanding: the exchange programme with Turkish pupils	6	Sakamoto and Takizawa (2016)
Grades 5 & 6	Social studies: Names of countries, capitals and their places on a world map	6	Nigo (2014)
Grades 5 & 6	Dietary education: Making original *Bento* (lunch box)	3	Moteki (2013)
Grade 6	Mathematics: Addition and subtraction to make 100, multiplication	3	Nigo (2013)
Grade 5	Art & Craft, Science and Social Studies: Animals and their habitats	3	Yamano (2013)

Adapted from Moteki (2017)

At primary level, Moteki (2017) summarises several case studies of CLIL in public schools as shown in Table 3.2. As mentioned earlier, the CLIL practices have been implemented in Foreign Language Activities classes, and the contents vary from international or cultural issues to mathematics and science. In a more recent publication, Ikeda (2017) also reports CLIL practices in maths classrooms in a private primary school, where pupils in grades 1 and 2 study mathematics in English.

Although the number is limited, some cross-curricular lessons in primary education were also documented: Yamano (2013, and Chap. 5 in this volume) reports CLIL classrooms in Utsunomiya, where pupils learn animals and their habitats as part of the knowledge included in Art and Craft, Science and Social Studies. Another case study of a cross-curricular lesson was reported in Nigo (2016), which describes primary CLIL classrooms in Hiroshima, where times in different places of the world are learned, involving several subject areas: science, mathematics, geography and social studies.

Out of 21 articles in secondary CLIL practices, there are 8 cases in lower secondary schools and 13 in upper secondary schools. Again, various contents were chosen, such as global issues, environmental study (see Yamazaki's Chapter in this volume), scientific experiments and English literature. Some authors also focus on the effectiveness of CLIL to improve particular language skills, i.e., English writing and oral presentation.

These articles show overall positive effects of CLIL on learning. However, some challenges and difficulties in the implementation of CLIL in the Japanese context were also recognised. Harada and Sawaki (2017) listed concerns about CLIL classes in Japan which were raised during the discussion at a workshop of Content Based Instruction (CBI), CLIL and EMI, and added possible solutions to the problems:

1. Teachers' expertise and workload	→	Teacher collaboration
2. Concerns about mother tongue use	→	Translanguaging
3. Less content knowledge	→	Task Design (LOTS to HOTS)
4. Concerns about linguistic skills	→	Extra time for language learning
5. Various English-speaking teachers	→	English as a Lingua Franca

Adapted from Harada and Sawaki (2017, p. 85)

The first concern is that teachers need broader expertise both in language and content, and the second one is the increase in workload as teachers are expected to plan and prepare for CLIL lessons. This, however, can be solved by collaborating with colleagues (also see Chap. 14 for the topic of teacher collaboration). The third concern is the domain loss of Japanese, to which the authors provided a solution, referring to the concept of *translanguaging* (García & Li Wei, 2014). This point is further discussed in the following section (also see Chap. 11 for a study of translanguaging in a CLIL classroom).

The other two concerns are related to content and language learning: in terms of content, there is a worry that students may learn less subject knowledge through CLIL because of the difficulty in learning content in an additional language. To solve this problem, more careful task planning is suggested with consideration of students' cognitive skills (i.e., to plan tasks from LOTS to HOTS). In terms of language, there is concern that CLIL classes may hinder students' language learning, considering the typological differences between Japanese and English, to which the authors advise that teachers can also take time to focus on language in CLIL, responding to students' needs of language support. The last issue concerns the still prevalent idea of *English Native Speakerism* in Japan and the need to raise learners' and teachers' awareness of *English as a Lingua Franca* (Ishikawa, 2018; Murata, Iino, & Konakahra, 2017). Further discussion is necessary to overcome these concerns, but some positive changes can be expected through CLIL practices, which the following section explains.

4   CLIL to Come

CLIL can be expected to bring two paradigm shifts in language education in Japan: (1) reconceptualising the learning aims of language education from acquiring language abilities to developing *competences* or *pluriliteracies* through using language as a learning tool, and (2) altering learners' learning experience and their perceptions of language learning through *languaging* and *translanguaging* in CLIL practices.

On the basis of the guidelines of *key competences for lifelong learning* in the EU (European Commission, 2007) and the framework of *twenty-first-century skills* in the US (P21, 2015), Ikeda (2015, 2017) summarised the competences for learning, which leaners can obtain through CLIL, into three categories: *cognitive competency, social competency* and *moral competency* (see Chap. 7 for the details). In terms of the *cognitive competency* in Ikeda's framework, the Graz Group in Europe has already established a more refined model for the CLIL pedagogy, which they call *pluriliteracies* (Meyer, Coyle, Imhof, & Connolly, 2018). Four dimensions teachers should consider in CLIL classrooms are illustrated in the model: generating and sustaining learners' commitment and achievement, monitoring learners' learning and personal growth, activating prior knowledge and developing skills to conceptualise and refine ideas, and providing learners opportunities to demonstrate and communicate their understanding. These conceptual frameworks also benefit CLIL practices in the Japanese context, and the shift in the learning aims also brings the change in learners' language use in classrooms as construed in existing studies (Dalton-Puffer, 2007; Llinares & Morton, 2017; Llinares, Morton, & Whittaker, 2012; Morton, 2018, also see the chapters in Part III in this volume).

The other change that CLIL could bring relates to learners' learning experience and their perception of language learning. Genesee and Hamayan (2016, p. 8) categorise CLIL in the school curriculum into three types: (1) *CLIL in immersion*, (2) *CLIL in education for immigrant and indigenous-language students*, which has two sub-categories, *Dual-language CLIL* and *Monolingual CLIL*, and (3) *CLIL in foreign language programmes*. In their definition, most CLIL practices in Japan can be classified into the third category, with which, according to the authors, students can achieve "low bilingual proficiency" (ibid., p. 8). However, the description of low in bilingual proficiency can be controversial since the authors seem to judge the proficiency from a monolingual perspective, where a bilingual is assumed as a person with native speaker proficiency in two languages. The idea was criticised in Grosjean (1985), and in the current trend in language learning and education after the multilingual turn (May, 2014), a more holistic view has been introduced where bi/multilingual individuals activate their linguistic repertoire appropriate in the specific context, cf. the concepts of *translingual practice* (Canagarajah, 2013), *translanguaging* (García & Li Wei, 2014) and *becoming and being multilingual* (Cenoz & Gorter, 2011). CLIL offers opportunities where learners can experience *languaging* and *translanguaging* through classroom practices, even in the CLIL in foreign language programmes. This would be a different experience for learners from learning linguistic knowledge to achieve native-speaker proficiency. Language learning through CLIL thus could be inter-related with learners' linguistic and social practices (cf. Chap. 15 in this volume for further discussion on this theme).

This chapter provided an overview of the language education policies in modern Japanese history, the current guidelines for English education and the school system in Japan, explaining that CLIL has been introduced in English classrooms in the Japanese context, first at the tertiary level, then in primary and secondary education. The challenges and positive changes expected through the CLIL implementations were also briefly discussed. It is hoped that this chapter will be a useful guide for those who wish to know the current state of CLIL in Japan, making it easier for readers to access the following chapters in this volume.

References

Aoki, S. (1947). Why was the course of study developed? [in Japanese, 学習指導要領はどうしてつくられたか]. In The Primary Education Research Association [初等教育研究協議会] (Ed.), *The Teaching Guidelines for Primary and Secondary Teachers [小学校・中学校教師のための学習指導必携 一般篇]* (pp. 55–64). Tokyo: Japan Educational Material Association [日本教育用品協会].

Butler-Goto, Y., & Iino, M. (2005). Current Japanese reforms in English language education: The 2003 "Action Plan". *Language Policy, 4*(1), 25–45.

Cabinet. (2011). *An Interim Report of The Council on Promotion of Human Resource for Globalization Development.* Cabinet Office, Government of Japan. Retrieved from http://www.kantei.go.jp/jp/singi/global/1206011 interim_report.pdf

Canagarajah, S. A. (2013). *Translingual Practice: Global Englishes and Cosmopolitan Relations.* London: Routledge.

Cenoz, J., & Gorter, D. (2011). Focus on multilingualism: A study of trilingual writing. *The Modern Language Journal, 95*(3), 356–369.

CiNii. (2018). *CiNii Articles Database.* Tokyo: NII (National Institute of Informatics). Retrieved from https://ci.nii.ac.jp/

CLAIR. (2015). *The Japan Exchange and Teaching Programme*. Council of Local Authorities for International Relations. Retrieved from http://jet-programme.org

Dalton-Puffer, C. (2007). *Discourse in Content and Language Integrated Learning (CLIL) Classrooms*. Amsterdam: John Benjamins Publishing Company.

European Commission. (2007). *Key Competences for Lifelong Learning*. Luxembourg: European Commission. Retrieved from https://ec.europa.eu/education/

Fujita-Round, S., & Maher, J. C. (2008). Language education policy in Japan. In S. May & N. Hornberger (Eds.), *Language Policy and Political Issues in Education* (pp. 393–404). New York: Springer.

García, O., & Li Wei (2014). *Translanguaging*. London: Palgrave Macmillan.

Genesee, F., & Hamayan, E. (2016). *CLIL in Context: Practical Guidance for Educators*. Cambridge: Cambridge University Press.

Grosjean, F. (1985). The bilingual as a competent but specific speaker-hearer. *Journal of Multilingual & Multicultural Development, 6*(6), 467–477.

Harada, T., & Sawaki, Y. (2017). The problems of CBI, CLIL and EMI [in Japanese, CBI・CLIL・EMIの課題]. In T. Harada & Y. Sawaki (Eds.), *Learning Subject Contents in English: CBI, CLIL and EMI [in Japanese, 英語で教科内容や専門を学ぶ: 内容重視指導(CBI)、内容言語統合学習(CLIL)と英語による専門科目の指導の視点から]* (pp. 85–90). Tokyo: Institute for Advanced Studies in Education Waseda University, Gakubunsha [学文社].

Hashimoto, K. (2000). 'Internationalisation' is 'Japanisation': Japan's foreign language education and national identity. *Journal of Intercultural Studies, 21*(1), 39–51.

Heinrich, P. (2012). *The Making of Monolingual Japan: Language Ideology and Japanese Modernity*. Bristol: Multilingual Matters.

Ikeda, M. (2015). English lessons—From language ability to competency [in Japanese, 英語科—語学能力の育成から汎用能力の育成へ]. In M. Nasu & F. Ema (Eds.), *Competency-based Lessons [in Japanese, コンピテンシー・ベイスの授業づくり]* (pp. 157–181). Tokyo: Tosho Bunka Sha (図書文化社).

Ikeda, M. (2017). From language ability to generic purpose competences: Fostering competence through CLIL [in Japanese, 言語能力から汎用能力へ:CLILによるコンピテンシーの育成]. In T. Harada & Y. Sawaki (Eds.), *Learning Subject Contents in English: CBI, CLIL and EMI [in Japanese, 英語で教科内容や専門を学ぶ: 内容重視指導(CBI)、内容言語統合*

学習*(CLIL)*と英語による専門科目の指導の視点から*]* (pp. 5–30). Tokyo: Gakubunsha (学文社).

Ishikawa, T. (2018). From English native-speakerism to multilingualism: A conceptual note. *JACET ELF SIG Journal, 2*, 9–17.

Izumi, S., Ikeda, M., & Watanabe, Y. (2012). *CLIL (Content and Language Integrated Learning): New Challenges in Foreign Language Education at Sophia University. Volume 2: Practice and Applications.* Tokyo: Sophia University Press.

Kobayashi, Y. (2013). Global English capital and the domestic economy: The case of Japan from the 1970s to early 2012. *Journal of Multilingual and Multicultural Development, 34*(1), 1–13.

Kubota, R. (2002). The impact of globalization on language teaching in Japan. In D. Block & D. Cameron (Eds.), *Globalization and Language Teaching* (pp. 13–28). London: Routledge.

Llinares, A., & Morton, T. (2017). *Applied Linguistics Perspectives on CLIL.* Amsterdam: John Benjamins Publications.

Llinares, A., Morton, T., & Whittaker, R. (2012). *The Role of Language in CLIL.* Cambridge: Cambridge University Press.

May, S. (Ed.). (2014). *The Multilingual Turn: Implications for SLA, TESOL and Bilingual Education.* London: Routledge.

MEXT. (1900). *The Elementary School Ordinance (Shogakko-rei).* The Ministry of Education, Culture, Sports, Science and Technology (MEXT). Retrieved from http://www.mext.go.jp/b_menu/hakusho/html/others/detail/1318016.htm

MEXT. (1901). *The Secondary School Ordinance (Chugakko-rei).* The Ministry of Education, Culture, Sports, Science and Technology (MEXT). Retrieved from http://www.mext.go.jp/b_menu/hakusho/html/others/detail/1318040.htm

MEXT. (2002a). *Developing a Strategic Plan to Cultivate "Japanese With English Abilities".* Tokyo: The Ministry of Education, Culture, Sports, Science and Technology (MEXT). Retrieved from http://unpan1.un.org/intradoc/groups/public/documents/APCITY/UNPAN008142.htm

MEXT. (2002b). *The Strategic Plan to Cultivate "Japanese with English Abilities" [in Japanese,* 「英語が使える日本人」の育成のための戦略構想*].* Tokyo: Ministry of Education, Culture, Sports, Science and Technology Japan (MEXT). Retrieved from http://www.mext.go.jp/b_menu/shingi/chousa/shotou/020/sesaku/020702.htm#plan

MEXT. (2003). *The Action Plan to Cultivate 'Japanese with English Abilities' [in Japanese,* 「英語が使える日本人」の育成のための行動計画*].* Tokyo. Retrieved from http://www.mext.go.jp/b_menu/shingi/chukyo/chukyo3/004/siryo/04031601/005.pdf

MEXT. (2008). *The Course of Study [in Japanese, 学習指導要領]*. 東京: 文部科学省. Retrieved from http://www.mext.go.jp/a_menu/shotou/new-cs/youryou/index.htm

MEXT. (2011a). *学習指導要領等の改訂の経過. [The Reforms of Course of Study]* Tokyo. Retrieved from http://www.mext.go.jp/a_menu/shotou/new-cs/idea/1304372.htm

MEXT. (2011b). *The Course of Study for Elementary Schools: Chapter 5 the Period for Integrated Studies*. Tokyo: Ministry of Education, Culture, Sports, Science and Technology Retrieved from http://www.mext.go.jp/component/english/__icsFiles/afieldfile/2011/03/17/1303755_012.pdf

MEXT. (2012). *Higher Education in Japan*. Japan: Higher Education Bureau, Ministry of Education, Culture, Sports, Science and Technology. Retrieved from http://www.mext.go.jp/english/highered/__icsFiles/afieldfile/2012/06/19/1302653_1.pdf

MEXT. (2014a). *English Education Reform Plan Corresponding to Globalization*. Tokyo: Ministry of Education, Culture, Sports, Science and Technology. Retrieved from http://www.mext.go.jp/english/topics/1343591.htm

MEXT. (2014b). *The Report on Foreign Language Education Other than English in School [in Japanese, 英語以外の外国語の科目を開設している学校の状況について]*. Tokyo: MEXT (Ministry of Education, Culture, Sports, Science & Technology). Retrieved from http://www.mext.go.jp/b_menu/shingi/chukyo/chukyo3/058/siryo/__icsFiles/afieldfile/2016/05/25/1371098_1.pdf

MEXT. (2017a). *The Course of Study for Lower Secondary Schools [in Japanese, 中学校学習指導要領]*. Tokyo: MEXT (Ministry of Education, Culture, Sports, Science & Technology). Retrieved from http://www.mext.go.jp/component/a_menu/education/micro_detail/__icsFiles/afieldfile/2018/06/05/1384661_5_1_2_1.pdf

MEXT. (2017b). *The Course of Study for Primary Schools [in Japanese, 小学校学習指導要領]*. Tokyo: MEXT (Ministry of Education, Culture, Sports, Science & Technology). Retrieved from http://www.mext.go.jp/component/a_menu/education/micro_detail/__icsFiles/afieldfile/2018/05/07/1384661_4_3_2.pdf

MEXT. (2017c). *Current Status of Higher Education Reform in FY2015 [in Japanese, 大学における教育内容等の改革状況について (平成27年度)]*. Retrieved from http://www.mext.go.jp/a_menu/koutou/daigaku/04052801/__icsFiles/afieldfile/2017/12/13/1398426_1.pdf

MEXT. (2017d). *The Notice of the Partial Reform of the Ordinance for Enforcement of the School Education Act, the Major Reform of the Educational Guidelines for*

Pre-schools and the Major Reforms of the Course of Study for Primary and Lower Secondary Schools [in Japanese, 学校教育法施行規則の一部を改正する省令の制定並びに幼稚園教育要領の全部を改正する告示、小学校学習指導要領の全部を改正する告示及び中学校学習指導要領の全部を改正する告示等の公示について]. Tokyo. Retrieved from http://www.mext.go.jp/component/a_menu/education/micro_detail/__icsFiles/afieldfile/2011/03/31/1304440_001.pdf

MEXT. (2018a). *The Course of Study for Upper Secondary Schools [in Japanese, 高等学校学習指導要領].* Tokyo: MEXT (Ministry of Education, Culture, Sports, Science & Technology). Retrieved from http://www.mext.go.jp/component/a_menu/education/micro_detail/__icsFiles/afieldfile/2018/07/13/1407085_12.pdf

MEXT. (2018b). *An Interim Report of the Super Global High School Programme [in Japanese, スーパーグローバルハイスクール(SGH)事業検証に関する中間まとめ].* Tokyo: MEXT (Ministry of Education, Culture, Sports, Science & Technology). Retrieved from http://www.mext.go.jp/a_menu/kokusai/sgh/__icsFiles/afieldfile/2018/08/24/1408438_001.pdf

MEXT. (2018c). *The School Survey FY2018.* Tokyo: MEXT (Ministry of Education, Culture, Sports, Science & Technology). Retrieved from http://www.mext.go.jp/b_menu/toukei/chousa01/kihon/kekka/k_detail/1407849.htm

Meyer, O., Coyle, D., Imhof, M., & Connolly, T. (2018). Beyond CLIL: Fostering student and teacher engagement for personal growth and deeper learning. In M. Agudo & J. de Dios (Eds.), *Emotions in Second Language Teaching: Theory, Research and Teacher Education* (pp. 277–297). Cham: Springer.

Morton, T. (2018). Reconceptualizing and describing teacher's knowledge of language for content and language integrated learning (CLIL). *International Journal of Bilingual Education and Bilingualism, 21*(3), 275–286.

Moteki, J. (2013). Practice of foreign language activities with CLIL and the outcome [in Japanese, CLIL (内容言語統合学習) 的外国語活動の実践とその効果]. *Education Practice Research, Joetsu Educational University [in Japanese, 上越教育大学 教育実践研究], 23,* 13–18.

Moteki, J. (2017). Developing a CLIL based programme and the outcome (in Japanese, CLILと連携した学習プログラムの開発とその効果). *Education Practice Research, Joetsu Educational University (in Japanese, 上越教育大学 教育実践研究), 27,* 163–168.

Mozumi, J. (2004). A brief chronological table of English teaching in Japan: The Edo period [in Japanese, 日本英語教育史略年表 : 江戸時代]. *Takushoku Language Studies, 107*, 217–231.

Murata, K., Iino, M., & Konakahra, M. (2017). An investigation into the use of and attitudes toward ELF (English as a Lingua Franca) in English-medium Instruction (EMI) classes and its implications for English language teaching [in Japanese, EMI (英語を媒介とする授業)における「共通語としての英語」の使用の現状把握と意識調査、および英語教育への提言]. *Waseda Kyoiku Hyoron (早稲田教育評論), 31*(1), 21–38.

Nigo, Y. (2013). Cross-curricular English instruction utilizing calculation: Through learning of English numbers for upper grade pupils. *JES (the Japan Associate of English Teaching in Elementary Schools) Journal, 13*, 84–99.

Nigo, Y. (2014). Possibility of two-sword English instruction in the application of CLIL: With social studies content for upper grade pupils. *JES (the Japan Associate of English Teaching in Elementary Schools) Journal, 14*(1), 66–81.

Nigo, Y. (2016). *A Cross-curricular English Teaching Method with Eight Intelligences: The Multiple Intelligences Theory and CLIL [in Japanese, 8つの知能を生かした横断的な英語指導法]*. Hiroshima: Keisuisha (渓水社).

Ogawa, S. (2017). The historical development of English education in Japan: The analysis of its characteristics and strengths [in Japanese, 英語教育の歴史的展開にみられるその特徴と長所]. *The Journal of Morioka University, 34*, 55–66.

Ohmori, A. (2014). Exploring the potential of CLIL in English language teaching in Japanese universities: An innovation for the development of effective teaching and global awareness. *The Journal of Rikkyo University Language Center, 32*, 39–51.

P21. (2015). *P21 Framework*. The Partnership for 21st Century Learning. Retrieved from http://www.p21.org/storage/documents/docs/P21_Framework_Definitions_New_Logo_2015.pdf

Saitoh, Y. (2007). *Japanese People and English: Another History of English Language [in Japanese, 日本人と英語 : もうひとつの英語百年史]*. Tokyo: Kenkyusha.

Sakamoto, H., & Takizawa, M. (2016). Environmental education project in English to connect children in Fukushima with children in Turkey: An attempt to raise WTC using CLIL [in Japanese, 福島とトルコの子どもを結ぶ英語環境教育プロジェクト:CLILによってWTCを高める試み]. *Bulletin of Toyo Women College [in Japanese, 東洋女子短期大学紀要], 24*, 163–180.

Sasajima, S. (Ed.). (2011). *CLIL: Content and Language Integrated Learning [in Japanese, CLIL: 新しい発想の授業]*. Tokyo: Sanshusha.

Tanabe, Y. (1987). The use of Katakana letters for English pronunciation: The history of English language education in Japan [in Japanese, 英語教育史に於ける発音の片仮名表記]. *Historical Studies of English Learning and Teaching in Japan, 2*, 37–60.

Tsuchiya, K. (2018). 'English' in the course of the study documents: A diachronic corpus assisted discourse analysis. *Waseda Working Papers in ELF (English as a Lingua Franca), 7*, 65–84.

Tsuchiya, K., & Pérez Murillo, M. D. (2015). Comparing the language policies and the students' perceptions of CLIL in tertiary education in Spain and Japan. *LACLIL, 8*(1), 25–35.

Watanabe, Y., Ikeda, M., & Izumi, S. (2011). *CLIL (Content and Language Integrated Learning): New Challenges in Foreign Language Education at Sophia University. Volume 1: Principles and Methodologies*. Tokyo: Sophia University Press.

Yamano, Y. (2013). Exploring the use of content and language integrated learning (CLIL) in foreign language activities. *JES (the Japan Associate of English Teaching in Elementary Schools) Journal, 13*, 20–35.

Part II

Practices in CLIL Classrooms

4

Practices to Scaffold CLIL at Transition to Primary

María Teresa Fleta Guillén

1 Introduction

In today's globalized world, the teaching of second languages (L2s) has been shaped by the many changes that advances in technology and neuroscience have brought about (Conkbayir, 2017; Kuhl, 2010). At all academic levels, "different forms of education are offered through the medium of English to non-English speakers" (Murphy & Evangelou, 2016, p. 4). In some countries, the immersion model (Baker & Wright, 2017; Cummins, 1979; Genesee, 2008) or the bilingual programmes under the Content and Language Integrated Learning (CLIL) umbrella have proliferated in primary and secondary education (Coyle, Hood, & Marsh, 2010). Moreover, English as the Medium of Instruction (EMI) has also rocketed in the sphere of tertiary education around the world (Dearden, 2015). As stated by the European Commission (2011b), the L2 must be a communication tool integrated into the normal day-to-day routines and should be used during the development of other activities;

M. T. Fleta Guillén (✉)
School of Education, Complutense University of Madrid, Madrid, Spain
e-mail: tfleta@perlaunion.es

© The Author(s) 2019
K. Tsuchiya, M. D. Pérez Murillo (eds.), *Content and Language Integrated Learning in Spanish and Japanese Contexts*, https://doi.org/10.1007/978-3-030-27443-6_4

children "should be exposed to the target language in meaningful and if possible, authentic settings, in such a way that the language is spontaneously acquired rather that consciously learnt" (p. 17).

In Spain, CLIL bilingual programmes have been implanted in the mainstream state primary education schools nationwide for more than a decade supported by national or regional educational authorities. One of the aims of CLIL programmes is to introduce students to subject content knowledge through studying the curriculum in an L2 (mostly English). According to a British Council study, English is positioned as the most offered language in both private and state institutions (Rixon, 2013).

In CLIL-based contexts, primary curricular content is taught in the bilingual modality (Coyle et al., 2010, p. 1). This initiative seeks to obtain greater integration between language and content in a teaching context which demands rethinking the training that pre-primary and primary education teachers receive. Despite this rapid increase of bilingual education programmes through the medium of English, little research has been undertaken in relation to the effective practices that scaffold CLIL methodology and ensure success in the early stages of bilingual education thereafter. In this regard, recent studies indicate that foreign language teachers working with young children suffer from a lack of suitable teacher education and the necessary methodological training (Mourão & Ferreirinha, 2016; Murphy & Evangelou, 2016; Rixon, 2013).

This chapter is intended to fill this niche by investigating the current situation of the initial stages of bilingual education in the Madrid Autonomous Community. To that end, the chapter starts by framing the topic of bilingual education against the backdrop of early L2 acquisition and by outlining the pedagogical grounds for applying CLIL. Then, it presents an overview of pre-primary education and foreign language teaching in the Madrid region. Finally, the chapter proposes a range of key practices to consider at the transition to primary CLIL bilingual education.

The topic of learning another language in childhood is not only relevant in Spain because of the increase of bilingual programmes, but also in other countries with a longer or shorter tradition of bilingual education (Kersten, Rohde, Schelletter, & Steinlen, 2010; Mourão, 2019; Mourão & Ferreirinha, 2016; Mourão & Lourenço, 2015; Murphy & Evangelou,

2016; Rokita-Jaskow, 2015). We consider that this chapter may encourage the opening of new research avenues relating to child acquisition of English in instructed settings.

1.1 Theoretical Underpinnings

Children have a "huge learning potential" (Cameron, 2001, p. xii). They learn languages by listening, by understanding the messages and by speaking (Fleta, 2015; Long, 1996; Mackey, 2007). Accordingly, oral exposure to the target language is of outmost relevance "because children who start learning a foreign language very young may encounter nothing but the spoken language for several years" (Cameron, 2001, p. 17). Meisel (2011) differentiates between *simultaneous* language acquisition which emerges if exposure to two (or more) languages occurs within a week after birth onwards, and *successive/sequential* acquisition of bilingualism which arises when children start an L2 before the age of five. In Meisel's words: "The suspicion thus is that whatever enables the child to acquire the mother tongue might not be lost forever, rather that it could be hidden somewhere among or underneath our other cognitive faculties" (Meisel, 2011, p. 1). Later, after five years of age, the acquisition of an L2 is considered a second language acquisition. In spite of this, from a language acquisition perspective, there seem to be close links between both *simultaneous* language acquisition and *successive/sequential* learning at school as the same psycholinguistic mechanisms to process language apply to young learners in naturalistic settings and in a classroom setting (Cutler, 2012, p. 304; Lightbown & Spada, 2013, p. 41).

In the case of L2 learning at an early age, Cameron (2001) highlights that the "new language is largely introduced orally, understood orally and aurally, practiced and automatized orally" (p. 18). As far as the acquisition of the first language (henceforth L1) is concerned, the amount of time that children are exposed to their L1 before attending school is approximately 20,000 hours (Lightbown & Spada, 2013, p. 13). By contrast, the amount of exposure time to an L2 varies from setting to setting. This implies that having a smaller amount of contact hours to the L2 equals less exposure to input data, and hence, the quality and intensity of instruction in these settings should be higher (ibid., p. 93). In the main, the greatest difference between L1 acquisition and L2 acquisition of bilingualism lies in the onset and the ultimate attainment. The reason being that unlike in L1 acquisition, child learners who face new languages have already gone through the process of building up the grammatical structure of their L1:

> [...] those who have learnt a language know a great deal about many other languages without realizing that they do. The learning of further languages generally facilitates the activation of this knowledge and increases awareness of it, which is a factor to be taken into account rather than proceeding as if it did not exist. (Council of Europe, 2001, p. 170)

Moreover, the ultimate attainment in L2 learning is not guaranteed, not only due to the age of onset, motivation or the individual differences among child learners but also due to social and pedagogical factors. In this regard, the learning setting, the amount and intensity of interaction in the target language, the quality and quantity of the input learners receive, the output they produce and the teacher's L2 competence, they all have an impact on child's L2 development.

Notwithstanding, a number of studies on L2 acquisition have revealed that "language learning in a bilingual kindergarten is not fundamentally different from naturalistic L2 acquisition scenario" (Kersten & Rohde, 2013, p. 111). Given adequate conditions of rich and meaningful input and time, young learners acquire L2s in a natural and subconscious manner (Cameron, 2001; Lightbown & Spada, 2013; Moon, 2000). As Cameron (2001, p. 18) suggests: "For young learners, spoken language is the medium through which the new language is encountered, understood, practiced and learnt". However, what children have to overcome in instructed settings is the dearth of exposure when the target is a foreign language; the main reason being that "in foreign language teaching, there is an onus on the teacher to provide exposure to the language and to provide opportunities for learning through classroom activities" (Cameron, 2001, p. 11).

Figure 4.1 presents an analogy in which L2 learning is depicted as a house. "For the preschool context, L2 intensity would rather include

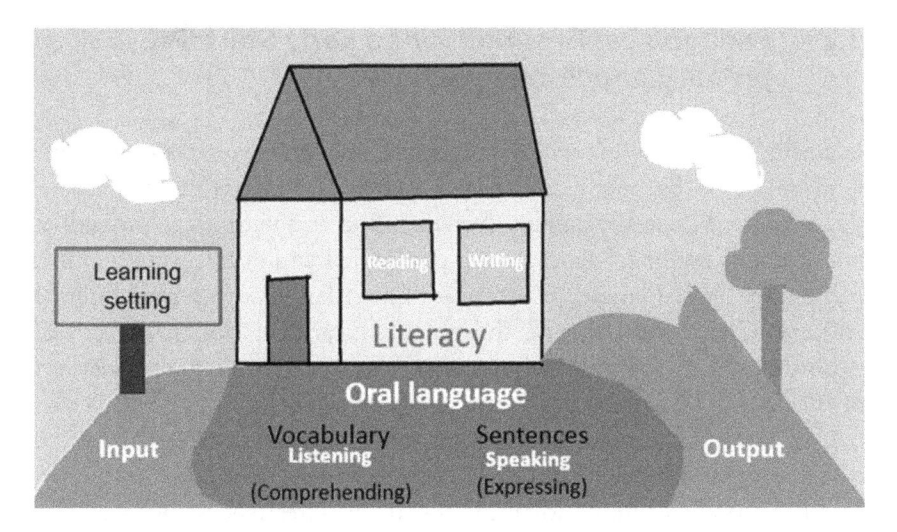

Fig. 4.1   The house of L2 learning (adapted from Cox Campus)

factors such as L2 teachers' and children's attendance time in the pre-school per week, opening hours of the preschool and number of children in the institution" (Kersten et al., 2010, p. 37). As can be observed, the learning setting as well as the input and output are the main forces driving the L2 learning.

Figure 4.1 highlights that the listening and speaking skills are the foundational support of the literacy (reading and writing) skills: "the knowledge that forms the foundation for reading and writing is built throughout early childhood through play, language and literary experiences" (Pinnel & Fountas, 2011, p. 21). Hence, to build strong literacy skills necessary for CLIL-based learning, it is of utmost importance to have a good base in oral skills with which learners comprehend messages and express their thoughts. Unlike listening and speaking, reading and writing are not acquired naturally: "The ability to read and write does not develop naturally, without careful planning and instruction. Children need regular and active interactions with print" (Pinnel & Fountas, 2011, p. 25). For that reason, reading and writing need to be taught in both L1 and L2.

1.2   Pedagogical Grounds for an Early Start: Pre-primary and Primary School

In Spain, more than one official language is spoken in some Autonomous Communities (Basque, Galician and Catalan). What is more, the language policy and responsibility for education rest within the individual autonomous regions. Madrid is a monolingual community and Spanish is the only official language. However, in the last few decades, bilingual education has been one of the chief educational policy objectives. According to the Institute of Statistics (INE, 2018, p. 1), the population of the Madrid Autonomous Community at the beginning of 2018 was 6.4 million inhabitants. This number of inhabitants makes it to some extent comparable to Finland with a population of 5.5 million, a country that has attracted international interest in the effectiveness of its educational system and the teaching of English (García Ruíz, 2009).

The first section of this chapter describes the bilingual education scenario of the Madrid Autonomous Community, where there are currently two bilingual programmes in operation: the bilingual programme of the Madrid Autonomous Community and the Ministry of Education-British Council Agreement project. The second section discusses the conceptualization and pedagogical implementation of CLIL.

2   Course Design

2.1   Bilingual Programmes of the Madrid Autonomous Community

After the publication of the first call for the selection of schools in the *Boletín Oficial de la Comunidad* (henceforth BOCM) in 2004, 26 primary schools joined the bilingual programme of Madrid Autonomous Community. Since then, the number of schools has increased steadily (Table 4.1).

In the school year 2018/2019, bilingual education reached 369 state primary schools (45, 6%) and also 152 state secondary schools (50, 3%)

Table 4.1 Number of primary schools and students

Year	2005	2008	2010	2014	2018
Primary schools	26	147	206	336	369
Students	1481	27,248	48,689	86,670	114,096

(Consejería de Educación e Investigación, 2018–2019)

as well as five state vocational schools. Aside from these schools, the bilingual programme has been recently implemented in 35 pre-primary schools to three-, four- and five-year-old children (BOCM 2018). In addition to the Spanish–English bilingual institutions, the Madrid bilingual programme has a total of 15 French and 4 German linguistic sections in secondary education institutions.

Along with this bilingual programme in public schools, bilingual education is implemented in 204 charter schools as well as in ten schools of the Ministry of Education-British Council Agreement project. These ten schools are a part of a pioneering bilingual project signed up in 1996. This project was implanted in different autonomous communities nationwide in pre-primary, primary and secondary education. The main goal of the Ministry of Education-British Council Agreement project was to increase the English language level of students in public schools by providing them with the opportunity to follow an official bilingual and bicultural curriculum through an integrated curriculum, based on the Spanish and British national curriculums (Llinares & Dafouz, 2010; Muñoz & Naves, 2007). The schools belonging to this programme start bilingual education in pre-primary, and teaching in the L2 takes up 40% of the school week (Dobson, Johnstone, & Pérez Murillo, 2010; Reilly & Medrano, 2009).

The increase in the number of schools offering bilingual education in the Madrid region can be put down to several factors (Pérez-Vidal, 2013). One is the need to redress historical deficiencies in teaching foreign languages (Dalton-Puffer, 2011, p. 185). Another is the European Commission's drive (2011a) for multilingualism which started in the 1990s. The launch of the White Paper on Education and Training in 1995 responded to a primary objective of the European Commission. The two major objectives included the acquisition and lifelong improvement of communicative skills and the command of three Community languages through the Formula 1 + 2 (mother tongue + 2) from an early age (European Commission, 1995). This formula specifies that, during their time in school, all children in the European Union should have the chance to learn at least three languages at a functionally appropriate level.

Based on the White Paper (1995), many Spanish schools developed bilingual programmes, most of them adopting CLIL as an approach to teach cross-curricular subjects through the medium of English. As stated in the European Council document (2002):

> It is a priority for Member States to ensure that language learning in kindergarten and primary school is effective, for it is here that key attitudes towards other languages and cultures are formed, and the foundations for later language learning are laid [...], in particular by teaching at least two foreign languages from a very early age. (European Council, 2002, p. 19)

Within CLIL-based contexts, English is used as a medium of instruction for teaching academic content. However, learning content through a foreign language is very demanding and "teachers involved in CLIL recognize the importance to change established needs which might be used in the L1 when teaching the same content in L2" (Papaja & Swiatek, 2016, p. 46).

2.2   Conceptualization of CLIL

The acronym CLIL "is used as a generic term to describe all types of provision in which a second language (a foreign, regional or minority language and/or another official state language) is used to teach certain subjects in the curriculum other than language lessons themselves" (Eurydice, 2006, p. 8). CLIL emerged in Europe in the mid-1990s as "a pragmatic European solution to a European need" (Marsh, 2002, p. 11), as "the ultimate opportunity to practice and improve a foreign language" (Pérez-Vidal, 2013, p. 59). This "dual-focused educational approach in which an additional language is used for the learning and teaching of both content and language" (Coyle et al., 2010, p. 1) has been implemented nationwide in Spain at all educational levels: pre-primary,

primary, secondary and tertiary education. In these CLIL-based contexts, the L2 plays the role of not only a language of communication but also a language of instruction (Bonnet, 2012; Coyle, 2010; Dalton-Puffer & Smit, 2007; Lyster, 2007; Mehisto, 2007). In short, the introduction of CLIL requires methodological shifts in both language skills and knowledge of methodology, since both are of utmost relevance in preparing teachers for bilingual education.

Within the European landscape for teaching foreign languages, Spain is in a prominent position. As Coyle (2010, p. viii) contends, Spain has taken a leading role in CLIL bilingual education programmes implementation: "Spain is rapidly becoming one of the European leaders in CLIL practice and research". Within the Spanish bilingual education scenario, the bilingual community of the Basque Country and the monolingual Madrid Autonomous Community stand out.

CLIL methodology draws upon social constructivist approaches to learning (Vygotsky, 1978; Bruner, 1996) and upon second language acquisition theories (Cummins, 1979; Genesee, 2008; Krashen, 1982). Social constructivist theories of learning "emphasise that learning is a social, dynamic process, and that learners learn when interacting with one another" (Dale & Tanner, 2012, p. 12). To help develop students' understanding and to reach the learning outcomes, students work in groups and are supported by the teacher to construct knowledge and understanding of the subject matter through the use of the vehicular language (Coonan, 2005).

Moreover, CLIL methodology relies heavily on the concept of *scaffolding*, a term which was originally coined by Wood, Bruner, and Ross (1976). As illustrated by Dale and Tanner (2012) in the scaffolding process, "[b]uilders use temporary scaffolds to support a building during construction, and then, once the building can stand alone, the scaffolds to support a building are removed" (p. 31). What is more, CLIL methodology draws on Vygotsky's Zone of Proximal Development: "The Distance between actual development level—determined by independent problem resolution—and potential—determined by problem solving under the guidance of an adult or in collaboration with more expert companions" (Vygotsky, 1978, p. 86). Within CLIL-based contexts, "Passing on knowledge and skill like any human exchange, involves a subcommunity in interaction" (Bruner, 1996, p. 20). For that reason, involving learners in meaning-driven interaction enables them to be involved in the learning process of the target language and also in the acquisition of new concepts.

As noted above, the CLIL distinct methodology, far from ignoring conventional teaching pedagogies, presents a challenging curriculum in which language learning skills and concept knowledge are presented to learners in meaningful contexts (Gibbons, 2009, p. 12). In a CLIL-based context, "content classrooms have the potential to be the best contexts for developing a second language in school" (Gibbons, 2009, p. 9). To push in high quality and quantity input in CLIL-based contexts, teachers' linguistic and pedagogical competence should be thorough. Furthermore, teaching a subject in a non-native language is different from teaching a subject in the teachers' and students' mother tongue. To teach through an L2 is challenging for teachers in that it may limit their ability to explain concepts. Moreover, in CLIL-based contexts, "there is an intimate relationship between content and language" (Ball, Kelly, & Clegg, 2015, p. 63). Students are not only expected to develop the skills related to the subject content but also to do something with that knowledge using the language. However, in non-bilingual schools where foreign languages are taught only as a subject, students focus primarily on the subject content in non-language lessons and only learn the L2 during language lessons.

Early pre-primary and primary education is perhaps the most influential stage for learning in general and for language learning in particular (Cameron, 2001; Kuhl, 2010). The knowledge and skills that students acquire in the early school years will allow them to go more deeply into different disciplines later in their schooling. What is more, "the degree to which learners are literate in L1 and have acquired strong cognitive academic language proficiency (CALP) in L1" is a determining factor influencing L2 learning (Ball et al., 2015, p. 6). As indicated in Sect. 1.2, at the beginning of the foreign language learning process, there is a need to build a strong oral foundation where skills such as listening, understanding and speaking become the support of literacy of reading and writing to express concepts and ideas thereafter (Fleta, 2015; Long, 1996; Mackey, 2007).

One of the key aspects of the CLIL methodological approach is the collaborative work between foreign language specialist teachers and teachers who use the language to teach academic content in non-linguistic curricular areas (Coyle et al., 2010). The systematic collaboration between both groups of teachers has an impact on both in planning CLIL lessons and their implementation. Furthermore, it creates rich learning contexts in which the foreign language and the communicative skills are enhanced.

Another added value of CLIL is "its planned pedagogic integration of contextualized content, cognition, communication and culture into teaching and learning practice" (Coyle et al., 2010, p. 6). The 4C's framework (content, communication, cognition and culture), together with the language Triptych and the CLIL Matrix, adapted by Coyle (2002) from Cummins' work (1984), are three essential entities underpinning CLIL methodology. The language used for communication is categorized by Coyle et al. (2010, p. 36) from three different perspectives: language of/for/through learning. It is also important to incorporate the seven competences, which, according to the recommendation of the European Parliament and of the Council (2006), need to be acquired by learners through life span: Linguistic communication; Digital Competence; Cultural awareness and expression; Mathematical and Basic competence in Science and Technology; Learning to learn; Sense of Initiative and Entrepreneurship; Cultural awareness and Expression; and Social and Civic competence. These different aspects of CLIL methodology are illustrated in Fig. 4.2.

Teachers who plan their lessons through CLIL methodology must be first aware of the content they want to teach, since the content determines the language which goes with it (Bentley, 2010, p. 54). Moreover, the key competences should also be integrated in CLIL-based contexts in line with a cross-curricular perspective.

2.3 Pre-primary Education and Foreign Languages in the Madrid Autonomous Community

Education in Spain consists of ten years of schooling. Primary education for students aged 6–12 years and secondary education for students

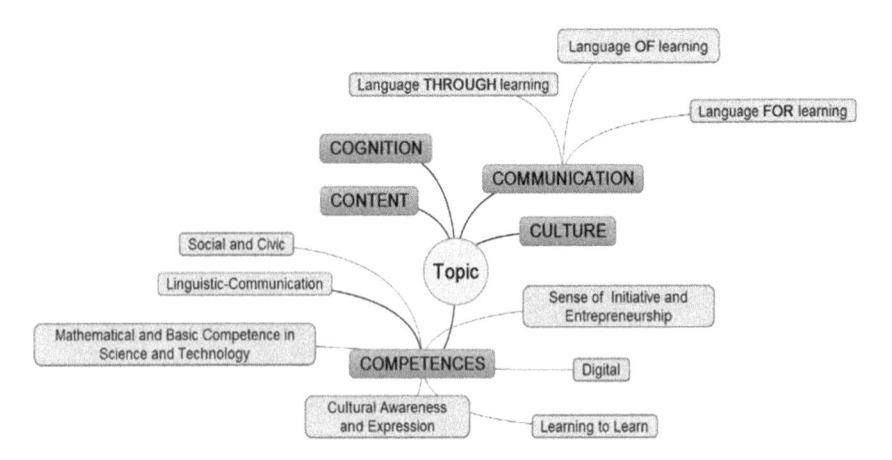

Fig. 4.2 Aspects of CLIL methodology

Table 4.2 Percentage of students learning foreign language in school year 2016–2017

First foreign language	English	French	Other foreign languages	Total
2nd Cycle of Pre-school	83.4	0.5	0.3	84.1
Primary	99.1	0.6	0.3	100.0

(Ministerio de Educación y Formación Profesional, 2017–2018)

between 12 and 16 years (BOE, 2006). Both primary and secondary education are compulsory, and at least one foreign language must be studied at both levels of education (Ley Orgánica para la Mejora de la Calidad Educativa, 2013). Conversely, pre-primary education in Spain is not mandatory. It is divided into two cycles: the first cycle accommodates children aged zero to three years (BOE, 2006). This type of school is usually run either by local or autonomous administrations or by privately owned educational institutions. The second cycle encompasses children three to six years of age and except for private institutions, the teaching is subsidized for all those children who choose to be enrolled in them. In pre-primary education, curricular content is organized by areas related to children's interests. Furthermore, the promotion of L2 teaching is the responsibility of the regional education authorities. As Table 4.2 illustrates, English is the most popular language usually implemented in the second cycle of pre-primary and in primary education.

In the Madrid region, it was established that L2 teaching was to be initiated in the second cycle of pre-primary education when children are three to six years of age with weekly periods of one or one and a half hours (BOCM, 2004). Table 4.3 presents the average number of English sessions in pre-primary education. Although the bilingual programme starts in primary, the law states that if the specialist teacher has time availability, the tuition in English in pre-primary can be increased. Later, it was established that the minimum number of hours of English in pre-school should be one and a half hours with a minimum of two weekly sessions (BOCM, 2008).

The primary CLIL bilingual programme of the Madrid Autonomous Community begins in Grade 1 and runs throughout its full six years. The choice of the subjects taught through the foreign language is determined by the school staff and resources available. According to Gibbons (2009, p. 10), "A program that integrates subject content and language takes a functional approach to language teaching and learning, in that it focuses on the subject-specific language needed for learning rather than aspects of language taught in isolation and taken out of a meaningful context". Table 4.4 illustrates the number of sessions of subjects commonly delivered in English in Grade 1 of CLIL primary education. Apart from English language tuition (4 hours per week, 1 hour per day), bilingual primary schools in the Madrid region much teach at least 30% of the syllabus in the foreign language (7.5 hours per week), up to a maximum of 50%. This means that curricular subjects other than Mathematics and Spanish Language and Literature can be taught through CLIL methodology.

As can be inferred from Tables 4.3 and 4.4, there seems to be a huge contrast between the degree of exposure to English in pre-primary and in primary CLIL bilingual education. As shown in Table 4.3, the amount of exposure to English in Pre-primary is around two hours weekly. In

Table 4.3 Average number of English sessions in pre-primary education

Age	Weekly sessions	Sessions length minutes
3	2	45'
4	2	45'
5	3	45'

Table 4.4 Subjects and number of teaching hours in bilingual primary schools in Madrid

Subject	Weekly sessions
English Language	4
Social Science (History and Geography)	3
Arts and Crafts	1
Physical Education	1
Music	1

Table 4.5 Minimum number of sessions in the second cycle of bilingual pre-primary education

Age	Weekly sessions	Sessions length minutes
3	3	45'
4	4	45'
5	5	45'

contrast, children starting CLIL in primary are exposed not only to the English language but also to content subjects through the medium of English, which means around ten hours of instruction a week.

As described in Sect. 3, the bilingual Spanish-English programme has recently been extended to some second cycle pre-primary public schools (BOCM, 2017). The implementation of early bilingual programmes seeks to lay the ground for CLIL primary education and depends upon the availability of appropriately qualified teachers. This novel programme consists of approximately 3 weekly sessions of 45 minutes each with a total of 9 hours a week. Table 4.5 presents the minimum number of sessions to be taught in English in the different years of the second cycle of bilingual pre-primary education.

One essential requirement to teach in the pre-primary and primary bilingual programmes is to have a sufficient number of teachers who have obtained the *Habilitación*, which is a language proficiency certificate required for bilingual teaching positions. To be able to teach subjects in bilingual schools, foreign language specialists must obtain this linguistic accreditation; otherwise, they can only teach English as a subject. Furthermore, the minimum language proficiency level required in the Madrid region to teach in pre-primary and primary is C1, according to the Common European Framework of Reference for languages (henceforth CEFR).

All in all, it seems that educational authorities in the Madrid region are increasingly recognizing the importance of introducing English in preschool to support the continuity of learning as children transition to primary CLIL bilingual education. This period of transition to CLIL-based teaching occurs over time and should be a dynamic process of continuity as children move from preschool to the first year of CLIL bilingual education. As Enever and Lindgren (2016) put it, "This challenge is even more evident at the preschool phase of education. Rapid changes in policy have not always been accompanied by the equally rapid development of suitable pre- and in-service teacher education courses" (p. 2).

3 Implementation of the Course

3.1 Age-Appropriate Practices to Scaffold CLIL at Transition to Primary

It is undeniable that the implementation of early bilingual programmes is necessary at the transition to primary bilingual education. Since bilingual education is very demanding for the teachers and learners, it requires a very different approach to the curriculum to that where the focus is only on learning English as a foreign language. It demands from teachers' understanding of young children's capacities, likes and needs as well as awareness of teaching strategies "to suit more implicit and naturalistic foreign language learning" (Kersten & Rohde, 2013, p. 113). The objective of the new teaching approach should focus on designing and implementing age-appropriate practices that promote the acquisition and learning of both the L1 and the L2 through an integrated content-based curriculum.

Thus, the practices described in this section are intended to help children to be well equipped for primary bilingual education. They can be inspirational ideas for pre- and in-service teachers by helping them to develop a conceptual framework based on current methodological approaches. To meet the CLIL methodology challenges, prospective teachers need to be trained in CLIL pedagogy: "Teaching in an L2 requires a specialist pedagogy. It is not the kind of pedagogy which a teacher would normally use when teaching in L1 or acquire in initial teacher education" (Ball et al., 2015, p. 252). Since at an early age (before six years of age), children are still developing their L1 and at a pre-literate stage, the learning should not be separated from all education areas but built on what they already know, even though their conceptual knowledge about the world is restricted. As pointed out in Sect. 2 of this chapter, to learn new languages, children use the same language learning strategies they use for acquiring their L1:

> Language is used as a means of communication, which implies two things: firstly, children have to be able to deduce the meaning of each situation and the reason for each activity from the context, i.e. from other information which the teacher has to provide in addition to the language; and secondly, by understanding the context and the meaning of the activity, the children are enabled to understand the language, and are thus able to gradually build up the language system of the L2 by themselves. (Kersten et al., 2010, p. 91)

Within CLIL-based contexts, both the teachers' language ability and their knowledge of the methodology are paramount for the effective teaching of curricular content. They need to foster the learners' input and output as well as to support their thinking skills. It is also importantly that methodology for early L2 teaching should not only focus on memorizing songs or learning single words in isolation. Rather, they should be based on the idea that early L2 learning runs in parallel with content learning and that, at an early age, children learn languages in a natural and subconscious manner by listening, understanding the messages and speaking (Cameron, 2001; Lightbown & Spada, 2013; Moon, 2000). Accordingly, the classroom focus should be on meaning and on fluency, rather than on form and accuracy (ibid., p. 38). In particular, the best practices to help language learning in a formal setting should be those which foster oral communicative interaction through listening and speaking.

All the ideas and suggestions in this section present a wide range of resources. They have been tested out and arise from classroom research in preschool settings based on principles that have successfully been used in bilingual immersion preschools (Fleta, 1999, 2001, 2003, 2018; Kersten et al., 2010). The suggested practices promote the implementation of CLIL and can be easily adapted to the learner's age and language level. They can be included in the pre-primary curriculum and embedded into all learning areas if they are planned in advance according to the children's different levels of ability and stages of language development. All the practices promote personal, emotional and social interactions through a myriad of multisensory learning experiences.

3.2   Practices for Supporting Listening

The practices described in this section propose a way of working which dovetails learning how to learn to listen in general and learning how to learn to listen to an L2 in particular. As illustrated in Fig. 4.1, listening is a prerequisite for developing other skills (Curtain & Dalhberg, 2010). Before children become readers and writers, they need to be proficient listeners and speakers. Young children can be easily distracted because their attention and memory are still developing (Perry, 1995). In this regard, to expand children's auditory awareness and to develop the listening skills in pre-primary education, children should be playing with sounds of all sorts (exploring the sounds around them, the sounds of common objects, sounds of musical instruments, sounds in picture books, speech sounds). Activities in Practice 4.1 help to expand children's auditory awareness through being conscious of the presence and absence of sounds.

As a follow-up, a list of the sound sources can be presented, either drawn or using pictures or photographs of the sound makers, and these can be classified into sound families: machines, weather, animals or people. The use of multisensory elements with auditory and visual clues provides learners with meaningful contexts in which they interpret the information and develop their comprehension in the L2 (Cameron, 2001). As Rost (1994) puts it, "Listening is vital for the language

Aims	For the learner to: • Expand attention span • Encourage children to listen for short periods of time (3 to 5 minutes) • Localise sounds • Discriminate sounds • Attach meaning to what is heard
Age	3 +
Level	Beginner
Language	Function: vocabulary and formulaic language development. Vocabulary: traffic, ambulance, fire-engine, bus, train, birds, dogs, children playing, people talking, teacher talking to children next door, wind blowing, rain, footsteps, drip of water, wind in trees, rustling paper; key jingling; telephone ringing; ringing bells; barking dog; a knock on the door; a creaking door. Structures: Keep quiet. Listen. Have your ears and eyes open/ready. What can you hear?
Resources	None
Procedure	In the classroom children listen in silence to the sounds they can hear (traffic, ambulance, fire-engine, bus, train, birds, children playing, people talking, next door teacher, the wind, the rain, etc.). The teacher can make a list of the sounds in English. The teacher can use pictures or photographs of the sound sources. The children can draw pictures of the sources of sound or write a list of words. The sounds can be recorded and played back during another lesson in order to make associations and to review the vocabulary and structures learned.
Variations	1. In silence, children can go for a walk-through school to identify sounds: in the dining room, toilets, playground, gym, etc. 2. This activity can also be carried out during school visits. Children can make a list of pictures or words of the sounds they can hear. Back in the classroom, the children can report on the sounds. 3. Teachers can hide an alarm clock, a timer, a toy that makes a sound in the classroom, and the children in silence guess where the sound comes from and the object that makes it. 4. Children can make a hair-band and big ears with card in the Arts and Crafts class to be worn during these activities (Template in: http://www.letters-and-sounds.com/phase-1-resources.html) 5. Teachers can provide children with a list of pictures or words of the sound source and children draw a circle/tick when they hear the sounds (dog, car, bird, airplane, music, etc.). If children can hear more sounds they add them to the list. 6. Teachers can set a 'Sounds Table' to make sound or create rhythm with classroom materials (rulers, crayons, scissors, paper, wooden blocks) or with other objects (dry leaves, sticks, shells, stones, coins, dice, safety pin, marbles, clothes peg). 7. The sounds can be classified into sound families: machines, weather, animals, people.

Practice 4.1   Listening to sounds in and around the classroom

	8. Teachers put objects in a box: school material: rulers, pencils, scissors, stapler, different types of paper, bubble paper. Musical instruments: tambourine, triangle, drum, whistle. Other objects: bag of crisps, a bunch of keys, a bell, snap fasteners, elastic bands, clock or a telephone, naming them while making them sound. Then, the teacher takes out an unseen object making it sound while singing the 'Old MacDonald' tune: *Mrs…has a box ee i ee i o* *And in that box she has a…* The children must listen carefully and have to guess what it is. The teacher can take the object/instrument out sounding it loudly, softly, quickly or slowly. Children can learn that common objects can make sounds: scrap/bump chair; opening/closing, fanning pages of book; crumpling/tearing/rattling newspaper.
Length	5/10 minutes

Practice 4.1 (continued)

classroom because it provides input for the learner. Without understanding input and the right level, any language simply cannot begin. Listening is fundamental for speaking" (pp. 141–142). Teachers can help children to develop their listening skills by localizing, identifying and remembering the sounds that are a part of the environment. Moreover, talking about environmental sounds will help to develop children's speaking skills.

3.3 Practices for Supporting Speaking

Listening and speaking are the foundation of the other skills. Unlike listening, speaking is a productive language skill. To support speaking, teachers can use music, language and movement by creating and adapting melodies, songs, chants, rhymes and poems to normal day-to-day routines. As acknowledged by some researchers, it seems that the brain remembers better the words and expressions of language if they are learnt with music and movement (Kuhl, 2010; Mithen, 2006; Patel, 2008). As acknowledged by Pinter (2017):

[…] learners are not yet able to analyse and manipulate language in an abstract way. They are learning by understanding meaningful messages. For example, in a song, children will not understand every word, but they will have an idea about what they are singing. (p. 167)

To encourage speaking and to maximize children' participation, teachers can take advantage of day-to-day routines and sing, recite and do actions in the classroom, in the playground, in the dining room or in the corridors at all times. Teachers can also make up their own songs: first, they decide on a language structure useful for the children at a specific time of the day; and then, on a familiar tune and some actions, gestures or movements to go with it.

Children can learn to discriminate the speech sounds, intonation patterns and the rhythm of English through stories, songs, chants, finger plays and rhymes and during choral speaking sessions: "Songs and rhymes increase their awareness of the sounds in words" (Pinnel & Fountas, 2011, p. 27). Activities in Practice 4.2, used with or without actions, gestures and movement, stimulate both sides of the brain and help children to develop holistically. Furthermore, informal singing and storytelling sessions tune the young learner' ears to the sounds and structures of English, increase the children's attention span and enhance the short-term and long-term memory.

Exposing children to songs, poems, rhymes, chants and creating opportunities for activities that support wordplay such as choral speaking, provide children with the opportunities to play with the sounds of any language during the early stages of learning how to speak (Patel, 2008). Hence, preschoolers should be provided with a wide range of sounds, pitches and intonation patterns in the target language in order to adjust their ears to the sounds and to the melody of the new language.

3.4   Practices for Supporting Emergent Readers

Young learners who face English as a new language at school must pay attention to the phonemes that make up English syllables, words and sentences in order to make sense of the continuous stream of speech sounds from the speakers around them since. This is because, as Cook (1997) points out, "a good deal of language remains primarily driven by

Aims	For the learner to: • Discriminate speech sounds • Interpret the nature and characteristics of speech sounds by increasing phonological awareness • Accent syllables
Age	3+
Level	Beginner
Language	<u>Function</u>: place the accent on syllables <u>Vocabulary</u>: rhyming words (snail-rail; mouse-house). Adjectives and adverbs <u>Structures</u>: Simple sentences in present tense.
Resources	Pictures of snake and bee
Procedure	Children can explore quality of speech sounds such as volume (quiet and loud), tempo (fast and slow), pitch (high and slow), rhythm (long and short), and they can play the 'Starting and stopping game'. This game helps children to be attentive as they all start a sound together and stop at a certain time: /s/ or /z/
Variations	1. The teachers can invite the children to set the slow beat of a snail and the quick beat of a mouse clapping their hands, tapping their fingers, skipping or bouncing a ball and emphasizing the accented syllables in this poem: 'Slowly, quickly' Slowly, slowly, very slowly Creeps the garden snail. Quickly, quickly, very quickly Runs the little mouse (Clark, 2002, p.46) 2. Very young children can set the beat with their index fingers as if they were windscreen wipers while reciting this poem: 'Tick-Tock' How does grandfather's clock sound? Tick---tock---tick---tock *(slowly)* How does mummy's little watch go? It goes tick-tock-tick-tock *(quickly)*
Length	5/10 minutes

Practice 4.2 Discrimination of English sounds

sound rather than meaning" (p. 228). In order for non-native children to absorb the phonemes and prosody of English, teachers need to understand which phonological skills acquired for the L1 can be transferred into English L2 and which ones are not equivalent in both languages and need to be learned. Even though young children are at the pre-literate stage, still unable to read written texts, they are able to read images in a

Aims	For the learner to: • Encourage emergent reading • Develop understanding of how reading works • Sequence sounds • Practice rhythm and rhyme
Age	3+
Level	Beginner
Language	Function: Pre-reading activity. To learn how to read from left to right, and from top to bottom using symbols. Vocabulary: Shapes. Names of sounds related to different body parts: hands, fingers, knees, legs, mouth. Click tongue, clap hands, click fingers, tap knees, pop finger out of mouth, thump chest, rub hand up and down arm or leg, scratch head, slap arm or leg. Children's names. Structures: Imperative. Simple sentences in present tense.
Resources	A card/digital board with a sequence of symbols: □ □○△ ☆ ○ □ □△
Procedure	Each symbol has an associated movement and sound. Children follow the pattern and make the sound and the movement while reading the symbols of the shapes. Square □ give a jump. Circle ○ touch the head. Triangle △ Hop. Star ☆ give a clap.
Variations	1. Different movements and sounds can be associated to symbols or shapes. 2. Children can explore the different sounds that the body parts can make with one hand, two hands, fingers, feet, with/ without shoes, heels (clap hands, click fingers, tap knees, pop finger out of mouth, thump chest, rub hand up and down arm or leg, scratch head, slap arm or leg). 3. Sitting in a circle, teacher passes a sound made with body part to a child. Children copy the sound, rhythm and so on until it has gone full circle. 4. Children can move around the classroom/playground marching to the clapping rhythm. 5. Children can clap according to the number of syllables of children's names. Explain to the children that each clap is a syllable in a word. For instance: 'cat' has only one syllable and that 'elephant' has three syllables 'e-le-phant'. The same happens to the children's names: 'Te-re-sa', 'John', 'Pe-ter'. 6. Children can pass round an instrument (drum, triangle, tambourine) and recite the following rhyme to the tune of 'London bridge'. 'Pass the drum' Pass the drum round the ring, Round the ring, round the ring, Pass the drum round the ring, Who is the one to tap and sing? 7. A child holds the instrument and at the end of the poem, says his or her name and plays the drum according to the number of syllables in the name. 8. The days of the week, months, numbers, etc., can be practiced in this way.

Practice 4.3 Pre-reading activity

	9. Children can play 'Copy the sound game', a child makes a sound with a body part, the group copies the sound. They take turns. 10. Children can play the 'Teddy Bear says game' and only repeat the sound when after they hear 'Teddy Bear says'. 11. The teacher can play the 'Soundmakers on/off game' as an attention getter by making sounds with different parts of the body.
Length	5/10 minutes

Practice 4.3   (continued)

quest for meaning. Likewise, by attaching actions, gestures and movements to illustrations, activities such as those in Practice 4.3 may play a significant role in the early stages of reading.

This fun game on rhythm patterns is a pre-reading activity that teaches preschoolers how to read from left to right and from top to bottom. As young learners play these games, they gain proficiency not only in localizing, identifying or attaching sounds to symbols but also in interacting both with the teacher and with each other. As underscored by Cooper (2010), "Some of the key skills for interaction are good eye contact, turn taking, showing an interest in the other person, listening and responding. There are lots of games that encourage these skills" (p. 29). By clapping the musical rhythms, children develop their fine motor skills and by associating sounds and movements to illustrations, they improve L2 word and language structures retention.

3.5   Practices for Supporting Emergent Writers

There are many ways in which teachers can foster children's imagination and develop stimulating learning environments. According to some authors, there is a correlation among language, music and the brain (Patel, 2008). It is precisely because of this correlation and of the positive effects of exposing children to music and songs in the classroom that many educators have incorporated music, especially songs, in their teaching strategies. Furthermore, there is a close correlation between music and literacy, as both help to train the brain to notice rhythmic patterns and sound qualities. Therefore, the first step in the creative writing process of Practice 4.4 is to invite children to listen to a piece of music or,

Aims	For the learner to: • Develop imagination and creativity • Draw and label pictures • Spell words correctly • Create messages • Talk about what they write
Age	3+
Level	Beginner
Language	Function: Classroom experience to investigate the effects of music in encouraging artistic expression and listening, writing, reading and speaking skills. Vocabulary: Words related to colours, numbers, animals, plants. Structures: Imperative. Simple sentences in present tense.
Resources	CD, DVD player or any music reproducer. Suggested music: Brahms (Lullaby, Waltz in A flan major Op. 39/15); Grieg (March of the Dwarfs Op.54/3); Grieg (Peer-Gynt Suite: In the Hall of the Mountain King); Hovhaness (Symphony No.2: Mysterious Mountain, Op.132, III. Andante Expressivo); Holst (The Planets: Jupiter). A3-sized paper, cardboard or similar. Crayons, markers and pencils of various colours and thicknesses
Procedure	"Brainstorming": Teacher reviews colours, numbers, animals, etc. with the whole class. The teacher then explains the activities to be carried out. Children listen to a piece of classical music, close their eyes and think of a picture and the colours they would use to colour it in. After listening to the music, children draw and colour pictures and write English words or phrases about the drawing. Finally, children explain to the other children what they have drawn/painted and what they have written using as much English as possible.
Variations	1. Children individually visualize a character and think of a story that has a beginning, middle and end. Then, they write and illustrate the story. Finally, students present and read the story in class to their classmates. 2. Children are shown a piece of fine art while listening to the music and think and write about the story behind the picture. Then they share their stories with the whole class. 3. In the gym, children can move to the music as they think their character in their story would move and use different types of movement (for levels: high, low and medium; for speed: fast and slow; for directions: backwards, forwards or sideways; and for movements: jumping, skipping or running).
Length	45 minutes

Practice 4.4   Developing emergent writing

alternatively, to see a work of art while listening to the music. While listening individually to music or/and alternately observing a picture, children draw images that reflect their thoughts. When they listen to music, they visualize images and draw them. They then think of words in English to describe their drawings, because creative writing recreates and preserves experience and plays with words, ideas and patterns (Palmer & Corbett, 2003, p. 55).

The purpose of this activity is to work on the musical, spatial, kinaesthetic and linguistic intelligences and to tap into children's imagination and creativity. This type of teaching involves both sides of the brain: the visual–spatial right hemisphere and the linguistic left hemisphere, thus favouring the model of teaching intended to develop the linguistic, creative, personal and social areas of learning. As Cameron puts it, "(e)vidence that children work naturally with rules and patterns comes from their creative productions of utterances" (Cameron, 2001, p. 102).

4 Outcomes and Implications

Taking as a springboard L1 acquisition approaches for early L2 learning, this chapter aimed to examine how the initial stages of bilingual education are being implemented in pre-primary education in the Madrid Autonomous Community. One of the objectives was to show that successful early L2 learning is built upon the rich and meaningful input children get via intensive exposure through everyday interactions at school, hence the necessity of incorporating explicit teaching of communication skills during the first stages of the L2 learning process.

The transition from pre-primary to primary education seems to have an impact on children's physical, cognitive, emotional, personal and social development. To apply for the bilingual programme in pre-primary education, teachers should be confident about their target language proficiency and trained to plan and carry out activities that scaffold listening, speaking, reading and writing in order to provide learners with rich language input and output. Moreover, to lay the ground for solid bilingual education, teachers from the two levels of schooling should meet to discuss the transition. In order to plan activities that suit children with different levels of proficiency, primary teachers should be well informed about the type of work that has been done at pre-primary school.

The first step to develop effective pre- and in-service teacher education is to be aware of teacher's needs. When dealing with very young L2 learners, if teachers use the L2 as the medium of instruction, they need to adapt their speech to make sure that children understand the messages so that they are able to learn. Practices that scaffold CLIL at the transition to primary should aim to support children in comprehending messages because even though children do not necessarily understand the L2 grammatical structure, they are able to attach meaning to expressions related to routines, songs, chants, rhymes, illustrations, stories, gestures, actions, movements and the like. When planning English language practices at the transition to CLIL, teachers should take into consideration not only the learners' age, their linguistic development and knowledge of the world, but also the demands of the communication tasks.

The journey from pre-primary to primary bilingual education is of paramount importance because primary school students must learn non-linguistic subjects through foreign language. Therefore, in order to ensure a smooth transition to primary bilingual education, the following issues should be taken into consideration as a priority: increased exposure to the L2 rich input through more curricular time; greater communication, coordination and collaboration between teachers in both stages to improve teaching quality; increase of comprehensive initial teacher training in the faculties of education and in-service training in both language and methodology; creation of guides, materials and educational resources adapted to the context and specific students' needs; and promotion of auditory and oral skills at the beginning to facilitate reading–writing skills in the foreign language later on. To make the most of bilingual programmes and reduce the speed to catch up the appropriate language level and conceptual knowledge, teachers and school directors should be aware of the early foreign language learning principles and methodological approaches. To support quality teaching, it is important to improve the expertise of teacher education. What is more, to ensure progression in learning, educational authorities should create an appropriate infrastructure for a smooth transition from pre-primary to primary bilingual education.

References

Baker, C., & Wright, W. (2017). *Foundations of Bilingual Education and Bilingualism*. Bristol: Multilingual Matters.

Ball, P., Kelly, K., & Clegg, J. (2015). *Putting CLIL into Practice*. Oxford: Oxford University Press.

Bentley, K. (2010). *The TKT Course: CLIL Module*. Cambridge: Cambridge University Press.

Boletín Oficial del Estado (BOE). (2006). Ley Orgánica 2/2006, de 3 de mayo, de Educación, p. 17162. Retrieved from https://boe.es/boe/dias/2006/05/04/pdfs/A17158-17207.pdf

Boletín Oficial de la Comunidad de Madrid. (2004). *Selección de colegios públicos de Educación Infantil y Primaria de la Comunidad de Madrid en los que se llevará a cabo la implantación de la enseñanza bilingüe español-inglés*. Retrieved from http://www.madrid.org/dat_capital/upe/impresos_pdf/Biling2004_05.pdf

Boletín Oficial de la Comunidad de Madrid. (2008). *Las enseñanzas de la Educación Infantil*. Retrieved from http://www.madrid.org/wleg_pub/secure/normativas/contenidoNormativa.jsf?opcion=VerHtml&nmnorma=4922&cdestado=P#no-back-button

Boletín Oficial de la Comunidad de Madrid. (2017). *Autorización de la enseñanza bilingüe en segundo ciclo de Educación Infantil*. Retrieved from https://www.bocm.es/boletin/CM_Orden_BOCM/2017/06/21/BOCM-20170621-16.PDF

Boletín Oficial de la Comunidad de Madrid. (2018). Madrid, a Bilingual Community 2017–2018, p. 7. Retrieved from http://www.madrid.org/bvirtual/BVCM016411.pdf

Bonnet, A. (2012). Towards evidence base for CLIL: How to integrate qualitative and quantitative as well as process, product and participant perspectives in CLIL research. *International CLIL Research Journal, 1*(4), 65–78.

Bruner, J. (1996). *The Culture of Education*. Cambridge, MA: Harvard University Press.

Cameron, L. (2001). *Teaching Languages to Young Learners*. Cambridge: Cambridge University Press.

Clark, V. (2002). *High Low Dolly Pepper. Developing Music Skills with Young Children*. London: A&C Black.

Conkbayir, M. (2017). *Early Childhood and Neuroscience: Theory, Research and Implications for Practice*. London: Bloomsbury Academic.

Consejería de Educación e Investigación. (2018–2019). *Datos y Cifras de la Educación 2018–2019*. Retrieved from http://www.comunidad.madrid/sites/default/files/doc/educacion/sgea_datosycifras_presentacion_18_19.pdf

Cook, G. (1997). Language play, language learning. *ELT Journal, 51*(3), 224–231.

Coonan, C. M. (2005). The natural learning of a foreign language. CLIL as a possible partial solution for the primary school. *Scuola e Lingue Moderne*, 4–5.

Cooper, J. (2010). *The Early Years Communication Handbook: A Practical Guide to Creating a Communication Friendly Setting*. London: Practical Pre-school Books.

Council of European Union. (2001). *The Common European Framework of Reference for Languages: Learning, Teaching, Assessment*. Brussels: Council of Europe. Retrieved from https://www.coe.int/en/web/common-european-framework-reference-languages

Council of European Union. (2002, March 15–16). *Presidency Conclusions*. Barcelona European Council. Retrieved from http://ec.europa.eu/investinresearch/pdf/download_en/barcelona_european_council.pdf

Coyle, D. (2010). Foreword. In D. Lasagabaster & Y. R. de Zarobe (Eds.), *CLIL in Spain: Implementation, Results and Teacher Training* (pp. vii–viii). Newcastle upon Tyne: Cambridge Scholars Publishers.

Coyle, D., Hood, P., & Marsh, D. (2010). *CLIL. Content and Language Integrated Learning*. Cambridge: Cambridge University Press.

Cummins, J. (1979). Linguistic interdependence and the educational development of bilingual children. *Review of Educational Research, 49*(2), 222–251.

Cummins, J. (1984). *Bilingual Education and Special Education: Issues in Assessment and Pedagogy*. San Diego: College Hill.

Curtain, H., & Dalhberg, C. A. (2010). *Languages and Children. Making the Match: New Languages for Young Learners, Grades K-8* (4th ed.). Boston: Pearson.

Cutler, A. (2012). *Native Listening: Language Experience and the Recognition of Spoken Words*. Cambridge, MA: MIT Press.

Dale, L., & Tanner, R. (2012). *CLIL Activities. A Resource for Subject and Language Teachers*. Cambridge: Cambridge University Press.

Dalton-Puffer, C. (2011). Content and language integrated learning: From practice to principles. *Annual Review of Applied Linguistics, 31*, 182–204.

Dalton-Puffer, C., & Smit, U. (2007). Introduction. In C. Dalton-Puffer & U. Smit (Eds.), *Empirical Perspectives on CLIL Classroom Discourse* (pp. 7–23). Frankfurt: Peter Lang.

Dearden, J. (2015). *English as a Medium of Instruction—A Growing Global Phenomenon*. London: The British Council.

Dobson, A., Johnstone, R., & Pérez Murillo, M. (2010). *Evaluation Report of the Bilingual Education Project*. Madrid: Ministerio de Educación y British Council.

Enever, J., & Lindgren, E. (2016). Early language learning in instructed contexts—Editorial introduction. *Education Inquiry, 7*(1), 1–8.

European Commission. (1995). *White Paper on Education & Training: Towards the Learning Society*. Brussels: European Commission. Retrieved from https://publications.europa.eu/en/publication-detail/-/publication/d0a8aa7a-5311-4eee-904c-98fa541108d8/language-en

European Commission. (2011a). *Language Learning at Pre-primary School Level: Making it Efficient and Sustainable. A Policy Handbook*. Brussels: European Commission. Retrieved from http://ec.europa.eu/assets/eac/languages/policy/language-policy/documents/early-language-learning-handbook_en.pdf

European Commission. (2011b). *Early Childhood Education and Care: Providing All Our Children with the Best Start for the World of Tomorrow*. Retrieved from https://eur-lex.europa.eu/LexUriServ/LexUriServ.do?uri=COM:2011:0066:FIN:EN:PDF

Eurydice Network. (2006). *Content and Language Integrated Learning (CLIL) at School in Europe*. Brussels, Belgium: Eurydice.

Fleta, M. T. (1999). *La adquisición del inglés no-nativo por niños: el desarrollo de la cláusula*. Unpublished doctoral dissertation, Universidad Complutense de Madrid.

Fleta, M. T. (2001). Child L2 acquisition of interrogatives. In *Proceedings 8th Conference of the International Association for the Study of Child Language (IASCL)* (Vol. I, pp. 1356–1370). San Sebastian: Cascadilla Press.

Fleta, M. T. (2003). IS-insertion in child grammars of English: A step forward between developmental stages? In J. M. Liceras, H. Zobl, & H. Goodluck (Eds.), *Proceedings of the 6th Generative Approaches to Second Language Acquisition Conference (GASLA 2002)* (pp. 85–96). Somerville, MA: Cascadilla Proceedings Project.

Fleta, M. T. (2015). Active listening for second language learning in the early years. In S. Mourão & M. Lourenço (Eds.), *Early Years Second Language Education: International Perspectives on Theories and Practice*. Abingdon: Routledge.

Fleta, M. T. (2018). From research on child L2 acquisition of English to classroom practice. In J. Rokita-Jaśkow & M. Ellis (Eds.), *Early Instructed Second*

Language Acquisition: Pathways to Competence (Early Language Learning in School Contexts). Bristol: Multilingual Matters.

García Ruíz, M. J. (2009). *Estudio Comparativo de la educación: Finlandia y Comunidad de Madrid. Análisis y Recomendaciones*. Comunidad de Madrid Consejería de Educación. Retrieved from https://canal.uned.es/uploads/materials/resources/pdf/2/7/1273511761972.pdf

Genesee, F. (2008). Bilingual first language acquisition: Evidence from Montreal. *Diversité urbaine*, 9–26. http://www.psych.mcgill.ca/perpg/fac/genesee/6.pdf

Gibbons, P. (2009). *English Learners, Academic Literacy and Thinking*. Portsmouth: Heinemann.

Instituto Nacional de Estadística. (2018). Retrieved from https://www.ine.es/

Kersten, K. A., & Rohde, C. (2013). Teaching English to young learners. In A. Flyman Mattsson & C. Norrby (Eds.), *Language Acquisition and Use in Multilingual Contexts* (Travaux de l'Institut de Linguistique de Lund) (Vol. 52). Lund: Lund University.

Kersten, K., Rohde, A., Schelletter, C., & Steinlen, A. (2010). *Bilingual Preschools Best Practices* (Vol. II). WVT Wissenschaftlicher Verlag Trier.

Krashen, S. (1982). *Principles and Practice in Second Language Acquisition*. Oxford: Pergamon.

Kuhl, P. (2010). Brain mechanisms in early language acquisition. *Neuron, 67*(5), 713–727.

Lightbown, P., & Spada, N. (2013). *How Languages are Learned* (4th ed.). Oxford: Oxford University Press.

Llinares, A., & Dafouz, E. (2010). Content and language integrated programmes in the Madrid region: Overview of research findings. In D. Lagasabaster & Y. Ruiz de Zarobe (Eds.), *CLIL in Spain: Implementation, Results and Teacher Training* (pp. 95–114). Newcastle upon Tyne: Cambridge Scholars Publishers.

LOMCE (Ley Orgánica para la Mejora de la Calidad Educativa). (2013). Retrieved from https://www.boe.es/boe/dias/2013/12/10/pdfs/BOE-A-2013-12886.pdf

Long, M. (1996). The role of linguistic environment in second language acquisition. In W. Ritchie & T. Bhatia (Eds.), *Handbook of Second Language Acquisition* (pp. 413–468). London: Academic Press.

Lyster, R. (2007). *Learning and Teaching Languages through Content: A Counterbalanced Approach*. Amsterdam and Philadelphia: John Benjamins Publishing Company.

Mackey, A. (2007). *Conversational Interaction in Second Language Acquisition: A Series of Empirical Studies*. Oxford: Oxford University Press.

Marsh, D. (2002). *CLIL/EMILE: The European Dimension: Actions, Trends and Foresight Potential*. European Commission. Retrieved from http://europa. eu.int/comm/education/policies/lang/doc/david_marsh-report.pdf

Mehisto, P. (2007). What a school needs to consider before launching a CLIL programme. In D. Marsh & D. Wolff (Eds.), *Diverse Contexts—Converging Goals: CLIL in Europe*. Frankfurt am Main: Peter Lang.

Meisel, J. (2011). *First and Second Language Acquisition: Parallels and Differences*. Cambridge: Cambridge University Press.

Ministerio de Educación y Formación Profesional. (2018). Estadística de las Enseñanzas no universitarias. Enseñanza de Lenguas Extranjeras, Curso 2017–2018, p. 3. Retrieved from http://www.educacionyfp.gob.es/dam/jcr:0008fa9a-b207-48d1-a2fd-b4843bc61130/nota-17-18.pdf

Mithen, S. (2006). *The Singing Neanderthals: The Origins of Music, Language, Mind, and Body*. Boston: Harvard University Press.

Moon, J. (2000). *Children Learning English*. Oxford: Macmillan-Heinemann.

Mourão, S. (2019). Research into the teaching of English as a foreign language in early childhood education and care. In S. Garton & F. Copland (Eds.), *The Routledge Handbook of Teaching English to Young Learners* (pp. 425–441). Abingdon: Routledge.

Mourão, S., & Ferreirinha S. (2016). *Early Language Learning in Pre-primary Education in Portugal*. Unpublished report. APPI, Associação Portuguesa de Professores de Inglês. Retrieved from http://www.appi.pt/activeapp/wp-content/uploads/2016/07/Pre-primary-survey-report-July-FINAL-rev.pdf

Mourão, S., & Lourenço, M. (2015). *Early Years Second Language Education: International Perspectives on Theories and Practice*. Abingdon: Routledge.

Muñoz, C., & Naves, T. (2007). CLIL in Spain. In D. Marsh & D. Wolff (Eds.), *Windows on CLIL. Content and Language Integrated Learning in the European Spotlight* (pp. 160–165). The Netherlands: European Centre for Modern Languages.

Murphy, V., & Evangelou, M. (2016). *Early Childhood Education in English for Speakers of Other Languages*. London: British Council.

Official Journal of the European Union. (2006). *Recommendation of the European Parliament and of the Council on Key Competences for Lifelong Learning*. Retrieved from https://eurlex.europa.eu/legalcontent/EN/TXT/PDF/?uri=CELEX:32006H0962&from=EN

Palmer, S., & Corbett, P. (2003). *Literacy: What Works?* Cheltenham: Nelson Thornes.

Papaja, K., & Swiatek, A. (2016). *Modernizing Educational Practice. Perspectives in Content and Language Integrated Learning (CLIL)*. Newcastle upon Tyne: Cambridge Scholars Publishing.

Patel, A. D. (2008). *Music, Language, and the Brain*. Oxford: Oxford University Press.

Pérez-Vidal, C. (2013). Perspectives and challenge of CLIL experience. In C. Abello-Contesse, P. M. Chandler, M. D. López-Jiménez, & R. Chacón-Beltrán (Eds.), *Bilingual and Multilingual Education in the 21st Century. Buildings on Experience* (pp. 59–85). Bristol: Multilingual Matters.

Perry, R. (1995). Take some notice of me! Primary children and their learning potential. In J. Moyles (Ed.), *Beginning Teaching: Beginning Learning in Primary Education*. Buckingham: Open University Press.

Pinnel, G., & Fountas, I. (2011). *Literacy Beginnings. A Prekindergarten Handbook*. Portsmouth: Heinemann.

Pinter, A. M. (2017). *Teaching Young Language Learners* (2nd ed.). Oxford: Oxford University Press.

Reilly, T., & Medrano, P. (2009). MEC/British Council Bilingual Project. Twelve years of education and a smooth transition into secondary. In E. Dafouz & M. Guerrini (Eds.), *CLIL Across Educational Levels* (pp. 59–70). Madrid: Santillana Educación/Richmond Publishing.

Rixon, S. (2013). *British Council Survey of Policy and Practice in Primary English Language Teaching Worldwide*. London: British Council. Retrieved from http://englishagenda.britishcouncil.org/sites/ec/files/D120%20Survey%20of%20Teachers%20to%20YLs_FINAL_Med_res_online.pdf

Rokita-Jaskow, J. (2015, November 26). Language policy in Poland: An interplay of top-down and bottom-up influences. *Conference Presentation: Issues of Multilingualism in Early Childhood Education. Research into Early Years Language Learning*, Roma Tre University, Rome, Italy.

Rost, M. (1994). *Introducing Listening*. London: Penguin.

Vygotsky, L. A. (1978). *Mind in Society: The Development of Higher Psychological Processes*. Cambridge, MA: Harvard University Press.

Wood, D. J., Bruner, J. S., & Ross, G. (1976). The role of tutoring in problem solving. *Journal of Child Psychiatry and Psychology, 17*, 89–100.

5

Utilizing the CLIL Approach in a Japanese Primary School: A Comparative Study of CLIL and Regular EFL Lessons

Yuki Yamano

1 Introduction

In recent years, Content and Language Integrated Learning (CLIL) has received growing attention, especially in East Asian countries, due to the introduction of English as a Foreign Language (EFL) education in primary schools. However, few empirical studies have been conducted regarding the feasibility and potentiality of content- and language-integrated instruction in these contexts (Butler, 2005; Yamano, 2012; Yamano, 2013a, 2013b, 2013c; Yamano, 2015). Coyle (2007) has called for encouraging the CLIL research community "to be connected" by "involving more practitioner researchers in articulating theories of practice through learning communities" (p. 558). In regard to these issues, it is particularly important to investigate the possible outcomes of CLIL at Japanese primary schools, in which English education was formally implemented in April 2011. In this context, many teachers have been

Y. Yamano (✉)
School of Education, Utsunomiya University, Utsunomiya, Japan
e-mail: yyamano@cc.utsunomiya-u.ac.jp

© The Author(s) 2019
K. Tsuchiya, M. D. Pérez Murillo (eds.), *Content and Language Integrated Learning in Spanish and Japanese Contexts*, https://doi.org/10.1007/978-3-030-27443-6_5

searching for effective educational programs (the Society for Testing English Proficiency (STEP), 2012) while integrating CLIL research into Asian contexts. To meet this need, the present study explores the potentiality of CLIL at a Japanese primary school by utilizing the four principles of CLIL, known as the 4Cs: Content (subject matter), Communication (language), Cognition (cognitive skills), and Culture/Community (awareness toward learning community and pluricultural understanding) (Coyle, 2007; Coyle, Hood, & Marsh, 2010; Mehisto, Marsh, & Frigols, 2008).

1.1   Japanese Primary EFL Education

Before discussing the implementation of the CLIL approach at a Japanese public primary school, it is necessary to first define the goals and characteristics of Japanese primary EFL education as conducted in the context of this study.

According to the Ministry of Education, Culture, Sports, Science and Technology (MEXT), the formal name of Japanese primary EFL education is "foreign language activities" (MEXT, 2009). Although it does not include a specific language in its name, MEXT (2009) clarifies that "[i]n principle, English should be selected for foreign language activities" (p. 1). The name of the subject itself represents the uniqueness of Japanese elementary EFL education, which is in fact different from that in other Japanese contexts such as junior and senior high schools.

According to MEXT, the primary purpose of Foreign Language (FL) education is "to form the foundation of pupils' communication abilities through foreign languages" (MEXT, 2009, p. 1). More precisely, it includes three overall goals: (1) developing an understanding of languages and cultures through various experiences; (2) fostering a positive attitude toward communication; and (3) familiarizing pupils with the sounds and basic expressions of foreign languages (MEXT, 2009, p. 1). Through these objectives, foreign language education was initiated for all fifth and sixth graders in Japan. At the same time, it imposed certain responsibilities on Japanese elementary school teachers who were basically subject teachers. Such responsibilities included creating their own lesson plans for their English classes.

In this regard, MEXT recommends that teachers utilize their knowledge of other subjects in order to maintain the interest of their pupils as well as enhance the communication activities in the classroom (MEXT, 2009). On the one hand, this treatment imposes a certain burden on Japanese primary school teachers, who are basically subject teachers and different from English language specialists at junior and senior high schools. On the other hand, it provides an opportunity for primary teachers to utilize their knowledge of other subjects in the class. Therefore, it is expected that CLIL can be helpful for Japanese primary school teachers to conduct their lessons by informing them how to integrate content and language in the classroom.

As indicated by Yoshida (2011), the importance of experiential learning and the "practical and real use" was lacking in Japanese EFL education until its formal implementation in 2011 (p. 111). In order to define experiential learning, Yoshida (2011) cited several instances of other major subjects that pupils study in the class. For instance, as a part of social studies classes, they can visit a garbage disposal plant in order to observe how refuse is recycled and "to see how society functions" (Yoshida, 2011, p. 104). As a part of science classes, they can grow plants or raise animals as hands-on experiments. Through these study processes, pupils can engage in "practical, down-to-earth experiential learning" (Yoshida, 2011, p. 104).

Furthermore, Yoshida (2011) defined this phase of experiential learning as an "approach phase" (p. 104) and argued that this empowered pupils to "take off" where "abstract formulas and cognitively demanding de-contextualized content is introduced" (Yoshida, 2011, p. 104). In fact, English was the only major subject that lacked this particular "approach phase" (Yoshida, 2011, p. 104). Therefore, Yoshida (2011) attributed one of the reasons for the failure of Japanese English education to the lack of experiential learning in primary school.

In regard to evidence about the failure of Japanese English education, Yoshida (2011) referred to the result of a questionnaire conducted by the National Institute for Educational Policy Research (NIER, 2006). It suggested that the number of junior high school students who favored English declined as they became older. In addition, almost one-third of the junior high school students stated that they could not comprehend

English. It indicated that students experienced more difficulty in studying English than in other subjects, such as math or science, because of the lack of experiential learning at primary school (Yoshida, 2011).

In order to solve the aforementioned problem as well as accomplish the successful transition from "approach to take-off," Yoshida (2011) argued that Japanese primary EFL education should be taught not only "through exposure in the here-and-now cognitively undemanding communicative situation" (p. 111) but also by "learning the skills and knowledge necessary for higher level communication activities" (p. 111). Furthermore, Butler (2005) encouraged Japanese primary teachers, when creating their lesson plans, to include a balance between their pupils' cognition levels and their English competence. She also insisted that lowering the cognitive level of the activities or materials was not appropriate for pupils in the fifth and six grades even though their English was somewhat limited (Butler, 2005). Thus, the importance of experiential learning is acknowledged in this study based on the premise that CLIL would be useful to enrich experiential learning in regard to Cognition, the third principle of the CLIL approach.

In addition to the experiential study, Yoshida (2003, 2008) also suggested that another goal of Japanese primary English education was to develop an understanding of international issues such as global warming, environmental topics, and cultural diversity. The guidelines of MEXT (2009) also stipulated the importance of "deepen[ing] the experiential understanding of the languages and cultures of Japan and foreign languages" (p. 1). MEXT (2009) indicates that deepening the understanding of other cultures and languages can enhance the awareness of students toward their own culture and native language. Thus, the development of international understanding should be included as one of the important elements of Japanese primary school English education.

Thus, the goals and characteristics of Japanese primary EFL education involve an effective integration of content and language, experiential learning, and intercultural understanding. In other words, these objectives acknowledge the 4Cs: Content, Communication, Cognition (various types of experiential study), and Culture/Community (Coyle, 2007; Coyle et al., 2010; Ikeda, 2011; Mehisto et al., 2008). In the following section, the use of the CLIL approach in Japanese EFL education will be further explored based on the 4Cs perspective.

1.2 CLIL and Japanese Primary EFL Education

CLIL was developed in Europe at around the same time as the European Union (EU) was promoting a policy which aimed to develop its members' foreign language education by encouraging students to learn two other languages in addition to their native tongue (European Commission, 2003). Since then, the CLIL approach has proven to be a promising educational approach that has the potential to enhance students' proficiency in their second language by integrating learning content courses along with the non-native language (Coyle, 2007; Coyle et al., 2010; Eurydice, 2006; Ikeda, 2011; Marsh, 2000; Mehisto et al., 2008). The CLIL approach has proliferated in Europe and numerous studies have been conducted on its educational effects (Dalton-Puffer, Nikula, & Smit, 2010). In addition, insightful frameworks have been developed to clearly define CLIL practices, one of which is the four principles of CLIL (i.e., the 4Cs) (Coyle, 2007; Coyle et al., 2010). Results from evaluations have suggested that CLIL implementation in European primary schools is effective in improving pupil proficiency in the target language (Bentley, 2010; Lorenzo, Casal, & Moore, 2010; Serra, 2007) and fostering a positive attitude and motivation toward language acquisition (González, 2011). This then raises the question: is it possible to share these positive attributes in a different context and environment?

As explained in the previous section and elsewhere (Yamano, 2013a, 2013b, 2013c), Japanese primary EFL education places importance on Content and Communication, Cognition, and Culture/Community, which the CLIL approach values as the four crucial principles of the theory (Coyle, 2007;Coyle et al., 2010; Ikeda, 2011; Mehisto et al., 2008). Therefore, CLIL seems effective for Japanese primary EFL education; however, it is important to further comprehend the rationale for the use of the CLIL approach in Japanese primary EFL education in terms of the 4Cs perspective.

1.2.1   Content

The term "Content" refers to the subject matter studied in class. In other words, it is the "progression in new knowledge, skills and understanding" (Coyle et al., 2010, p. 53), which can be constructed not only through one subject, such as science or social studies, but also through several subjects depending on the theme of learning (Coyle et al., 2010; Ikeda, 2011; Mehisto et al., 2008). In addition, as mentioned above, the guidelines of Japanese primary school English education suggest that instruction in class should be in accordance with the students' interests by linking it with several other subjects (MEXT, 2009). This is in agreement with the description of one of the core features of CLIL methodology: "maximizing the accommodation of students' interests" (Mehisto et al., 2008, p. 29) by bringing authenticity to learning (Coyle et al., 2010; Marsh, 2000; Mehisto et al., 2008). Thus, it is expected that a CLIL classroom learning environment is an effective one (Coyle et al., 2010; Mehisto et al., 2008), since it may provide Japanese primary school pupils with meaningful and authentic educational context.

1.2.2   Communication

Under the term "Communication," CLIL recognizes the importance of three different types of language: (1) the language *of* learning (language required to learn the primary concepts of the content); (2) the language *for* learning (language required to engage in classroom activities or related tasks); and (3) the language *through* learning (language that was not planned beforehand but emerges during the lesson (Coyle, 2007; Coyle et al., 2010)). Particularly, "language through learning" never appears without the active participation of the teachers and the students (Coyle et al., 2010), which is one of the main objectives of Japanese early EFL education. In regard to these three types of language, this study places a special emphasis on the importance of the "language through learning" while investigating the differences between a CLIL and a non-CLIL environment.

1.2.3 Cognition

The term "cognition" refers to the cognitive skills that students employ during the lesson (Coyle et al., 2010; Mehisto et al., 2008). The CLIL approach encourages students to utilize various types of cognitive skills from cognitively less demanding ones such as understanding or memorizing key vocabulary to cognitively higher demanding skills that include creative thinking while using the target language (Coyle et al., 2010; Ikeda, 2011; Mehisto et al., 2008). As a result, CLIL teachers should take care to achieve a sufficient balance in terms of cognitively and linguistically demanding tasks when they plan CLIL units or lessons. In a similar vein, it has been explained in the previous section that the consideration of classroom activities in Japanese primary EFL education was crucial in order to fill in the gap between pupils' lower levels of foreign language competence and their relatively higher levels of cognitive skills (Butler, 2005; Yoshida, 2011). In order to facilitate this type of planning, Coyle et al. (2010) developed the CLIL Matrix, "an adapted version of Cummins' 1984 model" (p.43), which has high and low cognitive demands in the Y axis and high and low linguistic demands in the X axis (see Figs. 5.2 and 5.3 in Sect. 3.3).

According to this CLIL Matrix, Coyle et al. (2010) explain that the "tasks [should] follow the route from low linguistic and cognitive demands to high linguistic and cognitive demands" (p. 68). Quadrant 1 is the starting point and provides initial confidence to the learners by reducing the linguistic and cognitive demands. Quadrant 2 ensures that language demands do not impede the achievement of cognitive goals. In Quadrant 2, it can be assumed that already learned language is recycled while the students are engaged in tasks that utilize their higher-order thinking skills (HOTS). Quadrant 3 represents the final situation wherein the students engage in tasks by incorporating new language and high cognitive skills. Quadrant 4 is used only when high linguistic demands necessitate linguistic practices or grammar explanations in order to assist the progress of learning (Coyle et al., 2010). This matrix is applied in this study in order to investigate how CLIL and non-CLIL pupils cognitively engage in classroom activities.

1.2.4   Culture/Community

Although the terms "Culture and Community" are used interchangeably in CLIL theory (Ikeda, 2011, p. 8), Ikeda (2011) explained that the former refers to developing intercultural understanding and global citizenship, while Mehisto et al. (2008) defined the latter as the realization "that being members of the learning community is enriching" (p. 31). Thus, the CLIL approach aims to bring global issues into the class through the enrichment of learning communities, which is in line with one of the purposes of Japanese primary school English education (MEXT, 2009) as mentioned in Sect. 1.1.

Therefore, the goals and characteristics of Japanese primary school English education clearly coincide with the 4Cs of the CLIL approach, as seen in Fig. 5.1.

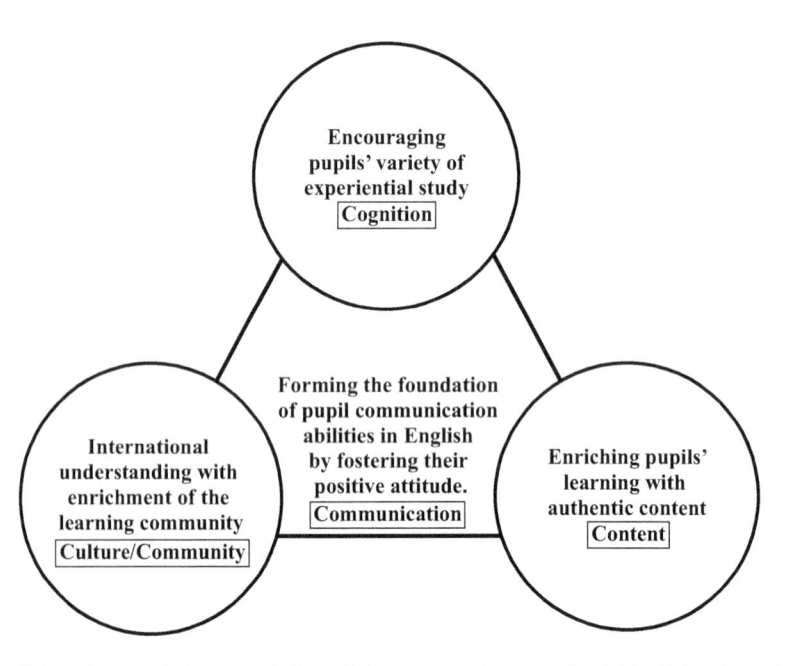

Fig. 5.1 Aims and characteristics of Japanese primary school English education based on the 4Cs of the CLIL approach

Based on these ideas, it is worthwhile to explore the feasibility and potentiality of the CLIL approach in a Japanese primary school by comparing the differences between CLIL and non-CLIL (standard) instruction through the 4Cs perspective.

2 Course Design

Three research lessons for both CLIL and non-CLIL classes were conducted in 2011 (see Appendix). The topic for this study was "animals," which was chosen beforehand on the basis of a needs-based analysis of the pupils and teachers. The lessons were aimed at familiarizing the pupils with the names of colors and animals, characteristics, and habitats of animals as well as using interrogative questions in English, such as "What animal do you like?" or "What animals live in the ocean?" and so forth.

In the non-CLIL class, English lessons were conducted using a conventional approach which solely focused on language learning. This involved: Presentation/Input; Practice (e.g., explicit practice using questions and visual aids such as picture cards or videos); and Production/ Output (e.g., playing fun games using the learned vocabulary). Furthermore, the teachers continued to focus on the overall objectives by providing the pupils with numerous fun learning activities to maintain their interest, familiarize them with the target vocabulary, and cultivate the pupils' positive attitude toward communication.

On the other hand, the CLIL lessons were conducted by incorporating the 4Cs. In regard to "Content," the instruction incorporated arts and crafts as well as science and social studies. In the first lesson, the pupils created their favorite animals with colored clay while using related vocabulary in English. At the beginning of the second lesson, which focused on science as well as arts and crafts, the pupils learned about the animals' habitats by categorizing the animals they had made in the previous lesson and then assembling all of the animals into a zoo constructed of colored clay. The third lesson was a social studies class in which the pupils studied various issues regarding endangered animals and attempted to devise solutions to save them.

In terms of "Communication," the language of learning, the target vocabulary, was the same as in the non-CLIL lessons. The "language for learning," the language for classroom participation entailing the use of specific phrases, was similar to that used in the non-CLIL class. The "language through learning," the unplanned emergent language, was accomplished by the augmentation of interaction and active involvement of the pupils and teachers.

As for "Cognition," keeping in mind that the pupils were still beginners in English, each lesson included activities that included "lower-order thinking skills" (LOTS) such as remembering, understanding, and applying (Ikeda, 2011, p. 8). Then they engaged in related tasks by using the target language and higher-order thinking skills (HOTS) such as "analyzing, evaluating, and creating" (Ikeda, 2011, p. 8). For instance, during the first CLIL lesson, since the colors of the clay were limited to five (red, blue, yellow, white, and black), it was assumed that the majority of the pupils would need a combination of the colors to make their favorite animals instead of just one. In other words, it required them to apply their existing knowledge about colors and use their newly learned English vocabulary in order to answer the teacher's question, "What color do you want?" In the second CLIL lesson, the pupils utilized the same cognitive skills to create their zoo while the third CLIL lesson demanded the pupils apply HOTS in English to think about solutions for saving endangered animals. It is obvious that it was the most challenging lesson for the pupils, since it required "creation," which is regarded as the most cognitively demanding process in the revised version of Bloom's taxonomy (Anderson & Krathwohl, 2001, p. 31).

Finally, regarding "Community," the pupils' learning was expanded from individual work to classroom discussion about animals during the sequence of lessons. Furthermore, the primary task in the second lesson required cooperative learning. As for "Culture," the understanding of international matters and learning about endangered animals were interwoven in order to raise the students' awareness regarding this particular global issue.

2.1 Participants

This experimental study was conducted on 71 fifth graders at a Japanese primary school. The pupils had just begun learning English six weeks prior to this project and they were hence still beginners in English. They were divided into two classes at the beginning of the school year. One class (n = 36, 20 boys and 16 girls) was assigned to the non-CLIL condition, a regular English class, in which English is taught as a main subject. The other class was a CLIL class (n = 35, 20 boys and 15 girls) in which English was used as a medium for content learning along with several other subjects.

This study involved four teachers: a native English-speaking teacher (NTE), a Japanese teacher of English (JTE, the researcher conducting this study), and two classroom teachers who were content teachers in charge of pupils' subject classes except for English. The English classes were carried out by the NTE and the JTE through a team-teaching approach while the role of the content teachers was to support their pupils during the class.

2.2 Instruments

This study utilized three different types of data: (1) recordings of the lessons, (2) pupils' responses to a questionnaire, and (3) teachers' interviews. First, three video cameras and eight integrated circuit (IC) recorders were used to record all of the classroom interactions as well as the pupils' reactions during the class. The collected data was then transcribed and utilized to identify the differences between the two classes. Second, a Likert-scale questionnaire and two open-ended questions were administrated to the pupils in both classes. The former was used to obtain the pupils' overall impressions toward their classes in terms of their understanding of the content and language, perceived difficulty of the class, and their level of satisfaction. The latter was used to examine individual and detailed reflections regarding the classes, which were answered voluntarily by the pupils. Finally, semi-structured interviews with the teachers were conducted in order to obtain their opinions regarding the classes.

In particular, since the CLIL instruction differed from non-CLIL instruction, the teacher of the CLIL class homeroom was interviewed in order to determine whether she perceived any potential problems in the lessons. Thus, all of the data was utilized to investigate the differences between the CLIL and non-CLIL instructions as well as explore the positive and negative aspects of CLIL application in a Japanese primary EFL context.

3   Implementation of the Course

Through the analysis of CLIL and non-CLIL classes conducted according to the aforementioned lesson plans, several differences were identified in relation to the 4Cs of CLIL.

3.1   Content: The CLIL Class and Its Diverse Emotions

A major difference between the CLIL and non-CLIL instruction was seen in the emotions experienced by the pupils during the classes. In fact, the CLIL class pupils perceived more diverse emotions compared to those in the non-CLIL class. One possible reason for this may be down to the difference in the content.

In the case of the non-CLIL class, fun learning games and activities were utilized to foster the pupils' interest in the target language. Consequently, the majority of the non-CLIL pupils reported that they enjoyed the games. In fact, English classes that involve playing games are very popular at Japanese primary schools, and the NTE of this study described it as a "regular" approach in his interview. This course of study follows the idea that teachers should provide pupils with the opportunity "to experience the joy of communication in the foreign language" (MEXT, 2009, p. 1).

On the other hand, CLIL pupils expressed not only enjoyment but a variety of other emotions such as sadness, sympathy, and satisfaction during the lessons. For example, during the first CLIL lesson, many pupils experienced pleasure and enjoyment when creating their favorite animals and working on their English skills. One CLIL pupil stated that it was the best class that she had taken over the last five years. In the third lesson, a number of CLIL pupils expressed deeper emotions such as grief and sympathy after becoming aware of the global issue regarding endangered animals; in fact, three CLIL pupils actually shed tears when they learned that endangered Sumatran elephants died from hunger due to deforestation. Furthermore, overall CLIL pupils' satisfaction was apparent in their responses to the questionnaires. CLIL pupils studied actual situations that endangered animals faced on a daily basis. Engaging with the topics and thinking about the solutions seemed to enrich the pupils' various types of emotions while using English. This appears to underscore the importance of "maximizing the accommodation of students' interests" (Mehisto et al., 2008, p. 29) by bringing authenticity to the class (Coyle et al., 2010; Marsh, 2000; Mehisto et al., 2008). In addition, it may be effective to realize one of the primary objectives of Japanese elementary school English education: deepening pupils' experiential learning that is appropriate to their ages and interest by enriching the content of the lessons.

3.2 Communication: "Language Through Learning" in the Lessons

The main vocabulary of the lessons and the phrases used for the class were planned beforehand and taught in both the non-CLIL and CLIL lessons. However, the emergence of "language through learning" (incidentally used or recycled language) could not be predicted (Coyle et al., 2010; Ikeda, 2011). Therefore, the advent of the language may influence active involvement in the class (Coyle, 2007; Coyle et al., 2010). Through the use of audio equipment, all of the classroom interactions and the "language through learning" were transcribed. The findings revealed that such language was rarely elicited from the non-CLIL pupils. Meanwhile, various examples of such language emerged in the CLIL class during the lessons as reactions or questions. Table 5.1 provides examples of these differences.

As shown in Table 5.1, there was a greater incidence of the emergence of "language through learning" in the CLIL class. It also reveals one apparent difference between the CLIL and the non-CLIL class: CLIL

Table 5.1 Language through learning in CLIL and non-CLIL classes

	CLIL class	Non-CLIL class
1st lesson	Total: $n = 72$ (LTL from the pupils: $n = 29$) Gray, brown, turtle, polar bear, whale, giraffe, pig, rabbit, tail, eyes, nose, mouth, teeth, ears, big, small, long, short, break, broke, connect, again, new, thank you, please, yes, no	Total: $n = 25$ (LTL from the pupils: $n= 2$) Yes, no,
	(LTL from the teachers: $n = 43$) Pretty, cute, wonderful, excellent, good, great, Be careful, Look at this, You're welcome, How much do you want? This much or more? A lot or a little? Do you need more? Do you understand it? Yes or no? Good job! You did it!	(LTL from the teachers: $n = 23$) Are you OK? Can you say the color in English? Do you understand the rule? Let's start. Ready go! Hang on! Good job!
2nd lesson	Total: $n = 79$ (LTL from the pupils: $n = 26$) Different, light green, dark green, light brown, dark brown, bird, sea, lake, fish, shark, treasure, pirates, grasses, desert, cold, deep, How do you say ~ in English?	Total: $n = 14$ (LTL from the pupils: $n = 0$) Nil
	(LTL from the teachers: $n = 53$) Sea lion, seals, salt water, fresh water, What color would you like? Do you have ~? Who made ~? Next is ~. Which do you want? In English, we say ~. We can say ~. Is this a ~? Both are OK, Over here, For example, Say sorry to your friend. Be nice to your friends. Great. It's interesting.	(LTL from the teachers: $n = 14$) Who won the game? Oh, that's great. Can you find the animals? Great. Wonderful.

(continued)

Table 5.1 (continued)

	CLIL class	Non-CLIL class
3rd lesson	Total: $n = 71$ (LTL from the pupils: $n = 44$) Don't throw dirty things in the ocean. Help animals. Protect our nature. Think about animals. Let's cooperate! Be kind to animals. Please take dirty things. Don't cut trees and recycle! Protect animals. Let's recycle. Don't make many dams. Don't waste electricity. Don't kill animals, (LTL from the teachers: $n = 36$) Why? Really? How do you feel? Japanese is OK. How wonderful your message is! Do you need a help? You're doing very well. Well done! Everyone did a wonderful job today. Please show us your pictures.	Total: $n = 18$ (LTL from the pupils: $n = 0$) Nil (LTL from the teachers: $n = 18$) Do you understand? Can you say that again? Be quiet. Try it again. Be nice to your friends.
Total	$n = 231$ (LTL from pupils: $n = 99$, LTL from teachers: $n = 132$)	$n = 57$ (LTL from the pupils: $n = 2$, LTL from the teachers: $n = 55$)

Note: *LTL* Language through learning

pupils actively engaged in the cognitively demanding interaction with teachers with more frequent use of "why?" or "how" questions. At the same time, CLIL teachers allowed the students to use the pupils' mother tongue, Japanese, during the CLIL activities. This accelerated pupils' thinking and teachers' feedback on their opinions, as most of the CLIL pupils needed to know how to explain their ideas in English. As a result, the teachers responded with a wider range of vocabulary compared to those in the non-CLIL class. In fact, in the non-CLIL class, the expressions that the pupils employed appeared to be fixed due to limited opportunities such as repeating the target vocabulary or using it in the games, both of which were introduced to reinforce the pupils' correct use of the target language. During the post-lesson interview, the NTE reported that he had more freedom to interact with the pupils in the CLIL class through the integration of content and language compared to those in the non-CLIL class.

Another interesting finding was that Basic Interpersonal Communicative Skills (BICS), the skills to use language necessary to communicate with people in everyday life situations (Cummins, 1981), appeared more frequently in the CLIL lessons than in the non-CLIL lessons. For instance, during the first lesson, all of the CLIL pupils had to engage with the teachers in order to receive their necessary colored clay, and several BICS expressions naturally emerged such as "Here you are," "Thank you," and "You are welcome." Furthermore, another example of BICS was identified in the second CLIL lesson when the school principal appeared and helped create the class zoo with the CLIL pupils. The English teacher asked the principal, "What color would you like?" instead of "What color do you want?" The expression seized CLIL pupils' interest and helped them realize the richness of the foreign language by learning a polite expression in English. Furthermore, the phrase was utilized as recycled "language through learning" in the teachers' skit during the next CLIL lesson. In the Japanese EFL public school environment, it is rare for students to engage in natural interactions involving BICS in a language class. In this regard, CLIL may be effective to enhance the natural use of the target language, which is necessary for basic interpersonal communication.

Thus, the results show that CLIL encouraged the use of "language through learning" during the lessons, which rarely appears in conventional EFL lessons. In other words, CLIL pupils more actively participated in language learning compared to those in the non-CLIL class. This difference may represent the potential of CLIL in deepening experiential learning by providing pupils with the opportunity to use the target language in a practical way as well as making them realize the need to express their individual thoughts.

3.3   Cognition

The overall results point to the positive effects of the CLIL experience. However, before the third CLIL lesson, three teachers had a disagreement about the extent to which cognitive burdens should be imposed on the pupils. In particular, the content teacher of the CLIL class anticipated problems regarding the tasks and believed that such activities were too difficult for CLIL pupils because of their high cognitive and linguistic demands.

In regard to high cognitive demand, it was assumed that two cognitively demanding tasks would be imposed on the CLIL pupils: difficulty in both the content and task. In fact, the content of the third lesson, the problems facing endangered animals, was to be studied in the sixth grade according to the syllabi of social studies as well as of science in the Japanese curriculum published by MEXT. This meant that pupils would be studying this particular subject more than one year ahead of time. In terms of the difficulty of the task, pupils were required to think about how to save endangered animals and write their ideas in both Japanese and English. Unlike the non-CLIL class in which the target vocabulary was acquired through fun games, the final CLIL class required higher cognitive engagement in order to comprehend the content and engage in the serious and relatively abstract task. As for high linguistic demand, vocabulary and expressions required to understand the aforementioned difficult content would be in English, despite the fact that they had just begun learning English. Thus, the CLIL class content teacher was deeply aware of the challenge and was concerned that it might even discourage the students while undermining the positive responses from the previous two lessons. The NTE also made a similar plea to decrease the level of difficulty in the lessons. However, having observed the CLIL pupils' engagement and involvement in the previous two lessons, the JTE had faith in the potential of the final lesson and attempted to convince the other teachers to continue with the original plan. After several meetings with the three CLIL teachers, it was finally agreed that strengthening the linguistic scaffolding during the lesson by a systematic use of both the target and the pupils' first language as well as the use of realia would stimulate interest in the pupils regarding endangered animals.

In fact, it turned out that the CLIL pupils participated actively and showed a high level of concentration during the final lesson. Their interest in learning about endangered animals was so keen that all of the CLIL pupils were eager to comprehend the content in English. As a result, they engaged in the final task by thinking of solutions to this particular global issue and expressing them in both English and Japanese, which increased their use of language through learning, as already mentioned in the previous section. This impressed all the CLIL teachers during the third CLIL lesson. In particular, this lesson worked as a catalyst in changing the content teacher's beliefs toward EFL teaching at primary school. In fact, this teacher created other CLIL lessons and materials with the collaboration of the JTE, which finally led to her teaching a CLIL class as a main teacher on her own (Yamano, 2015).

Thus, the third lesson revealed a clear distinction between the two classes in terms of the levels of cognitive skills presumably used in the lessons. The CLIL class pupils engaged in a wide range of tasks (from LOTS to HOTS) by learning both content and target language, whereas even after explicit practice, the target vocabulary acquired by the non-CLIL pupils was limited in range since they only employed low-level cognitive skills (understanding and memorizing the language) during the three lessons. The interrelation between how the pupils expanded their cognitive levels and linguistic demands in each lesson is shown in Figs. 5.2 and 5.3:

Drawing upon these findings, it can be claimed that CLIL lessons have the potential to help pupils utilize various levels of cognition by stimulating their interests with authentic content while also challenging them with high linguistic demands. They may also motivate content teachers to create better EFL lessons with the use of their knowledge and experience.

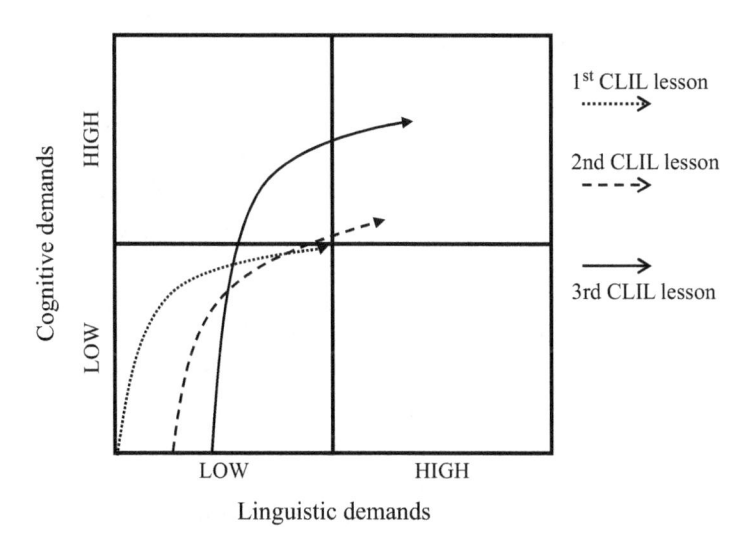

Fig. 5.2 CLIL lessons in the CLIL matrix (adapted from Coyle et al., 2010, p. 43, and Cummins, 1984)

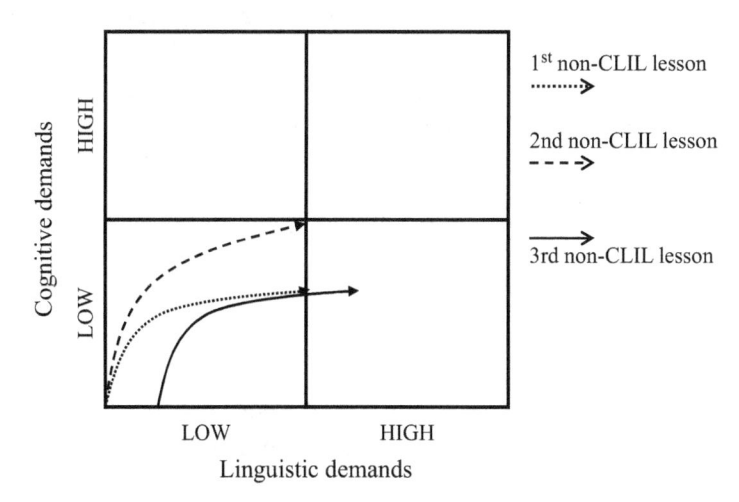

Fig. 5.3 Non-CLIL lessons in the CLIL matrix (adapted from Coyle et al., 2010, p. 43, and Cummins, 1984)

3.4   Community/Culture

Two differences were found between the CLIL and non-CLIL lessons under Community/Culture: (1) cooperative learning in the CLIL lessons versus playing learning games together in the non-CLIL lessons; and (2) active participation of CLIL students in the task related to certain global issues.

In the CLIL class, cooperative learning was interwoven with one of the 4Cs, enrichment of learning community. Interestingly, despite the fact that several mishaps occurred during the second lesson in the form of disagreements, none of the CLIL pupils responded negatively to the question related to satisfaction. This ambivalent result appears to be connected with the experience of cooperative learning. For instance, one CLIL pupil described her frustration about a conflict that had occurred during the cooperative learning lesson with the negative expression, "it was not fun today." Nevertheless, she responded positively to her Likert-scale questionnaire with "I am satisfied with the lesson." The pupil subsequently explained the inconsistency of her responses on the questionnaire by stating that although she had had a quarrel with one of the group members during the lesson, the product of the group work (i.e., the class zoo) had made a positive impression on her.

On the contrary, despite learning English through playing fun games, the non-CLIL pupils reported lower levels of satisfaction on the questionnaire. One non-CLIL pupil reported that she had been pinched by another person in her group since she was procrastinating during the game. As a result, she responded negatively to her Likert-scale questionnaire. It is apparent that although playing games was favored by many primary pupils and assumed by teachers to be effective for encouraging pupils to actively participate in a foreign language class in Japan, it may actually increase competitiveness, which may ultimately demotivate the pupils.

Thus, these differences reinforce the importance of cooperative learning, as indicated by numerous scholars (Johnson, Johnson, & Holubec, 1994; Kagan, 1992; Slavin, 1994). In addition, such differences elucidate the overall effectiveness of the implementation of cooperative student-centered activities into CLIL lessons (Mehisto et al., 2008; Meyer, 2010).

Another clear difference between CLIL and non-CLIL classes also appeared during the third lesson. That is, endangered animals as a global issue was considered by the CLIL pupils to be an important topic for classroom discussion. However, it might not be appropriate to compare the CLIL and non-CLIL classes since the non-CLIL class did not engage in discussing this issue. One can assume that just by learning vocabulary related to global issues without a streamlined lesson, a pupil would find it difficult to recognize the seriousness of global issues and thus enhance their participation in the world community. In contrast, the CLIL lessons provided the pupils with the opportunity to participate in a task related to one of the world's serious problems. Thus, it is apparent that CLIL has the potential to help students develop their understanding of international matters, which also resonates with the overall purpose of Japanese primary EFL education.

4 Outcomes and Implications

The present study explored the usefulness of CLIL courses by examining them in comparison with non-CLIL regular mainstream EFL classes in a Japanese primary school. The results of the in-depth analysis of classroom observations, students' questionnaires, and teacher interviews revealed that differences did exist between the two different types of instruction. For instance, in terms of Communication, the richness of "language *through* learning" appeared in the CLIL class, whereas unplanned language rarely appeared in the non-CLIL class. This finding shows that CLIL enhanced classroom communication by fostering a positive student attitude. As for Community, the enhancement of CLIL student cooperative learning was apparent, which enriched the learning environment compared to that of the non-CLIL class.

However, some of the results suggest that the reality is much more complex. Although the present study began with the expectation that the results would reveal the differential contribution of the 4Cs: Content,

Communication, Cognition, and Culture/Community, it is the interaction among the 4Cs that seems to have the most effect on enhancing the learning experience. For example, with authentic content (i.e., Content), the CLIL students experienced a wider range of emotions, which also encouraged them to actively engage in the linguistically and cognitively demanding tasks (i.e., Communication and Cognition) related to global issues (Culture). This can be seen as the contribution of the Content aspect of CLIL. Nevertheless, without the integration of the 4Cs, this positive synergy might not have worked in this study. Thus, it may not be possible to individually separate the four components, nor would it be effective to do so. However, in order to help CLIL instructors understand the four principles of CLIL, it may be advisable to characterize the expected contributing factors in terms of the individual components. Such an attempt is shown in the diagram in Fig. 5.4. The shaded portion

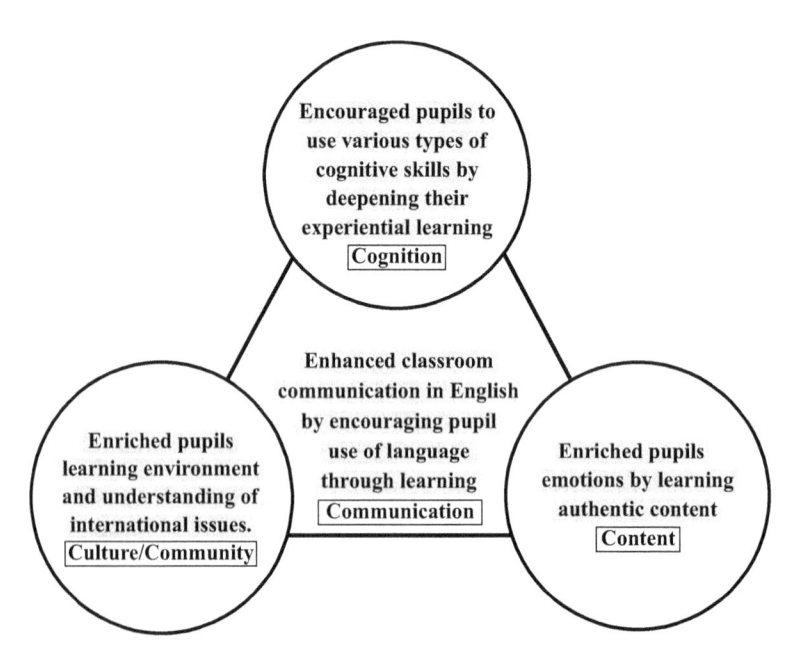

Fig. 5.4 The potentials of CLIL application in Japanese primary EFL education found in this study

illustrates the positive effects of the CLIL program conducted in this study.

Thus, this research study concludes that utilizing the CLIL approach in a Japanese primary school has the potential to improve Japanese primary EFL education. However, there were two limitations in this study: (1) this was only a single exploratory study regarding the application of a CLIL program; and (2) the numbers of the participants were restricted. Consequently, the results of this research may not be applicable to other school contexts. Therefore, additional research in more varied contexts is necessary in order to verify the overall feasibility and potential of CLIL implementation.

CLIL has emerged as a promising instrument for the development of language education, not only in the European context but also in Asia. Since CLIL has developed in Europe by finding ways to share experiences and address problems among the various countries, it is expected that the same phenomena will occur in the Asian context. Hopefully, this exploratory study can form a basis for future research and contribute to providing a firm foundation for the implementation of CLIL to the benefit of students and teachers who seek to enhance their English language education.

Acknowledgments This paper originally comes from the author's work, "Utilizing the CLIL Approach in a Japanese Primary School: A Comparative Study of CLIL and Regular EFL Lessons" (Yamano, 2013a). It is republished with permission by *Asian EFL Journal*. In addition, this study is based on the author's master's dissertation, "Content and language integrated learning (CLIL) in a Japanese elementary school: A comparative study of a CLIL program in early EFL education" (Yamano, 2012) submitted to the Graduate School of Language and Linguistics of Sophia University. I would like to express my most sincere gratitude to my MA's supervisor, Professor Kensaku Yoshida and members of the MA thesis committee, Professor Yoshinori Watanabe, Professor Shinichi Izumi, and Professor Makoto Ikeda. I would also like to express my profound gratitude to the participants. Without their help, this paper could never have been written.

Appendix

The First Non-CLIL lesson procedure

Activities and aim	Teachers (Ts)	Pupils (Ps)	Community and time
Warming up (Familiarize the pupils with the expression about their feelings)	Greeting in English.	Greet each other in English	Class (5 min)
Introduction to the new vocabulary about colors. (Provide input by using visual aids)	1. Show the pupils color picture cards. 2. Ask them the names in English and catch the pupils answer. 3. Provide them feedback depending on the pupils' responses.	1. Listen to the English teachers. 2. Try to answer the questions as much as possible.	Class (8 min)
Asking the pupils the name of the colors. (Familiarize the pupils with the vocabulary)	Ask each pupil the names of the colors in face-to-face interaction with extrinsic rewards.	Try to answer the teacher's question.	Pair (10 min)
Game "color relay game" (Provide the pupils an opportunity to use the target vocabulary and provide them an enjoyable experience)	Explain the game rules to the pupils and begin the game.	Listen to the teachers talk and participate in the game by using the target vocabulary.	Group (13 min)
Introduction to the new vocabulary about animals (Provide the pupils input by using visual aids)	1. Show the pupils animal picture cards. 2. Ask them the names in English and catch the pupils' answers.	1. Listen to the English teachers. 2. Try to answer the questions as much as possible.	Class (8 min)

The Second Non-CLIL lesson procedure

Activities and aim	Teachers (Ts)	Pupils (Ps)	Community and time
Warming up (Familiarize the pupils with the expression about their feelings)	Greeting in English "Good morning, everyone! How are you today?"	Greet each other and in English.	Class (3 min)
Review of the previous lesson. (Have the pupils review the learned vocabulary)	1. Ask the pupils the names of the color in English 2. Provide the pupils the first sound of the color as a hint.	No answer to the question. Rarely answer the question.	Only teachers (2 min)
Additional review of the previous lesson. (Provide the pupils with input and an opportunity for output)	1. Show the pupils a skit. 2. Ask the pupils the colors of their clothes	1. Watch the skit. 2. Raise their hand depending to the question.	Class (7 min)
Task 1: Game "Bingo" (Familiarize the pupils with the vocabulary and provide them an enjoyable experience)	Have the pupils play the game.	Play the game.	Solo (10 min)
Review of the names of the colors. (Have the pupils review the learned vocabulary)	1. Show the pupils color picture cards. 2. Ask them the names in English and catch the pupils answer. 3. Provide them feedback depending on the pupils' responses.	1. Listen to the English teachers. 2. Try to answer the question as much as possible.	Class (3 min)

(continued)

Activities and aim	Teachers (Ts)	Pupils (Ps)	Community and time
Review of the vocabulary of animals. (Have the pupils review the learned vocabulary)	1. Show the pupils animal picture cards. 2. Ask them the names in English and catch the pupils answer. 3. Provide them feedback depending on the pupils' reactions.	1. Listen to the English teachers. 2. Try to answer the question as much as possible.	Class (5 min)
Task 2: "Looking for the hidden animals." (Familiarize the pupils with the vocabulary and provide them an enjoyable experience)	1. Ask the pupils to look for the hidden animals on the pages. 2. Confirm what animals were on the pages with the pupils.	1. Look for the hidden animals on the page. 2. Confirm what animals were on the pages with the teachers.	Solo (15 min)

The Third Non-CLIL lesson procedure

Activities and aim	Teachers (Ts)	Pupils (Ps)	Community and time
Warming up. (familiarize the pupils with the expression about their feelings)	Greeting in English "Good morning, everyone! How are you today?"	Greet each other and answer the teachers' questions.	Class (5 min)
Review of the previous lesson. (Have the pupils review the learned vocabulary)	1. Show the pupils animal picture cards. 2. Ask them the names in English and catch the pupils answer. 3. Provide them feedback depending on the pupils' responses. Next, do the same procedure with the use of the pages of Eigo-note 1.	1. Listen to the English teachers. 2. Try to answer the questions as much as possible.	Class (8 min)

(*continued*)

Activities and aim	Teachers (Ts)	Pupils (Ps)	Community and time
Introduction to the new vocabulary about animals' habitats (Provide the pupils input while utilizing their existing knowledge of animals and the visual aids)	1. Show the pupils animals' habitat picture cards. 2. Ask them what animals live there and the names of the habitats by allowing them to use Japanese, then try to catch the pupils' answer. 3. Provide them feedback depending on the pupils' responses.	1. Listen to the English teachers. 2. Try to answer the question as much as possible.	Class (15 min)
Task: "animal relay game" (Familiarize the pupils with the vocabulary and provide them an enjoyable experience)	1. Explain the game rules to the pupils and have the pupils play the game.	Participate in the game.	Group (15 min)

The First CLIL lesson procedure

Activity and aim	Teachers (Ts)	Pupils (Ps)	Community and time
Warming up. (Familiarize the pupils with the expression about their feelings)	Greeting in English "Good morning, everyone! How are you today?"	Greet each other and answer the teachers' questions.	Class (3 min)
Introduction to the vocabulary about colors and animals. (Provide input by using visual aids)	1. Show the pupils color picture cards. 2. Ask them the names in English and catch the pupils answer. 3. Provide them feedback depending on the pupils' responses.	1. Listen to the English teachers 2. Try to answer the questions as much as possible.	Class (8 min)

(continued)

Activity and aim	Teachers (Ts)	Pupils (Ps)	Community and time
Task 1: Distribute the colored clay. (Provide the pupils the opportunity for output of the target vocabulary)	Ask the pupils their required colors and distribute the colored clay.	Answer the teachers' question in order to obtain the colored clay in order to make a favorite animal.	Pair (8 min)
Task 2: "Let's make your favorite animal!" (Familiarize the pupils with the vocabulary and provide them an enjoyable experience)	Have as much interaction as possible with the pupils by asking them questions, such as "What color is this?", "What animal are you making?", or "What's this?" Also provide instructions to help the pupils make their animals effectively.	Make a favorite animal in the lunch group while having interaction with three teachers and their peers. Also ask teachers if they need a help or have a question about the animals or the procedure.	Solo Pair Group (26 min)

The Second CLIL lesson procedure

Activity and aim	Teachers (Ts)	Pupils(Ps)	Community and time
Warming up (Familiarize the pupils with the expression about their feelings)	Greeting in English "Good morning, everyone! How are you today?"	Greet each other and answer the teachers' questions.	Class (3 min)
Review of the previous lesson. (Have the pupils review the learned vocabulary)	Ask the pupils, "What animal did you make?" and ask the questions about the English vocabulary of colors and animals to the pupils.	Listen to and answer the questions.	Class (5 min)

(continued)

Activity and aim	Teachers (Ts)	Pupils(Ps)	Community and time
Task 1: (science) Introduction to the vocabulary for the animals' habitats and natural things while categorizing the animals based on their five habitats. (Provide the pupils input by utilizing their existing knowledge of animals and visual aids)	1. Ask the pupils where their animals live and what natural features are in the habitat. 2. Provide correct feedback and encourage them to think about where their animals live. 3. Have the pupils organize the animals into the five habitats.	1. Listen to and answer the teachers' questions. 2. Receive teachers' feedback and think about what animals live in the habitat. 3. Try to categorize the animals into the five habitats using cognitive skills.	Class (10 min)
Task 2: (Arts and handicrafts) Let's make a class zoo! (Familiarize the pupils with the vocabulary and provide them an enjoyable experience)	1. Have the pupils organize themselves into five habitat groups according to the animals the pupils made. 2. Ask each group members what color paper and clay are needed to make their animals' habitat. 3. Have the pupils begin to make the habitats. 4. Ask the pupils what they are making, also answer the pupils' questions and support them if trouble occurs. 5. Praise the pupils' work and their class zoo.	1. Regroup into five habitat groups by thinking about which group is appropriate for the animals. 2. Think and choose the required color paper and clay to make the group's habitat in cooperation with the group members. 3. Start to make the group habitat. 4. Answer the teachers' questions and ask the teachers if they have questions. 5. Be confident of the work they did for the class zoo.	Group (27 min)

The Third CLIL lesson procedure

Activity	Teachers (Ts)	Pupils (Ps)	Community and time
Warming up. (Familiarize the pupils with the expression about their feelings)	Greet in English "Good morning, everyone! How are you today?"	Greet each other and answer the teachers' questions. (No one answered that they were sad today.)	Class (3 min)
Review of the previous lesson. (Have the pupils review the learned vocabulary)	Ask the pupils about their habitats, natural things they made in the previous lesson by showing pictures.	Answer the teachers' questions.	Class (3 min)
Introduction to the new vocabulary	Introduce the new vocabulary, "clean'" and "dirty" with the use of picture cards.	Listen to the teachers talk and answer their questions.	Class (6 min)
Skits about the issue of endangered animals. (Social study)	1. Provide first skit about the problem of the "dirty ocean" 2. After the first skit, show the picture of a dead turtle and introduce one more new word, "die." 3. Provide second skit about the problem of "the dirty forest." 4. After the skit, show a picture of a dead elephant. 5. Ask the pupils how they feel now by put the same questions at the beginning of the lesson.	1. Watch the skit-show. 2. Listen to the teachers' talk. 3. Watch the second skit-show. 4. Look at the picture. 5. Answer the teachers' questions. (All the pupils answered that they feel sad now because of understanding the issue of endangered animals.) (Three pupils shed tears.)	Class (8 min)

(continued)

Activity	Teachers (Ts)	Pupils (Ps)	Community and time
Class discussion	1. Ask the pupils their ideas to save the endangered animals. 2. Translate the pupils' ideas into English by confirming the ideas with the speaker and writing it down on the blackboard.	1. Think about and express the ideas to the class. 2. Negotiate meaning with the English teachers to translate the speaker's ideas into English.	Class (6 min)
TaskLet's think about how to save the endangered animals and write a message to the WWF.	1. Distribute a WWF's pamphlet and a worksheet about the endangered animals and white paper. 2. Help the pupils translate their ideas into English. 3. Help the pupils write their message in English. 4. After making sure that all the pupils finished writing their message, show them a picture of smiling children with a baby elephant in a regenerated forest.	1. Start to think about ideas. 2. Discuss their ideas with the teachers when they have help from the teachers. 3. Write down their message both in Japanese and English. 4. Watch the picture and hopefully feel happy to see it.	Solo Pair (18 min) Class (1 min)

References

Anderson, L. W., & Krathwohl, D. R. (2001). *A Taxonomy for Learning, Teaching, and Assessing: A Revision of Bloom's Taxonomy of Educational Objectives*. New York: Longman.

Bentley, K. (2010). *The TKT Course CLIL Module*. Cambridge: Cambridge University Press.

Butler, G. Y. (2005). *Nihon no shougakkou eigo wo kangaeru: ajia no shiten karano kensho to teigen [Thinking about Japanese Elementary School English: Inspection and Suggestion from Asian Perspective]*. Tokyo: Sanseidou.

Coyle, D. (2007). Content and language integrated learning: Towards a connected research agenda for CLIL pedagogies. *The International Journal of Bilingual Education and Bilingualism, 10*, 543–562.

Coyle, D., Hood, P., & Marsh, D. (2010). *CLIL: Content and Language Integrated Learning*. Cambridge: Cambridge University Press.

Cummins, J. (1981). The role of primary language development in promoting educational success for language minority students. In California State Department of Education (Ed.), *Schooling and Language Minority Students: A Theoretical Framework*. Los Angeles, CA: California State Department of Education.

Cummins, J. (1984). *Bilingualism and Special Education: Issues in Assessment and Pedagogy*. Clevedon: Multilingual Matters.

Dalton-Puffer, C., Nikula, T., & Smit, U. (2010). Charting policies, premises and research on content and language integrated learning. In C. Dalton-Puffer, T. Nikula, & U. Smit (Eds.), *Language Use and Language Learning in CLIL Classrooms* (pp. 1–19). Amsterdam: John Benjamins Publishing Company.

European Commission. (2003). *Promoting Language Learning and Linguistic Diversity: An Action Plan 2004–2006*. Brussels: European Unit.

Eurydice Report. (2006). *Content and Language Integrated Learning (CLIL) at School in Europe*. Brussels: Eurydice European Unit.

González, A. V. (2011). Implementing CLIL in the primary classroom: Results and future challenges. In C. E. Urmeneta, N. Evnitskaya, E. Moore, & A. Patino (Eds.), *AICLE-CLIL-EMILE Educacio Plurilingue: Experiencias, Research & Politiques* (pp. 151–158). Barcelona: Universitat Autónoma de Barcelona.

Ikeda, M. (2011). CLIL no kihon genri [The basic principles of CLIL]. In Y. Watanabe, M. Ikeda, & S. Izumi (Eds.), *CLIL [Naiyou gengo tougou gata gakushu]: Jyouchi daigaku eigo kyouiku no aratanaru chousen: dai 1 kan: genri to houhou [CLIL (Content and Language Integrated Learning): New Challenges in Foreign Language Education at Sophia University: Vol. 1: Principles and Methodologies]* (pp. 1–12). Tokyo: Sophia University Press.

Japanese Government Ministry of Education, Culture, Sports, Science and Technology. (2009). *Elementary School Course of Study Explanation: Compilation of Foreign Language Activity*. Retrieved from http://www.mext.go.jp/component/a_menu/education/micro_detail/__icsFiles/afield-file/2010/10/20/1261037_12.pdf

Johnson, D. W., Johnson, R. T., & Holubec, E. J. (1994). *The New Circles of Learning: Cooperation in the Classroom and School*. Alexandria: Association for Supervision and Curriculum.

Kagan, S. (1992). *Cooperative Learning*. San Juan Capistrano, CA: Kagan Cooperative Learning.

Lorenzo, F., Casal, S., & Moore, P. (2010). The effects of content and language integrated learning in European education: Key findings from the Andalusian Bilingual Sections Evaluation Project. *Applied Linguistics, 31*, 418–442.

Marsh, D. (2000). *Using Languages to Learn and Learning to Use Languages.* Finland: University of Jyväskylä.

Mehisto, P., Marsh, D., & Frigols, M. (2008). *Uncovering CLIL: Content and Language Integrated Learning in Bilingual and Multilingual Education.* Oxford: Palgrave Macmillan.

Meyer, O. (2010). Towards quality CLIL: Successful planning and teaching strategies. *Pulso: revista de educación, 33*, 11–29. Retrieved from http://dialnet.unirioja.es/servlet/articulo?codigo=3311569

National Institute for Educational Policy Research. (2006). Heisei 15 nen kyouiku katei jisshi jokyo chosa: kyokabetsu bunseki to kaizenten [chugakko eigo] [The Heisei 15 survey on the implementation of the national curriculum: Analysis and points of improvement] [junior high school English]. In *The Heisei 15 Elementary and Junior High School Students Survey on the Implementation of the National Curriculum: English Results.* Retrieved from http://www.nier.go.jp/kaihatsu/katei_h15/H15/03001051000007003.pdf

Serra, C. (2007). Assessing CLIL at primary school: A longitudinal study. *International Journal of Bilingual Education and Bilingualism, 10*, 582–602.

Slavin, R. E. (1994). *Cooperative Learning: Theory, Research, and Practice.* Boston: Allyn & Bacon.

The Society for Testing English Proficiency (STEP). (2012). Shougakkou no gaigokugo katudou ni kansuru genjo chosa (*Shougakkou taisho) chosa kekka houkoku* [A report for the results of a present survey to foreign language activities at primary schools]. Retrieved from http://www.eiken.or.jp/news/kyoukai/120518r01.html

Yamano, Y. (2012). *Content and Language Integrated Learning (CLIL) in a Japanese Elementary School: A Comparative Study of a CLIL Program in Early EFL Education.* Unpublished Master's thesis, Sophia University, Tokyo.

Yamano, Y. (2013a). Utilizing the CLIL approach in a Japanese primary school: A comparative study of CLIL and EFL lessons. *The Asian EFL Journal, 15*(4), 70–92.

Yamano, Y. (2013b). Exploring the use of content and language integrated learning (CLIL) in foreign language activities. *JES Journal, 13*, 20–35.

Yamano, Y. (2013c). CLIL in a Japanese primary school: Exploring the potential of CLIL in a Japanese EFL context. *International CLIL Research Journal, 2*(1), 19–30.

Yamano, Y. (2015). Exploring the cognitive change of an elementary school teacher through CLIL practices. *Bulletin of Utsunomiya University, Division of Educational Department, 65,* 205–219.

Yoshida, K. (2003). *Atarashii eigo kyouiku eno chalenji: Shougakkou kara eigo wo oshieru tameni [A New Challenge in English Education: To Teach English from Elementary School].* Tokyo: Kumon Shuppan.

Yoshida, K. (2008). Shougakkou no gaigokugo (eigo) katudou no kihonteki na kangaekata [A basic way of thinking about elementary school foreign language (English) activities]. In K. Yoshida (Ed.), *21 nendo kara torikumu shougakkou eigo: zenmen jisshi madeni koredake ha [Elementary School English to Cope with from 2011: These [We Have to Learn] Before the Whole Implementation].* Tokyo: Kyouiku kaihatsu kenkyujo.

Yoshida, K. (2011). Issues in the transition of English education from elementary schools to secondary schools. In K. Yoshida, H. Mori, T. Suzuki, M. Sakamoto, H. Toyoda, Y. Watanabe, & S. Izumi (Eds.), *Souki Eigo gakushuu eno eikyou -jyoui youin oyobi Can-do ishiki nochousa kara- kenkyuu seika houkokusho [A Report of the Research Results of "The Influence of Early English Education"-from a Survey based Affective and Can-do Factors]* (pp. 101–112). Tokyo: Sophia Linguistic Institute for International Communication.

6

CLIL in Secondary Classrooms: History Contents on the Move

Elena del Pozo

"Bilingual education has to do with education, not just with being bilingual"
(Prof. Baetens-Beardsmore, Vrije Universiteit Brussels, 2008)

1 Introduction

1.1 The CLIL Course

Bilingual programs adopting a Content and Language Integrated Learning (CLIL) methodology involve an innovation in teaching practice (Morton, 2018) because they require a wider focus in teaching: both meaningful content and the target language. CLIL teachers in bilingual settings can no longer give traditional lectures since the students' profile has changed: bilingual students require a more dynamic, innovative and interactive approach to learning. The search for and development of resources appropriate to CLIL learners is a demanding task. In this

E. del Pozo (✉)
Madrid, Spain
e-mail: elena.delpozo@madrid.org

© The Author(s) 2019
K. Tsuchiya, M. D. Pérez Murillo (eds.), *Content and Language Integrated Learning in Spanish and Japanese Contexts*, https://doi.org/10.1007/978-3-030-27443-6_6

chapter, a one-term team project about the evolution of democracy through history in Western Europe is portrayed. Students are prompted to engage with different resources to construe the idea of democracy and understand that the process of democratization has not been easy in some contexts. The assessment of the project by the teacher and peers and students' self-assessment through the portfolio are also depicted (del Pozo, 2009).

The setting is a public secondary school located in Madrid, Spain. At present, the school enrolls 530 students and a staff of 69 teachers. It offers the Spanish National Curriculum for Secondary Education and Baccalaureate (12–18 years). Secondary students get their certificate in Secondary Education within an English-Spanish bilingual program (henceforth Bilingual Section). This consists of some subjects to be taught through English: geography, history, natural sciences, PE, technology, citizenship and arts. The average class size is 30 students. The academic year starts in September and finishes in June.

The project depicted here was originated by the exchange of views among history teachers from the Bilingual Section about how the teaching of a topic like democracy through English could become meaningful to students when following the CLIL approach (Coyle, Hood & Marsh, 2010; Coffin, 2006). The model chosen to contextualize content and language in CLIL in this project is Dalton-Puffer's cognitive discourse functions (henceforth CDFs) since they "constitute such a zone of convergence as the cognitive processes involving subject specific facts, concepts and categories are verbalized in recurring and patterned ways during the event of co-creating knowledge in the classroom" (Dalton-Puffer, 2013, p. 216).

The target students participating in the project were 52Y4 (Grade 10) Secondary Compulsory Education (Educación Secundaria Obligatoria, henceforth ESO) students (15–16 years) from two cohorts. All of them had studied history through English in Bilingual Sections in both primary and secondary education. There was a double motivation behind the choice of these groups: on the one hand, the topic of democracy matches a large part of the four-year ESO history syllabus; on the other, Y4 is the last year of secondary education before the baccalaureate and the author thought that it was a milestone for students to look into the history contents from a more global and analytical perspective. Thus, students are encouraged to evaluate historical events and to improve their critical thinking skills which are not always embedded in history textbooks (Myskow, 2018a, 2018b).

The learning objectives of this reading experience are:

- To exploit inquiry-based activities as well as historical critical thinking
- To identify the links between how democracy was originally designed in Ancient Greece and today
- To categorize events, people and changes into correct periods of time
- To recognize the diversity of civilizations where democracy has developed
- To show an understanding of and explain the hard path toward democracy
- To describe the most relevant aspects of democratic governments in Western Europe
- To appreciate the similarities and differences between the evolutions of democracy in Western Europe with a specific focus on Spain
- To learn the practical rules for carrying out a task domain
- To develop the thinking mechanisms to solve problems

1.2 Learning History Through a CLIL Approach

History teachers' main goal is to help students to construe the characteristics of each historical era and certain events that have determined fundamental changes in the course of history, distinguishing periods that facilitate its study and interpretation (Ley Orgánica de Mejora de la Calidad de la Educación, LOMCE, 2013). Teaching history through a CLIL approach goes a step beyond this goal. It involves not only the ability of the teaching to enable students to develop subject literacy, but also the capacity to acknowledge, produce and interpret different genres (Llinares, Morton, & Whittaker, 2012). Learners who study a substantial part of the secondary school curriculum through English need an approach that is very different from the traditional instruction that had the teacher at the center of the learning process. Bilingual students need a double focus on the content and the target language and that means that content teachers tend to use different input at the same time in order to make the content meaningful to the teenage learners. Visual displays, the use of synonyms in class to reinforce the teacher's instruction (vocabulary and concepts), project-based learning, oral presentations and the development of historical thinking skills (Egea, Arias, & Casanova, 2018) are some of the tools that help bilingual instruction to succeed. The atmosphere in the classrooms also changes: visual layouts such as common instructional commands and patterns (Fig. 6.1) support teaching, help students and enhance the acquisition of concepts.

The art of history teaching is about teachers making appropriate and meaningful selections from the discipline and the complexity of the ideas which underpin it (Pendry, Husbands, Arthur, & Davison, 1998) and making them comprehensible to students. Approaching those history contents for secondary students is a forensic job which involves searches for the decisions that made events change. Students learn not just to

Fig. 6.1 Wall displays in a bilingual secondary school

enumerate those events but to relate them to one another, establishing their historical significance and analyzing cause and consequence (Myskow, 2018a). Dates are to be used as an integral part of historical enquiry since historical facts mean very little in isolation (Champagne, 2016). However, the dates when historical events happened should be seen as knots of relationships, or as an intersection. It is more important for students to learn the intrinsic trends of the moment than the date itself (González, 1988), and this involves complex thinking processes (Gómez & Sáiz, 2017). Beyond the transmission of collective memory and cultural heritage, time, space and society, it is the teacher's role to articulate these processes in the mental representations of students so as they learn to interpret them critically (Carretero & Montanero, 2008). One essential goal of this hands-on team project is for students to be able to build their own learning of history. They are able to do this through cooperative learning in interactive groups, as is described below.

Along with the subject content learning, the development of oral and written competences is one of the objectives of the CLIL approach. Learning a subject through a foreign language exposes students to new types of texts and genres that interpret new findings of disciplinary knowledge (Schleppegrell, 2004). It is the teachers' choice whether to use this resource to elicit students' own ideas as part of a dialogic interactive communication system in the CLIL classroom (Llinares et al., 2012, p. 54). School language should then be tailored to the cognitive and linguistic abilities of the learners, so that it is engaging and comprehensible (Myskow, 2018b). History contributes to the learning of content and language in two ways: through academic language as well as peripheral language (the language used by the teacher in his/her classroom management) (Kelly, 2014).

In carrying out the project, students have to take into account not only historical, social and economic aspects, but also political issues happening at the moment and how they are related to ways to preserve democracy (Pedwell & Perrons, 2007). Students develop both communication and cognition skills during the sessions, such as agreeing, interrupting, turn-taking, summarizing, gaining autonomy and decision making. The language tasks are evaluated along the two dimensions identified by Cummins (1984) according to the contextual information (content subject) and according to the cognitive demand in which language is used to construe knowledge (Cummins, 1984). These dimensions can also be applied to assessing the content. The level of cognitive demand of a particular question depends on the teacher's goals, what the students have already learned and the point in the lesson at which the question is asked (Schleppegrell, 2004). This means it is not just the teacher's question that could be more or less cognitively demanding, but also the relationship between the type of task and the learner.

Although most of the materials that students are reading for the project may be abridged to their learning level, for page 5 of the project (see Appendix 1), they are expected to work with original (not abridged) sources in English language (e.g., the Magna Carta) at their own level of knowledge. While complex at first and requiring close monitoring from the teacher, the work with sources contributes to building historical critical thinking skills in secondary students (Cooper & Chapman, 2009).

2   Course Design

2.1   Evolution of Democracy in Western Civilizations

Grade 10 (15–16 years) is a suitable moment in school to turn to critical thinking tasks in the form of an inquiry project. Students seem to be more comfortable participating in a group project, sharing their learning and having the chance to distribute the tasks. That said, it is essential to provide students with both an example of the kind of projects we expect from them (e.g., a sample project from previous years about the evolution of religion or the cities in history) (del Pozo, 2012) and the goals that teachers would like to achieve with them:

- Apply contents learned in class in different subjects (history, philosophy, citizenship and social sciences) to a specific issue (the path to democracy)
- Distribute the work among the members of the team
- Search for photographs and clips
- Prepare a PowerPoint presentation for the class

- Make a poster about the topic
- Reflect on findings

In carrying out the projects, students develop not only the knowledge of the history content studied in class but also linguistic and non-linguistic skills, such as:

- Selecting and putting information in order (cognitive, reading and writing skills)
- Kinesthetic and artistic skills
- ICT skills
- Written and oral communication skills
- Decision-making skills
- Evaluation of historical events and consequences

Projects can be more cognitively demanding than most common activities. In this sense, it is important to prime students to take up viewpoints in response to tasks that go further than the reading comprehension activities that accompany excerpts in textbooks (Myskow, 2018a). Thus, the aim of this project is to develop historical critical thinking that enhances the creative process historians follow to construe sources from the past and generate historical narratives (Seixas & Morton, 2013). History teachers are concerned that students provide supportive evidence of their findings throughout the project, and in doing so, they make sure conceptual contents are not missed for the sake of "low-value skills" (Gómez & Sáiz, 2017). Close guidance by the teacher during the whole process is necessary since some students could struggle with the tasks (Appendix 2).

Students tend to take democracy for granted, but the path to a democratic government was complex in most countries. How does a country improve governance? History teachers know there are no simple answers, but there are some pivotal concepts that students can enhance their knowledge of with the project depicted here. The United Nations Development Programme (UNDP) issued a report in 2010 to answer this question in an easy way for secondary students. The government becomes more efficient when institutions work to increase equality, transparency, participation, responsiveness, accountability and the rule of law. Most Western countries agree today that governance must be democratized to maximize effectiveness. In order to achieve democratic governance, three key areas need to be strengthened within a given state: inclusive participation, responsive institutions and international principles (UNDP, 2010). These ideas form the core of this project and the basis for its design. Some students may be more familiar with the topic than others. For some, they may have learned about the origins and development in previous school years, and for others, the topic will be completely new. This should not discourage students since the tasks and procedures are carefully planned step by step and monitored by the teacher weekly.

Every critical inquiry task in the project is based on one CDF (Dalton-Puffer, 2013) (see Table 6.1). "The potential meaning of the text that

Table 6.1 Dalton-Puffer's cognitive discourse functions (CFDs)

Function type	Communicative Intention	Label	Prompts in the project
CLASSIFY	I tell you how we can cut up the world according to certain ideas	Categorize, contrast, match	*Compare* the different types of democracy in…
DEFINE	I tell you about the extension of this object of specialist knowledge	Identify, characterize	*Identify* the oration by a famous…
DESCRIBE	I tell you details of what can be seen (also metaphorically)	Label, name, specify	*Label* the democratic elements (political parties,…
EVALUATE	I tell you what my position is vis a vis X	Judge, argue, justify, reflect	*Do you think there is a relationship between education and democracy?*
EXPLAIN	I give you reasons for and tell you cause/s of X	Reason, express cause/effect, deduce	*Identify the* traces of democratic institutions in…
EXPLORE	I tell you something that is potential	Hypothesize, speculate, predict	*Reflect on why democracy struggled in…*
REPORT	I tell you about something external to our immediate context on which I have a legitimate knowledge claim	Inform, recount, narrate	*Recount: Is democracy a difficult issue to preserve?*

students produce depends on the historical functions they express" when dealing with historical school content (Lorenzo, 2017, p. 35).

3 Implementation of the Course

The project will last a whole school term. The teacher devotes the first class session to recalling previous knowledge about democracy and informing students about the project: learning objectives, grouping, procedure and assessment. It is important that students agree on how much the project is going to count in the final mark since it will require hard work from everyone and commitment within the group to the job. Each cohort is grouped into teams of five or six members. Heterogeneous groups are advised, so as the weakest students are not marginalized and have the opportunity to learn from their peers. Each team distributes the roles: speaker, reporters, writers, designer, photographer/video producer. The teacher distributes the guidelines and schedule of the project (Appendix 2) and goes over any doubts. Students fill out Question Sheet #1 (Appendix 3) as a warm-up and share answers with the group. Students are expected to start researching at once but they will need supervision during the first steps to avoid plagiarism or feeling overwhelmed by the amount of information, especially online sources, which are not always reliable.

The second session should be devoted to problem solving, if possible, in the ICT classroom. Plagiarism is usually an issue in secondary schools. It is important for students to get used to researching without *copying and pasting* from the Internet. In most cases, the problem is that students find it hard to spot what is relevant from the source. The support of the teacher to model for the group is essential. It is recommended that showing the class online examples of what plagiarism is and explaining how to summarize, will help ease the stress of the work involved in the project.

There are ten more sessions distributed between the classroom, the school library and the ICT classroom according to the students' needs. During the sessions, students will work through an *interactive group's* strategy (Flecha, 2015): every member of the team shows the result of his/her research done during the week to teammates. Together they sort

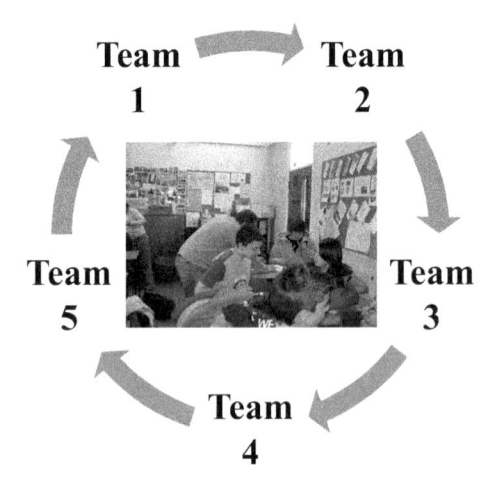

Fig. 6.2 Students update their projects in an interactive group session

out and shape the valid information and agree if more research is needed. The speaker coordinates the debate, informs the members of the team about the work that has been done, the problems that arose and future tasks. Meanwhile, the content teacher and the English teaching assistant (if applicable)[1] monitor the whole process. Every seven to ten minutes the team members will move to take the place of another team in a clockwise rotation while the speaker remains (Fig. 6.2). Every speaker provides the same information to the different teams in turns as they rotate. The goal is that all the students are aware of the difficulties that other teams had, learn about new resources that could be used and share opinions about the ongoing work. This strategy places the students in the center of their learning since they manage their own work in the team. It is also time-saving for the content teacher, who has the opportunity to observe how students react in every situation, assess every session by moving from group to group, solve doubts and find points for improvement. The English teaching assistant (or the co-teacher) may help students with their written and spoken production.

---

[1] In most bilingual schools in Spain, there are native English teaching assistants who share at least one session a week with every English or CLIL teacher to help students with pronunciation and vocabulary.

The resources that students used during the process comprise the guidelines (including observations about how to avoid plagiarism), project schedule (Appendix 1), the ministry-approved Y4 ESO history textbook (Eleanitz Project, 2010), blank maps of Europe and the Mediterranean basin, handouts with relevant information about the main political systems and an Internet connection. Limiting the space for the project report to about 20 pages seems to be restrictive but it proved to be effective. The first time the teacher implemented this project in school, there was no length restriction and students did not feel the need to synthesize the information. Summarizing and selecting the most significant ideas described in a source involve developing cognitive skills that should not be disregarded.

The project also requires adding a few lines at the end of every section, under a specific heading, for students to reflect on the section and give an opinion. This helps them focus when they have to answer the initial question of the project at the end of the work (see page 10 in Appendix 1).

The final task of the project is to choose one of the chapters of the topic or a specific aspect that students enjoyed and to prepare a PowerPoint presentation for the whole class. Students show more involvement in a task if it is going to be exhibited to peers, and they feel encouraged to make it appealing and surprise classmates. Choosing a classmate from a different team to give feedback (peer assessment) during the presentation makes them feel more confident. The peer assessment should not be seen by students as a form of criticism but as part of the assessment for the learning process, emphasizing both the strongest points and points for improvement of the project.

4   Outcomes and Implications

4.1   Assessment for Learning in History Through CLIL

Assessment in CLIL is a relatively unexplored area for content teachers (Reierstam, 2015). In this context, it is important that assessment in history through CLIL keeps the focus on the learning, not just on assessing the historical knowledge in examinations. The approach to assessment taken here can be illustrated by an analogy from Finnish folklore. Mielikki is the Finnish deity of the forest. Her husband, Tapio, with a beard of lichen and eyebrows of moss, is a tree and she is the solid ground where he buries his roots. She's the benchmark of land, solid as a rock, and helps little bushes grow silently but strong. This analogy explains the success of assessment: the stability of the substantial. Neither sophisticated curriculum design nor policymakers' complex outlines for instruction, but rather the effectiveness of simplicity. Formative assessment is preferred over summative assessment (Gómez & Miralles, 2018). Formative assessment provides responses to students' misconceptions and is specific to the aspect of the project to be tackled, encouraging students to establish links between factors that are no longer isolated events. Thus, time would be given for students to respond to comments, improve their work and embed their new understanding (Ford, 2015).

Inquiry projects like this contribute to assessing students for learning. Luff (2016) claims that inquiry as a tool for structuring planning and teaching for assessment in history is both holistic and authentic to the discipline and is thus truly useful to teachers and pupils. As described above, an assessment of the project was agreed between the teacher and students as a building commitment to the task job. This consisted of three forms of assessment: teacher assessment (Appendix 4), peer assessment and students' self-assessment (Appendixes 3 and 5). Although the teacher assessment grid applies a mark per section, qualitative comments should go with them, together with examples on how to improve the work.

History projects in CLIL help students develop their own learning and integrate content and process goals with the improvement of their linguistic skills (Fig. 6.3). Another useful tool is a portfolio that allows to reflect on the whole process. The CLIP (Content and Language Integrated Portfolio) contributes to the enhancement of formative assessment when evaluating the teaching and learning process (del Pozo, 2009, p. 37). This portfolio was inspired by the original Council of Europe's European Portfolio of Languages (ELP), linked to the Common European Framework of Reference for Languages (CEFR's proficiency levels) (Little, 2009).

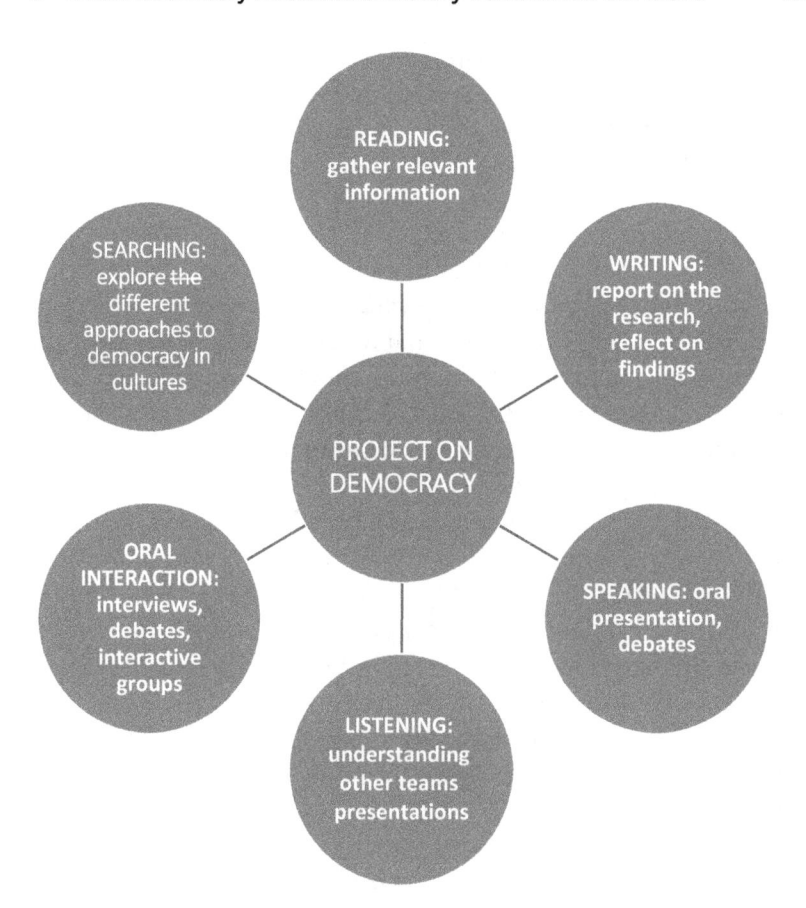

Fig. 6.3 The project presentation: portfolio assessment

Assessing the project does not necessarily mean testing students on whether they have met the goals of the course. The focus should be placed on the learning process.

4.2 Pedagogical Implications

According to Finnish professor Arja Virta:

[history teachers] should become able to transform their philosophy of teaching history into practical teaching activities, and to find such teaching methodologies that they can support their students' independent thinking and motivation. Prospective teachers should learn how to use methods supporting critical thinking and reflectivity on the one hand and empathy on the other hand. (Virta, 2001, p. 10)

Projects like the one depicted here have been shown to be very effective for working with history content in a meaningful way (del Pozo, 2012). Students are building their own learning as they use the same tools as historians: the sources. They read and develop their writing skills, which is usually challenging for 15-year-olds. Teachers and students focus on constructive learning based through inquiry-based projects. The teacher is a facilitator, a coach who guides students to develop their critical thinking and analytic skills in authentic learning scenarios. It is as simple as dropping a pebble in the middle of a lake, and waiting for the "ricochets" as feedback; or as complicated as using assessment as a means for reflection (Darling-Hammond & McCloskey, 2008). Students' outcomes show how critical thinking tasks work to foster a historical thinking mind-set. Myskow (2018a, 2018b) points out how they also draw attention to key points of the historical narrative.

The pedagogical implications are considerable. Students show a deeper awareness of social issues in history and other subjects related to social sciences (Tedick & Wesely, 2015). They learn how to think critically since they have to connect abstract facts and think *as a historian*. They strengthen the links between implicit, explicit and subliminal messages in visual and textual images together with the presentation of historical topics to their peers. Projects that cover several topics on one subject contribute to saving teaching time while students enhance their learning. Further examples of classroom applications of this technique could include inquiry projects about the progression of the major religions in the world, or the creation of cities in history.

The effect of project-based instruction enhances learning and motivation. Both content and language teachers can exploit the potential of inquiry projects as students are encouraged to select passages, read them to learn, speculate about the events that follow and write about their conclusions. Inquiry projects are also popular among students. They not only learn to search for information, summarize and improve their

English command but also develop an interest in historical events and how these help to understand the social and political matters in the media.

Professor Cummins said "Bilingual and immersion programmes shouldn't decrease the quality of education [for the language sake]" (Cummins, 2017, p. 3). CLIL-focused tasks contribute to meaningful learning of both the content and the language through practices that work in secondary education.

Appendices

Appendix 1

Guidelines Y4 ESO project: Evolution of democracy
How has democracy evolved in history?

About 20 pages (including the cover and contents page)
Team task: Write down the heading of every page's activity, you may include maps, photographs or graphs (they won't count in the paging). *At the end of every section, under a specific heading, include a few lines with your opinion on how democracy evolved in that specific period.* Always write in your own words. Plagiarism from texts or the Internet will gain a 0 mark. You may use your History 4 textbook as a basic context, then follow your teacher's advice on how to research. Send the file to your teacher prior deadline: May 30th, no projects will be collected after that date.
Choose one of the chapters of the topic or a specific aspect that you like and prepare a Power Point presentation for the class. Have a classmate from a different team to give you peer assessment after your presentation. Be ready to provide individual written feedback (Self-assessment Sheet).

PAGE	HEADING	TASKS
Contents page		
1	THE BIRTH OF DEMOCRACY	Define democracy. Do a map and mark where democracy was originated, mention who introduced it, what were the most important politicians of the time, the different assemblies and their functions. Identify the oration by a famous Greek historian to Pericles' funeral. Label the democratic elements (political parties, elections when applicable, etc.), the political systems associated to democracy. Name at least a philosopher who wrote about it.
2	ANCIENT ROME	Identify how did democracy develop during the Roman era? Mention the important assemblies and representative chambers. Specify the assemblies in Roman Hispania and where they were settled. Do you think the lack of democracy caused the decline of the Roman Empire? Justify your answer.
3	THE DARK AGES FOR DEMOCRACY	Reflect on why democracy struggled in the Mediaeval Era. Name here and how the first parliament appeared.
4	MODERN AGES: ORIGIN OF PARLIAMENTARISM	Compare the relationship between democracy and parliamentarism; identify the opposite trend: absolutism. Identify the traces of democratic institutions in the Modern States: English Monarchy (Henry VII and Henry VIII) and the Spanish Monarchy (Charles I and Philip II).
5	BRITAIN, A CASE STUDY	Search on the origin of democracy in Britain and the relationship with Parliamentarism (mention the Magna Carta, the Civil War, the first English Parliament, main politicians, etc.)
6	REVOLUTION AND LIBERALISM	Find the link between the 18th and 19th centuries revolutions, the new political trends: liberalism, and democracy.
7	DEMOCRACY AT WAR	How did the two world wars affect democracy in Europe?
8	CONTEMPORARY DEMOCRACY: A CIVILISING PROCESS	Compare the different types of democracy in Western, Islamic and Eastern civilizations.
9	SPAIN, A CASE STUDY	Search on the evolution of the Spanish democracy throughout the 20th century: pay special attention to the II Republic, the Civil War, the Dictatorship and the Transition periods. Write an essay about the milestones of this evolution.

10	HOW HAS DEMOCRACY EVOLVED IN HISTORY?	Recount: Is democracy a difficult issue to preserve? Reflect on your answer and mention its advantages and disadvantages. Why is democracy a fragile topic? Justify your answer. Do you think there is a relationship between education and democracy? Justify your answer. Answer the initial question 'How has democracy evolved in history?' summarizing briefly all your work and giving your opinion on the project.
BIBLIOGRAPHY AND WEBLIOGRAPHY		Add bibliography and sources following the pattern: Author surname, Author initial. (year). *Title of the book*. Publisher, place, webpage e.g.: Reynoldson, F. (2000). *KS3 History*.London:Letts Educational. http://www.schoolhistory.co.uk

Appendix 2

PERIOD	CLASS	TIMING	
One term (March-May)	Y4 ESO (15-16 years old)	15 sessions (50'/week)	
STUDENTS' AGE			15-16
STUDENTS' LANGUAGE LEVEL			B1
SUBJECTS	History, Social Sciences, Philosophy, Citizenship		
UNIT FROM SYLLABUS		TOPIC	
The Relationship between the Past, the Present and the Future along History		*The Evolution of Democracy in Western Civilizations*	
KEY ELEMENTS		COGNITIVE DISCOURSE FUNCTIONS	
<ul><li>Chronology</li><li>Historical knowledge and understanding</li><li>Interpretations</li><li>Historical Enquiry</li><li>Organization & Communication</li></ul>		<ul><li>Classify</li><li>Define</li><li>Describe</li><li>Evaluate</li><li>Explain</li><li>Explore</li><li>Report</li></ul>	

LEARNING GOALS	<ul><li>Exploit enquiry-based activities and historical critical thinking.</li><li>Identify the links between related ideas: democracy in the origins and today.</li><li>Categorize events, people and changes into correct periods of time.</li><li>Recognise the diversity of civilizations where democracy has developed.</li><li>Show an understanding of and explain the hard path towards democracy in some countries.</li><li>Describe the most relevant aspects of democratic governments in Western Europe.</li><li>Appreciate the similarities and differences between the evolution to democracy in Western Europe and in Spain.</li><li>Learn the practical rules for carrying out a task domain.</li><li>Develop and use thinking mechanisms to solve problems.</li></ul>
SUCCESS CRITERIA (be able to..)	<ul><li>Students understand the reasons that took governments to democratic governance.</li><li>Students acquire knowledge about inclusive participation, responsive institutions, national and international principles.</li><li>Students recognize the main features of different political systems in Western Europe.</li><li>Students have opportunities to share information, practice research skills and make decisions based on their findings.</li><li>Students are able to use new words in context.</li></ul>

LANGUAGE FOCUS	• Express content using academic vocabulary and verbal tenses. • Describe main situations and changes. • Select, read and record relevant information from different sources: make comparisons (philosophers bios, Magna Carta, constitutions,…) • Communicate knowledge and understanding in a variety of ways: ask and answer questions. • Writereports about findings based on research, give personal opinion.
SUBJECT CONTENTS	• Ancient Greece and Rome. • Middle Ages. • Idea of democracy and parliamentarism. • Age of Revolutions: liberalism, citizenship, elections. • World War I, World War II. • Contemporary Europe. • Contemporary Spain.
STUDENTS' WORKLOAD	• Students are to read texts, fill in worksheets, use maps and graphs to obtain information and draw conclusions. • Students are to select and use primary and secondary sources, including the Internet. • Students will produce written material based on the sources consulted to be presented in class.
RESOURCES AND MATERIALS	• Project guidelines, textbook, notes • Internet connection • Computer and projector • Blank maps of Europe • Blank Venn diagrams (for chapters 4 and 8, to contrast ideas) • Selection of extracts about the origins and evolution of democracy
TEACHER RESOURCES	• Computer with Internet connection, projector, clips on the history of democracy (as a complement to the students'research), screen, maps.
TEACHER PRODUCED OR DISTRIBUTED MATERIALS	• Guidelines, checklist, handouts, photocopies, Power Point presentations.
STUDENTS' PRINTED RESOURCES	• Adams, S. (2001). *Word War I*. London: Dorling Kindersley Ltd. • Eleanitz Project (2010). *History 4. Compulsory Secondary Education. Second Cycle*. Donostia: IkastolenElkartea • Lane, C. (2005). History. Revise KS3. London: Letts Educational. • Reynoldson, F. (2000) *KS3 History,* London, Letts Educational. • Shephard,C., Hinton, C., Hite, J. and Lomas, T. (2002). *Discovering the Past Y8. Societies in Change*. London: John Murray Publishers Ltd. • English monolingual and bilingual dictionaries

LEARNING ENVIRONMENTS	Students spend two sessions in the ICT Room, one session in the school library and one more sessions in their classroom.
LESSON PLAN	Session 1: project presentation • <u>Plenary</u>: brainstorm about democracy. What do you know about it? How does it work? Which countries can be called 'democratic' today? • <u>Small groups</u>: distribution of roles, agreement on how to schedule the tasks weekly. • <u>Individually</u>: fill up the Questions Sheet #1. Session 2: ICT Session • <u>Plenary</u>: problem solving, plagiarism, how to rephrase and summarize. Research. Sessions 3 - 12: • <u>Small group</u>: project update in interactive groups. • <u>Individually</u>: Questions Sheet #2 (only in session 7). Sessions 13-14: teams present a chapter of the project of their choice. Peer assessment. Session 15: • <u>Individually</u>: students' self assessment. Questions Sheet #3. • <u>Plenary</u>: teacher feedback and project wrap up.
ASSESSMENT FOR LEARNING (AfL)	• Content assessment: weekly observation of students in interactive groups (individual), development of contents in the project(teacher assessment grid - group) • Students' presentations: peer assessment (group) • Students self-assessment (individually) • Question Sheet (individually) • Language assessment: written production (group), oral production (interactive groups, peer assessment and teacher assessment grid)
ASSESSMENT CRITERIA	• **Continuous assessment** of every week work: Classroom, updateproject…………………………………………………………….20% • **Practical** assessment (weekly): active participation in interactive groups, observations, , maps, timelines, research, conclusions…………………………………………20% • **Project** final product **and presentation** …………………………………………………………………………50% • **Attitude**: care over work, enthusiasm, GW collaboration, doing work on time …10%

SUGGESTED WEBLIOGRAPHY FOR PROJECT	http://www.bbc.co.uk/schools/ancientgreece/main_menu.shtml http://www.historyforkids.org/learn/greeks/ http://www.schoolhistory.co.uk/year7links/romans/romanrepublic.pdf http://www.roman-empire.net/ http://www.fordham.edu/halsall/mod/modsbook.html http://www.eyewitnesstohistory.com/mefrm.htm http://www.historylearningsite.co.uk/France.htm http://www.historiasiglo20.org http://www.2travellingacrosstime.com http://www.4travellingacrosstime.com
TEACHER'S PRINTED RESOURCES	• Collins, M.E., Henry, G. and Tonge, S. (2004). *Living History* (1 and 2). Ireland: The Educational Company. • Counsell, C. (2004). *History and Literacy in Year 7: Building the Lesson Around the Text(History in Practice)*. Hodder Murray: London. • *Guidelines for the developments of the Integrated Curriculum in Secondary Education: Geography and History* (2004). Madrid: Convenio M.E.C.D./British Council. • LOMCE (Spanish Organic Law for the Quality of Education) (2013). Spain: Ministry of Education, Culture, and Sports. • Pedwell, C. and Perrons, D. (2007). *Politics of Democratic Governance*. London School of Economics Gender Institute: London. • Tarr, R. (2016). A History Teaching Toolbox. Practical Classroom Strategies. Garamond: Great Britain. • Walsh, B. (2001). *GCSE Modern World History*. London: John Murray Publishers Ltd.

Appendix 3: Self-assessment questions (student)

Class_____

Group
members_____

Question Sheet #1

Questions I have prior to researching (keep in mind all these questions during your research):

1. Why_____

2. How was it possible that

3. I wonder if

4. What would happen if

Question Sheet #2 (after some research has been done)

New questions I have now that I have done some reading:

5. Why_____

6. How was it possible that

7. I wonder if

8. What would have happened if

Question Sheet #3 (after some research has been done)

New questions I have after my research:

9. Why_____

10. How was it possible that

11. I wonder if

12. What would have happened if

Appendix 4: Assessment grid (teacher)

Name:				Group:		Mark:	

Subject: History				Topic: Evolution of Democracy			

Linguistic skills and project procedure (3 points)	Excellent 0.5	Very good 0.4	Good 0.3	Satisfactory 0.2	Improvement needed 0.1	Considerable improvement needed 0
Research skills						
Language/vocabulary/links						
Relevant information Generating ideas						
Maps/graphs/photographs						
Proper use of Internet resources, Bibliography and/or Webliography Presentation of work						

Subject criteria (7 points)	Excellent 1	Very good 0.8	Good 0.6	Satisfactory 0.4	Improvement needed 0.2	Considerable improvement needed 0
1. THE BIRTH OF DEMOCRACY / ANCIENT ROME						
2. THE DARK AGES FOR DEMOCRACY						
3. MODERN AGES: ORIGIN OF PARLIAMENTARISM / BRITAIN, A CASE STUDY						
4. REVOLUTION AND LIBERALISM / DEMOCRACY AT WAR						
5. CONTEMPORARY DEMOCRACY: A CIVILISING PROCESS						
7. SPAIN, A CASE STUDY / HOW HAS DEMOCRACY EVOLVED IN HISTORY?						

TEACHER COMMENTS:

Appendix 5: Portfolio self-assessment (student)

	My Comments	Which piece(s) of work show evidence of this?
Something that demonstrates my skills		
Something that made me think in a new way		
Something I found difficult or challenging		
Something I might do differently another time		
Something I really enjoyed		
Something that made me think…		

References

Beardsmore, B. H. (2008). Multilingualism, cognition and creativity. *International CLIL Research Journal, 1*(1), 4–19.

Carretero, M., & Montanero, M. (2008). Enseñanza y aprendizaje de la Historia: aspectos cognitivos y culturales. *Cultura y Educación, 20*(2), 133–142. https://doi.org/10.1174/113564008784490361

Champagne, M. (2016). Diagrams of the past: How timelines can aid the growth of historical knowledge. *Cognitive Semiotics, 9*(1), 11–44. https://doi.org/10.1515/cogsem-2016-0002

Coffin, C. (2006). *Historical Discourse*. London: Continuum.

Cooper, H., & Chapman, A. (Eds.). (2009). *Constructing History*. London: Sage.

Coyle, D., Hood, P., & Marsh, D. (2010). *CLIL. Content and Language Integrated Learning*. Cambridge: Cambridge University Press.

Cummins, J. (1984). *Bilingualism and Special Education: Issues in Assessment and Pedagogy*. Clevedon: Multilingual Matters.

Cummins, J. (2017, January 28). *Pedagogies of Powerful Communication in CLIL and Bilingual Education*. Conference read at the congress 'Evidence-Based Strategies to Support Bilingual Education in Spain and the US', University of Salamanca.

Dalton-Puffer, C. (2013). A construct of cognitive discourse functions for conceptualising content-language integration in CLIL and multilingual education. *European Journal of Applied Linguistics, 1*(2), 1–38.

Darling-Hammond, L., & McCloskey, L. (2008). Assessment for learning around the world. What would it mean to be internationally competitive? *Phi Delta Kappan, 90*(4), 263–272.

del Pozo, E. (2009). Portfolio: un paso más allá en CLIL. *Prácticas en EducaciónBilingüe y Plurilingüe*, 1. Castilla y León: Ediciones Prácticas en Educación y Centro de Estudios Hispánicos.

del Pozo, E. (2012). Experiencia pedagógica de la enseñanza de Geografía e Historia en inglés en secundaria. *Los proyectos de trabajo en el aula*. Madrid: Graó. Retrieved from http://www.grao.com/llibres/nivell-educatiu/ensenanza-reglada/los-proyectos-de-trabajo-en-el-aula

Egea, A., Arias, L., & Casanova, E. (2018). La metodología por proyectos como oportunidad para la introducción de la historia y el patrimonio en las aulas de Educación Infantil. *Contextos Educativos, 22*, 79–95. Universidad de Murcia. https://doi.org/10.18172/con.3185

Eleanitz Project. (2010). *History 4. Compulsory Secondary Education. Second Cycle.* Donostia: IkastolenElkartea.

Flecha, R. (Ed.) (2015). Successful educational actions in/outside the classroom. In *Successful Educational Actions for Inclusion and Social Cohesion in Europe* (Springer Briefs in Education) (pp. 31–45). Cham: Springer. https://doi. org/10.1007/978-3-319-11176-6_4

Ford, A. (2015). *Progression in Historical Thinking.* Association of School and College Leaders. Retrieved from https://www.ascl.co.uk/help-and-advice/guidance-paper-progression-and-assessment-in-history.html

Gómez, C. J., & Miralles, P. (2018). Las competencias históricas en perspectiva comparada. Enfoques internacionales sobre su desarrollo y evaluación. *Educatio Siglo XXI, 36*(1), 11–20. Servicio de Publicaciones de la Universidad de Murcia.

Gómez, C. J., & Sáiz, J. (2017). Narrative inquiry and historical skills. A study in teacher training. *RevistaElectrónica de InvestigaciónEducativa, 19*(4), 19–32. https://doi.org/10.24320/redie.2017.19.4.910

González, I. (1988). *Una didáctica de la Historia.* Madrid: Ediciones de la Torre.

Kelly, K. (2014). *Ingredients for Successful CLIL.* British Council-BBC. Retrieved from https://www.teachingenglish.org.uk/article/keith-kelly-ingredients-successful-clil-0

Little, D. (2009). *The European Language Portfolio: Where Pedagogy and Assessment Meet.* Graz: Council of Europe. Retrieved from https://www.coe.int/en/web/portfolio/elp-related-publications

Llinares, A., Morton, T., & Whittaker, R. (2012). *The Roles of Language in CLIL.* Cambridge: Language Teaching Library.

LOMCE (Spanish Organic Law for the Quality of Education). (2013). Spain: Ministry of Education, Culture, and Sports.

Lorenzo, F. (2017). Historical literacy in bilingual settings: Cognitive academic language in CLIL history narratives. *Linguistics and Education, 37*, 32–41.

Luff, I. (2016). Cutting the Gordian Knot: Taking control of assessment. *Teaching History, 164*, 38–44. London: Historical Association.

Morton, T. (2018). Reconceptualizing and describing teachers' knowledge of language for content and language integrated learning (CLIL). *International Journal of Bilingual Education and Bilingualism, 21*(3), 275–286. https://doi.org/10.1080/13670050.2017.1383352

Myskow, G. (2018a). Calibrating the 'right values': The role of critical inquiry tasks in social studies textbooks. *Visual Communication, 18*(1), 1–24. https://doi.org/10.1177/1470357218778876

Myskow, G. (2018b). Changes in attitude: Evaluative language in secondary school and university history textbooks. *Linguistics and Education, 43*, 53–63. https://doi.org/10.1016/j.linged.2017.12.001

Pedwell, C., & Perrons, D. (2007). *Politics of Democratic Governance.* London: LSE Gender Institute.

Pendry, A., Husbands, C., Arthur, J., & Davison, J. (1998). *History Teachers in the Making: Professional Learning.* Buckingham: Open University Press.

Reierstam, H. (2015). *Assessing Language or Content? A Comparative Study of the Assessment Practices in Three Swedish Upper Secondary CLIL Schools.* Gothenburg University Publications Electronic Archive (GUPEA), University Publications Electronic Archive (GUPEA). Retrieved from http://hdl.handle.net/2077/40701

Schleppegrell, M. J. (2004). *The Language of Schooling. A Functional Linguistic Perspective.* Mahwah, NJ: Lawrence Erlbaum Associates, Inc., Publishers.

Seixas, P., & Morton, T. (2013). *The Big Six Historical Thinking Concepts.* Toronto: Nelson.

Tedick, D. J., & Wesely, P. M. (2015). A review of research on content-based foreign/second language education in US K-12 contexts. *Language, Culture and Curriculum, 28*(1), 25–40. https://doi.org/10.1080/07908318.2014.1000923

UNDP. (2010). A Guide to UNDP Democratic Governance Practice. UN Development Programme. Retrieved from http://content.undp.org/go/cms-service/download/publication/?version=live&id=2551865

Virta, A. (2001). Student teachers' conceptions of history. *International Journal of Historical Learning, Teaching and Research, 2*(1). Retrieved from http://www.ex.ac.uk/historyresource/journal3/journalstart.htm

7

Collaborative Learning Through CLIL in Secondary English Classrooms in Japan

Masaru Yamazaki

1 Introduction

A Content and Language Integrated Learning (CLIL) programme has been implemented in English classes in Wako Kokusai High School in Saitama, Japan, since 2011 (Yamazaki, 2017, 2018). A method of *collaborative learning* called the *knowledge constructive jigsaw* (KCJ) (Miyake, CoREF, & Kawai-juku, 2016) has been applied to the programme and also integrated with *Content and Language Integrated Learning* (CLIL) (Coyle, 2007; Coyle, Hood, & Marsh, 2010; Mehisto, Marsh, Frigols, & Jesus, 2008). Saitama Prefectural Board of Education has been promoting *collaborative learning* in all the subject areas in secondary education

---

Translated by Keiko Tsuchiya
This chapter is based on two previously published articles written in Japanese by Masaru Yamazaki (Yamazaki, 2017, 2018). Keiko Tsuchiya (KT) translated these Japanese articles to English, adding the information provided through her observation of a CLIL class at Wako Kokusai High School and an interview with Masaru Yamazaki in 2018. KT also added explanations of concepts discussed in this chapter and references where necessary

---

M. Yamazaki (✉)
Wako Kokusai High School, Saitama, Japan
e-mail: yamazaki.masaru.ca@spec.ed.jp

© The Author(s) 2019   **153**
K. Tsuchiya, M. D. Pérez Murillo (eds.), *Content and Language Integrated Learning in Spanish and Japanese Contexts*, https://doi.org/10.1007/978-3-030-27443-6_7

since 2010, under the supervision of the *Consortium for Renovating Education of the Future* (CoREF) at the University of Tokyo. The project led by Saitama Prefectural Board of Education is called *Learning for Paving the Way to the Future* (in Japanese, 未来を拓く「学び」プロジェクト), which started in 2010, implementing lessons through the KCJ for "proactive, interactive and deep learning" (MEXT, 2016, p. 8), and 562 teachers in 133 Saitama Prefectural High Schools are involved in the project in 2018. I have also been engaged in the project as a teacher researcher to advocate *collaborative learning* in English classrooms, introducing the new teaching and learning approach to Wako Kokusai High School.

Our school, which is a public upper secondary school, was chosen to be an associate institution for the project since it offers two strands: a general course (six classes per grade) and a specialized course for foreign language (an English major course, two classes per grade). The latter provides more English classes than the general course, and there is more flexibility and freedom for teachers to plan and develop the lesson contents of the modules for the specialized course, that is, we can choose teaching materials which are not authorized textbooks by the government (see Chap. 3 for details of the national guidelines). This educational environment creates a space where we can try out the new pedagogical approach, CLIL and collaborative learning, with the support of the prefectural educational board and CoREF.

The concept of CLIL has also been introduced through another pedagogical development project with CLIL researchers at Sophia University, Tokyo (Izumi, Ikeda, & Watanabe, 2012; Watanabe, Ikeda, & Izumi, 2011), which commenced in 2011. Since then, the implementation of CLIL has been supervised by Prof Makoto Ikeda and his fellow researchers, and we have been striving to create lessons where the two approaches, collaborative learning and CLIL, are integrated for the foreign language course in our school.

1.1 The Knowledge Constructive Jigsaw Method

As a method for collaborative learning, the knowledge constructive jigsaw (KCJ) was suggested by CoREF and introduced in the English classes of the specialized course. *Jigsaw learning* is not a new idea (cf. Aronson, Blaney, Cookie, Sikes, & Snapp, 1978). However, KCJ was developed by Prof Miyake and researchers in CoREF (Miyake et al., 2016) and they differentiate KCJ from the traditional jigsaw learning, which was: originally developed "to promote interaction among pupils with different ethnic backgrounds" in the context of the US. In contrast, KCJ places an emphasis on "deeper learning of individuals through interaction" (CoREF, 2018, my translation). For that purpose, "KCJ requires the teacher to set an explicit question in the task and students answer the question twice—before and after the activity" (ibid.).

To conduct a KCJ task, first, a teacher sets a question which can be solved with learners' prior knowledge and new knowledge they learn through the activity (CoREF, 2017, p. 3). Learners follow the five steps to answer the question:

Step 1: *Become conscious of what you know*
Learners write down their answers individually.

Step 2: *Become an expert through the expert activity*
In the expert activity, learners form groups and each of the groups has a different piece of reading material. Learners read and discuss the content and meaning of the material in groups and become knowledgeable about the materials they are responsible for.

Step 3: *Exchange and integrate through the jigsaw activity*
In the jigsaw activity, a new group is assembled where each learner in the group has read different materials and each learner explains what they understood in the expert activity they participated in earlier while reflecting their own understanding (see Fig. 7.1). When deeper understanding has been achieved, the learners integrate their knowledge of each part and create an answer to the question.

Step 4: *Present and find expressions in the cross-talk activity*
Once the learners have finalized their answers, the learners present them to the class, providing reasons.

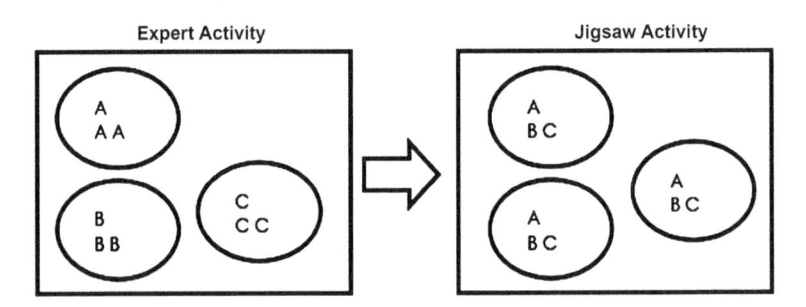

Fig. 7.1 The knowledge constructive jigsaw method (Adapted from: CoREF, 2017, p. 32)

Step 5:   *Go back to individual answers*
The learners once again look at the question which was set at the beginning, and rewrite answers by themselves at the end of the class. (Adapted from: CoREF, 2017, p. 3)

In the next section, we describe the paradigm shift in our teaching and our students' learning practices we experienced through the introduction of this method as a part of the CoREF project, and we explain how collaborative learning can be integrated with a CLIL approach.

1.2   From *Learning English* to *Learning Through English*

When we plan a lesson for collaborative learning, we have to start with a discussion with teaching colleagues to decide a topic which can engage learners. This process inevitably leads to a shift in our focus in lesson planning from the acquisition of linguistic skills, such as English grammar and vocabulary, to the content knowledge for learning. In traditional language lessons, we would choose materials to teach target English words and sentences, and our central concern was on whether the grammatical difficulty and lexical levels of the materials were appropriate to the English proficiency of our students, rather than the content knowledge they learn. Learners learn English language in a conventional English lesson, in contrast with the collaborative learning lesson which requires learners to learn content knowledge through English. Thus, the aim of the lesson is to integrate *content* and *language learning*, which chimes with the approach of CLIL.

The new pedagogical approach, collaborative learning through CLIL, has driven the improvement of our teaching practices and also provided an opportunity for us to reconsider the aims of the lessons. The main practice in collaborative learning is for students to exchange their opinions with peers. Therefore, the lesson aim of a collaborative learning classroom is that learners can express their opinions in their own words. Learners are expected to express their ideas in a creative manner based on the knowledge they have learnt rather than just explain the subject knowledge they remember. In collaborative learning, learners are asked to answer a question which has no clear answer. That is a difference from exercises for English grammar in a conventional English language class where learners check their answers with the ones a teacher provides. Thus, the aim of the lesson for collaborative learning, and also CLIL, should be that learners can achieve the *competency* to apply the content knowledge they learn in classrooms to their daily lives (Nasu & Ema, 2015; Sturgis & Patrick, 2010). These aspects are closely related to the components of *cognition* and *community* in the 4Cs framework in the CLIL approach (Coyle, 2007; Coyle et al., 2010; Mehisto et al., 2008).

The concept of *competency* has been adapted to the *framework of 21st century learning* (P21, 2015) and the guidelines of *key competences for lifelong learning* in the EU (European Commission, 2007). Reframing the concept of *competency*, Ikeda (2015, 2017) summarizes the competences for learning aims of CLIL lessons (see Table 7.1, and see also Chap. 3 for discussion).

There are three supracategories of competences in the framework: *cognitive competency, social competency* and *moral competency*. Cognitive competency includes seven sub-competences: relating *knowledge activation, critical thinking, problem setting, problem solving, innovation and creativity, willingness to act* and *meta-learning*. Three sub-competences are listed in the second and third competences, respectively: skills for *communication, collaboration* and *global citizenship* in *social competency*, and *individual, societal* and *international responsibilities* for *moral*

Table 7.1 The competences for learning

Cognitive competency	Social competency	Moral competency
Knowledge Activation	Communication	Individual Responsibility
Critical Thinking	Collaboration	Social Responsibility
Problem Setting	Global Citizenship	International Responsibility
Problem Solving		
Innovation and Creativity		
Willingness to Act		
Meta-learning		

(Adapted from: Ikeda, 2015, pp. 170–171)

competency. We aim to create a space in a CLIL classroom where learners acquire the competences through collaborative learning.

2   Course Design

The CLIL lessons are mainly implemented in the 11th grade in the foreign language course, where five English modules are offered through the 10th to 12th grades (see Table 7.2):

The first three classes focus on English language skills, that is, learning paragraph writing in the English Expression class, and the last two are advanced classes for 12th grade students. CLIL has been implemented in *Cross-cultural Understanding.* This section and the following section describe a lesson plan of a teaching unit in the module; *Can Mt. Fuji survive tourists?* (see Appendix 1 for the lesson plan). The unit was developed by the author with CoREF and Saitama Prefectural Board of Education with support of Google Education.[1] Students in the foreign language course have the Cross-cultural Understanding class twice a week: one lesson is conducted by a Japanese language specialist (JLS) and the other by two teachers, JLS and an assistant language teacher (ALT). The first lesson is a 55-minute preparatory session (one lesson unit), where the JLS helps students to prepare for the language and content knowledge necessary to participate in a CLIL class in the following

---

[1] The lesson plan and materials presented in this chapter were produced by Saitama Prefectural Board of Education, supervised by CoREF, The University of Tokyo, and drafted by Masaru Yamazaki at Saitama Prefectural Wako Kokusai High School. They are available on the websites of Google Education for Japan: https://www.google.com/earth/education/japan/.

Table 7.2 English modules and the units per grade

Subjects	10th Grade	11th Grade	12th Grade
Comprehensive English	4	3	4
English Expression	3	3	3
Cross-cultural Understanding		3	
Current English			3
English Comprehension			3

session. The second and third lessons are combined in a collaborative learning session, which lasts 110 minutes (two lesson units), which is described in detail in this section.

The specialized course attracts students who are interested in foreign languages and they are motivated to study English and other foreign languages. The course also offers introductory classes in other foreign languages (German, French, Chinese and Spanish) from the 10th grade. There are some returnees and international students in the course. We have about 40 students in a class, but students are divided into two for the Cross-cultural Understanding class, so about 20 students are in the class. The guidelines define the length of a lesson unit at 55 minutes. However, after we tried a few CLIL lessons, we realized that it was difficult to conduct all the activities we planned within the time allocated for one lesson unit (55 minutes). To allow students to have sufficient time to discuss a content topic with peers, we decided to change the lesson schedule and combined two lesson units to make a longer lesson unit (110-minute lesson unit).

When we first started this programme in 2011, we developed the teaching materials by ourselves, the topics of which included *energy resources, global warming, film studies* and *fashion culture*. These materials were refined together with my colleagues and CLIL practitioners in several schools and institutions in the Kanto area in Japan. The fruit of the activity was published as a textbook: *CLIL Global Issues* (Sasajima et al., 2014), which is now used as a textbook for the Cross-cultural Understanding class. The lesson plan I describe here was planned and conducted as a lesson in the unit of *ecosystem and humans*. Students learnt the topic of *tourism and ecosystems* in the previous lesson, and in this lesson, students were engaged in collaborative learning in CLIL on the topic of the environmental conservation of Mt. Fuji: *Can Mt. Fuji survive tourists?* Then in the following class, students work on a writing assignment to summarize the discussion in the previous class with their thoughts.

The question students were asked to discuss in the collaborative learning lesson is: *how can we solve the problems Mt. Fuji is facing now as a result of receiving more tourists?* Mt. Fuji is one of Japan's world heritage sites and students were asked to consider the environmental conservational measures through the activities. This lesson had six stages:

1. Oral Introduction[2]
2. First individual writing
3. Expert activity
4. Jigsaw activity
5. Mutual discussion among students
6. Second individual writing

The teaching materials were developed with visual images of Mt. Fuji, utilizing the online geographic application, *Google Earth* (Google, 2018), as seen in the lesson plan in Appendix 1. The reading materials were created on the basis of several resources, considering key vocabulary which were expected to be used in learners' speaking and writing activities (see Appendix 2). How these materials are used in the lesson is described in the next section.

3   Implementation of the Course

The lesson started with the teacher's *Oral Introduction* about Mt. Fuji as a world heritage site, showing its graphic images on *Google Earth*.

After the introduction, students wrote their own thoughts about the topic individually in silence (first individual writing), answering the two questions below:

---

[2] *Oral Introduction* is a teacher's brief introduction of a content topic in simple English, which is based on Palmer's *Oral Method* and has been introduced to Japanese secondary classrooms along with the approach of *Communicative Language Teaching* since the late 1990s (Nishino, 2011).

- What problems do you think Mt. Fuji is facing now as a result of receiving more tourists?
- How can we solve the problems?

Then they moved on to the *expert activity*, where students were divided into six teams. Each team consisted of three or four students. For the expert activity, three different types of materials for three expert groups were provided (see the sample material of Group A in Appendix 2).

Group A: Congestion—increasing number of tourists to Mt. Fuji
Group B: Toilets—lack of toilets in Mt. Fuji
Group C: Trash—trash dump on Mt. Fuji

A list of key vocabulary in English and Japanese is attached to the short piece of reading material. Two teams each were assigned as one of the three expert groups. Students first read the material individually in silence and then discussed the problem and the causes with peers, summarizing the main points on the worksheet.

After they had understood the information in the reading material, students formed different groups for the *jigsaw activity*. One or two students from each expert group assembled a new group for the activity to share the expert knowledge with the other students, organizing the information on the worksheet (see Worksheet (2) in Appendix 3), expressing their opinions in groups. The next activity is the *mutual discussion* where each group presented the summary of their discussion to the class. The teacher invited comments and questions from other teams and facilitated the exchange of ideas among groups to solve the problems of *Mt. Fuji*. At the end of the class, students had time to reflect their own learning and rewrite their thoughts individually (second individual writing), which is used as notes for the writing assignment students work on in the following lesson.

In sum, five states of activities could be discerned in this CLIL lesson:

1. Oral Introduction: a teacher introduces the topic of the content with visuals.

2. Silent reading: students read the material by themselves. Reading materials should be modified, considering learners' English proficiency. When preparing the materials, the teacher needs to consider how students can apply the knowledge obtained from the reading in the following tasks, that is, students can use the vocabulary they learnt through reading in speaking and writing at a later stage.
3. Question–Answer: students answer the questions provided based on the reading and discussions with the teacher and peers, organizing the information in a table on a worksheet.
4. Story retelling: a student explains the information they learnt from reading and discussion by looking at the summary, and his or her partner takes notes while listening.
5. Giving opinions: students present the ideas they discussed in groups to class. The teacher facilities the interaction among groups.

Students were familiar with the first four activities and they could manage them easily since they experienced those activities in general English classes, but not the last one. The last activity thus is crucial in collaborative learning and CLIL, through which students can achieve the competence to develop their thoughts by having dialogues with peers.

4   Outcomes and Implications

Before the introduction of the new pedagogy, our main focus was on *what should be taught*, especially in terms of linguistic knowledge, but we did not pay much attention to *how content and language knowledge should be learnt and taught in an integrative manner*. Without necessary scaffolding, some students, especially learners with low English proficiency, had a hard time keeping up with the classes. To improve the quality of our lesson, we adapted the approaches of collaborative learning through CLIL and used the 4Cs framework to evaluate our lesson practice, concerning the relationship between the four elements:

- Content and Language: if content and language learning are not integrated, students cannot understand content knowledge in English.

- Content, Language and Cognition: if content and language learning are not integrated with cognitive skills, students cannot develop and logically express their opinions based on the knowledge acquired although they may be able to retell what they understand.
- Cognition and Language: if cognition and language learning are not integrated, learners will first think in Japanese and then translate the thoughts into English.
- Content, Cognition and Collaborative Learning: if collaborative learning is conducted without considering content and cognition, the activity will become just a drill or a quiz.

In the new pedagogy, we consider a classroom as a community for learning and the main purpose of learning is to promote dialogues among students to develop their thoughts to tackle a question which does not have a clear answer. With carefully planned scaffolding, the pedagogy could benefit students with different proficiency levels. However, we noticed two areas where there is room for improvement in the class:

1. Teacher talking time in the CLIL class is still long and more time should be allocated for student-student interaction.
2. More active participation of students should be encouraged in the mutual discussion activity to exchange their opinions.

Through the observation of students' learning practice, contents, tasks and instructions should be refined further to enhance students' engagement with learning in the CLIL classroom.

We have been encouraged to see that this integrative approach to collaborative learning and CLIL has spread beyond our classroom and the region. We are constantly welcoming visiting teachers from all over the world and we also visit other institutions abroad to teach this method and learn about their practices. For example, we observed science classrooms in a secondary school in Cebu in the Philippines in 2017, sharing our teaching method with the local teachers. There was a follow-up visit by some of the Filipino science teachers to our school in 2018. We developed a unit together with them, and they taught our students as a part of the collaborative teacher development project organized by Saitama

Prefectural Board of Education and Japan International Cooperation Agency (JICA) (2017). Through this experience, we noticed the importance of collaboration between content teachers and language specialists. This will be the next area to be improved in the practice of our CLIL lessons.

Acknowledgement These lessons reported in this chapter were conducted as a part of the project, *Learning for Paving the Way to the Future* (in Japanese, 未来を拓く「学び」プロジェクト), led by Saitama Prefectural Board of Education and the Consortium for Renovating Education of the Future (CoREF) at the University of Tokyo in collaboration with Google Education.

Appendices

Appendix 1: Lesson Plan: *Can Mt. Fuji Survive Tourists?*

CoREF, The University of Tokyo
Lesson plan of collaborative learning based on The Knowledge Constructive Jigsaw method

School name: Saitama Prefectural Wako Kokusai High School
Teacher & Lesson planner: Masaru Yamazaki

Subjects	Foreign Languages Intercultural Understanding	School grade	11th grade of Foreign Language Department
No. of students	21	Learning unit	Ecosystems and Humans (Topic 9)
Session No. / Total session times	3/3	Textbook/Publisher	CLIL GLOBAL ISSUES (Sanshusha Publishing)

Purpose of the lesson (What are the students expected to learn? What kind of learning does this lesson lead to?)

To consider the environmental conservation measures for Mt. Fuji, one of Japan's world heritage sites.

Key assignment (Applying jigsaw activities as a main component of the lesson)

How can we solve the problems Mt. Fuji is facing now as a result of receiving more tourists?

Expectations for the current knowledge/learning of the students (How successfully can they answer the question above before the lesson? What would they struggle over?)

They may have learned from TV/newspapers that Mt. Fuji has been registered as a world heritage site, but they are probably not aware of the details of the issues around the mountain. They should be able to consider possible issues by leveraging their current knowledge of environment problems. However, they may not have thought about how the issues are connected to one another.

Elements of expected answers (By the end of the session, what kind of story should they be able to tell? What should their answers include? Think about the criteria for evaluating their understanding of the lesson contents.)

· Restricting the numbers of climbers by making it mandatory to pay an admission fee
· Promoting car regulations
· Setting up a mountain railway as a replacement of motorways
· Requesting climbers to bring their trash back home
· Installing bio toilets

Each expert <What are the students expected to learn in each expert in order to answer the given question successfully? What contents/activities should they go through?>

(Introduction) World Heritage site
Registered as a world heritage site in 2013 / Geographically registered area / Cultural heritage, not natural heritage / Popular tourist destination / Increasing number of tourists and climbers / Negative impact caused by tourism?

Expert A: Congestion
World heritage / Increasing number of tourists / Goraiko (Magnificent sunrise) / Four climbing routes / Reasons for congestion / Restrictions on the number of climbers / Climbing regulations / Any impact caused by the Tokyo Olympic Games 2020?

Expert B: Toilets
Climbing routes without toilets / How can the landscape be maintained? / Lack of toilets / "White river" caused by discharged excretions / Bio toilets

Expert C: Trash
Trash dump / Climbers' awareness / Illegally dumped trash / Litter cleanup activities by volunteers

Next assignments/learning contents based on what the students have learned through their jigsaw activities

Re-writing about the main assignment individually.

The relationship among the previous, current and next sessions

Session	Learning contents/activities	Expected learning goals
Preliminary	Ecosystems and Humans	What is an ecosystem? How is it related to humans?
Previous	Tourism and Ecosystems	Tourism and development / environmental problems
Current	"Can Mt. Fuji survive tourists?"	Considering the environmental conservation measures for Mt. Fuji (a world heritage site)
Next	Writing about the main assignment of this session	Summary of this session
Afterward	Endangered Species	Endangered Species

Learning objective for the students
Being able to explain what they have learned using their own words.

How to design the learning activities for this session

Grouping
21 students per class Expert group   3 people × 3 groups + 4 people × 3 groups Jigsaw group   3 people × 3 groups + 4 people × 3 groups

Time	Learning activities	Support from the teacher
5 mins	Give an oral introduction to the current situation of Mt. Fuji. Visually examine the mountain with Google Earth. [Using Google Earth] Top: Checking Mt. Fuji from a range of angles. Middle/Bottom: Observing some cultural assets including the Sengen Shrine and the Shiraito Falls.	Describe the impact caused by the growing number of tourists and climbers. Use Google Earth's 3D mode and Street View as visual aids in order to understand the current situation of Mt. Fuji and its cultural assets as well as their geographic relationships. Lead an interactive discussion to confirm the students' understanding of the lesson. Reference: · The Complete Guide to Mt. Fuji

5 mins	Each student writes down their own thought.	Writing on the Worksheet (1).
15 mins	**Expert activities (A / B / C)**	Organize key points on each Worksheet (A, B, C), and prepare to explain them during the jigsaw activities.
	Expert A: Congestion on Mt. Fuji [**Things to consider**] Increasing number of tourists after the registration of Mt. Fuji as a world heritage site / Four climbing routes / Reasons for congestion / Restrictions on the number of climbers / Possible climbing regulations / Any impact caused by the Tokyo Olympic Games 2020? [**Using Google Earth**] As a way of reflecting on the congestion of Mt. Fuji, examine the location and geographic features of the main climbing routes with Google Earth. Consider how these can be related to the congestion of the mountain. Click the icon of Pegman on the lower right corner to view the climbing routes highlighted in blue in Street View.	By referring to the official website of Mt. Fuji, use the Street View feature of Google Earth to check the main climbing routes. This can be a useful visual aid in contemplating what makes the mountain so crowded. References: • The Official Website for Mt. Fuji Climbing • The "Access / Vehicle Restrictions" section of the same official website
	Expert B: Toilet-related issues on Mt. Fuji [**Things to consider**] Climbing routes without toilets / How can the landscape be maintained? / Lack of toilets / "White river" caused by discharged excretions / Bio toilets [**Using Google Earth**] Search the locations of the toilets on Mt. Fuji with some words, such as "Mt. Fuji toilets" or "Mountain huts." Use your findings to think about the relationships between each climbing route and its number of toilets. Check the current situation of the actual sites with Street View. All of these help consider the toilet-related issues on the mountain. Searching for the toilets around the summit of Mt. Fuji	By referring to the official website of Mt. Fuji, encourage the participating students to check the locations of the toilets on the mountain. Use the Street View feature of Google Earth to take a look at each location in detail. This will be a useful visual aid in contemplating the toilet-related issues. References: • The "Toilets on Mt. Fuji" section of the same official website • The "Rules and Manners for the toilets on Mt. Fuji" section of the official website for Shizuoka prefecture [Japanese only]

15 mins	

Using Street View to see images of shared toilets on the summit near Yoshida/Subashiri routes.

Expert C: Trash Issues on Mt. Fuji

[Things to consider]
Trash dump / Climbers' awareness / large-sized trash illegally dumped / Impact caused by the growing number of tourists / Installation of trash cans / Litter cleanup activities by volunteers

[Using Google Earth]
As a way of reflecting on the trash issues, it's important to take into account the activity areas of climbers/tourists. With Google Earth, search for parking lots around Mt. Fuji. Then think about their locations in relation to their surrounding towns by zoom in and out on Google Earth.

Above: Enter the following in the search field and see the current situations of the parking lots: "Fuji Subaruline Fifth Station," "Fuji Miyaguchi Fifth Station," "Subashiriguchi Fifth Station Parking Lot," "Gotenbaguchi Mountain Trail New Fifth Station."
Below: Switch to 2D mode, and zoom in and out to consider the geographic relations between the parking lots and their surrounding urban areas.

By referring to the official websites of Mt. Fuji and Shizuoka prefecture, encourage the participating students to consider the current situation of trash issues on the mountain and the behavior of the climbers/tourists.

If there is a correlation between the trash issues and the increasing number of tourists, it's crucial to consider the parking lots in the area used by the climbers/tourists. For example, trash issues could arise in an area with a parking lot which is large or closer to the urban area, because many tourists are likely to use it. Use Google Earth as a visual aid to understand the geographic relationships among the locations of each parking lot, the surrounding urban areas, and popular routes.

References:
- The "Regulation and Rules for Climbing Mt. Fuji" section of the official website for Mt. Fuji Climbing
- The "Nature Conservation Division and Environmental Conservation for Mt. Fuji" section of the official website for Shizuoka prefecture [Japanese only]
- The "Access / Vehicle Restrictions" section of the official website for Mt. Fuji Climbing

15 mins	**Jigsaw activities**	Discuss key points from A, B, and C, and organize them on the Worksheet (2).
		Combine the contents of each Expert material, and have the Jigsaw groups think about the given question and put their answers on the Worksheet (3).
10 mins	**Mutual discussion**	Each Jigsaw group shares their thoughts and the reasoning behind them. Use the Worksheet (3) to record each presentation.
(Next) 15 mins	**Each student re-writes about the main assignment individually**	Use the Worksheet (4).

Appendix 2: Worksheet (1) for the Knowledge Constructive Jigsaw

"Can Mt. Fuji survive tourists?"

Worksheet A: Congestion

Mt. Fuji has become so crowded that it has reached the breaking point. Being a famous cultural icon and the most beautiful mountain in Japan, Mt. Fuji has become a hot spot that every tourist must see. So many tourists try to see the sunrise on the summit and it causes congestion. Mt. Fuji has four trails leading up to the summit, and by studying the characteristics of each trail, the reasons for congestion are revealed. Congestion often occurred whenever visitors entering the Fujinomiya trail, the shortest route up the mountain, exceeded 2,000 in a day. In contrast, no blockage was seen at the Subashiri and Gotemba entrances. The Yoshida trail is the longest but it is the gentlest in terms of slope inclination, which makes it the most popular route. There were four days in a year when climbers on this trail exceeded 4,000 per day, from around 4 a.m. to 5:30 a.m. between the months of July and September. The Fujisan World Cultural Heritage Council is currently aiming to reduce the number of visitors to less than 4,000 at any one time by restricting entry if it does exceed. The 2020 Olympics is just around the corner, and the event will bring even more tourists and problems, so the council should take measures soon.

Task:
• **What is the problem?**

• **What are the causes of the problem?**

Name:

Appendix 3: Worksheet (2) for the Knowledge Constructive Jigsaw

"Can Mt. Fuji survive tourists?"

Worksheet (2)

Task
- Listen to each other and take notes to share information about the problems and the causes.

	Problem	Causes
A		
B		
C		

Name:

References

Aronson, E., Blaney, N., Cookie, S., Sikes, J., & Snapp, M. (1978). *The Jigsaw Classroom*. London: Sage Publications.

CoREF. (2017). *CoREF Brochure 2017*. Tokyo: The University of Tokyo. Retrieved from http://coref.u-tokyo.ac.jp/newcoref/wp-content/uploads/2017/08/brochure2017english_A4web.pdf

CoREF. (2018). *Consortium for Renovating Education of the Future, The University of Tokyo*. Tokyo: The University of Tokyo. Retrieved from http://coref.u-tokyo.ac.jp/

Coyle, D. (2007). Content and language integrated learning: Towards a connected research agenda for CLIL pedagogies. *International Journal of Bilingual Education and Bilingualism, 10*(5), 543–562.

Coyle, D., Hood, P., & Marsh, D. (2010). *Content and Language Integrated Learning*. Cambridge: Cambridge University Press.

European Commission. (2007). *Key Competences for Lifelong Learning*. Luxembourg: European Commission. Retrieved from https://ec.europa.eu/education/

Google. (2018). Google Earth Education for Japan. Retrieved from https://www.google.com/earth/education/japan/

Ikeda, M. (2015). English lessons—From language ability to competency (in Japanese, 英語科―語学能力の育成から汎用能力の育成へ). In M. Nasu & F. Ema (Eds.), *Competency-Based Lessons [in Japanese, コンピテンシー・ベイスの授業づくり]* (pp. 157–181). Tokyo: Tosho Bunka Sha (図書文化社).

Ikeda, M. (2017). From language ability to generic purpose competences: Fostering competence through CLIL (in Japanese, 言語能力から汎用能力へ:CLILによるコンピテンシーの育成). In T. Harada & Y. Sawaki (Eds.), *Learning Subject Contents in English: CBI, CLIL and EMI [in Japanese, 英語で教科内容や専門を学ぶ: 内容重視指導(CBI)、内容言語統合学習(CLIL)と英語による専門科目の指導の視点から]* (pp. 5–30). Tokyo: Gakubunsha (学文社).

Izumi, S., Ikeda, M., & Watanabe, Y. (2012). *CLIL (Content and Language Integrated Learning): New Challenges in Foreign Language Education at Sophia University. Volume 2: Practice and Applications*. Tokyo: Sophia University Press.

JICA. (2017). *Saitama Prefecture Shares Japanese Active Learning Model in Cebu Schools*. Tokyo: The Japan International Cooperation Agency (JICA). Retrieved from https://www.jica.go.jp/philippine/english/office/topics/news/171012.html

Mehisto, P., Marsh, D., Frigols, M., & Jesus. (2008). *Uncovering CLIL: Content and Language Integrated Learning in Bilingual and Multilingual Education.* Oxford: Macmillan Education.

MEXT. (2016). *Overview of the Ministry of Education, Culture, Sports, Science and Technology.* Tokyo. Retrieved from http://www.mext.go.jp/en/about/pablication/__icsFiles/afieldfile/2019/03/13/1374478_001.pdf

Miyake, N., CoREF, & Kawai-juku (Eds.). (2016). *Collaborative Learning—Active Learning Lessons to Deepen the Understanding through Dialogues [in Japanese, 協調学習とは—対話を通して理解を深めるアクティブラーニング型授業].* Kitaoji Shobo (北大路書房): Kyoto.

Nasu, M., & Ema, F. (Eds.). (2015). *Competency-based Lessons [in Japanese, コンピテンシー・ベイスの授業づくり].* Tokyo: Tosho Bunka Sha (図書文化社).

Nishino, T. (2011). Japanese high school teachers' beliefs and practices regarding communicative language teaching. *JALT Journal, 33*(2), 131–155.

P21. (2015). *P21 Framework.* The Partnership for 21st Century Learning. Retrieved from http://www.p21.org/storage/documents/docs/P21_Framework_Definitions_New_Logo_2015.pdf

Sasajima, S., Ikeda, M., Yamazaki, M., Chida, T., Fujisawa, S., & Fukushima, J. (2014). *CLIL Global Issues [in Japanese, CLIL英語で学ぶ国際問題].* Tokyo: Sanshusha (三修社).

Sturgis, C., & Patrick, S. (2010). *When Success is the Only Option: Designing Competency-based Pathways for Next Generation Learning.* Vienna, VA: iNACOL (International Association for K-12 Online Learning). Retrieved from https://files.eric.ed.gov/fulltext/ED514891.pdf

Watanabe, Y., Ikeda, M., & Izumi, S. (2011). *CLIL (Content and Language Integrated Learning): New Challenges in Foreign Language Education at Sophia University. Volume 1: Principles and Methodologies.* Tokyo: Sophia University Press.

Yamazaki, M. (2017). CLIL, collaborative learning and Oral Method [in Japanese, クリル、協調学習とオーラルメソッド]. *The IRLT Journal (The Institute for Research in Language Teaching, Tokyo, Japan), 16*, 28–32.

Yamazaki, M. (2018). Collaborative learning through CLIL: From 'learning English' to 'learning through English' [in Japanese, CLILによる協調学習の実践——「英語を学ぶ」から「英語で学ぶ」へ]. *J-CLIL Newsletter, 1*, 7–10.

8

Testing the Water: Implementing a Soft CLIL Approach for Future Global Engineers at a Japanese University

Takashi Uemura, Graeme J. Gilmour, and Luis Fernando Costa

1 Introduction

1.1 The Go Global Japan (GGJ) National Project and a New English Course for Undergraduate Engineering Students

This chapter reports a series of new English courses tailored to second, third, and fourth-year undergraduate engineering students, in an effort to find the best educational practice during the Ministry of Education, Culture, Science, Sports and Technology (MEXT) Go Global Japan (GGJ) national project from 2012 to 2017. The MEXT GGJ national

The development of these textbooks was supported by Yamaguchi University's fund from the MEXT Go Global Japan (GGJ) project.

T. Uemura (✉) • G. J. Gilmour • L. F. Costa
Faculty of Engineering, Yamaguchi University, Yamaguchi, Japan
e-mail: t-uemura@yamaguchi-u.ac.jp; gjg68@yamaguchi-u.ac.jp; luis@yamaguchi-u.ac.jp

175

K. Tsuchiya, M. D. Pérez Murillo (eds.), *Content and Language Integrated Learning in Spanish and Japanese Contexts*, https://doi.org/10.1007/978-3-030-27443-6_8

project (formerly known as the Project for Promotion of Global Human Resources Development) was aimed at overcoming Japanese youngsters' "inward tendency" and developing professionals who can positively tackle challenges and prosper on the global stage as a springboard for enhancing Japanese global competitiveness and strengthening bonds between nations (MEXT, 2018). With this objective in mind, the courses were designed by three teachers with different backgrounds and nationalities at Yamaguchi University in Japan. Takashi Uemura is an associate professor in the Faculty of Engineering. Prior to his English language teaching career, he worked in the banking, auditing, and finance industries for approximately ten years. Graeme Gilmour is Associate Professor of English. He comes from Scotland and has taught English at a variety of levels in Japan from conversation schools to undergraduate students at the university level. Luis Costa studied Computer Science and Engineering at Instituto Superior Técnico in Portugal. Luis worked in industrial and research positions in Portugal and Norway, where he contributed to national and international projects.

Yamaguchi University's (2012) GGJ proposal to MEXT had the double aim of developing students as global professionals in STEM (Science, technology, engineering, and mathematics), especially in engineering in this course, and improving their English proficiency. The former is intended to develop professionals who understand different cultures and possess an awareness of working overseas through the university curricula. The latter is intended to produce students who hold TOEIC® Listening & Reading Test[1] 650, which is the proficiency level the university considers adequate for demonstrating students' ability to work in overseas branch offices or factories. Improvement of linguistic abilities also includes launching an instructional programme to develop academic writing, logical explanation, and discussion skills. In sum, a combination of challenges was encountered by the three teachers: (1) developing globally aware professionals, (2) improving

---

[1] TOEIC is a registered trademark of Educational Testing Service (ETS). This publication is not endorsed or approved by ETS.

TOEIC® Program[2] scores, (3) developing academic writing skills, and (4) improving logical explanation and discussion skills.

It was decided that a Content and Language Integrated Learning (CLIL) approach would fit our English as a Foreign Language (EFL) context due to its dual-focused educational approach to teaching and learning both content and language simultaneously by means of an additional language (Coyle, Hood, & Marsh, 2010). In other words, content will be the topics that inspire engineering students who wish to prosper as full-fledged global engineers, and language will be English for academic writing, and presentations and discussions, which is inevitably beneficial for students to achieve the target TOEIC® Program score.

1.2 Development of Technical Communication Courses

With the positive inspirations and potential of CLIL in mind, the three language practitioners introduced a series of English courses that are individually designed to cater for future global engineers. The courses are also carefully sequenced from the second to the third and fourth years of the engineering degree. Takashi Uemura is in charge of Basic Technical Communication (BTC) for second-year undergraduate students. Graeme Gilmour is responsible for Technical Communication I and II (TCI and II) for third- and fourth-year students, and Luis Costa is in charge of Advanced Technical Communication (ATC) for third- and fourth-year students (see Table 8.1).

BTC is a one-year practical English business communication course which is designed to teach business as content and business English as target language skills, simultaneously preparing for the TOEIC® Program. Both components are closely intertwined since business-oriented lexical items and context are frequently occurring in the TOEIC® Program. Thus, CLIL has enabled the "dual-focused educational approach" for effective learning for future engineers (Coyle et al., 2010, p. 1).

---

[2] The Test of English for International Communication® (TOEIC) is an English language test designed specifically to measure the everyday English skills of people working in an international environment.

Table 8.1 The classes for the GGJ project

Lecturer	Students	Module name
Uemura	2nd year students	Basic Technical Communication (BTC)
Gilmour	3rd and 4th year students	Technical Communication I and II (TCI and II)
Costa	3rd and 4th year students	Advanced Technical Communication (ATC)

TCI is an academic writing course with a focus on engineering topics, while TCII is an ESP course devised specifically for undergraduate engineering students. Classes consist of students from a variety of international backgrounds. Although the majority of students are Japanese, there are also Malaysian, South Korean, and Chinese participants. The students' English language level ranges between B1 and B2 on the Common European Framework of Reference for Languages (CEFR) scale.

The ATC class was devised to support the development of essential English skills for engineers and researchers: oral presentations, academic writing, and technical discussions.

As the class is available to students studying different fields of engineering such as Civil, Electrical, or Chemical, a varied set of topics was selected to foster technical discussions. These topics are driverless cars, Japan's energy crisis, cloud computing, natural materials, genomics, and remote sensing. Last year, students were asked to choose an additional technical topic that they would like to discuss in class. The topic chosen was "Diversity", which is not strictly a technical topic. However, this topic was used in class since it was possible to find materials enabling the discussion of the relation between diversity and the development of technology.

2   Course Design

Due to space limitations, this section selects only one lesson plan of a unit from the BTC course regarding corporate structure and corporate profile research (see Appendix 1). Section 3, however, describes the classroom practices of all three courses.

2.1 Warmer

The initial activity is intended to activate what students know about business content and relevant English vocabulary and expressions. The teacher shows pictures of departments in a typical manufacturing company such as *production department, human resources (HR) department,* and *research and development (R&D) department* (see Appendix 2). Each picture contains an employee doing a specific task. The students are asked to answer what each employee is doing through the teacher's open-ended questions and multiple-choice questions. These activities are designed to prepare the students for TOEIC® Program listening comprehension tasks since similar tasks can be seen in the test. With students' knowledge of what is being done in each picture, the teacher introduces what each department is termed in English. This way, students' prior knowledge will be associated with their new learning.

2.2 Main Activities

Through the use of the audio materials originally developed by Uemura, the students have rich input and immersion into business conversations featuring both American and British accents (see Appendix 3). For example, in the recorded dialogue for this unit, an American HR staff member is taking a new British recruit on an office tour at a multinational company. Key terms include departments such as General Administration Department and Shipping Department, and business terms and expressions related to personnel, such as *supervisor, clerical work, incentive, quota,* and *climb the corporate ladder.* One of the main topics to be learned in this unit is corporate structure. Therefore, it is essential that the students understand the departments in a typical manufacturing company while inferring their functions from business genre-specific terms purposefully spread throughout the dialogue.

Multiple-choice questions catering for the TOEIC® Program are followed by peer and group discussions. That is, answers for the multiple-choice questions based on the audio dialogue are first discussed in pairs. Then, the students listen to the dialogue again and share their understanding and expressions that they have picked up in groups of four to six. To consolidate the personnel-related content of the dialogue, the teacher gives a short lecture on meritocracy and the seniority system entirely in English. The students are then asked to demonstrate their understanding of the short lecture using their notes in pairs. This activity helps cement students' understanding before moving on to group discussion about the pros and cons of meritocracy or the seniority system. Group leaders are assigned to give a presentation to the whole class about the pros and cons using a whiteboard.

The other topic covered in the lesson is corporate profile research. The teacher selects two or three listed companies before class and shows their online annual reports to the whole class. This corporate profile research will also be helpful for students' future job-hunting and global career development. The students are asked to find designated information in groups using the annual reports such as strengths of the company and the company's philosophy (see Appendix 4). Since authentic materials like these often include a great deal of less frequent genre-specific vocabulary, the teacher's intervention is necessary to facilitate and encourage student group learning. This is done by guiding students to the parts they should skim-read or read for detail by collaboratively checking new vocabulary in the dictionary. Student groups need to compare, analyse, and evaluate the introduced companies after the corporate profile research. Finally, group leaders are assigned to give a presentation on designated information about each company and explain why they prefer one of the companies.

2.3   Reflections

The students are instructed to close their textbooks and notebooks and should answer three or four comprehension questions in the distributed worksheet (e.g., (1) Write as many departments as possible of a typical manufacturing company. (2) Select three departments and write what the people in those departments generally do. (3) Why do you think annual reports are useful when looking for a job?). This reflection is followed by pair discussion and peer teaching. If time allows, teacher-student assessment is conducted. The students are randomly chosen by the teacher, and they should answer the aforementioned questions without looking at their answers written in their report.

3 Implementation of the Course

3.1 BTC Course

The content is aimed at developing engineering students' mindset as future global engineers who can become successful in a highly competitive global labour market. For that purpose, topics include corporate structure (introducing what departments there are in a typical manufacturing company and what they do in daily operations) and corporate research (a small project to grasp the meaning of a corporate profile through the examination of annual reports) as described in the lesson plan in the previous section. These topics are closely intertwined with what students should know before attending future job interviews. Therefore, the content is practical and motivational for the learners.

As Coyle et al. (2010) state, communication in CLIL is synonymous with language which consists of three components: language *of* learning, language *for* learning, and language *through* learning. This section summarises each definition by Coyle et al. (2010) along with examples used in the BTC class that overlap with frequently occurring items in the TOEIC® Program. Language *of* learning is genre-specific language such as *research and development (R&D), human resources (HR), shipping*, and *general and administration* that collocate department (of companies). Language *for* learning is characterised as the kind of language necessary to access new knowledge or learning in a foreign language classroom setting. For example, BTC classes involve a lot of group discussions, where the students need to apply expressions for clarification (e.g., *Are you saying that* Company A has more advanced technology?), eliciting ideas from their classmates (e.g., *What do you all think?*), demonstrating agreement and disagreement in a polite fashion (e.g., *I'm afraid I don't agree.*). Finally, language *through* learning posits the principle that effective learning cannot be realised without actively involving language and thinking amongst learners. Therefore, CLIL entails rich interactions in which learners' articulation of understanding leads to deeper learning. New linguistic items and associated meanings encountered in the CLIL classroom need to be captured, recycled, and strategically developed through teacher-student collaboration. Some examples are the aforementioned departments of a company and the terms appearing in annual reports such as *procurement, relocate, retail store*, and *headquarters*.

The BTC class involves three pedagogical strategies: (1) Performances of Understanding (PoUs) for facilitating learner cognitive development from lower-order thinking skills (LOTS) to higher-order thinking skills (HOTS) (Bloom, Engelhart, Furst, Hill, & Krathwohl, 1956), (2) comparison and analysis of two listed companies by means of examining their annual reports, and (3) presenting which company the learners want to work for in the future using their own words and ideas and pointing out the potentials of the company that are not explicitly stated in the annual reports. The cognitive facet of CLIL tends to focus on the importance of HOTS development. Nevertheless, there seem to be few pedagogical debates on how learners can effectively shift their LOTS to HOTS in a CLIL context. The first element of PoUs refers to the activities provided for the learners to demonstrate their understanding by applying the knowledge gained in the lecture or lesson materials in new and visible ways (Blythe, 1998). For example, CLIL lessons generally entail rich input. Thus, CLIL teachers are often concerned about whether their input has been understood correctly. Likewise, CLIL learners may also want to confirm that their understanding is accurate. It is proposed that the teacher's input be divided into several parts, and, at the end of each part, the students can choose to demonstrate their understanding by giving an oral or graphical presentation to their classmates and the teacher so that the input can be digestible for the learners and their understanding can be visibly demonstrated. PoUs will enable the learners to solidify and apply their understanding in their own fashion. Therefore, PoUs will help bridge learners' LOTS and HOTS. The sequence of strategies outlined above aims to gradually enable the learners to create new perspectives, which are deemed to be the highest level of HOTS.

Another aspect to be considered in the CLIL class is authenticity. Uemura (2013) points out that because of his previous international professional experiences in auditing, banking, and finance and accounting and his current position as a Japanese EFL teacher, he can be considered both a content and a language teacher. When the class encounters a complex business term, the teacher purposefully includes anecdotes associated with the term. Authenticity rests with the teacher narrative, which contributes to attracting the learners' attention, arouses their curiosity, and enhances their motivation in class. Furthermore, the students are instructed to access authentic annual reports of two designated listed companies online in class.

In the BTC class, the students are guided to which sections they should skim-read or read carefully so that they can comfortably grasp the content of the authentic annual reports and recognise their novelty and usefulness for their future job-hunting. For example, before the project, the teacher asks several discussion questions that the groups of students need to answer through a collaborative project such as *What does the company do?*, *What are the strengths of the company?*, and *What is the company's philosophy?* First, the teacher demonstrates how annual reports are generally organised using the table of contents and corresponding pages. Then, the teacher has the students scan the headlines and skim-read the relevant summary to get the gist of where in the report they should focus on to answer the discussion questions. If the students have time and ability, they are guided to skim-read topic sentences of the passage they become interested in. Then, the teacher introduces frequently occurring vocabulary and expressions in the TOEIC® Program, which can also be seen in the annual reports. This teacher intervention often brings about new cultural discovery for the learners: the connection between authentic English annual reports and an English proficiency test. In other words, the students are invited into the broader global business world from a narrower context of classroom English learning exclusively for an English proficiency test. Finally, the students are instructed to read the summary and passages they are interested in to answer the discussion questions more precisely.

The following section moves on to discuss the compatibility of Technical Communication I and II with a CLIL approach.

3.2 TCI and TCII Courses

There is a lot of potential for CLIL in a Japanese university setting in general and in Yamaguchi University's faculty of engineering in particular. The much-touted flexibility of the approach is perhaps its greatest strength: Ioannou Georgiou (2012, p. 479) states that "the rapid and widespread adoption of CLIL as a practical solution has resulted in a range of models being developed to fit specific contexts". To exploit this apparent flexibility, TCI and TCII (both developed *without* using a CLIL framework) were examined closely in order to identify areas of possible overlap and compatibility. Throughout the course of the current semester, it has become increasingly apparent that aspects of all four of Coyle's components, content, communication, cognition, and culture, are touched upon regularly. Of the four essential elements, culture is perhaps the most prominent. According to Dale and Tanner (2012, p. 13), "CLIL learners learn about the 'culture' of a subject, and how to think, write and speak like specialists". These are essential skills for students looking to thrive as engineers in an increasingly globalised workplace. This aspect of culture is emphasised in the courses, particularly within academic writing, where a selection of essential genre structures relevant to science and engineering students are analysed during the courses. Content is delivered using the *Teaching Learning Cycle*: the *Teaching Learning Cycle* is a scaffolded approach which helps students to engage with and construct authentic texts. It is based largely on the work of Halliday and Painter, who characterised the essence of successful language learning as needing "guidance through interaction in the context of shared experience" (Martin & Rose, 2012, p. 58).

An example of this approach can be found in TCII (Gilmour, 2015) where students are asked to focus on the language used in engineering product descriptions. In this lesson, participants are required to use authentic text examples from an online shop selling construction equipment. They are shown examples of target texts and are directed towards common language features and similarities in the structure of the genre examples. In small groups, the students are then asked to jointly *deconstruct* one of the texts (step one of the *Teaching Learning Cycle*) and to place the relevant parts into corresponding sections in a simple table in the TCII textbook (see Fig. 8.1). This part of the cycle is repeated with a number of similar texts. Once they have familiarised themselves with the genre features, they move on to *joint construction*, the next step of the *Teaching Learning Cycle*. Working in groups, they select a product relevant to their field of study and attempt to jointly construct a product description. They are again asked to focus on recurrent language patterns of the genre. Other language features such as common collocations and phrases used to highlight features and benefits are introduced at this point. Once their understanding of the genre structure is consolidated, they move on to the final part of the cycle; *independent construction*. This part is completed as a homework assignment in which students are

What it is	What it does/what was it invented for?
What it looks like/what parts it has	How it works

Fig. 8.1 TCII product description template

required to compose a product description of an imaginary new engineering product. The cycle is used regularly in both TCI and TCII.

It could be argued that a carefully scaffolded approach like genre analysis and the associated *Teaching Learning Cycle* are tailor made for CLIL. Indeed, the parallels and apparent compatibility are striking. The method incorporates not only the cultural aspect discussed at length above, but also content (authentic science and engineering texts are used throughout the course and are approached using the *Teaching Learning Cycle*), communication (students work in groups throughout the cycle to work towards jointly constructing coherent texts) and cognition (students are required to develop their higher-order thinking skills when researching and producing a variety of texts throughout the courses). Some relatively minor modifications to the *Teaching Learning Cycle* may be necessary in order to more closely mirror a truly CLIL approach. However, the incorporation of the approach into a more CLIL based curriculum going forward has the potential to bear fruit and merits further investigation.

3.3   ATC Course

The main purpose of the ATC class was to develop students' English skills, not teaching engineering. However, the heterogeneity of both students and topics also allows students to complement their knowledge of the engineering field that they are studying with knowledge of other engineering fields.

While designing materials for the ATC class, one of the main goals was authenticity; all the texts and videos used in the activities are either authentic materials (not specifically produced for language teaching) or based on authentic materials. We were aware that these materials could be challenging for the students, but as this class was intended for the students at Yamaguchi University possessing the best English skills, we were hoping that this difficulty could be overcome by the students' strong motivation and genuine interest in developing their skills. The materials developed for the ATC class were compiled in a textbook which is currently being used at Yamaguchi University (Hoysted & Costa, 2015) (see Appendix 5).

The ATC class includes activities based on authentic texts and videos about a selection of technical topics. To get a maximal benefit from the ATC class, students are expected to read the texts and watch the videos before the class. These activities are intended to introduce the students to vocabulary related to the topic and enable them to practise their listening and reading skills. The vocabulary exercises are based on words present in the texts and videos for which students may have greater difficulties. These are mainly technical words or words included in the Academic Word List (Coxhead, 2000).

Additionally, the ATC textbook also includes a number of pictures and illustrations to motivate the students for discussion around the technical topics. All these activities build into the discussion itself, which is further motivated by questions related to each topic.

The class was not designed specifically following a CLIL approach, but eventually it ended up including a good number of the features generally identified with CLIL. In different degrees, all the key features of Coyle's 4Cs framework are present in the ATC class. There is obviously content in the texts, videos, and illustrations used in the ATC textbook to foster the discussion about the different technical topics. Besides this content, students have the option to select an additional technical topic that they would like to discuss in class. They are also encouraged to suggest materials to be used in that class (texts, videos, etc.).

Communication in different forms (presentations, discussions and written) is fostered in the ATC class. The activities done in class (such as quizzes, vocabulary exercises, comprehension questions, paraphrase exercises, note-taking, and writing summaries) prepare students step by step to perform efficiently in each of these communication contexts.

Regarding cognition, some of the ATC class activities require students to use HOTS. For example, students are asked to create a presentation about a technical topic and to be able to do that they are required to learn enough about that topic to be able to explain it to their peers. The technical discussions also allow students to analyse different technical solutions and evaluate their advantages and disadvantages.

Students are exposed to different cultures both through the classroom environment and through the class materials. Yamaguchi University has a considerable some number of international students (mainly from

Asian countries such as China, Korea, Malaysia, Vietnam, and Indonesia). The participation of these students in the ATC class enriches the class experience. Having a heterogeneous group of students allows for exposure to different accents of English. The technical discussions enable the comparison of realities in the different countries. Technology is the main focus, but the discussions end up touching other areas such as society, the economy, politics, and history.

4 Outcomes and Implications

The number of students participating in TC courses increased significantly despite the fact that they are elective. First, the dramatic increase in BTC participants among second-year engineering students was striking (from 28 students in 2013 to 98 in 2016). This may have demonstrated learners' enhanced motivation towards English studies by incorporating a *soft CLIL* approach into the courses. *Soft CLIL* defined by Bentley (2010) is curricular topic teaching that can be partially seen within some language courses, while *hard CLIL* involves curricular teaching with more target language immersion nearing half of the curriculum. Second, the number of students participating in TCI and TCII and TCA courses culminated in the third year of the project at more than 30 in the former and about 20 in the latter, while, there were only 4 students in each class in the first year. To our knowledge, this kind of autonomous English learning through participating in official courses provided by the university among senior year students was not seen before the project.

For the last three years, students were asked to evaluate how interesting and difficult they found the content of the ATC class. The following scale from 1 to 5 was used: 1—not interesting/not difficult, 5—very interesting/very difficult. Fig. 8.2 shows students' feedback about the technical topics used for discussion in the ATC class. All the topics seem to be fairly interesting to the students, but the topics "driverless cars" and "remote sensing" were considered to be slightly more stimulating throughout the years. For these topics, interest seems to be independent of their difficulty.

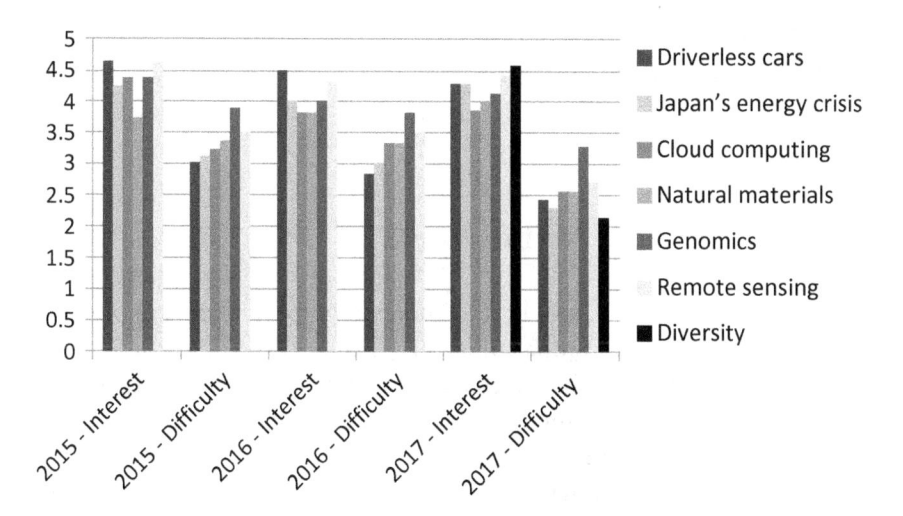

Fig. 8.2 Feedback about the technical topics used for discussion in the ATC class

Whereas "driverless cars" was one of the topics where students felt fewer difficulties, "remote sensing" was considered one of the most difficult topics. In all the studied years, "genomics" was considered to be the hardest topic. Perhaps not surprisingly, diversity, the topic chosen by the students, was considered the most interesting topic last year.

4.1 CLIL Workshop and Collaboration with Subject Teachers

In an effort to outline the benefits of adopting a CLIL approach in delivering course content in the Faculty of Engineering at Yamaguchi University, a three-hour-CLIL workshop was organised by the three language practitioners. Participants included content teachers from the departments of engineering, mathematics, and economics at Yamaguchi University as well as high school teachers from Yamaguchi Prefecture with an interest in CLIL. One of the purposes of holding the workshop was to encourage collaboration between content and language teachers. The workshop outlined the underlying principles of the approach and underlined its relevance to content teachers. Although participant feedback was generally positive, additional events of this kind will be needed to further reinforce the importance of the pedagogy to content teachers.

4.2   Implications for the Future

For TCI and TCII it would be interesting to further explore and develop the apparent compatibility of CLIL with Genre Analysis and other aspects of English for Academic Purposes (EAP)/English for Specific Purposes (ESP) methodology over the course of future semesters. It would also be useful to foster further CLIL collaboration between content and language specialists. There has been recent cooperation of this kind with teachers from the department of mechanical engineering at Yamaguchi University (YU). Gilmour was invited to participate in the Summer Programme for Innovative Engineering Design (SPIED) at Kunsan National University in South Korea. SPIED is a two-week summer programme designed for fourth-year undergraduate and graduate engineering students from Japan, China, and South Korea. Participants work collaboratively in planning, designing, producing, and presenting a prototype product following set programme themes. The course content has been designed by content teachers from YU's mechanical engineering department and is delivered entirely in English.

The main purpose of attending the programme was to observe and provide formative and summative feedback to programme participants for collaborative presentations. Qualitative data was also collected in the form of field notes and video recordings with the intention of producing tailor-made teaching materials for future participants in the programme. From initial observations, however, the potential for a CLIL approach in developing both English teaching materials and an overall course curriculum with content specialists appeared obvious. From a language specialist perspective, attending the event provided a further opportunity to incorporate the *Teaching Learning Cycle* (in this instance for developing English presentation skills). It also indicated that creating teaching materials that develop skills in product and process description, meetings and discussions, and describing data, and so on will be important for future programmes.

There has also been successful collaboration with other departments within the faculty of engineering. Uemura (2017) was involved in task design and materials development for an experiential learning class with a civil engineering teacher. Unlike formal lectures, experiential learning classes generally allow flexibility in the syllabus and cater for solidifying and applying students' knowledge gained in the subject L1 lecture. Thus, it was suggested that CLIL in these kinds of classes could be practically implemented with a collaboration between subject and language specialist. Fostering further partnerships with content specialists from other disciplines will be essential when a CLIL approach is to gain a foothold in the faculty of engineering at YU. In order to do this, efforts must be made to emphasise the beneficial nature of the current joint effort with SPIED and similar projects.

Appendices

Appendix 1

BTC lesson plan for corporate structure and corporate profile research.

Topic: corporate structure and corporate profile research.

Lesson objectives:

- To develop learners' abilities to describe what each department of typical manufacturing companies does **(content)**
- To develop learners' abilities to understand and apply business terms and expressions used when indicating specific departments in spoken English **(communication)**
- To develop learners' abilities to identify target information from authentic annual reports **(culture)**
- To develop learners' abilities to compare a selection of annual reports and present the advantages of the company while explaining their reasons **(cognition)**

Level: Upper beginner to Lower intermediate

Time: 90 minutes.

Lesson procedure:

Warmer (10 mins.)	<ul><li>Show pictures of departments in a typical manufacturing company (see appendix 2).</li><li>Have the students discuss in pairs what each employee is doing in each department picture.</li><li>The teacher should ask some open-ended questions such as "What is the man doing?" and also additional questions with multiple choice answers such as "What is the woman doing? … a. She is fixing a computer…. b. She is preparing some documents for her colleagues….c. She is thinking about tonight's dinner." Then, elicit answers.</li></ul>

	• After the students have grasped what the people in each picture are doing, the teacher should demonstrate the names of the departments and have them repeat these terms after the teacher.
Main activities (65 mins.)	**Pre-listening activity (2 mins.)** The teacher should show a picture or an illustration, which represents a job-interview. Then, elicit expressions such as job-hunting, interview, and career to provide the students with an opportunity to guess what the dialogue will be about in the following listening task. **Listening comprehension activity (12 mins.)** • Play the audio dialogue and have the students get the gist of the content (see appendix 3). • Have the students discuss the content of the dialogue in pairs, and ask some capable students what the dialogue is about and expressions that they have caught. • Play the audio dialogue again, and have the students answer multiple choice questions. **Post-listening activity (12 mins.)** • Have the students check their answers in groups of 4 to 6. • Have the whole class answer the questions and check if their answers are correct. • Get the students to open their transcript and check the content. • The teacher should highlight the business terms that are considered to be frequently occurring in TOEIC® Program such as supervisor, clerical work, incentive, quota, meritocracy, and seniority system. **Short lecture and discussions (15 mins.)** • In association with the personnel related content of the dialogue, the teacher should give a short lecture on what meritocracy and seniority systems are. • The students should demonstrate their understanding of the short lecture using their notes in pairs.

	• Have the students form groups of 4 to 6 and have them discuss pros and cons of a meritocracy or seniority system. • Group leaders are assigned to give a presentation about the pros and cons using a whiteboard to the whole class. **PBL (Project-based Learning) using an annual report (24 mins)** • Ask the students what resource they might check before going to their future job interviews, and introduce an annual report as one of the resources helpful for learning about companies. • The teacher should select two or three listed companies and show their online annual reports to the whole class. • Show how annual reports are generally organised using the table of contents. • Have the students find designated information in groups using the annual reports such as who the CEO or President is, strengths of the company and company's philosophy. Then, have them write their answers on the allocated whiteboard. • Student groups should compare, analyse, and evaluate the companies after the corporate profile research and decide which company will be the best for each group. • Group leaders should be assigned to give a presentation on designated information about each company and explain why they prefer one of the companies.
Reflections (12 mins.)	**Reflections (7 mins.)** • Have students close all of their lesson materials. • The teacher should show about three to four comprehension questions or classroom written assignment on the presentation slide (e.g. 1. Write as many departments as possible of a typical manufacturing company. 2. Select three departments, and write what the people in those departments generally do. 3. Why do you think annual reports will be useful in your future job-hunting?) and have the students write their answers in the classroom report.

Peer-to-peer assessment and teaching (5 mins.)

- Have the students turn over the report and pair up with a classmate.
- One student should read the comprehension questions and the classroom written assignment shown on the presentation slide. Then, the other student should orally answer the questions.
- If the student struggles to answer, his or her partner should help while checking the report and lesson materials (if necessary).

Appendix 2

Excerpts from Uemura (2015a, p. 46) : Pictures of departments in a typical manufacturing company

Appendix 3

TRANSCRIPTS

Unit 1

A: Good morning, Greg. I'm Sophia from the HR Department. I'll take you on an office tour this morning.

B: Thank you for taking the time, Sophia.

A: It's my pleasure, Greg. Please follow me. I heard that you are majoring in commerce. Which type of work environment do you prefer, a seniority system or a meritocracy?

B: I prefer the latter. The more achievements I make, the more incentives I'd like to earn.

A: Alright. Then, you'll have a lot of opportunities to climb the corporate ladder if you are hired as a full-timer after you successfully complete your apprenticeship.

B: That's exciting. I'll give it my all. May I ask what my responsibilities are?

A: That's a good question. Mainly, you will be dedicated to clerical work. Because of our business expansion, everybody has been hectic and the backlog has been growing. So, we would like you to assist with paperwork. You will not be assigned to Sales, so please be assured that you won't have any quota. However, it is sedentary work, so I suggest you regularly take a break and stretch.

B: Thank you. I will. Could I have a chance to talk with my supervisor today?

A: I'm afraid he is tied up in a business meeting. Probably tomorrow. Oh, when you show up tomorrow morning, be sure to punch in and punch out when you leave the office.

B: Sure.

A: Look. This is the General Affairs Department. If you need office supplies, such as whiteout, a stapler, and cardboard boxes, just fill out the request form and email it to this department. You can collect the requested items here usually in 2 days.

B: OK. By the way, I wonder where I can make photocopies.

A: Oh, if you go down the corridor, you'll find the copier on your left. Please bear in mind that you need to refill the copier's paper tray and fix any paper jams by yourself.

Excerpt from Uemura's (2015b, p. 17) BTC classroom audio transcript

Appendix 4

Speaking frame

I would like to work in the field of _____ .

or

I hope that I can be successful in the field of _____ .

In fact, one of the strengths of your company is _____ .

or

Actually, the major strength of your company is_____ .

So, I strongly feel that I will be able to realize my career goals by working for
_____ .

Speaking frame for eliciting and practicing the information about strengths of the companies used in the classroom

Appendix 5

B *Match the computer specifications on the left with their respective values on the right.*

1.	_____ Storage capacity	a.	1366 × 768
2.	_____ Weight	b.	20 hours
3.	_____ Screen size	c.	750 GB
4.	_____ Battery life	d.	2.3 GHz
5.	_____ Screen resolution	e.	15.6"
6.	_____ Processor speed	f.	3 kg

Activity designed to activate prior knowledge about the technical topic cloud computing (Hoysted & Costa, 2015, p. 17)

C *Match the underlined words in the previous text with the following synonyms.*

combined	_____
precise	_____
remarkable	_____
means	_____
possible	_____
payment	_____
use	_____
manufacture	_____

D *Read the text 'An Overview of Cloud Computing' and answer the following questions.*

a) According to the text, what is cloud computing?

b) Which companies are using cloud computing?

c) Why is it now possible to build powerful systems from inexpensive components?

E *Discussion*

a) Which of the following cloud computing services do you use? Why? / Why not? How do you use them?

    i) E-mail
    ii) Office suites
    iii) Photo and video sharing
    iv) Backup
    v) Social networks

b) Do you have concerns about any of the following aspects of cloud computing? Why? / Why not?

    i) Efficiency
    ii) Reliability
    iii) Privacy
    iv) Cost

Main activities and reflection activities related to the technical topic cloud computing (Hoysted & Costa, 2015, p. 19)

References

Bentley, K. (2010). *The TKT Course CLIL Module.* Cambridge: Cambridge University Press.

Bloom, B., Engelhart, M., Furst, E., Hill, W., & Krathwohl, D. (1956). *Taxonomy of Educational Objectives: The Classification of Educational Goals. Handbook 1: Cognitive Domain.* New York: David McKay.

Blythe, T. (1998). *The Teaching for Understanding Guide.* San Francisco: Jossey-Bass.

Coxhead, A. (2000). A new academic word list. *TESOL Quarterly, 34*(2), 213–238.

Coyle, D., Hood, P., & Marsh, D. (2010). *CLIL: Content and Language Integrated Learning.* Cambridge: Cambridge University Press.

Dale, L., & Tanner, R. (2012). *CLIL Activities: A Resource for Subject and Language Teachers.* Cambridge, UK: Cambridge University Press.

Gilmour, G. (2015). *Technical Communication.* Ube, Japan: Electronic Media Education Publishing.

Hoysted, A., & Costa, L. F. (2015). *Advanced Technical Communication.* Ube, Japan: Electronic Media Education Publishing.

Ioannou Georgiou, S. (2012). Reviewing the puzzle of CLIL. *ELT Journal, 66*(4), 495–504. https://doi.org/10.1093/elt/ccs047

Martin, J., & Rose, D. (2012). *Learning to Write/Reading to Learn.* London: Equinox Publishing.

Ministry of Education, Culture, Sports, Science and Technology (MEXT). (2018). *Project for Promotion of Global Human Resources Development.* Retrieved from http://www.mext.go.jp/en/policy/education/highered/title02/detail02/sdetail02/1373895.htm

Uemura, T. (2013). Implementing content and language integrated learning (CLIL) approach to TOEIC preparatory lessons. *Asian EFL Journal, 15*(4), 305–323.

Uemura, T. (2015a). *Technical Communication (Basic)—Workplace English for Global Engineers—BOOK I.* Ube, Yamaguchi: Yamaguchi University.

Uemura, T. (2015b). *Technical Communication (Basic)—Workplace English for Global Engineers—BOOK I Answer Key & Transcript.* Ube, Yamaguchi: Yamaguchi University.

Uemura, T. (2017). CLIL and its possible application to engineering education to enhance undergraduates' academic and subject-specific English literacy. *International Journal of Engineering Innovation and Management, 7*(2), 13–21.

Yamaguchi University. (2012). *Proposal for Project for Promotion of Global Human Resources Development in 2012 [in Japanese,* 平成24年度グローバル人材育成推進事業構想調書*]*. Retrieved from https://www.jsps.go.jp/j-gjinzai/data/shinsa/h24/gjinzai_chousho_b11.pdf

Part III

Interactions in CLIL Classrooms

9

Co-construction of Knowledge in Primary CLIL Group Work Activities

Amanda Pastrana

1 Introduction of the Study

The central and distinguishing element of Content and Language Integrated Learning (CLIL) is its dual-focused educational approach, which seeks to fuse goals of content and language learning (Coyle, Hood, & Marsh, 2010). In this line, many researchers are calling for the fusion of the content and language perspectives in CLIL research as well as teaching. As Dalton-Puffer et al. write, "either applied linguistics or content pedagogy fusional understanding would require a similarly 'fused' investigative take" (2010, p. 289).

Other researchers have also defended this fusion of language and content in research, teaching and learning. Two volumes on CLIL (Llinares, Morton, & Whittaker, 2012; Nikula, Dafouz, Moore, & Smit, 2016) have highlighted integration as the main aspect to be addressed in CLIL. Many researchers have demanded more work on principled approaches to content and language integration (e.g. Cenoz, Genesee, &

A. Pastrana (✉)
Chanhassen, MN, USA

© The Author(s) 2019
K. Tsuchiya, M. D. Pérez Murillo (eds.), *Content and Language Integrated Learning in Spanish and Japanese Contexts*, https://doi.org/10.1007/978-3-030-27443-6_9

Gorter, 2014; Dalton-Puffer, Nikula, & Smit, 2010; Gajo, 2007). A decade ago, Leung (2005) proposed to integrate two pedagogic issues that were still seen in a separate way: curriculum content learning and language learning in classroom-based bilingual research (2005, p. 240). Specifically in CLIL, a pioneer study was by Llinares et al. (2012) on the roles of language. This chapter responds to the need to bring content and language issues together, doing so through a focus on the roles of classroom interaction and drawing on the constructs of genres and registers. Two recent studies have proposed a conceptual framework for the analysis and implementation of CLIL (Llinares, 2015; Meyer, Coyle, Halbach, Schuck, & Ting, 2015). The present study stands by the statement that Llinares et al. (2012, p. 10) make when they write: "The theory needs to show, in a principled way how, at the same time, social activities such as education shape language use and how language itself constructs knowledge". However, in Nikula et al.'s (2016, p. 2) words, "operationalising such considerations to the more concrete level of research and educational practice still remains a challenge".

This study seeks to operationalise these considerations by proposing a multi-layered analytical model that addresses both the language and the content elements present in CLIL students' group discussions in a fused manner. Moreover, in order to delve deeper into the integrative aspect of CLIL, the intertwined process of language constructs knowledge and how participating in educational activity shapes language use must be dealt with. Dalton-Puffer et al. (2010) suggest that "research based on CLIL as 'fusion' presupposes an inter-, perhaps even transdisciplinary research construct" (2010, p. 289). It is with this idea in mind that the present study proposes an analytical model based on both a sociocultural view of learning and a functional linguistics conception of language. This will be further presented in Part III, the Data and Method section.

The implementation of CLIL in Europe at a primary level is growing steadily. However, according to Nikula, Dalton-Puffer, and Llinares (2013), CLIL research at this educational level is still in its infancy and very scarce. Among the few existing studies, there is Buchholz's (2007) analysis of Austrian primary school students' participation in classroom interaction and Massler's (2012) account of children's, parents' and teachers' perspectives on CLIL in Germany. An example of a more longitudinal research is Serra's (2007) study assessing integrative bilingual learning implemented through CLIL in three Swiss primary schools. In addition, there are also a few comparative studies, such as Llinares and Lyster's (2014) comparison of the use and effect of corrective feedback in immersion and CLIL classrooms in Spain and Canada, and Llinares and Pastrana's (2013) comparison of primary and secondary school students' oral production in Spain.

Although research at the primary level in other bilingual education contexts, such as immersion, is more abundant and is definitely relevant for CLIL, we need more studies contextualised in settings where the school represents the only contact that students have with the foreign language (Dalton-Puffer et al., 2010). This is an important difference with immersion contexts where students' possibilities to have contact with the L2 outside school are much higher (for a further discussion, see, e.g. Lasagabaster & Sierra, 2009). The present study addresses the above-mentioned gap in research by focusing on primary school CLIL students in a "foreign" language context.

In addition, although some studies on CLIL have shown the advantages of group activities when compared to whole-class activities (e.g.Buchholz, 2007; Llinares & Pastrana, 2013; Nikula, 2005; Pastrana, 2010), a deeper examination of the type of language that CLIL students use in such activities is necessary: "we still know rather little about how different classroom contexts and activity environments constrain language use" (Nikula, 2005, p. 29). In order to further research this topic, the present study focuses on small group interaction in CLIL settings. Therefore, the aim of this study is to get a deeper understanding of the relation between language and knowledge construction in group work sessions in CLIL primary classrooms in Spain.

2 Literature Review

The analysis of group interaction in the classroom can be approached from multiple perspectives. In the pedagogical or educational field, the debate is set around learning in general, and educational experts often focus on learning per se and build on the methodologies and the types of talk and interaction that promote that learning. In contrast, in the linguistic field, the main focus is on language and language learning since linguists consider language as a carrier or maker of meanings and concepts to be learnt. This two-fold interest is parallel to the focus of interest shared by the CLIL research and teaching communities: how best to integrate content and language.

Some applications of applied linguistics have shown concern for investigating the way language is connected to learning in general. This is particularly the case of systemic-functional linguistics (henceforth SFL), an approach that is centred on meanings and how these are built through language use (Halliday, 1977). Within the educational field, sociocultural theory (henceforth SCT) views learning as a social process immersed in the act of communicating (Lantolf, 2000). In order to deeply analyse this two-fold focus on language and knowledge, the present study combines the educational and the linguistic fields to gain a better understanding of how language and knowledge are co-constructed in group work interaction. In this way, from the linguistic field, the systemic-functional and a cognitive discourse approaches to language were used while from the educational field, a sociocultural perspective was taken.

The synergies between SCT and SFL have been demonstrated by several researchers (Gibbons, 2002, 2008; Hammond, 2002; Schleppegrell, 2004; Wells, 1999), who have combined the two models in their research on language and education. This link has been possible due to the parallel vision both frameworks have on conceiving language learning as taking place in interaction with others. Within the CLIL framework, Llinares et al. (2012) also demonstrated the compatibility of these approaches since both view language as a social process. Namely they write: "[i]n SFL, language use is shaped by what kind of activity we are doing and who we are doing it with, and for Vygotsky, such language use with others is the essential tool in our cognitive development" (2012, p. 11).

The three-layered analytical model designed for this study brings together the linguistic and the educational perspectives. The linguistic analysis comprises the *discourse layer* (based on Eggins and Slade's model of speech functions) and the *knowledge layer* (based on Christie's model of classroom registers and Dalton-Puffer's cognitive discourse functions,

CDFs henceforth). The combination of these models allows us to examine language as it is used in group work interaction (speech functions) and to connect specific linguistic realisations to their meaning (CDFs).

Meanwhile, the educationally based sociocultural analysis corresponds to the *interactional layer* (based on Storch's interactional patterns of pair work). The *interactional layer* adds the social element of interaction among peers to the multi-layered analysis of the learning process that takes place while working in groups in the CLIL class (see Fig. 9.1).

Therefore, by combining SFL and SCT, the present study aims at going beyond language as it seeks to analyse the process that unites and integrates language and knowledge. This combined perspective sees talk as enabling learners to reason and acquire common knowledge whilst immersed in a meaning-making activity. This primacy of language and its interrelation with thought can maintain and integrate the language and content goals of CLIL. Moreover, it also "provides the fundamental basis for the negotiated relationship between these dual goals" (Moate, 2010, p. 43).

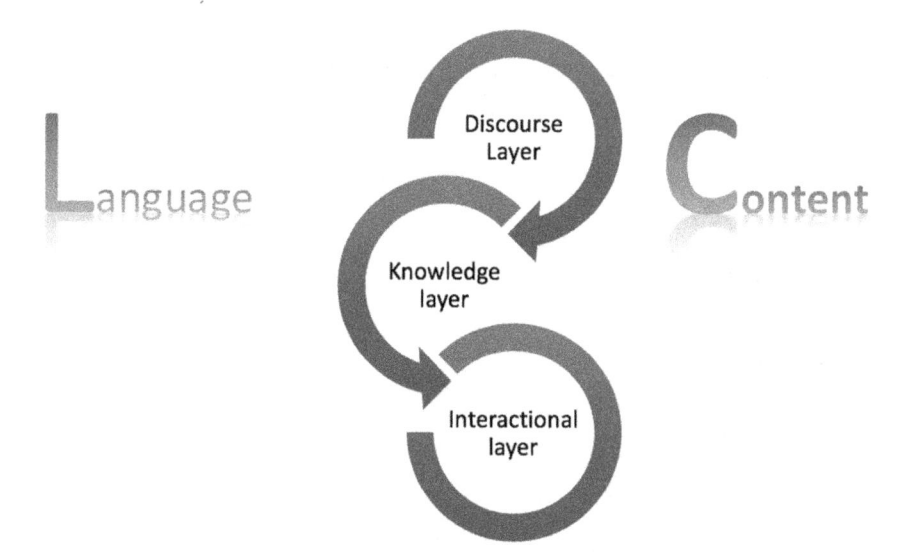

Fig. 9.1 Representation of the multi-layered analytical model designed for this study

2.1 Multi-model and Multi-level Conceptual Framework for the Study

As already pointed out, in order to describe the practice of small group co-construction of knowledge and thereby answer this study's research questions (RQs), a multi-model and multi-layer framework was designed and applied to the collected data corpus. In the present study, three aspects, *discourse, knowledge and interaction*, have been considered influential in the learning process (in any context in general and in CLIL specifically) that takes place while performing group communicative activities. Two main theoretical models support these layers: systemic-functional linguistics and sociocultural theory. For the discourse layer, SFL discourse analysis, and more specifically, the speech functions model (Eggins & Slade, 1997), was used. For the knowledge layer, SFL register theory, as applied to formal contexts in the classroom registers model (Christie, 2002), together with a construct of cognitive discourse functions (Dalton-Puffer, 2013) were heavily drawn on. The interactional layer is mainly based on the socioculturally framed patterns of interaction identified by Storch (2002).

In sum, the analytical model comprises the following layers whose elements will be explained in more detail:

1. A *discourse layer*: An adaptation of the model developed by Eggins and Slade (1997, pp. 192–213).
2. A *knowledge layer*: Which comprises the types of talk and registers presented by Christie (2002: 3) and an adapted version of cognitive discourse functions as proposed by Dalton-Puffer (2013, p. 19).
3. An *interactional layer*: Which deals with equality and mutuality dimensions of group interactions as presented by Storch (2002, pp. 127–128).

These three layers were used in the analysis through a mixed-methods quantitative and qualitative design. The following sub-sections further describe the moves and functions in the three layers.

2.1.1 Discourse Layer

The first layer operates at the discourse level for which Eggins and Slade's (1997) systemic-functional model for the analysis of speech functions as realised as conversational moves in casual conversation was adapted. Some of the levels of delicacy described by Eggins and Slade (1997, pp. 192–213) were omitted in order to simplify the model and reduce it to the ones that would be expected to be most frequently found in a primary classroom context. The level comprises two moves: (1) *Initiating moves*: where a speaker initiates an interaction either by *demanding* (normally realised in question format) or *giving information*. (2) *Sustaining moves*: where there are two types: *continue* and *react*. The first one is the move in which the same participant who has done the initiating move *continues* with yet another move whist the second is the one where another participant produces a *reacting* move to the initiation performed by the previous speaker. Within *continuing* moves, only the categories of *monitor* and *prolong* were used in this study. *Monitor* moves are all those moves where "the speaker focuses on the state of the interactive situation" (1997, p. 195). *Prolonging* moves are those where the students added to something they had said before "by providing further information" (1997, p. 196). Under *reacting* moves there are, as Eggins and Slade (1997) also identify, *responses* and *rejoinders*. *Responses* help to move the exchange towards completion and *rejoinders* are reactions which, in some way, prolong the exchange. There are two types of *responses*, *support* and *confront*. Supporting responses would be the expected responses, whereas *confronting* responses would represent discretionary alternatives. Within these two sub-categories, Eggins and Slade (1997) establish yet another level of delicacy which has not been used in the multi-layered analytical model developed for this study, except for two further categories within the category of *replying* moves: *agree* and *disagree*. In the original framework, *replying* moves are the *responding* moves that imply more negotiation. Hence, *support-reply-agree* (labelled in this model just as *agree* within *support*) is defined as the move performed to indicate support of the information given whereas *confront-reply-disagree* (used here only as a disagreeing move within confront) is the move that provides a negative response to the question. In the analytical model developed here, *support-reply-agree* is used here as an agreeing move within support (*support-agree*), and *confront-reply-disagree* is used here as a disagreeing move within confront (*confront-disagree*). Finally, and also within the reacting moves, *rejoinder* was omitted as a general category, and only one type of rejoinder at a further level of delicacy was used, namely *rejoinder-track* (see Eggins & Slade, 1997), which elicits repetition of a misheard element or move. This was justified by the constant use of clarification requests in the corpus that could be done by the same speaker (*monitoring moves*) or another speaker, in which case the analytical category of *rejoinder-track* was needed.

2.1.2 Knowledge Layer

The next level of delicacy, linked to knowledge, was based on a different model, namely CDFs. Eggins and Slade's (1997) distinction of information as facts, opinions and reasons was initially considered in earlier versions of the multi-layered model proposed in this study. However, in the final version, and inspired in the CDF model proposed by Dalton-Puffer (2013), this level finally included three types of knowledge functions: facts, explanations and evaluations (see Figs. 9.2 and 9.3). The CDF model proposes seven types of functions:

– Type 1: Classify; used to tell how we can cut up the world according to certain ideas.

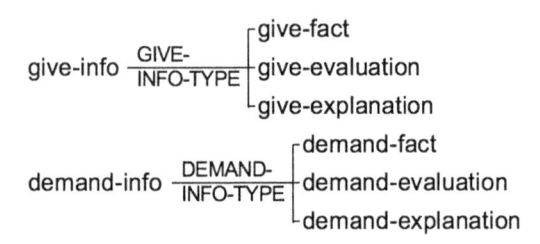

Fig. 9.2 Details of initiating moves in the third level of delicacy taken from the final version of the model as represented in Fig. 9.3

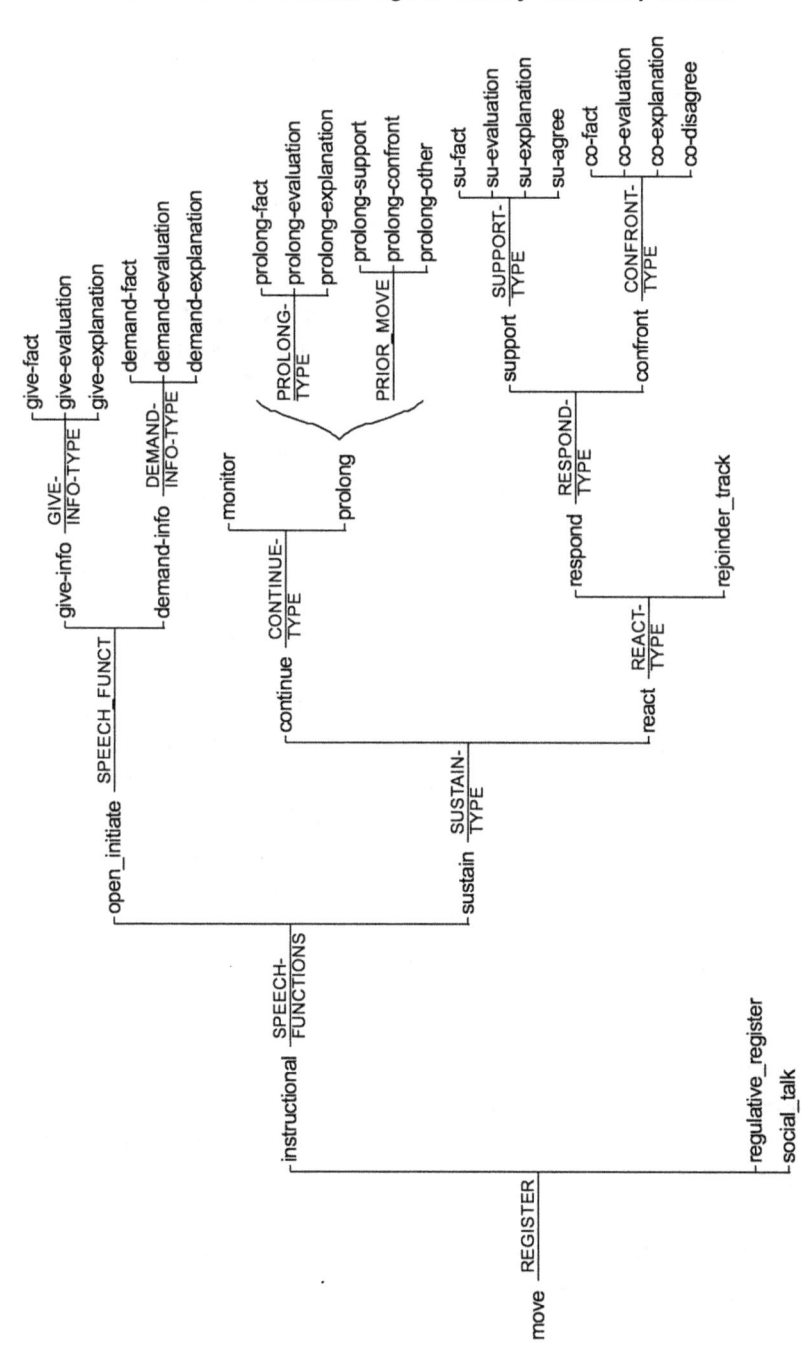

Fig. 9.3 Discourse and knowledge layers in the final version of the multi-layered analytical model

- Type 2: Define; used to tell about the extension of an object of specialist knowledge.
- Type 3: Describe; used to tell details of what can be seen (also metaphorically).
- Type 4: Evaluate; used to tell the position of the speaker vis a vis X.
- Type 5: Explain; used to give reasons for and tell cause/s of X.
- Type 6: Explore; used to tell something that has potential.
- Type 7: Report; used to tell about something external to the speakers and the listener's immediate context on which the speaker has a legitimate knowledge claim (Dalton-Puffer, 2013, p. 19).

To simplify the CDF model for the present study, the seven types were grouped into three broader categories: explanations (type 5); facts (types 1, 2, 3 and 7) and evaluations (types 4 and 7). Report (type 7) could be seen as either fact or evaluation while exploring (type 6) was not found in the data corpus. Figure 9.2 is an amplified section of the final version of the analytical model developed in this thesis for initiating moves.

Therefore, facts, explanations and evaluations could be used as initiating moves: *initiating facts* (*give-fact* and *demand-fact*), *initiating explanations* (*give-explanation* and *demand-explanation*) and *initiating evaluations* (*give-evaluation* and *demand-evaluation*). They were also used as sustaining moves: *sustaining facts* (*prolong-fact*, *support-fact* and *confront-fact*), *sustaining explanations* (*prolong-explanation*, *support-explanation* and *confront-explanation*) and *sustaining evaluations* (*prolong-evaluation*, *support-evaluation* and *confront-evaluation*).

Another model used for the knowledge layer was the model of classroom registers and social talk developed by Christie (2002). Christie (2002) defines classroom activity as composed by curriculum genres and macrogenres. In addition, she argues that this type of discourse has to be analysed and understood in terms of the operation of two registers, the first, the *regulative* register and the second, the *instructional* register (ibid., p. 3):

a *first order or regulative register*, to do with the overall goals, directions, pacing and sequencing of classroom activity, and a second order or *instruc-*

tional register, to do with the particular 'content' being taught and learned. (Christie, 2002, p. 3, original emphasis)

The *instructional* register was the only one further analysed at the discourse and knowledge layer. Another type of talk that can be classified as neither *regulative* nor *instructional* and that is not directly associated with the academic classroom activity is *social talk*. This category was added to Christie's (2002) registers in order to account for the presence of this type of talk in the data corpus. This talk is often used by students when they are "off-task" and talk about more personal topics. The introduction of the concepts of *regulative* and *instructional* registers (Christie, 2002) and *social talk* was motivated by the need to distinguish between talk about the content at hand, talk related to organisational purposes and unrelated off-task issues. In the present study, only the *instructional* register (related to the content to be taught and learnt) was analysed at the discourse and knowledge layers.

2.1.3 Interactional Layer

The third layer of the multi-layered model used in the present study is closely connected to the group interaction. This level of analysis is based on four distinct patterns of interactions: collaborative pattern, expert/novice (or peer tutoring in Damon & Phelps, 1989), dominant/passive and dominant/dominant. These four patterns are based on two descriptive indexes proposed by van Lier (1996): *equality* and *mutuality*. *Equality* is the type of interaction which describes more than merely an equal distribution of turns or equal contributions but an equal degree of control over the direction of the task at hand, meanwhile, *mutuality* is the learners' level of engagement with their partners' contributions (van Lier, 1996).

In the model developed in this study, these two indexes and patterns of interactions were used to analyse the data corpus. As already mentioned in Sect. 3.5, the analytical tool used in this study was the UAM Corpus Tool. Using this programme, a mixed-methods approach was adopted for the analysis of the data corpus. Thus, equality was measured quantitatively, whereas mutuality was examined qualitatively. A separate layer for equality was created within the interactional layer in order to retrieve equality elements of the interaction, and the data corpus was analysed quantitatively. In this way, the degree of equality in the group was measured in terms of the following two aspects: (i) the distribution of turns among group members and (ii) the distribution of *regulative* register as a way of measuring the control over the task exercised by each student. Figure 9.4 shows the interactional layer of the analytical model developed for this study:

This layer of analysis was then added to the discourse and the knowledge layer of the analytical model. The combination of the three layers had the purpose of providing a detailed picture of the interplay between language, content, cognition and participation in group interaction in the CLIL classrooms under study.

The study hence examines students' group work discussions by analysing (a) the discourse, focusing on the moves used by students (layer 1), (b) the knowledge, analysing the registers and cognitive discourse functions (layer 2), and (c) the interaction, concentrating on the mutuality and equality present in the interaction. The developed model attempts to reflect on the process of language being used to express content in a group work activity and the resolution of the task, in other words, what happens between the: "You can start now" and the: "We've finished!".

Fig. 9.4 Interactional layer: Analytical framework

3   Data and Method

3.1   Objectives and Research Questions

This study's main objective is to develop a deep understanding of the learning opportunities in group work interaction in Spanish primary CLIL classrooms by focusing on the integration of language and content. This therefore aims at describing and comparing the language used by students working in small groups in CLIL settings and across two different activities. The research questions for this study are the following:

RQ1. How is knowledge co-constructed in CLIL group work activities?

RQ1.1 What type of speech functions do CLIL students produce?
RQ1.2 What type of knowledge is displayed in CLIL students' use of registers and cognitive discourse functions?
RQ1.3 What type of interaction takes place in CLIL group work in terms of the equality and mutuality fostered in the groups?

This study is descriptive. It seeks to obtain a thorough understanding of the connection between language and cognition in CLIL. In order to elaborate a precise description of this connection and a precise description of it, a multi-layered analytical model was designed which contains three layers: *discourse layer, knowledge layer* and *interactional layer*. The *discourse layer* delves into the way we use language to convey meaning by focusing on speech functions; the *knowledge layer* focuses on the type of content we transmit through the use of those functions, and finally, the *interactional layer* concentrates on the way students interact in the group. Each layer is represented by a corresponding sub question within RQ1 (RQ1.1, RQ1.2 and RQ1.3). The designed analytical model is described in the method section.

3.2   Corpus

The primary school where the CLIL data corpus was obtained is a private bilingual school situated in the north of Madrid. It is in a residential area still within the city limits but situated on the outskirts. It comprises nursery (age 2–5), primary (age 5–12) and secondary (age 12–18) educational levels.

The school where the CLIL data corpus used in this study was obtained fulfils all the legal requirements to be considered bilingual (a minimum of 30% and a maximum of 50% of the subject-matter curriculum has to be taught in English). In the primary section, where this study was carried out, children have a total of 22.5 hours of class per week. Half of that time, children attend classes in Spanish as their first language (L1), which is a total of 11.25 hours per week. The rest of the time they are taught in English, which are English as a Foreign Language (EFL) and CLIL science classes. This adds up to approximately 8.75 hours of English per week, which represents 38% of the total amount of the instruction hours. The classes examined in this study were grade 4 (age 9–10), which has three classes of 23–27 students. Most of the students who took part in this study have been attending the school since the age of three, although learning a content subject in English, in this case, science, starts only at the age of six, in grade 1 of primary school.

The CLIL data corpus comprises recordings from two of the three grade 4 classes. Each of the two classes (CLILA and CLILB) has 27 students who are all native speakers of Spanish. There were no students considered to be in different circumstances from the ones described above. Both classes worked in two group work sessions: a discussion activity and a problem-solving activity based on the Raven's test of progressive matrices (RTPM). However, out of the total of eight to nine small groups that took part in the activities in each class, only four were randomly selected for the analysis. This was due to the length and complexity of the original study (my PhD thesis).

3.3   Sessions

For the first and descriptive part of the study, two activities were designed. The first was a group discussion about a topic belonging to the grade 4 science curriculum, which was chosen together with the four teachers involved. This activity will be referred to as the science topic discussion activity (hereafter STA). The second activity was a problem-solving activity (PSA henceforth) based on the RTPM.

3.4 Data Collection

The two group activities were audio and video recorded with the use of iPads and video cameras. Each camera or iPad recorded one group, and in total there was a minimum of seven and a maximum of nine cameras or iPads recording each group work session simultaneously. The recordings for this study comprise two sessions (STA and PSA activities) performed by two classes (CLILA and CLILB), thus making a total of four sessions recorded. Each STA and PSA session lasted 45 minutes, and so the total length of the recording was 3 hours.

As indicated above, only 4 groups carrying out the two activities from each class were randomly chosen to be analysed, which makes a total of 8 groups and 16 video and audio recordings of both activities, that is, 8 recordings of the 4 groups doing the STA and 8 recordings of the PSA (approx. 12 hours). These recordings were transcribed using a specialised open source transcription and analysis software for audio and video data, Transana,[1] with the Santa Barbara conventions (Du Bois, 2003; Du Bois, Schuetze-Coburn, Cumming, & Paolino, 1993). The final data corpus consisted of approximately 56,000 words.

3.5 Analytical Procedure

As described above, in order to examine the complex connection between language, content and cognition, an analytical model containing three layers was designed: *discourse, knowledge* and *interaction*. Once the model was defined, the coding of the transcribed data and the quantitative analysis were performed using the UAM Corpus Tool (O'Donnell, 2008), a programme developed to assist in the annotation and retrieval of text corpora (see Fig. 9.5 for an example of coding).

First, a selection of approximately 5% of representative data from the whole corpus was coded using the UAM Corpus Tool. This dataset was coded by the researcher and by two colleagues who were also applied linguists in order to guarantee reliability and validate the model. Each

---

[1] For further information see: www.transana.com.

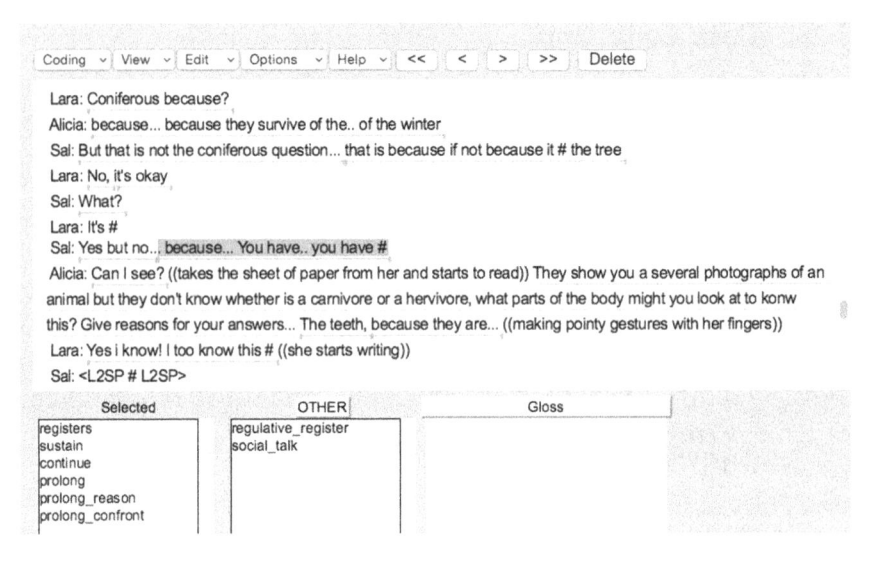

Fig. 9.5 Screenshot of the coding process in the UAM Corpus Tool

researcher coded the representative data sample separately using the UAM Corpus Tool. Disagreements were discussed, and the coding and the model were revised accordingly until the inter-rater reliability reached 0.05%.

4 Findings

4.1 Discourse Layer

Table 9.1 shows the speech functions produced by CLIL students in the two group discussion activities (STA and PSA) in the CLIL classroom. The two columns show the frequency and distribution of the different speech functions identified in the data. The results are presented locally, in other words, each category is considered as a whole, representing a total of 100%, as opposed to globally, where the 100% would be distributed through each category (including all *initiating* and all *sustaining* moves). When results are presented locally, it means that, for example, the category *initiation* represents 100%, and within it, the two options obtain a percentage according to their use by students.

The first category is *speech functions*, which differentiates between *initiating* (16.24%) and *sustaining* moves (83.76%). This unequal distribution is highly expected as, during casual conversation, *initiations* are followed by several turns of *sustaining* moves on the topic initiated. Moving further, we can observe that in both activities, CLIL students prefer *initiating* by *giving information* (63.54%) to *initiating* by *demanding information* (36.46%). They also prefer *sustaining* interaction with *reactions* (84.44%), which include *support* and *confront* (within *respond*) and *rejoinder-track*, to *sustaining* interaction with *continuing* moves (15.56%). This preference for *reactions* (produced in the next turn) over *continuing moves* (produced in the same turn) implies that the turns cannot be very long.

When we move towards a further level of delicacy of speech functions used by CLIL students, for the types of *continuing* moves, most were found to be of the *prolong* type (96.73%) rather than of the *monitor* type (3.27%). The high percentage of *prolong* and the low percentage of *monitor* is also a highly expected distribution. The low use of *monitor* can be explained by the fact that this speech function is only used in the CLIL

Table 9.1 Distribution of speech functions in the two group activities in the CLIL classroom

Feature	N	Per cent (%)
SPEECH FUNCTIONS	*N* = 4457	
Open_initiate	724	16.24
Sustain	3733	83.76
OPEN INITIATE	*N* = 724	
Give-info	460	63.54
Demand-info	264	36.46
SUSTAIN	*N* = 3733	
Continue	581	15.56
React	3152	84.44
CONTINUE	*N* = 581	
Monitor	19	3.27
Prolong	562	96.73
REACT	*N* = 3152	
Respond	3006	95.37
Rejoinder_track	146	4.63
RESPOND	*N* = 3006	
Support	2577	74.12
Confront	778	25.88

data to check if the rest of the group members follow the speaker. Typically, they use it when the students feel someone lags behind to make sure they followed. This was not a frequent situation. However, *prolong*, used to further explain something mentioned by the same speaker, was frequently used to help that students make their point and convince the other members of the group.

We find a similar distribution in *react*, with *respond* being the leading move (95.37%) and *rejoinder-track* being used highly infrequently (3.27%). This is also highly expected because *respond* accounts for all replies given to the first speaker by a second speaker, whereas *rejoinder-track* has a similar function to *monitor* as it tends to only check or clarify previous moves. Finally, in the *responsive* moves we see a clear tendency among CLIL students to use *support* (74.12%) more than *confront* (25.88%), which shows CLIL students' preference to use short supporting responses, probably with the objective of completing the activities at hand, keeping the discussion moving forward and arriving at a consensus.

This preference for the use of short turns and supporting responses in both activities (STA and PSA) is illustrated in Extracts 9.1 and 9.2:

1 *Jorge*[a]:	*This one, this one, this one here is not finished.. eh.. ((reading part of the*
2	*question again)) and explain the parts that help them live in that habitat..*
3 *Raúl:*	*Ah... eh the....*
4 *Jorge:*	*Tail?*
5 *Raúl:*	***Tail, tail* (SUPPORTING RESPONSE)[b]**
6 *Jorge:*	***Yes ((Eva writes)) (SUPPORTING RESPONSE)***
7 *Eva:*	*Tail... ((while writing)) second... the head?*
8 *Raúl:*	*No*
9 *Jorge:*	*No, no, no... eh... a large body..*
10 *Raúl:*	***Yes* (SUPPORTING RESPONSE)**
11 *Eva:*	*A large?*
12 *Jorge:*	*A large body <L1SP cuerpo largo SPL1>*

[a] All names are pseudonyms used to protect the identity of the real students.
[b] In each extract, the examined speech functions is presented in capital letters and in bold.

Extract 9.1 Clilb4 using short turns and supporting response in the STA

In Extract 9.1, Raúl and Jorge *support* each other (lines 5, 6 and 10) although, in lines 8 and 9 they use *confront* responses. However, the extract reveals a tendency to favour the resolution of the content question in the STA. It is also worth noticing how students' responses tend to be short and mostly contain one word (see lines 3–12). We can find examples of a similar type of discourse also in the PSA.

1 *Nono:*	*No, no ((Eva writes and Ana turns the page)).eh... then is my turn.. ehh.. I think, is this*
2	*((pointing)) because this have a point and this no and then this no and this yes.. You are agree?*
3 *Eva:*	***Yes ((Ana laughs))* (SUPPORTING RESPONSE)**

Extract 9.2 Clilb1 using slightly longer turns and supporting response in the PSA

In this example, after Nono's use of several *continuing* moves (lines 1, 2 and 3), Eva makes a *supporting* response (line 4).

4.2 Knowledge Layer

Following the same pattern of data presentation employed in the discourse layer, all results in this section are also presented locally. Table 9.2 shows the use of registers in the two activities (STA and PSA) by the CLIL group in terms of the frequency and distribution of *instructional* and *regulative* registers and of *social talk*. The results indicate that most of the talk produced by CLIL students in both activities is focused on the task: either for organisational aspects through the *regulative* register (22.65%) or content aspects by discussing the topic at hand through the *instructional* register (74.56%). Little space is left for the use of *social talk*.

Table 9.2 Registers used in the two group activities in the CLIL classroom

Feature	N	Per cent (%)
REGISTER		
Instructional	4457	74.56
Regulative	1354	22.65
Social_talk	167	2.79

Table 9.3 Facts, evaluations and explanations in initiating moves used in the two group activities in the CLIL classroom

Feature	N	Per cent (%)
GIVE-INFO-TYPE		
Give-fact	250	54.35
Give-evaluation	182	39.57
Give-explanation	28	6.09
DEMAND-INFO-TYPE		
Demand-fact	142	53.79
Demand-evaluation	75	28.41
Demand-explanation	47	17.80

Table 9.3 shows the results regarding the CDFs (*facts, evaluations* and *explanations*) in *initiating* moves. CLIL students tend to initiate mostly by *giving facts* (54.35%), closely followed by *giving evaluations* (39.57%). The use of *giving explanation* is minimal (6.09%). *Demands* show the same tendency: first are *facts* (53.79%), followed by *evaluations* (28.41%). *Explanations* are also used to a certain extent (17.80%). We must conclude here that in *initiations, facts* are the preferred option, both when *giving* and *demanding* information. *Evaluations* are more frequently used in the *giving* moves, whereas *explanations* are the least used type of moves but, when used, they are preferred in the form of *demands*.

When CLIL students use a *demanding information* move referring to *facts* it frequently takes the form of a metalinguistic inquiry in the STA:

1 *Jorge:*	*Okay ((he finishes writing and reads the next page))*
	name three vertebrates and three
2	*invertebrates and their main characteristics…((finishes reading))*
3 *Eva:*	**What is inver..? (DEMANDING FACTS)**
4 *Jorge:*	*They don't have a backbone.. ((Eva and Raúl laugh))*
	they don't have a backbone…
5 *Raúl:*	*Yes…((continues laughing)).. okay*

Extract 9.3 Clilb4 *demanding facts* in the STA

In this extract, Eva seems not to remember the definition of a concept used in the prompt (line 4), and Jorge reminds her (line 5). In the discourse layer it was suggested that the use of a questions in the prompt might trigger reformulated demands. These content demands could be related to a concept as in Extract 9.4, in which case they would be *demanding facts* moves, or to a reason, in which case they would be *demanding explanations* moves.

1 *Alicia:*	*what? # the.. ehmm*
2 *Lara:*	*They...((while writing)) have sharped teeth...*
3 *Alicia:*	*# ((Lara keeps writing))...*
4 *Saúl:*	*No! No, why,* ***why is sharped teeth?*** **(DEMAND EXPLANATION)**
5 *Alicia:*	*Because is...*

Extract 9.4   Clila3 initiating *demanding explanation* in the STA

In this extract, Saúl (line 4) *demands explanation* because the prompt question also asks for it, and he is reminding Alicia and Lara that they must give reasons for their statement by reformulating the question in the prompt.

In contrast, in the PSA, and as also found in the discourse layer, the first initiation move tended to be *giving facts* since the stimulus of the item was already a clearly stated problem in itself. Due to the fact that the booklet with problems showed an incomplete picture and required students to complete the pattern by choosing an option from 6 or 8 available, this activity can be seen as promoting the use of *giving facts* as the answer to the items. That is, the options are answered in the form of facts and neither reasons nor opinions are demanded. Extract 9.5 is such an example:

1 *Lara:*	*One moment ((she turns back the page))... yes okay*
2 *Dani:*	***This one*** **(GIVING FACTS)**
3 *Guille:*	*This, this one*
4 *Lara:*	*This*
5 *Guille:*	*No, no, no, no, no, no, no.. is this*
6 *Dani:*	*Yes, is this.. is this.. is... is this*

Extract 9.5   Clilb3 *giving facts* in the PSA

In Extract 9.5, Dani uses a *giving fact* move (line 2)—"This this one"—as the answer a part of the problem the group is trying to solve.

Table 9.4 shows the results regarding the CDFs (*facts, evaluations* and *explanations*) in *sustaining* moves. Taking into account that the CLIL stu-

Table 9.4 Facts, evaluations and explanations in sustaining moves used in the two group activities in the CLIL classroom

Feature	N	Per cent (%)
PROLONG-TYPE		
Prolong-fact	190	33.81
Prolong-evaluation	70	12.46
Prolong-explanation	302	53.74
PRIOR_MOVE		
Prolong-support	267	47.51
Prolong-confront	227	40.39
Prolong-other	68	12.10
SUPPORT-TYPE		
Su-fact	883	39.63
Su-evaluation	265	11.89
Su-explanation	397	17.82
Su-agree	683	30.66
CONFRONT-TYPE		
Co-fact	178	22.88
Co-evaluation	104	13.37
Co-explanation	162	20.82
Co-disagree	334	42.93

dents' participation in *supporting* and *confronting* moves within the *prolong-prior move* category is almost equal (47.51% vs. 40.39%), within *prolong*, the results show that *explanations* are the most commonly used functions (53.74%), followed by *facts* (33.81%) and finally *evaluations* (12.46%).

In the *responses* category, *support* and *confront* show slightly different results. Apart from facts, which are most frequently used type of *supporting* move (39.63%), the difference also affects the use of *agree* and *disagree*. *Disagree* is the most frequent move used in *confronting* moves (42.93%) while *agree* in *supporting* moves is the second most frequent (30.66%), after *facts*. These two moves can be comprised by a mere acknowledgement or opposition or could be accompanied by *prolonging* moves.

When *agree* and *disagree* were followed by *prolonging* moves, they revealed vivid discussions where each student justified their different opinion, as is the case in Extract 9.6.

1 *Alicia:*	*So... this is... I think is this because.*
2 *Lara:*	*No... No*
3 *Alicia:*	*Yes, it's this*
4 *Lara:*	**No because look, here is open and here isn't** (DISAGREE-PROLONG
5	EXPLANATION)
6 *Saúl:*	*But look here, is.. is the two, the two*
7 *Alicia:*	**No, this is open, this is open** (DISAGREE-PROLONG
	EXPLANATION)
8 *Saúl:*	*and this...*
9 *Alicia:*	**Yes... And this is so thin...** *two lines, this ((Lara looks at the picture*
10	*carefully)) ..This is come like this... yes, yes.. I think yes* (AGREE-
11	PROLONG EXPLANATION)
12 *Saúl:*	*This one?*
13 *Alicia:*	*Yes, this one...*

Extract 9.6 Clila3 using *explanations* in PSA

As mentioned before, the most frequent use of the *prolong*-type move was *prolong-explanation*. In Extract 9.6, Lara (line 4) and Alicia (line 7) introduce their chosen options first by *disagreeing* and then by justifying with a *prolonging* move that explains their position. Later (lines 9–10), Alicia uses a similar combination of moves to justify her *agreeing* with Saúl. It is frequent to find examples of students justifying a negative answer, especially after a strong disagreement. It is a resource to convince their partner that they are wrong.

As shown in Table 9.2 above, regarding the knowledge expressed in *supporting* moves, results indicate that CLIL students use *facts* as their first option (39.63%), then *agreeing* moves (30.66%), then *explanations* (17.82%) and lastly *evaluations* (11.89%). Regarding *confronting* moves, however, *disagree* is the most frequent one (42.93%), followed by *facts* (22.88%) and closely followed by *explanations* (20.82%) and then *evaluations* (13.37%). The high percentage of *facts* could be connected to students' attention to stating the preferred option in the PSA, as illustrated in Extract 9.7.

1 *Catalina:*	*We put it %X%*
2 *Blanca:*	*No, is circle, circle, circle... and **this.. this...** (SUPPORT-FACT)*
3 *Catalina:*	**This** (SUPPORT-FACT)
4 *Blanca:*	**This** (SUPPORT-FACT)
5 *Roberto:*	*<L1SP vosotras creeis? SPL1>...This*
6 *Blanca:*	*Yes is this one*

Extract 9.7 Clila8 using facts to support in PSA

In Extract 9.7, Blanca (lines 2 and 4) and Catalina (line 3) are supporting each other merely by pointing at what they think is the correct option. In general, we can conclude that the preferred option used by students in both activities is *facts*. The second option in *initiating* is *evaluations*, whereas when *responding* and *prolonging*, the preferred options are *explanations*. It also appears that *explanations* are mostly used when *confronting* or *disagreeing*. Therefore, descriptive results obtained in the knowledge layer illustrate students' high reliance on *facts* in all *initiating* moves (*giving* and *demanding*) and in the majority of *prolonging* and *responding* moves. Thus, when *initiating* their discourse, students also tend to use *evaluations* while they often prefer to end it or *sustain* it by *giving explanations*. They generally follow their *disagreeing* moves with *explanations*, in this way justifying their *confrontations*. When *supporting* a previous statement, they tend to do it with *facts*.

4.3   Interactional Layer

In this layer, the results for eight CLIL small groups from both CLILA and CLILB classes were analysed. After the analysis, three interactional patterns were identified:

1. Groups with *low equality* in distribution of turns led by one or two members (three small groups).
2. Groups with *high equality* in distribution of turns but *low equality* in control of the activity (three small groups).
3. Groups categorised as *high in equality* in both factors, distribution of turns and control of the activity (two small groups). These groups are further qualitatively analysed in terms of *mutuality*.

4.3.1   Groups Low in Equality in Terms of Distribution of Turns

Three groups emerged as *low in equality* in terms of distribution of turns. However, the interactional patterns that produced this inequality were of two kinds. The first one was produced due to the high participation of two group members and the low participation of one in terms of percentage of turns per each student. The second one was produced by a very high participation of one member and the low participation of the remaining two.

The first pattern, where two students participate more and the other one less, was found in two small groups: Clila2 and Clila5. The second pattern, where one member participates significantly more than the other two, was seen in only one small group: Clila8. Clia2 results will be sued as an illustrative example of how the quantitative analysis was done.

In Table 9.5, the first column presents the total number of turns per student with the percentage of turns out of the total number of turns of the group (Clila2 in this case) assigned to that number. An equal distribution of turns was assigned to those distributions that showed no more than a five-point difference in the percentage between the lowest and the next and then between the middle percentage and the highest. Considering that one student might have a large number of very short turns while another student might have fewer but longer turns, the number of words per student with the corresponding percentage and the average number of words per turn, excluding the ones produced in the L1, were also calculated, as shown in the second and fourth columns. These aspects were mainly considered in a descriptive way. Therefore, they were not used to determine equality in distribution of turns except in moments of doubt, when the five-point difference did not seem to be enough. These three columns (turns, words and average words per turn) provide information about one of the factors related to equality: the distribution of turns. In addition, another column was added referring to the number of words in

Table 9.5 Distribution of turns and words in Clila2 group

Clila2	Turns	Words	L1 words	Avg. words per turn (not L1)
Student 1	223	1812	106	7.6
Irene	42.72%	55.69%	32.51%	
Student 2	194	1099	166	4.8
Jimena	37.16%	33.77%	50.92%	
Student 3	110	343	54	2.6
Juan	21.07%	10.54%	16.56%	
Total	522	3254	326	
			10.01%	

the L1[2] produced by each student (column three). These words were excluded from the average number of words per turn as they were also excluded from the total word amount in the CLIL data.

None of the three groups (Clila2, Clila5 and Clila8), could be categorised as fostering *equality* in terms of distribution of turns and, therefore, they were not considered for the analysis of the second *equality factor*, which is control over the task.

4.3.2   Groups High in Equality in Distribution of Turns but Low in Control of the Activity

In groups with high level of equality in distribution of turns, that is, the ones presented in this section and the next section, another column with the distribution of the use of the *regulative* register per student was added to reflect the results on the second aspect related to *equality*, control of the activity. In this section, three groups were categorised as *high in equality* in terms of distribution of turns but *low in equality* in terms of control of the activity: Clila3, Clilb3 and Clilb4. Clilb3 will be used as an illustrative example of this.

The results of Clilb3 group, the second group in this interactional pattern (high in equality in terms of the distribution of turns but low in the distribution of control of the activity) are shown in Table 9.6.

After the quantitative analysis of Clila3, Clilb3 and Clilb4 groups, these groups could not be categorised as having *equality* in the second factor related to the control of the activity and, therefore, were not considered for the qualitative analysis.

---

[2] The words in Spanish were coded as L1 words and assigned to each group member using the UAM corpus tool. This tool was also used to later retrieve number of words per student and percentages of words in Spanish per member from the total produced in the group.

Table 9.6 Distribution of turns and words by the Clilb3 group

Clilb3	Turns	Words	L1 words	Av. words per turn (not L1)	Regulative register
Student 1	227	1158	96	4.6	69
Dani	36.55%	35.74%	46.83%		45.39%
Student 2	181	1045	36	5.5	36
Lara	29.15%	32.25%	17.56%		23.69%
Student 3	213	1037	73	4.5	47
Guille	34.3%	32.01%	35.61%		30.92%
Total	621	3240	205		152
			6.33%		

4.3.3 Groups High in Equality in Both Turn Distribution and Control of the Activity

Two groups were identified as high in both equality factors, distribution of turns and control of the activity: Clilb1 and Clilb6. The results of the first group, Clilb1, are presented in Table 9.7.

The second group that showed high *equality* in both factors (distribution of turns and of the *regulative* register) is group Clilb6. Table 9.8 shows the results for this group.

In order to confirm the use of the *regulative* register as a way to control the activity and to delve deeper into *mutuality factors* of these groups, a more contextual and detailed analysis was necessary. This detailed analysis, which cannot be shown here due to space limitations, showed a frequent use of *evaluations* and *supporting* moves, indicating the involvement in the task of all members and a tendency towards *agreement*. It also showed how the group members used *giving* reasons for their answers, dealing with *confrontations* in the process of seeking agreement.

In addition, Clilb1 group showed examples of using the *regulative* register in an evenly distributed way, which allowed for a more democratic organisation of each member's turns at talking and writing. This confirmed the second *equality factor*, an equal distribution in the control of the activity by all group members. In terms of *mutuality*, we seek a high level of learners' engagement with their partners' contributions or, as Damon and Phelps (1989, p. 127) describe, whether interactions are rich in reciprocal feedback with sharing of ideas during the task. The detailed analysis showed how group members were constantly giving feedback to

Table 9.7 Distribution of turns and words by the Clilb1 group

Clilb1	Turns	Words	L1 words	Av. words per turn (not L1)	Regulative register
Student 1	284	2021	149	6.5	77
Eva	33.85%	45.13%	27.14%		30.55%
Student 2	261	1205	88	4.2	84
Ana	31.11%	26.91%	16.03%		33.33%
Student 3	294	1252	312	3.1	91
Nono	35.04%	27.96%	56.83%		36.11%
Total	839	4478	549		252
			12.26%		

Table 9.8 Distribution of turns and words by the Clilb6 group

Clilb6	Turns	Words	L1 words	Av. words per turn (not L1)	Regulative register
Student 1	215	1213	16	5.5	54
Pedro	35.83%	40.22%	32.65%		37.5%
Student 2	189	962	22	4.9	41
Marta	31.5%	31.9%	44.9%		28.47%
Student 3	196	841	11	4.2	49
Covi	32.67%	27.88%	22.45%		34.03%
Total	600	3016	49		144
			1.62%		

each other in the particular group. Namely, they gave opinions about the content discussed and about what other members were saying and they were also concerned with including the other members when asking for their opinions.

Following Storch's model of dyadic interaction (2002) and drawing on these results, we can categorise the Clilb1 group as *collaborative*, that is, *high in equality* and *high in mutuality*. However, it must be pointed out that most of the examples of group interaction where mutuality was promoted were found in the PSA activity. After the quantitative analysis of both Clilb1 and Clilb6 and the qualitative analysis, it was concluded that Clilb1 was the only one of the two that appeared to meet all descriptive features of a collaborative group.

4.4 Summary of Results

In relation to RQ1, results have demonstrated that in the co-construction of knowledge, CLIL students tend to start their turns by *giving facts* or *evaluations* most of the time. When continuing their conversations, others tend to *respond* most of the time in a *supportive* way and through *explanations*; in addition, *disagreements* tend to be followed by *justifications*. CLIL students also favour the use of the *instructional* register and in their interaction they tend to distribute their turns fairly evenly, although some might have the control of the activity more than the others. Their model of interaction is familiar to the *expert/novice* dyadic pattern; however, some examples of the *dominant/passive* pattern may also occur.

5 Conclusion

This study has contributed with a multi-layer perspective on small group interaction in a primary CLIL context that takes into account not only the integration of content or knowledge being communicated and speech functions but also the presence of roles or different forms of interactivity within group interaction. Many authors have stated how the presence of certain roles or identities (Goffman, 1981; Wells, 1999) influences any type of interaction. These roles have also been proven to exercise a powerful influence within the task and language and content used in CLIL classrooms (Llinares & Morton, 2010). Llinares and Morton (2010) found that the interactional space generated by different activities triggered different participating roles as animators, principals or authors (Goffman, 1981) by CLIL students. Moreover, certain interactional styles have been shown to influence L2 effective learning more than others (see Ballinger, 2013; Storch, 2002). Therefore, the consideration of the interactional level within an analytical model is more than justified.

In sum, the use of this multi-layered analytical model has enriched data analysis and has provided a layer by layer account of how oral language reasoning helps acquire knowledge in group work in the CLIL classroom. Evidence of this is that the multi-layered analysis performed to the large corpus used in this study obtained results comparable to qualitative analysis performed in small corpora (Mercer, Wegerif, & Dawes, 1999; Rojas-Drummond, Pérez, Vélez, Gómez, & Mendoza, 2003). Investigating the integrative aspect of CLIL is, at present, a widespread interest among CLIL researchers. In line with this interest, this study presents an analytical model that could be used, not only with other primary CLIL data, but also at the secondary or even tertiary CLIL levels. In fact, it could be used in any classroom setting where learning through a communicative interaction among peers is valued.

References

Ballinger, S. (2013). Towards a cross-linguistic pedagogy: Biliteracy and reciprocal learning strategies in French immersion. *Journal of Immersion and Content-Based Language Education, 1*(1), 131–148.

Buchholz, B. (2007). Reframing young learner's discourse structure as a preliminary requirement for a CLIL- based ELT approach. An action research project in conversational language learning from primary students. In C. Dalton-Puffer & U. Smit (Eds.), *Empirical Perspectives on CLIL Classroom Discourse* (pp. 51–78). Frankfurt, Wien: Peter Lang.

Cenoz, J., Genesee, F., & Gorter, D. (2014). Critical analysis of CLIL: Taking stock and looking forward. *Applied Linguistics, 35*(3), 243–262.

Christie, F. (2002). *Classroom Discourse Analysis: A Functional Perspective.* London and New York: Bloomsbury Publishing.

Coyle, D., Hood, P., & Marsh, D. (2010). *CLIL: Content and Language Integrated Learning.* Cambridge: Cambridge University Press.

Dalton-Puffer, C. (2013). A construct of cognitive discourse functions for conceptualising content-language integration in CLIL and multilingual education. *European Journal of Applied Linguistics, 1*(2), 216–253.

Dalton-Puffer, C., Nikula, T., & Smit, U. (Eds.). (2010). *Language Use and Language Learning in CLIL Classrooms.* Amsterdam and Philadelphia: John Benjamins Publishing Company.

Damon, W., & Phelps, E. (1989). Critical distinctions among three approaches to peer education. *International Journal of Educational Research, 13*(1), 9–19.

Du Bois, J. W. (2003). Transcription convention updates introduction. *Discourse,* 1–3.

Du Bois, J. W., Schuetze-Coburn, S., Cumming, S., & Paolino, D. (1993). Outline of discourse transcription. In J. A. Edwards & M. D. Lampert (Eds.), *Talking Data: Transcription and Coding in Discourse Research* (pp. 45–89). Hillsdale, NJ: Lawrence Earl.

Eggins, S., & Slade, D. (1997). *Analysing Casual Conversation*. London: Equinox.

Gajo, L. (2007). Linguistic knowledge and subject knowledge: How does bilingualism contribute to subject development? *International Journal of Bilingual Education and Bilingualism, 10*(5), 563–579.

Gibbons, P. (2002). *Scaffolding Language, Scaffolding Learning: Teaching Second Language Learners in the Mainstream Classroom*. Portsmouth, NH: Heinemann.

Gibbons, P. (2008). *Bridging Discourses in the ESL Classroom: Students, Teachers and Researchers*. London and New York: Continuum.

Goffman, E. (1981). *Forms of Talk*. Philadelphia, PA: University of Pennsylvania Press.

Halliday, M. A. K. (1977). *Learning How to Mean: Explorations in the Development of Language*. Oxford: Elsevier.

Hammond, J. (Ed.). (2002). *Scaffolding Teaching and Learning in Language and Literacy Education*. Newtown, NSW: PETA.

Lantolf, J. P. (2000). *Sociocultural Theory and Second Language Learning*. Oxford: OUP.

Lasagabaster, D., & Sierra, J. M. (2009). Language attitudes in CLIL and traditional EFL classes. *International CLIL Research Journal, 1*, 4–17.

Leung, C. (2005). Language and content in bilingual education. *Linguistics and Education, 16*, 238–252.

Llinares, A. (2015). Integration in CLIL: A proposal to inform research and successful pedagogy. *Language, Culture and Curriculum, 28*(1), 58–73.

Llinares, A., & Lyster, R. (2014). The influence of context on patterns of corrective feedback and learner uptake: A comparison of CLIL and immersion classrooms. *The Language Learning Journal, 42*(2), 181–194.

Llinares, A., & Morton, T. (2010). Historical explanations as situated practice in content and language integrated learning. *Classroom Discourse, 1*(1), 46–65.

Llinares, A., Morton, T., & Whittaker, R. (2012). *The Roles of Language in CLIL. Cambridge Language Teaching Library*. Cambridge: Cambridge University Press.

Llinares, A., & Pastrana, A. (2013). CLIL students' communicative functions across activities and educational levels. *Journal of Pragmatics, 59*, 81–92.

Massler, U. (2012). Primary CLIL and its stakeholders: What children, parents and in, teachers think of the potential merits and pitfalls of CLIL modules teaching, primary. *International CLIL Research Journal, 1*(4), 36–46.

Mercer, N., Wegerif, R., & Dawes, L. (1999). Children's talk and the development of reasoning in the classroom. *British Educational Research Journal, 25*(1), 95–111.

Meyer, O., Coyle, D., Halbach, A., Schuck, K., & Ting, T. (2015). A pluriliteracies approach to content and language integrated learning—Mapping learner progressions in knowledge construction and meaning-making. *Language, Culture and Curriculum, 28*(1), 41–57.

Moate, J. (2010). The integrated nature of CLIL: A sociocultural perspective. *International CLIL Research Journal, 1*(3), 38–45.

Nikula, T. (2005). English as an object and tool of study in classrooms: Interactional effects and pragmatic implications. *Linguistics and Education, 16*(1), 27–58.

Nikula, T., Dafouz, E., Moore, P., & Smit, U. (2016). *Conceptualising Integration in CLIL and Multilingual Education*. Bristol: Multilingual Matters.

Nikula, T., Dalton-Puffer, C., & Llinares, A. (2013). CLIL classroom discourse: Research from Europe. *Journal of Immersion and Content-Based Language, 1*(1), 70–100.

O'Donnell, M. (2008). UAM Corpus Tool. Retrieved from http://www.wagsoft.com/CorpusTool/.

Pastrana, A. (2010). Language functions in CLIL classrooms: Students' oral production in different classroom activities. *Vienna English Working Papers, 19*(3), 72–82.

Rojas-Drummond, S., Pérez, V., Vélez, M., Gómez, L., & Mendoza, A. (2003). Talking for reasoning among Mexican primary school children. *Learning and Instruction, 13*(6), 653–670.

Schleppegrell, M. J. (2004). *The Language of Schooling: A Functional Linguistics Perspective*. London: Taylor & Francis.

Serra, C. (2007). Assessing CLIL at primary school: A longitudinal study. *International Journal of Bilingual Education and Bilingualism, 10*(5), 582–602.

Storch, N. (2002). Patterns of interaction in ESL pair work. *Language Learning, 52*, 119–158.

Van Lier, L. (1996). *Interaction in the Language Classroom: Awareness, Autonomy and Authenticity*. London: Longman.

Wells, G. (1999). *Dialogic Inquiry: Towards a Socio-cultural Practice and Theory of Education*. Cambridge: Cambridge University Press.

10

Constructing Cognitive Discourse Functions in Secondary CLIL Classrooms in Spain

Natalia Evnitskaya

1 Introduction of the Study

In a conference on education held some years ago in Gerona (Spain), where primary and secondary school children were invited to speak to adults, one ten-year-old told the audience the following when referring to the lessons taught in her L1: 'I would be good at maths if only I could understand the words that the teacher uses during the lessons'.[1] For this child, academic language is a sort of *foreign language* full of new terminology, false friends, obscure concepts and discourse rules that do not match those she is familiar with. From her story we can infer that her teacher is not aware of the fact that the lesson taught in the L1 often creates an illusion of a common transparent language shared by everyone in the classroom, which allows trouble-free communication and understanding.

---

[1] Escobar Urmeneta (2009), personal communication.

N. Evnitskaya (✉)
Institute for Multilingualism, Universitat Internacional de Catalunya, Barcelona, Spain

237
K. Tsuchiya, M. D. Pérez Murillo (eds.), *Content and Language Integrated Learning in Spanish and Japanese Contexts*, https://doi.org/10.1007/978-3-030-27443-6_10

In the case of this and many other students, however, the L1 acts as a thick glass screen, apparently transparent but impenetrable to academic messages and mutual understanding (for more on the 'glass' metaphor, see Escobar Urmeneta, 2009).

In today's increasingly multilingual and globalised society, innovation in education is essential to provide new generations with the knowledge and competences needed for participation in learning, work and leisure to help them become open minded and responsible citizens of the world and to promote plurilingualism (e.g., Council of Europe, 1992). Since the mid-1990s, Content and Language Integrated Learning (CLIL) has become one of the most popular educational approaches in Europe (Coyle, Hood, & Marsh, 2010). A solid body of research produced over the last 20 years in diverse sociocultural, sociolinguistic and educational contexts, age groups and subjects clearly point to overall positive effects of CLIL instruction on students' gains in *general language proficiency*, particularly in terms of lexis and grammar, and in the development of speaking skills (see, e.g., contributions in Ruiz de Zarobe & Jiménez Catalán, 2009).

However, much less research attention has been given so far to the development of students' *subject-specific academic language* in CLIL contexts. And yet, the quality of teaching academic content through the L2 and the effect it might have on CLIL students' learning of disciplinary content and the development of their academic language competence (both in the L2 and in the L1) represent one of the main concerns of different stakeholders involved in CLIL. Some recent attempts have been made to closely examine these issues in a range of CLIL subjects from different theoretical and analytical perspectives such as systemic-functional linguistics (Llinares, Morton, & Whittaker, 2012), discourse-pragmatic analysis (Nikula, 2015), multimodal conversation analysis (Kääntä, Kasper, & Piirainen-Marsh, 2018) and cognitive discourse functions (Dalton-Puffer et al., 2018). This chapter aims to push this area of research a step forward by examining teachers' use of subject-specific academic language in terms of *cognitive discourse functions* (CDFs), and more specifically teachers' classification practices, in CLIL classroom interaction in Spain.

2 Literature Review

2.1 Everyday Versus Academic Language at School: BICS and CALP

Research on immersion programmes in Canada in which English-speaking learners studied school subjects in French has shown that despite a considerable amount of years of schooling in such programmes, learners' gains in L2 French in certain areas (e.g., grammatical accuracy, subject-specific academic writing and speaking) were still notably lower than those of their L1 French-speaking classmates (e.g., Swain & Lapkin, 2005). Cummins (1991) explained this phenomenon with a two-dimensional conceptualisation of language proficiency, applicable to both learners' L2 and L1. His model has subsequently been used to help teachers develop learners' subject-specific academic skills in the L2.

According to Cummins, the first dimension, *Basic Interpersonal Communication Skills* (BICS), is activated in everyday informal interactions which are typically highly contextualised due to the presence of contextual clues (e.g., verbal referents, objects, gestures and intonation) which help participants in interactions interpret what is being done and said at each moment. On the contrary, the second dimension, *Cognitive Academic Language Proficiency* (CALP), is necessary in situations which are usually characterised by the absence of contextual clues. This is the case when we need to understand, read, talk or write about abstract and complex topics such as those that can often be found in school textbooks. We can therefore say that CALP forms an essential part of students' *literacy skills* in school contexts.

Cummins (1991) also argues that in immersion and content-based contexts, learners acquire BICS in the target language rather quickly and can become fluent in using everyday L2 within a year or two, or even earlier. However, achieving the level of CALP necessary for the understanding and production of school academic texts might take L2 learners up to seven or eight years. This process requires teachers' explicit and continuous support and guidance since merely being exposed to, or even engaged in, an activity in the L2 is not sufficient to ensure academic success (Swain & Lapkin, 2005).

2.2   Cognitive Discourse Functions

More recently, CLIL researchers and stakeholders have raised concerns about the possible mismatch between CLIL students' cognitive level of development and their L2 proficiency (especially in terms of CALP), arguing that this might lead to learning less and poorer quality content than in subject classes taught in the L1. Such concerns become particularly relevant in the case of learners with a low L2 level. With the aim to address these issues, Dalton-Puffer (2013) developed a transdisciplinary construct of *cognitive discourse functions* (CDFs) which combines linguistic and educational approaches to academic language and 'links subject-specific cognitive learning goals with the linguistic representations they receive in classroom interaction' (Dalton-Puffer, 2016, p. 30).

Dalton-Puffer (2013) suggests that the CDF construct allows us to conceptualise how language and content are integrated in CLIL, whether in classroom interaction, textbooks, or the school syllabus. It also allows us to identify subject-specific, academic language demands set by CLIL teaching materials, exams or official content-subject curricula. CDFs thus make content and academic language integration visible, understandable and meaningful not only to applied linguists and educational researchers but also to language and content-subject teacher educators and, most importantly, to language and content teachers (Dalton-Puffer et al., 2018). The construct is therefore a potential unit of analysis since it allows researchers to simultaneously identify subject-specific cognitive operations which can be grouped into seven types (classify, define, describe, evaluate, explain, explore and report; see Dalton-Puffer, 2013) and their corresponding discursive, lexical and grammatical realisations.

2.3   Classifications

One of the CDFs, namely *classifying*, which consists in establishing taxonomies and categories, is essential for knowledge construction in any school discipline as it helps learners move from specific to abstract

(Mohan, 1986). This explains why, although often based on direct observations of certain phenomena or features or the knowledge of facts, classifications and categories still require a degree of expertise in establishing relations among their elements. This is due to the fact that their basic components are an *object* to be classified, a *hypernym* denoting class and some *underlying principle*.

According to Trimble (1985, p. 86), structurally, *complete classifications* consist of 'the item/s being classified', 'the class to which the items (or members) belong to' and 'the basis of classification', with the latter commonly realised through *comparison*—by identifying features that the item has in common with other members of the same class or those that distinguish it from members of other classes. However, we can often come across *incomplete classifications*, that is, those which only contain the first two elements (item to be classified and the class) and omit the basis of classification.

Linguistically, classifications often tend to contain a set of recognisable distinctive sentence patterns and/or discourse markers (Widdowson, 1979). These are usually represented in syntactic structures such as 'X is Y', 'X is a member of Y' or 'X forms part of class Y' for classifications in which items are classified in relation to a higher order and a more general term (i.e., member → class), and 'Y comprises X and Z' for top-down classifications in which a more general group of items is sub-divided into more specific items (i.e., class → member). Some of these sentence patterns, especially of the type 'X is (a kind of) Y', strongly resemble another CDF, *defining*, since this syntactic structure belongs to the 'taxonomic relation type', that is, it expresses a hierarchical relationship between a specific term and a general class without providing any basis of classification and can therefore be also considered a 'non-formal definition' (Trimble, 1985, p. 78). This implies that we cannot establish a clear-cut boundary between different CDFs as very often they form part of each other. Thus, it is difficult to distinguish defining and classifying when a classification introduces the class and the member to be defined, or classifying and describing when a description constitutes part of comparison within the basis of classification.

2.4   Classifications in CLIL Classroom Interaction

Empirical research on how CDFs are realised in CLIL classroom interaction is still in its beginnings. However, a few recent attempts have been made to provide empirical validation of the CDF construct in CLIL settings by applying it to actual classroom interaction and identifying particular lexico-grammatical and interactional patterns through which different CDFs are realised (Bauer-Marschallinger, 2018; Dalton-Puffer et al., 2018; Kääntä et al., 2018; Lackner, 2012). Lackner's (2012) study is of particular relevance here since it is the only study which examined classifications (alongside another three CDFs) in greater detail and as realised in longer extracts of CLIL classroom interaction, beyond short illustrative examples. Lackner's analysis of CLIL history lessons in upper secondary vocational schools identified that classifying was among the most infrequently occurring CDFs, with less than one instance per lesson on average. Moreover, complete classifications, which can be considered the most explicit type of classifying because of the clear and recognisable expressions of semantic relations among the three constituting elements, were totally absent in his corpus, and teachers' classifications were predominantly incomplete and highly implicit. Finally, teachers hardly ever made explicit reference or used meta-discourse to raise students' awareness of the canonical lexico-grammatical features involved in classifying. Therefore, 'a significant aspect of this [CDF] in the CLIL history classroom lies in its implicit formulations, which require the students to infer a great amount of information' (Lackner, 2012, p. 96).

This chapter aims to contribute to this on-going research by examining one CLIL science teacher's classifying practices when constructing scientific knowledge from a multimodal conversation-analytic perspective.

3   Data and Method

The dataset examined in this chapter belongs to a larger data corpus comprising eight CLIL science lessons (a total of 5 hours and 57 minutes of video-recorded data) which were collected in a grade 7 (age 12) CLIL biology in English classroom in a public secondary school located in a middle-class neighbourhood in bilingual (Catalan-Spanish) Barcelona, Spain. Informed written consent regarding the audio and video-recording of CLIL lessons and the use of the collected data for the research and publication purposes were obtained from all participants who were a CLIL biology teacher and 16 students.[2] At the time of data collection, the teacher had 25 years of experience of teaching biology and geology in Catalan/L1 and was in her second year of teaching CLIL biology in English. During the lessons, the participants worked with teacher-made materials (dossier and handouts), lab instruments (e.g., light microscopes), models of internal organs, L1 reference books, bilingual dictionaries, posters and charts, and so on.

Selected video data excerpts were transcribed following standard conversation-analytic conventions for a talk (Jefferson, 2004) and multimodal transcription conventions for participants' embodied actions (Mondada, 2014). The transcripts were anonymised, and the pseudonyms were used to guarantee the participants' confidentiality. Whenever it was considered necessary, additional screenshots were embedded into the transcripts. Using a multimodal conversation-analysis approach, this study aims to produce a fine-grained examination of CLIL classroom interaction, and more specifically how one CLIL teacher constructs subject-specific classifications in her CLIL biology classroom using an array of semiotic resources such as language, gestures and material objects.

4 Findings

4.1 Constructing Scientific Knowledge Multimodally: Using Everyday L2 and Other Semiotic Resources

Extract 10.1 takes place during a lab session dedicated to the classification of different organisms into kingdoms in which students working in

---

[2] CLIL biology class only had 16 students (half of the regular class) since the other 16 students had biology classes taught by the same teacher in Catalan/L1.

pairs were carrying out an experiment on one-celled microorganism (Euglena) through the study of its main features. Students had to use a light microscope and a teacher-designed handout which contained a list of possible characteristics of Euglena to be checked during the experiment. The extract shows how two students (Quim, QUI, and Jaume, JAU)—who faced a problem related to one of the statements in the handout ('Euglena can change its shape')—resort to the teacher (TEA) who initiates an explanation sequence containing a classification and a comparison of the phenomenon that has triggered the students' question. To ease the analysis of Extract 10.1, it is divided into two parts, Extracts 10.1a and 10.1b. Extract 10.1a begins with one of the students, Quim, addressing his partner, Jaume:

```
01 QUI    ((to JAU)) ↑change the shape
02 JAU    ((to TEA)) Eug↑lena=
03 QUI    ((to TEA)) =change the shape?
<…>
04 TEA    ↓a:: (0.5) if it changes its ↑shape
          'oh::'
05 JAU    yes
06 TEA    I think so (0.5)
07        but we cannot see it today.
```

Extract 10.1a

Quim's utterance (line 1) seems to have emerged as a result of his previous private discussion with Jaume. The latter however orients himself to the teacher rather than to his classmate and initiates his turn by naming the microorganism (line 2). Both students produce their turns with slightly rising intonation which might indicate that they have not reached agreement on whether the microorganism can change its form and that they have therefore decided to resort to the teacher's expertise. Indeed, Quim reorients towards the teacher to whom he resends his utterance which he now clearly shapes intonationally as a question ('change the shape?', in line 3).

The teacher's turn begins with a 'news-receipt' (Heritage, 1984) in the L1 (line 4). Besides containing a change-of-state token 'oh' ('a::' in Catalan/Spanish), it also reveals the teacher's analysis of the students' previous interventions since in the rest of her turn she displays her understanding of their questions. More specifically, she solicits the students' confirmation of her interpretation which she articulates as a conditional with final raising intonation ('if it changes its ↑shape'). Her confirmation request may also be seen as an implicit other-repair of Quim's utterance focused on formal aspects of the L2 because her turn contains a subject, a correct third-person singular verb form and a possessive pronoun instead of a definite article (compare her 'if it changes its shape' with Quim's 'change the shape'). Once Jaume confirms that her interpretation is correct (line 5), the teacher gives her personal opinion (line 6) which concurs with the assumption expressed earlier by the students. After a brief pause, however, she makes a discourse shift (line 7) from her own perspective ('I') to that of a shared classroom experience ('we'). By referring to the impossibility of examining the phenomenon of Euglena changing its shape during the experiment, she introduces—though implicitly and in a negative form ('we cannot see it today')—the importance of using pieces of scientific evidence (in this case, observable through the physical act of seeing) in the construction of subject-specific knowledge.

In what follows (Extract 10.1b), the teacher builds a complex multimodal comparison which further develops her idea:

```
08 TEA    but if you (.) *look here (2.0) Euglena (3.2)
   tea                   *takes a reference book, searches through it
09        #*%is like this
   tea     *points at an image-->
   jau,qui %slightly lean forward towards the teacher
10 TEA    (in) this:: (0.7) #book.
   fig                      #fig10.1
```

Extract 10.1b

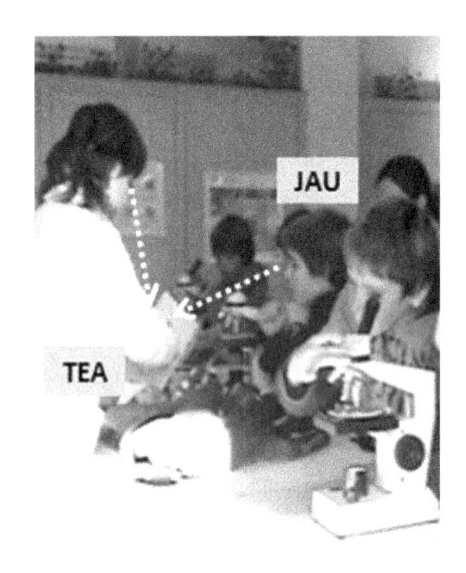

Fig. 10.1   A complex multimodal comparison (1)

```
11 TEA    and* #*your:: Euglena*
   tea    -->*  *points at QUI *
   fig          #fig10.2
```

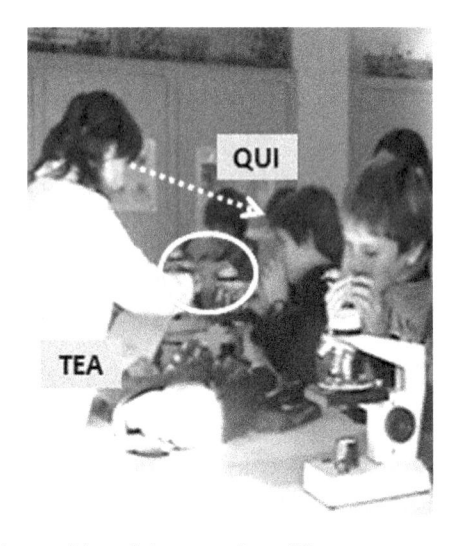

Fig. 10.2   A complex multimodal comparison (2)

```
12              *is not like this (0.5)*
   tea          *points at the image-->*
13              it's not #*so: long (0.5)
   tea                    *moves her index finger along the image
   fig                    #fig10.3
```

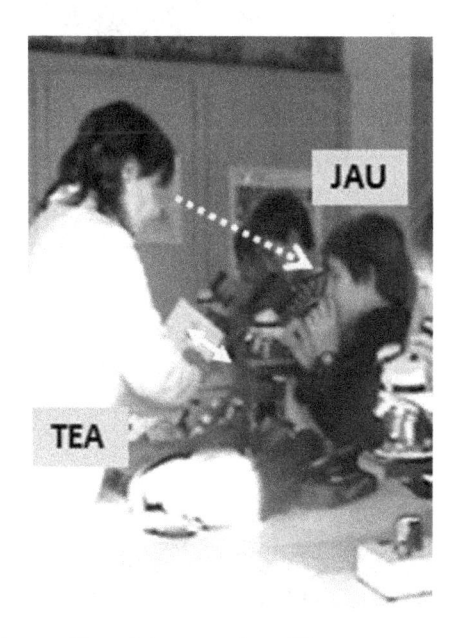

Fig. 10.3 A complex multimodal comparison (3)

```
14              it's #*%rounded.
   tea                 *draws circles on the image with her index finger
   jau                 %makes circling gestures with his index finger
   fig                 #fig10.4
```

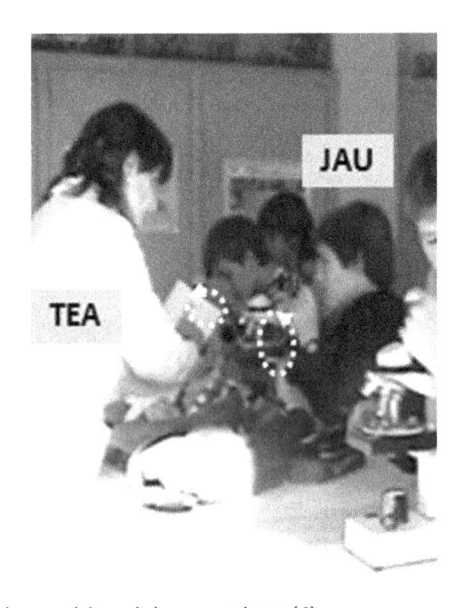

Fig. 10.4 A complex multimodal comparison (4)

```
15  TEA    ↓so (0.5) #what does it mean?
    fig              #fig10.5
```

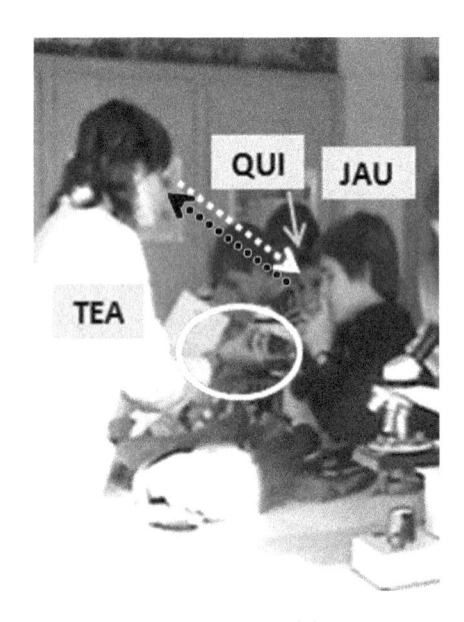

Fig. 10.5 A complex multimodal comparison (5)

```
16 QUI    change the shape?
17 TEA    *it can change shape.
   tea    *nods
```

The teacher starts her utterance (line 8) with a contrasting conjunction 'but' and then produces 'look here (2.0) Euglena' while taking an L1 biology reference book from the table next to Quim. She employs a verb of visual perception ('look') and a prosodically emphasised deictic ('here') to explicitly attract the students' attention to what she is going to say and/or do next. Her utterance contains several long pauses due to her simultaneous search through the artefact in her hands. She also names the microorganism under study thus signalling that what she is seeking for is relevant and they should pay attention to her. Having spent more than 5 seconds in her search, the teacher seems to have finally found what she was looking for ('is like this (in) this:: (0.7) book', in lines 9–10) since she shows an image in the reference book (from her utterance, it can be inferred that it is the image of Euglena) while pointing at it (lines 9–10, Fig. 10.1). The students' and the teacher's coordinated mutual gaze orientation (Fig. 10.1) can be interpreted as a sign of their 'joint attention' (Kidwell & Zimmerman, 2007) to the co-construction of a shared understanding.

While continuing to point at the image, the teacher initiates a comparison between the image and what the students have seen under the microscopes using everyday language full of deictics and simple vocabulary in the L2 (lines 11–12). She uses the conjunction 'and' to connect her previous utterance ('Euglena (3.5) is like this (in) this:: (0.7) book') to her next one ('your:: Euglena is not like this'). Moreover, she explicitly and multimodally makes the students' classroom experience as the observers of the phenomenon relevant for the comparison she is building by emphasising and stretching the pronoun 'your' as well as through gaze and a pointing gesture at Quim (line 11, Fig. 10.2). By pointing again at the image (line 12) while saying that the students' Euglena 'is not like this', that is, that what they have observed is different from what is depicted in the reference book, she effectively strengthens her comparison.

After a 0.5 second micro-pause, the teacher develops the comparison further by overtly explaining the difference between the two Euglenas. She employs a syntactic structure 'it's (not)+ADJ' twice: first to give a negative description of the microorganism observed by the students ('it's not so: long', in line 13) and then a positive one ('it's rounded', in line 14). To ensure their understanding of her message and highlight the importance of academic knowledge being constructed, here again she combines verbal means with non-verbal ones. In the first case, having uttered the first part of the statement, she then produces 'so: long' and simultaneously moves her right index finger down and up along the image while gazing at Jaume (Fig. 10.3). In the second case, she accompanies 'rounded' with a circling gesture (Fig. 10.4). It can be seen that the teacher effectively reinforces her verbal messages in the L2 by aiding them visually with iconic gestures. Concurrently to the teacher's gesture, Jaume also makes several rapid circles in the air with his index finger (line 14, Fig. 10.4). By producing the same non-verbal action synchronically with that of the teacher, he both displays his understanding of the comparison developed so far and actively contributes to its on-going construction in interaction.

The teacher's use of the discourse marker 'so' (line 15) is characterised by stress, falling pitch and its separation from the subsequent part of the utterance by a 0.5-second pause. All this clearly indicates the end of a prolonged sequence in which she developed the basis of classification through a comparison which evidenced the difference between the two Euglenas. At the same time, it can also be assumed that the teacher employs the marker as a means to relate what she is going to say to the preceding sequence as its logical inference. More particularly, it indicates that she is probably going to provide a recapped and final answer to the students' initial question regarding one of the characteristics of the microorganism, namely its ability to change its shape. However, instead, she passes the interactional floor to the students with a question and an open-hand gesture (line 15, Fig. 10.5), in this way positioning them as legitimate co-constructors of the knowledge claim in question. The establishment of mutual gaze between the teacher and Quim at the onset of the teacher's question allows him to self-select as the next speaker and contribute with a candidate response (line 16), which he produces with rising intonation thus requesting the teacher's confirmation.

The teacher legitimates his candidate response with a nod while reformulating Quim's utterance into a complete clause in a more appropriate and academic English ('it can change shape', in line 17), thereby finally legitimising it as a scientifically accepted statement. Here again, the teacher's turn may also be interpreted as an integrated, that is, linguistic and content-related, other-repair of the student's utterance. On the one hand, she incorporates a missing subject and eliminates the article and, on the other, she adds a modal verb 'can' which allows her to highlight the *capability* (as opposed to the inherent feature) of the microorganism to change its form. In this way the teacher implicitly models the appropriate way of talking school science (Lemke, 1990) in the L2.

4.2 Constructing Scientific Knowledge Multilingually: Moving Back and Forth Across Literacies and Languages

Extract 10.2 takes place during a lesson on the classification of living beings into different groups, starting from the biggest and most general group (kingdom) to the smallest and most specific group (species). This content was dealt with through the students' reading aloud sentence by sentence of a text from their dossier and a whole-class discussion of each sentence. Prior to the extract, one of the students read the sentence 'Elephants and earthworms belong to the animal kingdom because they have some common features, but elephants have a backbone and earthworms do not'. After a brief clarification of new terminology, the teacher and the students discussed the differentiating feature mentioned in the basis of classification ('elephants have a backbone and earthworms do not') which allowed them to classify the two members into two subgroups (vertebrates vs. invertebrates) within the same kingdom.

Extract 10.2 shows how the teacher further builds on the original classification from the text and guides the students towards the development of another basis of classification. In this case it is oriented towards the specification of one of the common features, namely nutrition, which allows the inclusion of certain types of living beings and not others into the animal kingdom based on the source of their nutrition (autotrophic vs. heterotrophic). To ease the analysis of Extract 10.2, it is also divided into two parts, Extracts 10.2a and 10.2b. Extract 10.2a begins with the teacher asking for the classification criteria according to which the two animals from the text should be classified into the same group of the animal kingdom:

```
01 TEA    can you tell me why elephants and earthworm
02        *belong (.) both to the animal kingdom?
   tea    *makes a grasping gesture with right hand
03        what do they (0.5) have in common?
04 AND    because they reproduce
05 TEA    yes (.) but plants also reproduce an::d (0.5)
06        a mushroom (.) also reproduce (1.0)
07        what do (.) they have in common? animals?
08 AND    they move?
09 TEA    they move (.) this is a:: [a good ↓answer
10 JAU                              [the plants also
11 TEA    yes but from *place to ↓place (0.7)
12        we can add *'they move| from place| to place' (0.7)
   tea                          *with both hands she marks each word
                                 while moving hands from left to right
13        and what about their nutrition? (2.5) animals?
14 AND    they- they find their nutrition (.)they don't make it
15 JAU    they-
16 JOA    they don't need-
17 JAU    they eat other::=
18 MAR    = (pla[nts)
19 AND         [animals
20 TEA    yes (.)
21 JAU    and ↓plants
```

Extract 10.2a

The teacher initiates the sequence with an open question containing prosodically stressed 'why' and an iconic gesture (lines 1–2), but she immediately narrows down her enquiry by specifying that students should look for similarities between the two living beings (line 3). Andrew volunteers a candidate answer starting with a direct 'because' (line 4), which the teacher seems to accept with a positive agreement token (line 5). Yet, in fact it serves to preface her disagreement in which she brings in other types of living beings (plants and mushrooms) which have the same feature, that is, reproduction (see her emphasis on 'also', in line 6), and yet belong to a different kingdom. The fact that the teacher builds an implicit counterargument to show that Andrew's candidate response is not correct implies that she expects students to know that plants and mushrooms are not animals and therefore the feature of reproduction by itself is not an exclusive classification criterion of the animal kingdom. This might be the reason why she insists on students focusing on common features among (only) animals (line 7).

Her repeated request triggers another candidate response from Andrew who now suggests the idea of motion. It seems that this time his answer is more appropriate as it is overtly accepted by the teacher as can be seen in her repetition and positive feedback (line 9). Her positive evaluation of Andrew's contribution however overlaps with Jaume's turn (line 10) in which the latter disagrees that moving is not an exclusive feature of animals. His contribution to the joint construction of the features constituting the basis of classification of the animal kingdom requires the teacher to be more explicit. She produces a delayed disagreement (prefaced with 'yes but', line 11) in which she adds a specification of motion in space. She first does it elliptically, and after a short pause, she frames it discursively and utters a fully formulated statement 'they move from place to place' (line 12) which she accompanies with a rhythmical beat gesture. In this way she multimodally delimitates the suggested characteristic, thereby allowing its ascription only to animals.

She further orients the class towards the expected answer by suggesting yet another feature: nutrition, and, after a noticeably long pause, by again referring specifically to animals (line 13). Andrew again is the first one to suggest a candidate response which he formulates twice, first in more academic English making use of the key term 'nutrition' and the second time in more colloquial English (line 14). Several more students attempt to provide an answer although they leave them incomplete (Jaume, in lines 15 and 17, and Joan, in line 16). Jaume's second attempt seems to be clearer for other classmates to build on because Marta and Andrew suggest, in a partial overlap, candidate lexical items eligible as 'food' (lines 17–18). This co-constructed contribution is briefly acknowledged by the teacher (line 20) and reformulated (or extended) by Jaume (line 21) who might have only caught Andrew's suggestion.

In Extract 10.2b the teacher finally explicitly states the scientific terms necessary for establishing the basis of classification of the animal kingdom she was asking for:

```
22  TEA   they are not (0.3) *'auto' what? *auto-?
    tea                      *stands up    *goes to the blackboard
23  JAU   autoserves?
24  S?    auto-
25  S?    °autotrophic°
26  TEA   trophic (.) plants are *auto-
    tea                           *writes 'auto' on the blackboard
27  GUI   tra:(h)phic
28  TEA   *tro::phic (1.0)
    tea   *writes 'trophic'
29  MAR   yes
30  TEA   'trophos' means 'alimentar' (0.5)
                               'feed'
31  JAU   yes
32  TEA   *↓'feed' (1.0)
    tea   *writes 'feed' under 'trophic'
33  MAR   ja (0.5) yes
          'yeah'
34  TEA   and *'auto' (0.3) ↓'self'
    tea        *writes 'self' under 'auto'
35        *<plants make their own food> (0.3)
    tea   *turns to the class, presses both hands to her chest
36        they are *autotrophic.
    tea            *points at 'autotrophic'
37  S?    ↓m::
38  TEA   animals are all (0.5) *<hetero: (0.5) trophic>
    tea                         *writes 'hetero' on the blackboard
39        because they feed on others.
    TEA   *ok?
    tea   *turns to the class, nods
41  S?    yes
```

Extract 10.2b

Interestingly enough, although the teacher has repeatedly requested a classifying feature to describe animals, she however starts her classification with a negative structure 'X is/are not Y' to introduce a feature of a different kingdom, namely plants (lines 22, 24 and 26). She uses a 'format-tying' mechanism, thus following the inherent context-shaping nature of human interactions (Sacks, 1992) since the immediately previous turn produced by Jaume mentions this very type of living beings. After a short pause (line 22), the teacher introduces the first part of a scientific term through a designedly incomplete utterance (DIU, Koshik, 2002) and leaves it for students to finish while she stands up and walks towards the blackboard.

Several students take the floor and make an attempt at providing the term. Thus, Jaume suggests a candidate response (line 23), meanwhile another student only repeats the same first part of the term already provided by the teacher (line 24). Yet another student produces the full term, that is, both the first and the second part of the term (line 25). None of the students' contributions are acknowledged by the teacher who rather directly provides the second, expected part of the term which she emphatically highlights (line 26).

The fact that there is no teacher's response to students' candidate answers might be because she is busy with her own agenda of providing the class with the term. This is evidenced in what she does next since she makes her statement even more explicit by clearly stating the type of living beings she is referring to and then following a similar pattern as in line 22 by this time employing a positive structure 'X is/are Y'. She supports her verbal classification with a written inscription of the term ('auto') on the board. Another student, Guillem, fills in the teacher's DIU with a candidate (line 27) which he pronounces with a slightly laughing intonation, which might be due to its phonetic resemblance to the Catalan/L1 word '*tràfic*' ('traffic' in English). The fact that the teacher repeats the term emphasising and stretching only the problematic syllable might be interpreted as a potential recast (Lyster, 2007) of the student's faulty (or inappropriate) candidate (line 28).

After that the teacher launches the explanation of the second part of the term ('trophic', in lines 30 and 32). She does so by engaging students in the interactional processes of 'unpacking/packing' or 'translating' knowledge (Lin, 2016) from academic language to everyday language and back again into academic language. To 'unpack' the scientific term which might be problematic and unfamiliar to the students due to the 'non-transparency' or 'opacity' of the L2 (Gajo, 2007), the teacher tackles it through the sequence of remediation, so common in foreign language classrooms. Namely, she provides the original Greek word '*trophós*' and then its corresponding translation into both everyday Catalan ('*alimentar*') and everyday English ('feed'). To foster students' comprehension, she also accompanies her verbal explanation with writing the key L2 words on the board (lines 28 and 32). Then she repeats the same multimodal remediation procedure for the first part of the term ('auto', line

34), this time however only providing a translation into everyday English ('self'), maybe because the original Greek word '*autós*' ('*auto*' in Catalan) is familiar and transparent to the Catalan-speaking students.

To further support the students in the understanding of the full term, she also orients to a potential problem of the conceptual complexity or 'density' of the subject-specific content encapsulated in the focal scientific concept (Gajo, 2007) which leads to the sequence of mediation, common in L1 content lessons. With this aim she provides an easily understandable gloss in everyday English ('plants make their own food', line 35) while turning to the students and using embodiment to express the idea of 'their own' with her hands. After that she packs the new knowledge back into academic English by providing a formal classification using the 'X is/are Y' structure (line 36) while pointing to the key term. The teacher further develops the basis of classification by establishing the difference between plants and animals. Namely, she again resorts to the 'X is/are Y' structure in order to introduce the opposite scientific term ('heterotrophic') and strengthens it by adding 'all' and only inscribing the new and dissimilar part of the term on the board (line 38). Although this time she provides no translation of the new part of the term into the L1 or everyday L2, she still offers the class a gloss in everyday English which aims to clarify the meaning of the Greek word 'hetero' ('they feed on others').

During the teacher's explanation, several students produce clearly audible brief displays of understanding and listenership at the moments of a possible speaker change (Marta, in line 29; Jaume, in line 31; Marta, in line 33; and an unidentified student in line 37). The explanation-classification sequence is closed with the teacher's brief comprehension check (line 40) which she produces while gazing at the students and nodding, which elicits a positive confirmation from one of the students (line 41).

5   Conclusion

The detailed multimodal analysis of two extended extracts showed how one CLIL teacher accomplished classification practices in one particular CLIL science classroom and the array of semiotic resources she used. The analysis revealed how the teacher intertwined linguistic and paralinguistic elements which constituted her verbal message with numerous non-verbal actions in the process of developing the explanation-classification sequences and the embedded comparisons. More specifically, she was observed to mobilise a range of lexico-grammatical features in several languages (English, Catalan and Greek), different registers (everyday and academic) and different language modes (oral and written). She also used prosodic elements of intonation, such as stress and stretching, pauses, gaze and gesture, and material objects (the reference book and the image in it, the blackboard and key inscriptions on it).

Such rich multimodality assisted the teacher in achieving three pedagogical goals. First, engaging the students in the construction of shared understanding of relevant empirical and academic knowledge encapsulated in the classifications and comparisons that she developed for the phenomenon of shape-changing (Extract 10.1) and nutrition (Extract 10.2). Second, modelling how to talk school science in the L2 rigorously, that is, how to construct school-science knowledge through the L2 academic discourse by establishing explicit relationships between an empirically observed phenomenon/characteristic and a credited source of knowledge as well as by establishing explicit similarities and differences between different elements.

Last but not least, the teacher's multimodal 'unpacking' and 're-packing' of academic knowledge (Lin, 2016) served as rich scaffolding for the students' learning of school science evidenced in the way she carefully and skilfully led them through the explanation-classification sequences. By 'bridging' different discourses (Gibbons, 2006), that is, everyday and academic ways of talking about the same topics, and explicitly showing similarities and differences between them, teachers develop learners' comprehension and correct use of subject-specific concepts and content which become increasingly more abstract, de-contextualised and cognitively complex as learners move up the school years (Lemke, 1990).

The analysis showed how the teacher sequentially and multimodally *guided* students in discovering school-science knowledge behind their empirical observations and *built* on their contributions, incorporating them into the on-going interaction as part of the co-constructed explanation-classification sequences. She also acknowledged and legitimised the students' claims and reports by transforming their everyday wordings into appropriate school-science statements. She also introduced the students into relevant scientific and discursive practices of school science such as moving from concrete and observable phenomena towards more abstract and general meanings through the construction of appropriate comparisons and classifications.

However, despite such multi-layered, multimodal and multilingual work accomplished by the teacher for the construction of subject-specific classifications and comparisons, the students were hardly ever provided with any kind of more explicit meta-linguistic talk on these CDFs in particular, neither there was any evidence of CALP-related awareness-raising in general. On the one hand, there were no instances of explicit discussion of what components are required to make appropriate classifications and comparisons or what linguistic means (lexis, grammar, logical-discourse connectors, etc.) are necessary to produce them. On the other hand, although the teacher skilfully moved between everyday and academic language, provided key terminology in different languages and accompanied her talk with written inscriptions on the blackboard to make scientific knowledge accessible to students, this was done implicitly without ever raising students' awareness or explicitly stating similarities and differences between different ways of talking about academic knowledge using CALP and BICS.

The kind of analysis presented in this study aspires to make CLIL teachers aware of the necessity to organise classroom interaction in such a way that students are given frequent opportunities to participate in the discursive practices relevant for the teaching-and-learning of subject-specific content in the L2, such as comparing and classifying. To achieve this goal, CLIL teachers need to provide students with necessary interactional scaffolding which will help them understand, produce and negotiate academic messages in the target language adopted as the medium of instruction. This includes not only explicit teaching and scaffolding on the academic content but also moments of explicit meta-talk on CALP-related aspects, 'unpacking' and 're-packing' of knowledge in different registers, modes and languages. As this chapter has argued, this could also include explicit modelling of CDFs, for example, how to do comparisons/classifications both orally and in written form, as well as affording lexico-grammatical resources necessary for the construction of different CDFs. In this way, language integration goes beyond focusing on only subject-specific terminology.

CLIL teachers should also be encouraged to make numerous, rich and varied use of multimodal meaning-making resources available to them in providing appropriate support to their students and guiding them in their learning process. As a consequence, there is the necessity for CLIL pre-service and in-service teacher education courses to pay more attention to furthering teachers' understanding of the role of language and other semiotic resources in scaffolding students' learning of both academic content and the target language through classroom interaction. Therefore, it is hoped that this study may contribute to helping policymakers and course developers make relevant decisions on these issues.

Appendix: Transcription Conventions

For talk (Jefferson, 2004):

JAU	Speaker's pseudonym.
(.)	Very brief, unmeasured (micro-) pause.
(1.5)	Measured pause.
=	'Latching' between utterances produced by the same speaker/different speakers.
over[lap] [overlap]	Start, and if relevant, end of the concurrent speech.
<u>word</u>	Speaker's emphasis.
↑↓	A marked rise/fall in pitch, not necessarily a question/ end of the utterance.
.	Falling intonation.
,	Low-rising intonation, suggesting continuation.
?	Rising intonation, not necessarily a question.
|	Speaker's rhythmical emphasis.
cu-	A sharp cut-off.
:	Stretching of the preceding sound, more colons more stretching.
>fast< <slow>	Talk is produced noticeably quicker or slower than the surrounding talk.
(word)	Best guess at an unclear fragment.
word	Utterances produced in any other language that is not English.
italics	Translations into English of utterances produced in other languages.

For multimodality (Mondada, 2014):
Embodied actions relevant for the analysis are described in the line following the line containing utterance, in italics, and are synchronised with talk thanks to a series of landmarks:

JAU/jau	Participant accomplishing the action is identified. Capital letters are used when the action accomplished by the participant is verbal; the lower case is used of embodied actions.
* *	Delimitate descriptions of the teacher's embodied actions.
% %	Delimitate descriptions of Jaume's embodied actions.
* / %*turns to ARN*	The instant when embodied action of a particular participant starts within turn at talk.
* / % -->	Described embodied action of a particular participant continues across subsequent lines.
-->* / %	Described embodied action of a particular participant continues until the same symbol is reached.
#fig1.1	The exact place/instant where the screenshot within turn at the talk was taken.

References

Bauer-Marschallinger, S. (2018). Integration of content and language pedagogies: Cognitive discourse functions in the CLIL history classroom. *CELT Matters, 2*, 19–28.

Council of Europe. (1992). *European Charter for Regional or Minority Languages CETS 148*. Strasbourg. Retrieved November 30, 2018, from https://www.coe.int/en/web/conventions/full-list/-/conventions/treaty/148

Coyle, D., Hood, P., & Marsh, D. (2010). *CLIL. Content and Language Integrated Learning*. Cambridge: Cambridge University Press.

Cummins, J. (1991). Conversational and academic language proficiency in bilingual contexts. In J. H. Hulstijn & J. F. Matter (Eds.), *Reading in Two Languages* (pp. 75–89). Amsterdam: AILA.

Dalton-Puffer, C. (2013). A construct of cognitive discourse functions for conceptualising content-language integration in CLIL and multilingual education. *European Journal of Applied Linguistics, 1*(2), 216–253.

Dalton-Puffer, C. (2016). Cognitive discourse functions: Specifying and integrative interdisciplinary construct. In T. Nikula, E. Dafouz, P. Moore, & U. Smit (Eds.), *Conceptualising Integration in CLIL and Multilingual Education* (pp. 29–54). Bristol and Buffalo and Toronto: Multilingual Matters.

Dalton-Puffer, C., Bauer-Marschallinger, S., Brückl-Mackey, K., Hofmann, V., Hopf, J., Kröss, L., et al. (2018). Cognitive discourse functions in Austrian CLIL lessons: Towards an empirical validation of the CDF construct. *European Journal of Applied Linguistics, 6*(1), 5–29.

Escobar Urmeneta, C. (2009). Cuando la lengua de la escuela es diferente de la lengua familiar. *Cuadernos de Pedagogía, 395*, 46–51.

Gajo, L. (2007). Linguistic knowledge and subject knowledge: How does bilingualism contribute to subject development? *The International Journal of Bilingual Education and Bilingualism, 10*(5), 563–581.

Gibbons, P. (2006). *Bridging Discourses in the ESL Classroom: Students, Teachers and Researchers.* London: Continuum.

Heritage, J. (1984). A change-of-state token and aspects of its sequential placement. In J. M. Atkinson & J. Heritage (Eds.), *Structures of Social Action: Studies in Conversation Analysis* (pp. 299–345). Cambridge: Cambridge University Press.

Jefferson, G. (2004). Glossary of transcript symbols with an introduction. *Conversation Analysis: Studies from the First Generation.* Retrieved from http://www.liso.ucsb.edu/liso_archives/Jefferson/Transcript.pdf

Kääntä, L., Kasper, G., & Piirainen-Marsh, A. (2018). Explaining Hooke's law: Definitional practices in a CLIL physics classroom. *Applied Linguistics, 39*(5), 694–717.

Kidwell, M., & Zimmerman, D. H. (2007). Joint attention as action. *Journal of Pragmatics, 39*(3), 592–611.

Koshik, I. (2002). Designedly incomplete utterances: A pedagogical practice for eliciting knowledge displays in error correction sequences. *Research on Language and Social Interaction, 35*, 277–309.

Lackner, M. (2012). *The Use of Subject-Related Discourse Functions in Upper Secondary CLIL History Classes.* MA thesis, University of Vienna, Vienna.

Lemke, J. L. (1990). *Talking Science: Language, Learning and Values.* Norwood, NJ: Ablex.

Lin, A. M. Y. (2016). *Language Across the Curriculum & CLIL in English as an Additional Language (EAL) Contexts: Theory and Practice.* Singapore: Springer Science+Business Media Singapore.

Llinares, A., Morton, T., & Whittaker, R. (2012). *The Roles of Language in CLIL.* Cambridge: Cambridge University Press.

Lyster, R. (2007). *Learning and Teaching Languages through Content: A Counterbalanced Approach.* London: Continuum.

Mohan, B. (1986). *Language and Content.* Reading, MA: Addison-Wesley Publishing Company.

Mondada, L. (2014). *Conventions for Multimodal Transcription*. Basel: Romanisches Seminar der Universität.

Nikula, T. (2015). Hands-on tasks in CLIL science classrooms as sites for subject-specific language use and learning. *System, 54*, 14–27.

Ruiz de Zarobe, Y., & Jiménez Catalán, M. (Eds.). (2009). *Content and Language Integrated Learning: Evidence from Research in Europe*. Bristol, UK: Multilingual Matters.

Sacks, H. (1992). *Lectures on Conversation*. Edited by G. Jefferson. 2 vols. Oxford: Basil Blackwell.

Swain, M., & Lapkin, S. (2005). The evolving sociopolitical context of immersion education in Canada: Some implications for program development. *International Journal of Applied Linguistics, 15*(12), 169–186.

Trimble, L. (1985). *English for Science and Technology. A Discourse Approach*. Cambridge: Cambridge University Press.

Widdowson, H. G. (Ed.). (1979). *Reading and Thinking in English. Discovering Discourse*. Oxford: Oxford University Press.

11

Translanguaging Performances in a CLIL Classroom at a Japanese University

Keiko Tsuchiya

1 Introduction of the Study

Translanguaging (TL) refers to 'both the complex language practices of plurilingual individuals and communities, as well as the pedagogical approaches that use those complex practices' (García & Li Wei, 2014, p. 20). It has been investigated by a number of researchers (García & Kleyn, 2016b; Llinares, Morton, & Whittaker, 2012; Nikula & Moore, 2016; Li Wei, 2015), and the theory has been (re)conceptualised in the field of bi/multilingual practice and education. Lin, Wu and Lemke (forthcoming) recently coined the term *translanguaging performances* to describe the nature of structuring of translanguaging, which is 'not as tightly structured as formal written grammars would dictate, but [...] not so loosely structured that anything is possible' (ibid., p. 3). This study focuses on the use of TL in a group discussion in a Content and Language

K. Tsuchiya (✉)
International College of Arts and Sciences, Yokohama City University, Yokohama, Japan
e-mail: ktsuchiy@yokohama-cu.ac.jp

© The Author(s) 2019   **263**
K. Tsuchiya, M. D. Pérez-Murillo (eds.), *Content and Language Integrated Learning in Spanish and Japanese Contexts*, https://doi.org/10.1007/978-3-030-27443-6_11

Integrated Learning (CLIL) classroom at a Japanese university where both English and Japanese were used. The group consisted of three Japanese students and one Saudi student. Thus, the English they used is English as a Lingua Franca (ELF).

One of the frequently quoted definitions of ELF is 'any use of English among speakers of different languages for whom English is the communicative medium or choice' (Seidlhofer, 2011, p. 7). The definition has recently been updated, placing ELF under the framework of multilingualism: '[m]ultilingual communication in which English is available as a contact language of choice, but is not necessarily chosen' (Jenkins, 2015). In the traditional English as a Foreign Language (EFL) framework, code-switching (CS) from English to a first language (L1) has been marked as 'error resulting from gap in knowledge', while, in the paradigm of ELF, CS is seen as 'bilingual resource' (Jenkins, 2014, p. 26), which chimes with the concept of TL. TL refers:

> not simply to a shift or shuttle between two languages, but to the speakers' construction and use of original and complex interrelated discursive practices that cannot be easily assigned to one or another traditional definition of a language, but that make up the speakers' complete language repertoire. (García & Li Wei, 2014, p. 22)

TL disrupts traditional bilingualism, which hypothesises that bilinguals have two separate linguistic systems, rather with TL occurring when bilingual speakers select multiple linguistic features appropriate to a given context.

Taking the definition in García and Li Wei (2014), this study investigates the structure of the participants' use of TL, where ELF emerges in particular, in a CLIL classroom at a Japanese university. The functions and forms of TL were analysed based on the existing studies of CS. The process of TL was also examined in relation to turn-taking structure (Tsuchiya, 2013), the use of response tokens (Gardner, 2002; O'Keeffe, McCarthy, & Carter, 2007) and metalanguage (Storch & Wigglesworth, 2003). The results from the analysis will be discussed from perspectives of *the social-interactional theory*, that is, participation framework (Goffman, 1981) and interactional/transactional talk (Brown & Yule, 1983).

According to Goffman (1981, p. 137), an interlocutor is not just a recipient or non-recipient of an utterance in a conversation. Interlocutors position themselves in relation to utterances, in what is termed *participation status*, in the participation framework in a conversation (ibid.). In terms of functions of talk, Brown and Yule (1983, p. 1) describe *transactional talk* as serving 'in the expression of 'content'', and *interactional talk* as being involved in 'expressing social relations'. These concepts will be adapted to the discussion.

2 Literature Review

The practice of translanguaging is often observed in CLIL classrooms. Lewis, Jones, and Baker (2012, p. 650) identified three areas of research in TL; *classroom translanguaging, universal translanguaging* (the use of translanguaging in the lives of bilinguals) and *neurolinguistic translanguaging*, stating that TL can promote 'a deeper and fuller understanding of the subject matter' (ibid., p. 5). For the first category in the study by Lewis et al. (2012), Cenoz (2015) uses a different term, *pedagogical translanguaging*, which is defined as translanguaging practices in language learning or CLIL and encouraged in the pedagogy of *focus on multilingualism* to activate learners' multilingual repertoire (Cenoz & Gorter, 2011, 2015). Teachers in CLIL classrooms, for example, use translanguaging between the target language and their L1 efficiently to support learning (Nikula & Moore, 2016) and to introduce key concepts and terms in both languages, bridging learners' knowledge in multiple languages (Lin & Lo, 2017; Llinares et al., 2012). Students also translanguage to understand subject contents (Espinosa, Herrera, & Gaudreau, 2016), to show their emotion (Seltzer, Collins, & Angeles, 2016) and to index their multilingual/cultural identities (Li Wei, 2011). By so doing, bi/multilingual individuals develop a 'linguistic capital' (Bourdieu, 1991) in a given context (Espinosa et al., 2016, p. 173).

With the concept of TL, García and Kleyn (2016a) distinguish two types of performances: *language-specific performances*, which concern 'the lexicon and linguistic structures of a specific-named language', and *general linguistic performances*, which include 'students' ability [...] to argue a point, express inferences, communicate complex thoughts, use text-based evidence, tell a story, identify main ideas and relationships in complex texts, tell jokes, and so forth' (ibid., p. 24). The latter is related to TL. The structure of TL is then termed as *translanguaging performances* in Lin et al. (forthcoming). However, the nature of ordering and structuring of translanguaging has not been fully uncovered. To fill the gap, this study examines forms/functions and the process of TL in a CLIL group discussion in detail.

In the literature on the forms and functions of CS, Romaine (1995 [1989]) defines three forms of CS: inter-sentential, intra-sentential and tag code-switching. I use just the first two in the analysis and include tag code-switching in the second. I also take a single lexical item which is recognisably pronounced in Japanese accent as a Japanese word, that is, America /əˈmerɪkə/ is an English word, while /amelika/ is a Japanese word in the analysis.[1] As to the functions, Gumperz (1982) recognised six conversational functions of CS: *quotation, addressee specification, interjection, reiteration, qualification* and *personalisation versus objectivization*. More recently, Klimpfinger (2007) analysed academic ELF conversations and identified four functions of CS in ELF: *specifying an addressee, appealing for assistance, introducing another idea* and *signalling culture*. Through the observation, four functions were identified in my data, which were annotated in the transcript: (1) *addressee specification*, (2) *assertion*, (3) *clarification* and (4) *appealing for assistance*. The detailed procedure of the analysis is described in the following section.

3   Data and Method

A 40-minute-long group discussion was audio-recorded and analysed using the approach of corpus-assisted discourse analysis, which integrates a quantitative corpus-based analysis and qualitative discourse/conversation analytic approaches (Partington, Duguid, & Taylor, 2013; Walsh, Morton, & O'Keeffe, 2011). The data was recorded in an introductory

---

[1] Which words are taken as English or Japanese was decided by me and the transcriber based on the pronunciation in the recording.

intercultural communication class at a university in Japan, where CLIL was implemented. The class was one of the elective courses and open to students from all departments. Fifty-two students were enrolled in the class, the majority of whom was Japanese students with six international students from Thailand, China, Korea and Saudi Arabia. The medium of language in the class is English, but students used both English and their mother tongues in group discussions. The aims of the course are as follows: (1) to understand the theories in intercultural communication and apply them to students' own analysis and (2) to develop skills to understand theories and studies in intercultural communication by reading a textbook and journal articles. Although students were required to deliver group presentations in English, they had a choice to write an essay either in Japanese or in English. Thus, both Japanese and English were used through the course, considering the diverse English proficiency among students.

In the discussion data, three Japanese students (one male student, Daiki, and two female students, Haru and Mari) and a Saudi Arabian student (Omar) were working on an assigned project, using both Japanese and ELF (see Table 11.1, all names are anonymised). This group volunteered for the research and allowed me to record the discussion. Their levels of English vary as indicated in the levels of the Common European Framework of Reference (CEFR). Daiki is a fourth-year Aviation student who spent his childhood in Thailand and Canada and also studied in the United States for a year as a part of the university course. The other three

Table 11.1 Participants

	Nationality	School	Year	CEFR	English speaking countries
Daiki (male)	Japan	Aviation	4	B2	US (1 year), Canada (1 year) Thailand (3 years)
Omar (male)	Saudi Arabia	International Studies	2	B1	US (2 months)
Haru (female)	Japan	International Studies	2	A2	Canada (2 months)
Mari (female)	Japan	International Studies	2	A2	

students are second-year students in International Studies. Omar has been in the United States for two months, and his level of English is B1. Omar is enrolled in the Japanese university, which requires international students to pass N1 (B2 in CEFR) in the Japanese proficiency test before entering the undergraduate course. The two female Japanese students have lower proficiency in English (A2) than the male students.

In the assigned project work, students make a short film where misunderstanding in intercultural communication occurs. They create a scenario, act in English and film themselves. I asked the group to audio-record their conversation during the preparation for the assignment and left the room to avoid their being too conscious about the recording. The group eventually decided to film four scenes, two in imaginary classrooms in Japan and two in America where one of them acts as a teacher and the others take the role of students. In each setting, one scene describes misunderstandings between Japanese and American students because of differences in their behaviours and values, and the other offers a solution to overcome the misunderstandings.

The audio-recorded group discussion was transcribed and time-stamped using an annotation software tool, Transana (Fassnacht & Woods, 2002). The conventions of the Cambridge and Nottingham Corpus of Discourse in English (CANCODE) were applied to the transcription (see Appendix). The number of the participants' utterances and the time lengths of their speaking turns both in Japanese and in ELF were measured using the time-aligned corpus (Tsuchiya, 2013) to obtain an overview of the data.

4   Findings

4.1   The Numbers of Turns and Words in the Discussions

The word count and speaking length in English and Japanese for each participant are summarised in Table 11.2. They discussed in Japanese for about 25 minutes and in English for about 8 minutes in total with about

Table 11.2 Word count and speaking time length

	Wordcount		Speaking English		
	English	Japanese	English	Japanese	Total
Daiki	636	2314	0:04:18	0:06:54	0:11:12
Omar	505	2147	0:03:04	0:07:42	0:10:46
Haru	92	1957	0:00:40	0:05:52	0:06:32
Mari	20	1290	0:00:12	0:04:30	0:04:42
Pause	–	–	–	–	0:06:48
Total	1253	7708	0:08:14	0:24:58	0:40:00

7 minutes of silence. From the lengths of time they spent in Japanese and ELF, the dominant language in the discussion seems to be Japanese, but they sometimes switched to ELF.

Daiki spoke for 4 minutes 18 seconds (636 words) in ELF and about 7 minutes (2314 letters) in Japanese, which is similar to Omar. Omar's English level was B1, and he also had sufficient Japanese proficiency to study subjects in Japanese at university. Haru and Mari, on the other hand, spoke in Japanese most of the time and used ELF for less than 1 minute during the discussion. Most of the ELF interactions occurred between Daiki and Omar.

These figures reflect the turn-taking patterns in which Daiki and Omar sometimes initiated translanguaging and used ELF, while Mari and Haru kept to speak Japanese. The following section looks at the forms of translanguaging the participants employed.

4.2 Forms of Translanguaging

Two forms of TL, inter-sentential and intra-sentential, were annotated in the transcription based on Romaine (1995 [1989]). Tag code-switching is taken as intra-sentential TL, and discourse markers (DMs) and back-channels, such as *okay* and *yeah*, are not counted as occurrences of TL and annotated as discourse markers (DMs). Borrowing is also included in TL although single words with obvious Japanese pronunciation are excluded.

Extract 11.1 shows occurrences of the two forms of TL, intra-/inter-sentential TL. Omar and Daiki were talking about which language they were going to use when they acted as Japanese students in the scene.

1	Omar	日本人でも英語 どっち?
		(Japanese students also speak English, which?)
2 →	Daiki	え だから たぶんアメリカの environment で 例えば あの その=
		(well, so perhaps, in an American environment, for example, erm=)
3	Omar	yeah but=
4	Daiki	アメリカ人のクラスじゃなくて 別に=
		(It's not a class for American students, but=)
5	Omar	ah yeah yeah
6	Daiki	あの なんて言うのかな=
		(erm what can I say=)
7 →	Omar	but we gonna make this the right thing now? or the wrong one?
8	Daiki	the answer?
9	Omar	yeah
10	Daiki	right? doesn't= it's just practice, it doesn't really matter.

Extract 11.1   (at 00:07:09) Forms of TL

In line 1, Omar raised a question in Japanese whether Japanese students also talk in English or Japanese in the scene they are going to film. Daiki answered him in Japanese, using intra-sentential TL, in line 2. Omar inserted several response tokens in English, 'yeah but=' in line 3 and 'ah yeah yeah' in line 5, and then asked another question 'but we gonna make this the right thing now? or the wrong one?' in ELF in line 7, which is an instance of inter-sentential TL.

Table 11.3 shows the numbers of occurrences of inter-sentential/intra-sentential TL and DM. The numbers include instances of borrowing except a single word with Japanese accent.

Most of the participants used inter-sentential TL more frequently than they used intra-sentential TL. The frequent use of inter-sentential TL in

Table 11.3 Forms of TL

	Inter-sentential	Intra-sentential	DM	Total
Daiki	31	14	41	86
Omar	45	21	24	90
Haru	6	4	15	25
Mari	3	3	5	11
Total	85	42	85	212

Omar (45 in total) and Daiki (31) was observed. Daiki also used DM 41 times, which is about twice of that in Omar. The use of all the forms in Haru and Mari was limited in number when compared with the male students. The following section will discuss functions of TL in relation to the forms.

4.3 Functions of Translanguaging

The functions of TL in the discussion are categorised into four types as stated: (1) addressee specification, (2) assertion, (3) clarification and (4) appealing for assistance, on the basis of the categorisations in Gumperz (1982) and Klimpfinger (2007). In the following, I will introduce examples of each type in this order.

TL was used to specify an addressee in the following examples. In Extract 11.2, Haru and Omar were seated at a desk in front of the whiteboard, and Daiki was looking at the camera lens for filming and adjusting the angle.

1		Omar	こっちからの方がいいじゃん
			(it's better to film from here.)
2		Daiki	あ いいよ
			(okay)
3		Pause	(2.0)
4		Haru	うん 映りますか？
			(can you see us?)
5		Daiki	あぁ大丈夫
			(yeah okay.)
6		Haru	大丈夫
			(okay)
7		Omar	yeah
8		Omar	大丈夫
			(okay)
9	→	Omar	Can you see?
10	→	Daiki	Yeah. Like front row er through=

Extract 11.2 (at 00:00:52) Addressee specification

In lines 1 to 8, Daiki was adjusting the position of the video camera, checking the scope together with Omar and Haru in Japanese. Omar then switched to ELF in line 9, asking Daiki, 'Can you see?', to which Daiki answered in ELF in line 10. This is an instance where Omar used TL to speak to Daiki. Omar's use of TL to ELF was often observed when he addressed Daiki, not the other two students, and the same practices were recognised when Daiki addressed Omar.

Extract 11.3 includes the second function, assertion. The four students were talking about lines they were going to say in the scene where Daiki in the role of teacher asked what is important in intercultural communication for the students.

1		Daiki	あー じゃあ なんか ス= ステレオタイプとかね
			(erm you can say stereotype.)
2		Haru	ああ
			(yeah.)
3		Omar	Understanding other culture
4		Daiki	Other culture um
5		Mari	うん
			(Okay.)
6		Haru	じゃあ understanding=
			(Then)
7		Omar	Understanding 一緒に入る
			(I will join at the same time.)
8	→	Daiki	Not= Not= Not= ああ そうだね Not judging people=
			(well yeah)
			だから別に (.) it doesn't really have to be this word, right?
			(so it doesn't have to be=)
			Like I mean it can be= if understanding can be like judgement
			or er I don't know= belief or whatever like that= can be other
			words if it's not the same= これじゃなかったら
			(if it's not this one.)

Extract 11.3 (at 00:10:57) Assertion

In lines 1 to 7, Daiki, Haru and Omar suggested some possible responses from the students to the question given by the teacher in the imaginary classroom. Then in line 8, Daiki asserted his opinion, switching from Japanese to ELF while slightly raising his voice. He inserts several short Japanese phrases: he uttered an acknowledgement phrase 'ああ そうだね (well yeah)' after 'Not=Not=Not', then switched to ELF, saying 'Not judging people' in ELF, followed by another Japanese phrase

'だから別に' (so it doesn't have to be=). He then drew on another available resource, ELF, for a while, then chose Japanese at the end, saying 'これじゃなかったら (if it's not this one.)'. Here he took a longer floor and led the discussion by suggesting what the students should utter in the scene.

The participants also used TL for clarification in the discussion. An example of TL for clarification is the confirmation initiation shown in Extract 11.4, where they were talking about the scene they were going to record next.

1	Omar	はい 今はアメリカで
		(Now in America)
2 →	Haru	in America?
3	Daiki	うん <$O1> in America </$O1>
		(Yeah)
4	Omar	<$O1> now it's </$O1> in America

Extract 11.4 (at 00:06:21) Clarification (confirmation)

In line 1, Omar said in Japanese that the next scene they were going to practise was a scene in America. Haru switched to ELF in line 2 and said, 'in America?', which functions as confirmation initiation. The following utterances by Daiki and Omar in lines 3 and 4 were taken as confirmation. Haru used Japanese most of the time in the discussion. However, she seemed to employ TL to initiate confirmation, which can be one of her clarification strategies. In fact, she used clarification in ELF five times in the discussion (see Table 11.4).

Table 11.4 Functions of TL

	Address	Assertion	Clarification	Assistance	Unclassified	Total
Daiki	19	22	1	2	1	45
Omar	27	26	4	6	3	66
Haru	0	3	5	1	1	10
Mari	0	3	3	0	0	6
Total	46	54	13	9	5	127

Note: In the data, the participants sometimes used ELF in acting a scene. The instances of TL to ELF in acting are excluded in the numbers

Extract 11.5 includes another example of clarification, this time in the form of repair. Before this extract, they started acting a scene, but they stopped here since they were not sure which scene they should act this time.

1		Omar	待って待って <$G?>さぁ
			(Wait, wait)
2	→	Haru	あ　これ2個目？Good manner?
			(Er is this the second scene?)
3		Omar	例えばね=
			(For example)
4	→	Mari	違う　3個目
			(No, this is the third one)
5	→	Daiki	え　これこっちじゃないの？
			(Oh is it not this one?)
6	→	Omar	3個目だったっけ？
			(Is it the third one?)
7	→	Haru	3個目
			(It's the third one)

Extract 11.5 (at 00:26:36) Clarification (repair)

Omar stopped acting in line 1, then Haru asked whether this was the second scene or the third one both in Japanese and ELF in line 2, saying 'あ これ2個目?(Er is this the second scene?) Good manner?' The scenes were given many names in the discussion in both Japanese and ELF, such as '良くないヤツ (a bad scene)' or 'first shot [sic]'. Haru then chose the term 'good manner' for clarification here (see Excerpt 5 for another case where Haru used ELF for clarification). Mari first repaired in line 4, saying, 'No, this is the third one' in Japanese, which was followed by Daiki and Omar's response to Haru's repair initiation and Mari's repair in lines 5 and 6. Finally, Haru self-repaired and confirmed in line 7, saying 'It's the third one' in Japanese.

There were a few occurrences of TL to ELF for clarification by Mari (five in total) and Haru (three; see Table 11.4). In these occurrences, Haru and Mari spoke to either Daiki or Omar as seen in Extract 11.4. Thus, TL for clarification by those students with relatively lower proficiency in ELF can be interpreted as their accommodation to the norm in interaction between Daiki and Omar, who tended to communicate in ELF between themselves.

Occurrences of TL in appealing for assistance were also observed in the data. One such example is shown in Extract 11.6.

1	→	Omar	まあいい 誰がとら=とれ= なんだっけ?
			(okay, who films= can film= how can I say?)
2	→	Omar	<$O1> someone= </$O1> someone must take for us
3		Daiki	<$O1> だから もし= </$O1>
			(So if=)
4		Daiki	<$O2> yeah </$O2>
5		Omar	<$O2> video </$O2>
6	→	Daiki	so if we are recording the eleventh then she can do it <$G?>

Extract 11.6 (at 00:03:05) Appealing for assistance

In line 1, Omar tried to ask who was going to film in Japanese first, but he could not conjugate the verb '撮る (the verb *film*)' in Japanese properly and sought assistance, saying 'なんだっけ? (how can I say?)', which was followed by an ELF equivalent 'someone = someone must take [a film] for us' as nobody offered help in Japanese. Daiki started responding to Omar's statement first in Japanese 'だから もし=', then uttered DM in ELF in line 4 and then eventually answered Omar's statement, switching to ELF in line 6.

The numbers of TL used by each participant are summarised in Table 11.4. TL for addressee specification (46 in total) and assertion (54) were observed more often than the other two functions, clarification (13) and appealing for assistance (9). Only Daiki and Omar used TL for addressee specification. Daiki used TL 15 times to address Omar, and Omar to address Daiki 18 times. The use of appealing for assistance was observed in Daiki, Omar and Haru. TL for assertion and clarification appeared in all the participants although most of the instances of assertion were seen in Daiki and Omar's data. The relationship between the forms and functions of TL are summarised in Table 11.5.

Inter-sentential TL in addressee specification was more frequently used than intra-sentential TL. Both forms were observed in the four functions. The results indicate that Daiki and Omar often used inter-sentential TL

Table 11.5 Forms and functions of TL

	Address	Assertion	Clarification	Assistance	Unclassified	Total
Inter-sentential	43	27	9	3	3	85
Intra-sentential	3	27	4	6	2	42
Total	46	54	13	9	5	127

in interaction between themselves. They seem to employ TL to ELF as a strategy to restrict their addressee, which thus can relate to the management of *participation framework* (Goffman, 1981) in the discussion (see Extract 11.2). In Extracts 11.4 and 11.5, Haru and Mari also used TL for clarification, simultaneously accommodating their language to ELF, which Daiki and Omar tended to use in their interaction. By so doing, the participants regulate a *translanguaging space* (Li Wei, 2011), utilising both languages available to them by shifting from Japanese to ELF and moving back to Japanese.

4.4   Shifting from Interactional Talk to Transactional Talk

A qualitative conversation and discourse analytic approach was also applied in this study. The use of TL in relation to interactional and transactional talk (Brown & Yule, 1983) was analysed, focusing on a longer sequence of interaction in the data.

As shown in Extract 11.7, some instances of TL seemed to indicate a shift from interactional talk to transactional talk. Here, intending to act as a teacher in the scene, Omar was writing about a topic they are going to use in the scene (e.g., stereotype or intercultural communication) on the whiteboard, in front of the desk where two female students, Haru and Mari, were seated. Daiki was setting up a video camera near the whiteboard.

1		Mari	書く? 大丈夫?
			(Do you want me to write? Are you alright?)
2		Omar	うん 大丈夫
			(Yeah I'm alright.)
3		Mari	ステレオ=
			(stereo=)
4		Omar	どっちでいい, intercultural?
			(which is better, intercultural?)
5		Mari	どっちでも[良いです]
			(whichever [you like.])
6		Omar	[あとで]聞くんでしょ
			([later] you will ask about it?)
7			(4.0)
8	→	Mari	Omar の字じゃ雑
			(Omar's hand writing is untidy.)
9		Haru	え あれの白のデイジー欲しい
			(I want that [Omar's T-shirt] with Daisy [a Disney character] and white one.)
10		Mari	あ デイジーあるの? かわいい
			(Oh is there one with Daisy? It's cute.)
11		Haru	[絶対ほしい]
			([I'll definitely buy one.])
12		Mari	[え かわいい] 絶対 かわいい
			([Oh it's cute] really cute.)
13		Omar	<$E> laugh </$E>
14		Haru	絶対 かわいいでしょ ミニーちゃんとかもあるよ
			(It must be really cute. There's the other one with Minnie.)
15		Mari	えー
			(Oh)
16	→	Omar	can you write for me? <$E> laugh </$E>
17		Daiki	what? write what?
18		Omar	Intercultural communication
19	→	Mari	汚い
20			(It's [=Omar's handwriting] untidy.)
21		Daiki	yes I can
22		Omar	Mm <$E> laugh </$E>

Extract 11.7 (at 00:04:01) TL to shift from interactional to transactional talk

Mari and Omar were discussing what topic they were going to use in the scene in Japanese from lines 1 to 6, including one instance of intra-sentential TL by Omar in line 4. After a 4-second pause, Mari complained that Omar's handwriting was untidy in line 8. Then, Haru initiated another topic in line 9, which was totally unrelated to the ongoing task, that is, about Omar's shirt with some Disney character, saying in Japanese, 'え あれの白のデイジー欲しい (I want that [Omar's T-shirt] with Daisy [a Disney character] and white one)'. Mari joined Haru, in pursuing this topic, at the following turn, which continued until line 15. Omar was listening to their talk but just laughed in line 13. This interactional talk between the two female students in Japanese was terminated in line 16 by Omar asking Daiki to write on the board instead of him in English, 'Can you write for me?' This was also taken as a request for Daiki to act as a teacher. This request from Omar seems to be his accepting Mari's complaint about his handwriting in line 8. From a conversation analytic view, this Mari's complaint in line 8 is the first pair part of an adjacency pair, which is completed with the delayed second pair part by Omar's request in line 16 for Daiki to change the roles, which was accepted by Daiki in line 21 (Schegloff, Jefferson, & Sacks, 1977). Meanwhile, Mari repeated her complaint in line 19, which served to strengthen her complaint in line 8, thus proving the legitimacy of the sequence (see *next-turn proof procedure* in Sacks, Schegloff, and Jefferson (1974, p. 729)).

Here we can see how Omar used TL to ELF to shift from the interactional talk to the transactional talk, which is also related to a transactional goal and decision-making on who is going to act as a teacher in the scene. This use of TL for the achievement of transactional goals was also observed in Extract 11.3, where Daiki asserted his opinion to decide what they should say in the scene.

Examining the transition process of translanguaging, two practices seemed to trigger translanguaging: (1) the use of English response tokens and (2) the use of metalanguage, before the floor-taking in ELF. Extract 11.2 is one such example where English response tokens were observed before floor-taking in ELF. In the first few lines, Haru and Daiki spoke in Japanese. However, Omar uttered an English response token *yeah* in line 7 before he took the floor in ELF in line 9. After Omar's translanguaging to ELF in line 9, Daiki responded to Omar in ELF in line 10, by which he seemed to co-construct a context where translanguaging was the norm in the discussion. Another discursive practice before floor-taking in ELF was the use of metalanguage. In line 1 in Extract 11.6, Omar was trying to ask who was going to film for them in Japanese, but as he could not produce a correct verb form, then he used a metalinguistic inquiry, なんだっけ? (how can I say [in Japanese]?). Thus, the bi/multilingual speakers strategically negotiated the discursive norms (language choice) and simultaneously claimed their bi/multilingual identities, utilising their linguistic repertoires.

5   Conclusion

This study examined the use of TL, mainly from Japanese to ELF, in relation to its forms and functions in a group discussion in a CLIL classroom at university, where both Japanese and ELF were available language resources for the participants. The quantitative analysis of speaking time in both languages indicates the use of Japanese seems to be the shared norm in the discussion, but simultaneously, the use of TL from Japanese to ELF is also accepted on some occasions. Most occurrences of TL to ELF are observed between Daiki and Omar in the form of inter-sentential TL, while limited use of TL occurs with Haru and Mari. Daiki and Omar used TL to specify their addressee and to assert their opinions, securing the floor of conversation. Haru and Mari, on the other hand, employed TL for clarification although the number of occurrences is small. The occurrences of TL for appealing for assistance were also observed most in Omar's data. The results from the qualitative analysis are summarised as below:

1. The use of TL to ELF by Daiki and Omar seems to relate to their indexicality of bi/multilingual self in the translanguaging space and also the management of participation framework (i.e., drawing on ELF to specify an addressee).
2. Haru and Mari's use of TL for clarification can be their accommodation to the norm in the interaction between the two male students although the number of the occurrences is limited.
3. The use of ELF seems to be used as a strategy to mark a shift from interactional talk to transactional talk.

From the practice of translanguaging especially in Daiki and Omar, three features of structuring of translanguaging were identified, which could be elements of translanguaging performances:

Aspects	Translanguaging performances
(1) Comprising subordinate communication	TL for participation framework: TL to select a recipient.
(2) Indicating a boundary between discourse frames	TL for discourse framework: TL to move from interactional talk to transactional talk.
(3) Claiming bi/multilingual self	TL for bi/multilingual identity: TL to develop linguistic capital.

First, the two male students' use of TL to ELF seems to comprise *subordinate communication*, in other words 'by play' (Goffman, 1981, pp. 134–135), which enabled them to talk each other by specifying an addressee, but not completely eliminating the other two participants from the discussion. Thus, TL can be used as a strategy to regulate participation framework in the interaction. Second, TL to ELF seems to indicate boundaries between different discourse frames. Poncini (2004, p. 258) found that a shift from a joking framework to seriousness was indicated by a change in the participants' choices of languages available at that moment in multicultural business meetings. Extract 11.7 shows a similar instance, where Omar's use of TL signalled a shift from interactional talk between Haru and Mari to transactional talk (see Sect. 4.4). Third, to create a translanguaging space, the two male students did not stay in ELF for long and went back and forth between ELF and Japanese. In Extract 11.3, for instance, Daiki first translanguaged from Japanese to ELF at the beginning of line 8, asserting his opinion about what student role actors should play in the scene, before going back to Japanese at the end, saying 'これじゃなかったら(if it's not this one)' in Japanese. A conversation in Japanese continued after the interaction in Extract 11.3. A similar tendency was observed in Omar's utterances. By engaging in these practices, they seem to represent a *bi/multilingual self,* that is not restricting themselves to either ELF or Japanese.

The results from the analysis of only one 41-minute long conversation cannot be generalised. However, this study highlights discursive practices of translanguaging between ELF and Japanese in the context of a CLIL classroom in tertiary education in Japan, illuminating possible features of translanguaging performances: their strategic use of TL from Japanese to ELF to regulate participation framework and interactional/transactional talk in the discussion, and students' presentation of themselves as bi/multilingual individuals. These features can be explored further in future research on translanguaging performances in CLIL classrooms.

Acknowledgement The article is written based on my previously published article, Tsuchiya (2017): 'co-constructing a translanguaging space: analysing a Japanese/ELF group discussion in a CLIL classroom at university' in *Translation and Translanguaging in Multilingual Contexts, 3*(2), 229–253, which was published by John Benjamins Publishing Company, Amsterdam/Philadelphia (https://benjamins.com/catalog/ttmc). I would like to thank the editor, Prof. Sara Laviosa, and the publisher for kindly providing the permission. I also extend my gratitude to the GRAPE (Group for Research on Academic and Professional English) at Universitat Jaume I for offering an excellent webinar programme of translanguaging in CLIL in higher education (http://www.grape. uji.es), which was inspiring. This study was supported in part by JSPS Grant-in-Aid for Young Scientists (B) No. 26870599.

Appendix: Annotation Conventions

Conventions	Symbol	Explanation
Extralinguistic information	<$E>...	This includes laughter, coughs and transcribers' comments.
Unintelligible Speech	<$G?>	Unintelligible speech is marked with these brackets.
Guess	<$H>...	Where the accuracy of the transcription is uncertain, the sequence of words in question is placed between these two angle brackets.
Overlap	<$O1>...	Some parts of the corpus have been coded for overlapping speech. For this purpose, the overlap is indicated by numbered angle brackets.
Interrupted sentence	+	When an utterance is interrupted by another speaker, this is indicated by using a + sign at the end of interrupted utterance and at the point where the speaker resumes his or her utterance.
Unfinished sentence	=	Unfinished sentences of any type are indicated with = sign at the end of unfinished utterances.

Adolphs (2008, pp. 137–138)

References

Adolphs, S. (2008). *Corpus and Context: Investigating Pragmatic Functions in Spoken Discourse*. Amsterdam: John Benjamins Publishing Company.

Bourdieu, P. (1991). *Language and Symbolic Power*. Cambridge: Polity Press.

Brown, G., & Yule, G. (1983). *Discourse Analysis*. Cambridge: Cambridge University Press.

Cenoz, J. (2015). Discussion: Some reflections on content-based education in Hong Kong as part of the paradigm shift. *International Journal of Bilingual Education and Bilingualism, 18*(3), 345–351.

Cenoz, J., & Gorter, D. (2011). Focus on multilingualism: A study of trilingual writing. *The Modern Language Journal, 95*(3), 356–369.

Cenoz, J., & Gorter, D. (Eds.). (2015). *Multilingual Education*. Cambridge: Cambridge University Press.

Espinosa, C., Herrera, L. Y., & Gaudreau, C. M. (2016). Reclaiming bilingualism: Translanguaging in a science class. In O. García & T. Kleyn (Eds.), *Translanguaging with Multilingual Students: Learning from Classroom Moments* (pp. 160–177). London: Routledge.

Fassnacht, C., & Woods, D. (2002). *Transana. Version 2.12—Win*. Wisconsin: University of Wisconsin-Madison.

García, O., & Kleyn, T. (2016a). Translanguaging theory in education. In O. García & T. Kleyn (Eds.), *Translanguaging with Multilingual Students: Learning from Classroom Moments* (pp. 9–33). London: Routledge.

García, O., & Kleyn, T. (Eds.). (2016b). *Translanguaging with Multilingual Students: Learning from Classroom Moments*. London: Routledge.

García, O., & Li Wei (2014). *Translanguaging*. London: Palgrave Macmillan.

Gardner, R. (2002). *When Listeners Talk: Response Tokens and Listener Stance*. Amsterdam: John Benjamins.

Goffman, E. (1981). *Forms of Talk*. Philadelphia, PA: University of Pennsylvania.

Gumperz, J. J. (1982). *Discourse Strategies*. Cambridge: Cambridge University Press.

Jenkins, J. (2014). *English as a Lingua Franca in the International University: The Politics of Academic English Language Policy*. Abingdon: Routledge.

Jenkins, J. (2015). Repositioning English and multilingualism in English as a Lingua Franca. *Englishes in Practice, 2*(3), 49–85.

Klimpfinger, T. (2007). 'Mind you, sometimes you have to mix'? The role of code-switching in English as a Lingua Franca. *Vienna English Working Papers, 16*(2), 36–61.

Lewis, G., Jones, B., & Baker, C. (2012). Translanguaging: Origins and development from school to street and beyond. *Educational Research and Evaluation, 18*(7), 641–654. https://doi.org/10.1080/13803611.2012.718488

Lin, A., & Lo, Y. Y. (2017). Trans/languaging and the triadic dialogue in content and language integrated learning (CLIL) classrooms. *Language and Education, 31*(1), 26–45. https://doi.org/10.1080/09500782.2016.1230125

Lin, A. M. Y., Wu, Y., & Lemke, J. (forthcoming). 'It takes a village to research a village': Conversations with Jay Lemke on contemporary issues in translanguaging. In S. Lau & S. Stille (Eds.), *Critical Plurilingual Pedagogies: Struggling Toward Equity Rather than Equality*. Switzerland: Springer.

Li Wei (2011). Moment analysis and translanguaging space: Discursive construction of identities by multilingual Chinese youth in Britain. *Journal of Pragmatics, 43*, 1222–1235.

Li Wei (2015). Complementary classrooms for multilingual minority ethnic children as a translanguaging space. In J. Cenoz & D. Gorter (Eds.), *Multilingual Education: Between Language Learning and Translanguaging* (pp. 177–198). Cambridge: Cambridge University Press.

Llinares, A., Morton, T., & Whittaker, R. (2012). *The Role of Language in CLIL*. Cambridge: Cambridge University Press.

Nikula, T., & Moore, P. (2016). Exploring translanguaging in CLIL. *International Journal of Bilingual Education and Bilingualism*. https://doi.org/10.1080/136 70050.2016.1254151

O'Keeffe, A., McCarthy, M., & Carter, R. (2007). *From Corpus to Class Room: Language Use and Language Teaching*. Cambridge: Cambridge University Press.

Partington, A., Duguid, A., & Taylor, C. (2013). *Patterns and Meanings in Discourse: Theory and Practice in Corpus Assisted-Discourse Studies (CADS)*. Amsterdam: John Benjamins Publishing Company.

Poncini, G. (2004). *Discursive Strategies in Multicultural Business Meetings*. Bern: Peter Lang.

Romaine, S. (1995 [1989]). *Bilingualism* (2nd ed.). Oxford: Blackwell.

Sacks, H., Schegloff, E. A., & Jefferson, G. (1974). A simplest systematics for the organization of turn-taking for conversation. *Language, 50*(4), 696–735.

Schegloff, E. A., Jefferson, G., & Sacks, H. (1977). The preference for self-correction in the organization of repair in conversation. *Language, 53*, 361–382.

Seidlhofer, B. (2011). *Understanding English as a Lingua Franca*. Oxford: Oxford University Press.

Seltzer, K., Collins, B. A., & Angeles, K. M. (2016). Navigating turbulent waters: Translanguaging to support academic and socioemotional well-being. In O. García & T. Kleyn (Eds.), *Translanguaging with Multilingual Students: Learning from Classroom Moments* (pp. 140–159). London: Routledge.

Storch, N., & Wigglesworth, G. (2003). Is there a role for the use of the L1 in an L2 setting? *TESOL Quarterly, 37*(4), 760–770.

Tsuchiya, K. (2013). *Listenership Behaviours in Intercultural Encounters: A Time-Aligned Multimodal Corpus Analysis*. Amsterdam: John Benjamins Publishing Company.

Tsuchiya, K. (2017). Co-constructing a translanguaging space: Analysing a Japanese/ELF group discussion in a CLIL classroom at university. *Translation and Translanguage in Multilingual in Multilingual Contexts, 3*(2), 229–253.

Walsh, S., Morton, T., & O'Keeffe, A. (2011). Analysing university spoken interaction: A CL/CA approach. *International Journal of Corpus Linguistics, 16*, 325–344.

Part IV

CLIL Pedagogy and Teacher Education

12

Teacher Development: J-CLIL

Shigeru Sasajima

1 Introduction

This chapter explores Content and Language Integrated Learning (CLIL) pedagogy and teacher education (TE) in a context beyond Europe, where CLIL has been developed as a curricular innovation in the teaching of non-language subjects supported by the European Commission (Eurydice, 2006). Today CLIL has been gradually implemented as an integrated language learning approach in Japan. CLIL pedagogy in Japan is thus seen as a way to improve the current situation of English language teaching (ELT) and as a means of fostering learners' cognitive development, language learning, and intercultural awareness. English knowledge and skills are exclusively focused on, especially in secondary education, and the aim is to help develop learners' English proficiency skills based on the *English Education Reform Plan* responding to the challenges of corresponding to globalization (MEXT, 2014a). In terms of CLIL TE, no

S. Sasajima (✉)
Department of International Communication, Toyo Eiwa University, Yokohama, Japan
e-mail: sasajima.s@toyoeiwa.ac.jp

© The Author(s) 2019
K. Tsuchiya, M. D. Pérez Murillo (eds.), *Content and Language Integrated Learning in Spanish and Japanese Contexts*, https://doi.org/10.1007/978-3-030-27443-6_12

official curriculum, teaching standards, or guidelines for CLIL are as yet available in the current primary and secondary education system, nor is there a CLIL curriculum for any educational level. It actually means that CLIL teacher education urgently needs to be provided for part of professional teacher development, including CLIL methodology, curriculum development, materials development, and practices (teaching knowledge and skills, lesson procedures, activities, etc.), which seems to be primarily related to ELT in some specific school subjects and themes.

As a teacher-researcher on ELT and CLIL pedagogy, I have been committed to the implementation of CLIL in Japan together with some colleagues since 2007. In this chapter, I describe the work that we have carried out as part of the CLIL-continuing professional development (CLIL-CPD), grassroots collaborative CLIL seminars, and lesson studies. The CLIL curriculum started as part of health sciences at a medical university with ELT teachers in 2008. From then onward I have published several CLIL textbooks with them to support teachers to teach CLIL in their own contexts while having collaborative research and study meetings with CLIL teachers and researchers. In the process of such CLIL-CPD activities, some ELT methodology courses including CLIL theory and practices at university have been provided over the past decade. In the following section, I first discuss CLIL pedagogy and TE, and then provide a definition of CLIL I have refined in the Japanese context, describing examples of implementation, materials, and pedagogies. This chapter also discusses the practice of lesson study to implement CLIL with task-based language teaching (TBLT) (Long, 2009), teacher development and teacher networks for CLIL, showing some implications for CLIL teacher education in Japan through J-CLIL activities, which primarily aim to support CLIL pedagogy.

2   CLIL Pedagogy and Teacher Education in Japan

The Japan CLIL Pedagogy Association (J-CLIL) was established in April 2017. Since then, this association has played a key role in promoting CLIL contextualized in Japan, in which different types of CLIL are applied at each educational stage. J-CLIL aims 'to study and promote practices for the implementation of integrated education called CLIL or Content-Based Language Teaching (CBLT)' (see the J-CLIL website: https://www.j-clil.com/english), which means that it seeks to support CLIL approaches in primary, secondary and tertiary education, building networks among teachers and researchers who are interested in CLIL (e.g., Marsh, 2002; Coyle, 1999) or CBLT (e.g., Lightbown, 2014; Lyster, 2007). Since CLIL was practically introduced into ELT in Japan a decade ago (Sasajima, 2011), more teachers have tried to implement CLIL in their classrooms. However, there is still confusion about what CLIL is because of the broad definition of the term. For example, Coyle, Hood, and Marsh (2010, p. 1) define CLIL as 'a dual-focused educational approach in which an additional language is used for the learning and teaching of both content and language.' However, many teachers need to know some specific teaching methods or materials of CLIL approaches.

2.1 English Teachers and Teacher Education in Japan

In Japan, CLIL has attracted attention mostly among ELT teachers, except some Japanese language teachers who are engaged in teaching Japanese in a European context and have taught Japanese to European citizens. Because of the growing interest among the ELT teachers, it is necessary to briefly look at the background of the national curriculum or the Course of Study, ELT, and the ELT teacher education system in Japan. Since 1945, the Japanese national curriculum has guided basic education up to ninth grade for all eligible children. English has been taught at secondary school since then, and accordingly from 2020 English will be introduced in the primary school curriculum (see the details in Chap. 3 in this volume). English has actually been taught as 'foreign language activities' but not as a subject in itself. The national curriculum has insisted on using the term 'foreign languages' in the document, and has maintained a rigid curriculum comprising accurate English language skills (listening, reading, speaking, and writing), the grammar syllabus and vocabulary size, although apparently referring to communicative language teaching (CLT) (for more details see Section 9 Foreign Languages in the Course of Study). As for foreign language teaching, the Course of

Study has exclusively focused on the English language and its knowledge and skills, which are often criticized as impractical. The Ministry of Education, Culture, Sports, Science and Technology (MEXT) nevertheless encourages ELT teachers and students to improve their English proficiency skills to use the language in the classroom. The reality is that ELT teachers find it difficult to change their teaching methods so drastically due to the complex teacher culture deeply-rooted in the teacher education system and their complex teacher cognitions (Sasajima, 2014a). There are also practical reasons why they could not teach their students communicative English although the MEXT (2008) requests them to do so: for example, the hidden curriculum (Jackson, 1968), large class size, students' language learning needs and the exam-oriented education system they work in. Japanese schoolteachers may have the most complex working conditions in the world, since they work the longest hours in the world, as the OECD Teaching and Learning International Survey (TALIS) (Ainley & Carstens, 2018) shows. I found through my research that many ELT teachers are worried about their teaching. They also try to establish better relationships with students, valuing emotional relationships with students, but concern dual burdens because they are required to have multiple burdens. In addition, they wonder what the goal is and find their teacher education irrelevant since it lacks practical classroom observation (Sasajima, 2014a).

In preservice or initial teacher education, teacher trainees are not able to gain sufficient knowledge and skills of English teaching since the programs only include a three-week teaching practicum and minimal course requirements in terms of ELT (English literature, English linguistics, English communication, and English cross-cultural understanding). Because of the flexible credit-based teacher education system, most teacher trainees unfortunately cannot focus on ELT knowledge and skills including practical classroom teaching practices and reflections and thus cannot cultivate their practical pedagogical content knowledge (PCK) (Shulman, 1987). Their PCK or the knowledge of ELT methodology may not be developed sufficiently enough to enable them to be professional language teachers who can make appropriate decisions in their classrooms. In many cases, they just follow the textbook syllabus provided by the publishing company, focusing on teaching grammatical knowledge by applying the traditional grammar-translation method, which they believe can help their students prepare for the entrance exams. It seems that the hidden curriculum hinders teacher trainees' thinking about their students' learning of communicative English use (cf. MEXT, 2014b).

In in-service teacher education or CPD, ELT teachers at secondary school cannot actually focus on ELT development since they have multiple roles at school: subject teaching, disciplines, pastoral care, career guidance, counseling, and other supporting activities. Compared to teachers in Europe, Japanese secondary school teachers have a greater workload apart from teaching their subjects at school. Their CPD can thus include a variety of professional fields and they may have difficulty in developing their subject teaching. Although ELT teachers certainly need to study ELT methodology and other theories of learning and teaching, they actually cannot have enough time to reflect on their teaching in the classroom. CLT has been popular among ELT teachers, but in spite of this, it has not been implemented in many ELT classrooms. Most ELT teachers can speak English well and have at least B1 or B2 on the Common European Framework of Reference of Languages (CEFR) proficiency scale (Council of Europe, 2001), but it could be hard to adopt a CLT approach in their classrooms, due to complex situations at school. For this reason, they should have opportunities for CPD and need to develop their career as ELT teachers by gaining pedagogical and didactic knowledge and skills. CLIL can be included in CPD as it is an integrated language learning approach with the potential to help change their mindsets on learning itself and raise their language awareness (Coyle, 2006). Moreover, CLIL teacher education can probably help promote their CPD, since ELT teachers can develop their competencies on integrated learning of content, cognition, communication, and culture through CLIL practices.

Language teacher education in Japan, compared to the EU, may be rather lacking in its attention to multilingual and multicultural perspectives, exclusively focusing on globalization and the English language (MEXT, 2014a). This seems to be due to sociolinguistic factors, as it is common in a large number of cities in Europe to always hear several languages spoken in the streets. The language and cultural awareness that ELT teachers in Japan can develop may naturally be different from language teachers in Europe. The awareness of CLIL may also be different between Japanese teachers and European teachers. The problem of the current ELT teacher education in Japan seems to be a lack of practical ideas focusing on developing the knowledge and skills of the English language (cf. MEXT, 2014b). There is thus a need for more interdisciplinary and intercultural viewpoints to develop the future educational approach, which should be more diverse and flexible in terms of learning and teaching. In such contexts, CLIL has some potential to help change ELT teachers' mindsets that currently insist on teaching standard American or British English which they have learned while studying English literature and linguistics in university education (Denman & Al-Mahrooqi, 2018; Sasajima, 2013). Generally speaking, ELT teachers are required to have intelligible pronunciation skills, appropriate grammatical knowledge, and sufficient vocabulary size to teach their students (Farell & Martin, 2009; Holliday, 2006), but CLIL pedagogy may help them think about what their students need to know through learning, communicating and understanding (de Graaff, Koopman, & Westhoff, 2007). Such integrated learning approaches in teacher education will encourage learners to develop their own competencies to cope with studying subjects and themes bilingually in English and Japanese and to improve their English proficiency practically.

2.2   CLIL: Definition and Implementation

CLIL may be difficult to define clearly, but it needs to be contextualized when considering its implementation in the Japanese context. Bearing this in mind, I propose the following definition:

> CLIL is a generic term to refer to integrated learning of content (knowledge, understanding, and skills related to subjects and courses) and language (bilingual: e.g., English and Japanese), focusing on cognition (thinking) and culture (intercultural awareness) based on Communicative Language Teaching. CLIL can/should be flexible in terms of language learning and use depending on its learning context. (Sasajima, 2014b)

Figure 12.1 illustrates how CLIL should be implemented in the current context and embodies the definition of CLIL in Japan on the basis of the

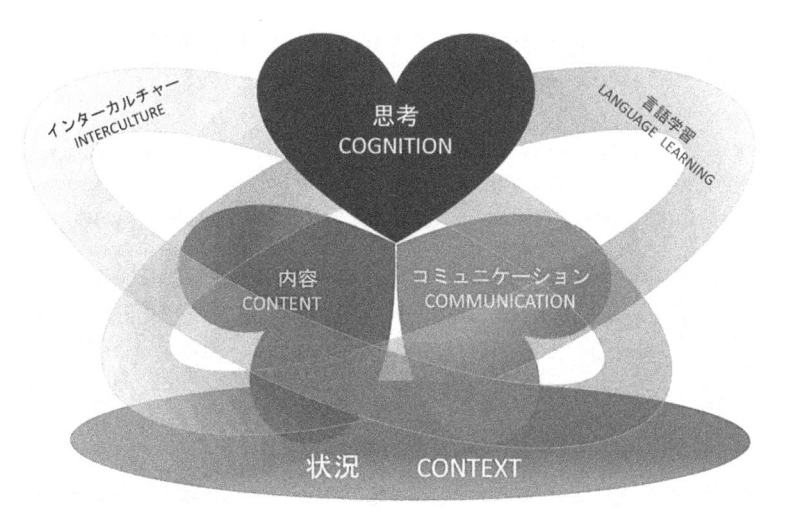

Fig. 12.1 Contextualized CLIL framework (Sasajima, 2017a)

4Cs framework (Coyle, 1999). The most important point is that we should consider *language learning*, which needs to be distinguished from *communication* because it is important for most Japanese students to have basic knowledge and skills of English, such as knowing grammar rules, understanding word meanings, and learning pronunciation skills. *Interculture*, instead of *culture*, also should be highlighted. In a context beyond Europe like Japan, *language learning* and *interculture* need to be taken into special consideration in CLIL pedagogy.

I first used a primitive version of this framework and started the CLIL implementation project with six ELT teachers in general English courses at a medical university in 2009. The project set two objectives: to design a contextualized CLIL curriculum and develop CLIL materials. Since then I have conducted both these activities as part of CLIL teacher education projects, in which teachers, whether they are language or subject teachers, discuss and deliver the curriculum in their contexts while developing a course syllabus, considering learning aims, content and language learning, teaching materials and assessment criteria. The first objective was the action-oriented teacher education for curriculum development because there had not been any CLIL models during the process of implementing CLIL at that time. In the first stage when we started teaching CLIL, one ELT teacher reflected on teaching and said that:

> This was the first time to teach a group of students using the CLIL approach, and I must say from the start I was nervous about it. When the course was first introduced, my thought was, 'What is CLIL? And how do I teach it?' After talking to some other teachers, they shared my concerns (especially the newest teachers). So, before preparing for my lessons, I did some online research to focus on the theory as well as the potential lesson structure. These hands-on CLIL teacher education activities were effective to understand what CLIL is and how to teach CLIL in their classrooms.

When implementing a CLIL curriculum, these hands-on practices, in which teachers are learning CLIL practices by teaching CLIL while sharing ideas with colleagues and studying themselves, can be very helpful for CLIL teacher education. In this project, the six ELT teachers, who happened to be all native speakers of English with no experience of CLIL teaching, taught health sciences and English under the guidance of the abovementioned framework. When using the framework, the context is much more relevant than whether the teachers are native or non-native speakers. However, it seems that a conceptual framework alone is not enough. The learning cycle of actual, collaborative and reflective practices (cf. Kolb, 1984) is necessary to activate CLIL in classrooms. After finishing the first-year course, the teachers gave the following reflective feedback in the lesson study meetings:

- *Students participated in CLIL. I really enjoyed teaching CLIL.*
- *CLIL had good interaction and enthusiasm.*
- *CLIL changed students' learning style.*
- *Activities are varied in CLIL class.*
- *I wish I would get lots of new ideas in teaching CLIL.*
- *It was hard to prepare the materials.*

In implementing CLIL, collaborative activities in which teachers share ideas with each other as in the case described above are the most important for CLIL teacher development. That is partly because CLIL aims to promote integrated learning and respect teachers' flexible teaching approaches and their students' learning needs.

2.3   CLIL Materials Development and Teacher Education

The second objective was to develop CLIL materials in the Japanese context. It is often said that CLIL resources should be authentic (cf. CLIL for Children, 2016) because content learning is one of the two learning objectives in CLIL. If the content is simplified for learners to improve English, then they will easily lose interest in what they want to know and think about. CLIL materials are strongly related to facts and realities, so authenticity is necessary for CLIL resources and materials. CLIL teachers need to develop competencies, such as knowledge, skills, abilities, and attributes, to find good resources and turn them into appropriate materials for their students (see McLagan, 1997). CLIL teacher education has to provide teachers with the opportunities to develop these competencies. In other words, CLIL materials development is essential for teacher development because CLIL methodology is still a new idea for language teachers as well as subject teachers. Many teachers and teacher educators do not know about the range of CLIL materials available for learners. In different contexts, they will have to cope with a variety of CLIL pedagogies, which include a wide range of subject topics, genres, and teaching resources. Developing CLIL materials could be more complex than expected because of their integrative nature.

Such complex characteristics of CLIL can hinder teachers from implementing CLIL in their classrooms. Although CLIL can provide learners with dual-focused activities, which include complex integrated learning, such as content, language, communication, cognition, and intercultural awareness, it is still rather hard for teachers to introduce CLIL in their classrooms. They usually wonder what to teach and how to teach CLIL. Some teachers need a coursebook or textbook to use in their classrooms, especially if they are beginners in CLIL teaching. In many cases, CLIL teachers tend to share resources with their colleagues or through their local CLIL networks. To meet these needs, we started a project to design a series of CLIL textbooks in 2012, because we thought creating a CLIL textbook collaboratively can be useful and helpful to develop our own CPD in terms of CLIL pedagogy.

There have been different types of CLIL textbooks published thus far in each context. It would take much time and effort to understand what kind of textbooks or materials are being used in CLIL classroom contexts in Europe and beyond. Without thinking about it deeply, some teachers tried to use a textbook which was used in international schools, bilingual schools, and International Baccalaureate (IB) schools. However, those textbooks were not always available or appropriate for each context, and neither could they be used in primary and secondary education due to the national curriculum. Teachers needed to have a CLIL textbook appropriate in their contexts. Also in many cases, CLIL was sometimes taught by subject teachers as one-off experiments, which means that CLIL was usually provided by ELT teachers. This type of CLIL may be called soft-CLIL or language-driven CLIL, but it actually is natural in the Japanese context, since such language-focused CLIL pedagogy matched the needs in the current curriculum which aims at integrated language learning in Japan. In other words, CLIL in Japan can/should be part of language learning which is integrated with content learning. For such teachers who want to teach CLIL in their classrooms, CLIL textbooks are necessary and the textbook writing project can support their CLIL teacher development.

We then thought that CLIL textbooks were necessary, so we cooperated with some publishing companies and compiled CLIL textbooks as follows: *CLIL Health Sciences* (2013), *CLIL Global Issues* (2014), *CLIL Seeing the World through Maps* (2015), *CLIL Human Biology* (2016), *CLIL Basic Science & Math* (2018), and *CLIL World Heritage* (2018) (see Fig. 12.2 and for more details see the publishers' website at http://www.sanshusha.co.jp/text/search_result/sgen/269/). In total, 20 teachers were involved in these publication projects. They all developed their CLIL pedagogical knowledge and skills through the textbook writing project.

Most of the textbooks were written by ELT teachers with the support of experts in each subject and topic. At the beginning, all the teachers lacked sufficient knowledge about the content (health sciences, global issues, the world through maps, human biology, basic science and math, and world heritage). However, they were able to build their knowledge in

Fig. 12.2 CLIL textbooks

many areas of content, language, and intercultural awareness while discussing and sharing ideas as well as referring to CLIL theory and resource books. Most of the authors attempted to use these textbooks in their own classrooms, so they developed good CLIL knowledge and skills in using them to make lesson plans and prepare for classroom activities. While discussing ideas in reading topics and tasks, some were particularly worried about their content knowledge and cognitive or thinking skills in English due to their insufficient spoken English skills. However, others argued that bilingual activities were natural when communicating with each other and such practices using English and Japanese bilingually were useful to develop their competencies for integrated learning. These practical discussions are part of teacher education, where teachers are aware that content and language in integrated learning should be intertwined with each other and other learning factors.

In terms of CLIL teacher education, there are a number of other advantages to add contributing to textbook writing. The most important point is that teachers realize CLIL textbooks are appropriate for students' learning background and teachers' teaching styles. Moreover, compared to ELT or CLIL textbooks published internationally for all contexts, these CLIL textbooks are compiled in Japanese local contexts by considering students' learning styles and cultures, which are related to their grammar knowledge, vocabulary size, and pronunciation problems. In the contextualized CLIL framework, language learning is an important principle for Japanese learners as well as teachers. If the contents of a textbook are obsolete, they cannot provide learners with authentic resources which motivate them to learn. When teachers have some know-how to make textbook materials, they can supplement them with hands-on materials depending on contexts. As such, materials development is one of the most important skills in implementing CLIL pedagogy in the Japanese context. If CLIL teachers find good resources and develop materials appropriate to their students, they can create a better learning environment for them, providing effective scaffoldings in their classroom activities.

3   CLIL Pedagogy and Lesson Study

Any good classrooms can be active and dynamic in that students enjoy learning autonomously while cooperating with each other with the support of teachers. Whether they are doing CLIL or not, students need to be interested in knowing something and motivated to use English. Teachers are all responsible for teaching well and supporting their students' learning. Active classroom activities are necessary for any good classroom, whether content-based or task-based approaches. Long (2009) suggests ten methodological principles of TBLT: (1) to use task, not text, as the unit of analysis, (2) to promote learning by doing, (3) to elaborate input, (4) to provide rich input, (5) to encourage inductive learning, (6) to focus on form, (7) to provide negative feedback, (8) to respect learner syllabuses, (9) to promote collaborative learning, and (10) to individualize instruction. They might be universal for any language learning activities or even CLIL. In terms of CLIL pedagogical knowledge and skills, CLIL teachers are required to have more diverse and flexible attitudes toward complex learning and teaching which could comprise a large number of teaching methods and techniques as well as learning styles and strategies.

In CLIL teacher education, teachers primarily need to develop their professional knowledge comprising seven categories of teacher knowledge (Shulman, 1987): content knowledge, general pedagogical knowledge, pedagogical content knowledge (PCK), curriculum knowledge, knowledge of educational contexts, knowledge of learners and their characteristics, and knowledge of educational goals. However, CLIL teacher knowledge can be considered to be more complex than this concept of teacher knowledge, which has been constructed in the tradition of the western education system. CLIL teachers in Japan, as in the contextualized CLIL framework mentioned above, should have more complex teacher knowledge, such as integrated learning knowledge and intercultural knowledge, which may be rooted in the Japanese context (cf. Sasajima, 2014a). Essentially the core knowledge of CLIL teachers is composed of PCK, which 'represents the blending of content and pedagogy into an understanding of how particular aspects of subject matter are organized, adapted, and represented for instruction' (Shulman, 1987, p. 8). In CLIL pedagogy, then, CLIL PCK, which is also the most important for CLIL teachers to develop, can comprise all the pedagogical competencies which are related to the contextualized CLIL framework (content, cognition, communication, language learning, and interculture). In CLIL teacher education, therefore, CLIL PCK will have to be developed as core professional teacher knowledge.

In order to do so, CLIL teachers and teacher trainees need to conduct teacher learning by doing or hands-on teacher practice while teaching students in the classroom and sharing ideas with colleagues. Lesson study (Fernandez & Yoshida, 2004), or *Jugyo Kenkyu* in Japanese, can be helpful and effective in this case. It is a Japanese traditional collaborative classroom research in which teachers observe a classroom, discuss the classroom activities, share ideas about teaching and learning, and reflect on them.

One of the cases is the collaborative CLIL lesson study project which aims to cultivate intercultural communicative competence (ICC) (Byram, 1997) through CLIL lesson study and to develop CLIL approaches in different contexts. Teachers teach CLIL in their classrooms, share CLIL lesson ideas and have reflective lesson study meetings. Another teacher learning activity is collaborative research meetings about CLIL practices. These meetings can cover a variety of CLIL topics: for example, lesson plans, methods, activities, teaching techniques, reading articles, workshops, and discussions. They can encourage CLIL colleagues to teach CLIL and develop their CLIL pedagogical knowledge and skills. The most useful point is that they can help build CLIL networks, which can work as communities of practice (Wenger, 1998).

CLIL methodology may comprise a mixture of different learning concepts and methods. CLIL therefore might be referred to as a patchwork pedagogy (Sasajima, 2017b), although it is a methodology as well. It means that CLIL is a flexible, dynamic and diverse framework. Although a wide range of features and principles of CLIL methodology has been described, the most widely accepted definition of CLIL is that it is a dual-focused educational approach to the integrated learning of content and language. The CLIL approach can have a variety of methods and techniques and both teachers and learners can create many interesting learning activities. They can enjoy learning themselves by utilizing several ways of learning, which can develop their general or critical thinking skills. When teachers and learners discuss problems or issues with others, they can cultivate their own ICC. When they are learning in such complex situations, they can be aware of *languaging* (Swain, 2006) or *translanguaging* (García, 2009). They can have good opportunities to develop their communication skills and have good knowledge of learning content. The role of a CLIL teacher should be to support such learners and design better CLIL learning contexts.

Regarding CLIL teacher education, teachers could develop better CLIL pedagogical knowledge and skills through collaborative CLIL lesson study. It also means that they need to develop appropriate CLIL teacher competencies to better understand CLIL pedagogy and teach CLIL well. European Parliament and the Council (2006, p. 3) define the eight key competences that 'each European citizen needs for personal fulfilment and development, employment, social inclusion and active citizenship' as follows: (1) communication in the mother tongue, (2) communication in foreign languages, (3) mathematical competence and basic competences in science and technology, (4) digital competence, (5) learning to learn, (6) social and civic competences, (7) sense of initiative and entrepreneurship, and (8) cultural awareness and expression. These competencies seem to share some common features with CLIL competencies, as CLIL has contributed to the cultivation of European citizens' competencies. As CLIL teachers in Japan need to develop bilingual communication and literacy skills and the awareness of intercultural communication, they need to be aware of developing CLIL pedagogical competencies through collaborative lesson study.

4   CLIL Teacher Development

In Japan or other areas beyond Europe, there are few if any examples of CLIL teacher qualifications at the present moment. Despite, there are CLIL teachers and teacher educators working at all educational levels, and CLIL is actually a very diverse phenomenon with different versions being adopted depending on diversified contexts. It is therefore important to take it into account, but it is not clear how different and diverse CLIL teachers' awareness and perceptions of CLIL pedagogy. The point is to know to what extent CLIL teachers in Japan think about the complex and complicated CLIL diversity. In order to investigate CLIL teachers' needs for teacher education, I conducted a questionnaire survey to 41 CLIL practitioners who taught CLIL to Japanese students at primary, secondary, and tertiary education in 2016. Most of them are also researchers and some are native or bilingual speakers of English. One of the questions was *What would CLIL be like to you? Please describe CLIL as in 'CLIL is like ....'* The answers were summarized and classified into six categories: Image, Language, Diversity, Integration, Flexibility, and Complexity. The summary results were very different as shown in Table 12.1. The results illustrate that CLIL still does not have any stable status as an educational approach in the Japanese context.

Table 12.1 CLIL is like …

Image	*almighty medicine, a treasure box, a trick art, Mt Everest, a dream with fun, high sky or deep ocean, an intermission of the play or a movie trailer, a ghost, Pegasus wings, rain showers, a beautiful mathematics formula*
Language	*a short-term study, a study abroad program, a practical situation to use English, facilitating English learning efficiently*
Diversity	*a chef enjoying eating and cooking, a Japanese pub, debating activities, an external hard drive, a Japanese food bowl, It's fun, a child's curiosity*
Flexibility	*very natural, holistic, an appropriate educational approach, soaking the earth, causing growth and changing worlds, scaffolding*
Integration	*CLT with some special skills and theoretical knowledge, a bicycle, a smartphone, a dual focus approach, developing language learning by integrating content, a bridge between language and knowledge*
Complexity	*a deep discussion topic, walking home up a steep hill*

This categorization suggests that CLIL has a variety of positive images, such as '*an appropriate educational approach*' and '*developing language learning by integrating content*,' but it may still be complex to understand and difficult to see what the 41 CLIL practitioners think CLIL is.

Based on the current situation in Japan, CLIL teacher development needs to be prioritized in order to design appropriate CLIL and develop effective CLIL pedagogy in each educational context. There is an urgent need to establish CLIL standards and teacher development programs which are contextualized for the needs for the learners who are motivated to understand CLIL and participate in CLIL classrooms. CLIL can be referred to as a European approach to bilingual education in Europe (Nikula, 2016), which means in the Japanese context that CLIL can encourage students to grow awareness of the new orientations to bilingual education. Students should be motivated but not forced to learn in the CLIL classroom, and they should be helped to understand the significance of CLIL pedagogy in bilingual education. As I have already argued, CLIL has been or should be taught as part of the English curriculum in Japan. In the English curriculum, which has been actually taught by ELT teachers primarily but by non-ELT teachers in some cases, especially at university or private school, CLIL pedagogies can be easily introduced into classrooms in primary and secondary education. In pre-primary and tertiary education, CLIL pedagogies are becoming more popular among ELT teachers. In a way, CLIL actually has been taught in part of the English curriculum in Japan, so CLIL teacher development should be provided to ELT teachers or teacher trainees, as well as other subject teachers who are interested in CLIL.

CLIL teacher education programs or courses are provided by some universities and language schools in Europe and Australia or by some CLIL teacher educators whose backgrounds seem to be bilingual education or applied linguistics and who have experience of CLIL teaching. Such program and course contents include CLIL theory, methodology, curriculum development, materials development, applied linguistics, and TESOL activities. However, the program or course contents do not always consider local educational needs and classroom language use practices. For example, Oxford TEFL Teacher Training (http://www.oxfordtefl.com) provides a CLIL teacher education course, which says that CLIL is a growing part of the ELT industry and consists of three modules: (1) CLIL and language learning; (2) resources, tasks, and materials; and (3) planning for CLIL. This course is designed for teachers who want to widen their CLIL pedagogical knowledge and skills, but it does not cover any content knowledge and English language knowledge and skills. Japanese ELT teachers' needs may be different from the needs catered for on this course.

In any situation where teachers and teacher trainees start to teach CLIL or develop their CLIL pedagogies in Japan, they need to develop their practical knowledge and skills to teach CLIL or practical ideas for CLIL classrooms in their own contexts. In addition, they need to improve their English proficiency in CLIL disciplinary areas. Furthermore, they wish to know what to teach in their CLIL classrooms and how to teach some specific knowledge and skills as well as English while using English and Japanese in the classroom. Considering CLIL teachers and teacher trainees in Japan, the following contextualized CLIL teacher education (TE) model (see Table 12.2) is proposed to better meet the needs for CLIL teachers' pedagogical development. The program has three stages: (1) Initial teacher education (ITE), (2) continuing professional development (CPD), and (3) content knowledge development (CKD). Each stage has several program contents and assessment criteria. ITE and CPD have a

Table 12.2 Contextualized CLIL teacher education (TE) model

Stage	Certificate	Program contents	Assessment criteria
ITE	Novice	CLIL methodology (theory and framework, etc.)CLIL lesson study (teaching practices, etc.)CLIL classroom managementCLIL activitiesCLIL classroom language use (translanguaging, etc.)ELT vs. CLIL	CLIL teachers can understand basic CLIL pedagogy and apply some CLIL methods in their classrooms.
CPD	Expert	CLIL classroom researchCLIL lesson studyCLIL materials developmentCLIL curriculum developmentCLIL cognitive developmentCLIL assessment	CLIL teachers can develop CLIL pedagogy and arrange CLIL methods in their classrooms.
CKD	N/A	Developing content knowledge and skills in EnglishFurther studies on content knowledge in English	N/A

certificate system and CKD, which focuses on developing content knowledge and skills, is an ad-hoc program for the purpose of teaching specific subject areas.

These three stages of the CLIL TE model all include practical action-oriented workshops and use a peer feedback assessment system

The definition of what a CLIL teacher is might be rather ambiguous in the Japanese context, compared to Europe. It is therefore necessary to set out the minimal requirements for CLIL teachers which are expected to be achieved in the abovementioned CLIL teacher education program in Japan. The item requirements for CLIL teachers comprise English proficiency, translanguaging, language learning, content knowledge, material development, cognition, ICC, assessment, creativity, and research, as shown in Table 12.3. The table just shows reference points for CLIL teachers without providing detailed descriptions of each criterion at this stage. The reference points are set for CLIL teachers' self-assessment on their own pedagogical competencies.

Table 12.3 Minimal requirements for CLIL teachers

Item requirement	Novice	Expert
English proficiency	CEFR B1	CEFR B2 or above
Translanguaging	Appropriate English use	Professional bilingual use
Language learning	Appropriate linguistic knowledge	Applied linguistic knowledge
Content knowledge	General & pedagogic	Professional & pedagogic
Materials development	Use of authentic materials	Use of hands-on materials
Cognition	Metacognitive awareness	Metacognitive development
ICC	Intercultural awareness	Intercultural development
Assessment	Assessment of/for learning	Assessment of/for/through learning
Creativity	Critical thinking	Critical and creative thinking
Research	Reflective teacher	Teacher research

There is little difference between novice and expert CLIL teachers at this preliminary version. However, I use the terms novice and expert depending on whether they have experiences of teaching CLIL lessons or not since in terms of metacognitive awareness and development, for example, novice CLIL practitioners become just aware of metacognitive skills and expert CLIL practitioners have developed them to some extent. While establishing these reference points for CLIL teachers may be challenging, they can be set as the first step in improving the status of CLIL teachers in Japan. Especially as there are no CLIL teacher education systems in Japan at the moment, the idea of this CLIL TE model will work as a pilot for future CLIL TE.

5 CLIL Teacher Networks

In Japan, the popularity of CLIL has been increasing in the past ten years and there are a variety of CLIL approaches from English conversation schools to life-long learning courses in Japan. It is therefore urgent to focus on teacher development in CLIL pedagogy. The diverse and flexible characteristics of CLIL and the patchwork methodology of CLIL can be beneficial, but any English Medium Instruction (EMI) or Content-based Instruction (CBI) may be liable to be called CLIL generically. Although the EU has the educational platform to implement CLIL and it has its own educational goal-setting for CLIL, Japan does not have any such platforms. To solve such diversified situations, I decided to establish CLIL teacher networks with other CLIL colleagues in 2015. At that time there were already several active research groups, and the idea was to bring these together. Within a year, a small CLIL research group started, having several meetings and preparing the ground to an association. J-CLIL was founded in 2017 and had some 300 members in 2018.

CLIL teachers and researchers need to share ideas and create practical teacher networks for better CLIL pedagogy, and J-CLIL fulfills this need for CLIL practitioners in Japan. In terms of providing CLIL teacher education, J-CLIL will be a key platform to arrange and coordinate programs for CLIL teachers. As of 2018, J-CLIL has the headquarters (in Tokyo) and two chapters (in Osaka and Sendai). The headquarters host several events annually: regular research meetings and one annual conference, in which the members can share ideas at lectures, presentations, and workshops. Moreover, ad-hoc seminars and special interest group (SIG) meetings are held. The two chapters also have their own local conferences and meetings to share ideas about CLIL pedagogy between members. In sessions, most topics are related to CLIL classroom ideas and practices (see the previous events at the J-CLIL website: https://www.j-clil.com/news, which can show the presentation or workshop reports including the slides that were used there). In addition, the online newsletters are published a couple of times a year and the online Journal of J-CLIL is published annually. The activities of J-CLIL aim to support teachers and researchers who are interested in CLIL and provide them with practical CLIL teacher education programs. J-CLIL is very active in Japan now and is going to accumulate the experiences and develop better CLIL pedagogies.

As one of the founders, I have been involved in the activities of J-CLIL, which have promoted CLIL pedagogy and research including teacher education for the past several years. Since I started to implement CLIL in my educational context, I have always been concerned about how to provide CLIL TE for teachers as well as teacher trainees. This has led to the development of the provisional program's design of CLIL TE based on the contextualized CLIL framework, which includes CLIL materials development, CLIL pedagogy, and CLIL teacher development. Table 12.4 shows the outline of the program, which is based on my previous project

Table 12.4 Program design of CLIL TE

Program descriptions	The programs provide ELT teachers or subject teachers with CLIL pedagogies and practices in the Japanese context, including primary, secondary and tertiary. The programs aim to develop and improve their CLIL professional (novice and expert) knowledge and skills to be able to teach CLIL in bilingual format (English and Japanese). The programs should be based on the minimal requirements for CLIL teachers and the CLIL teacher education programs (ITE, CPD and CKD). The program participants will earn the certificate as CLIL novice or expert teacher authorized by J-CLIL (except for CKD). In addition, there are some On-site programs in Europe on a temporal basis.
4 CLIL TE programs	ITE, CPD, CKD, and On-site CLIL
CLIL-ITE course(30 h in total)	CLIL methodology (theory and framework, etc.) (5 h)CLIL lesson study (teaching practices, etc.) (7 h)CLIL classroom management (5 h)CLIL activities (5 h)CLIL classroom language use (translanguaging, etc.) (5 h)ELT vs. CLIL (3 h)

Participants have some lectures and workshops, and after understanding CLIL methodology, they will have the opportunities to teach and observe CLIL lessons. During CLIL teaching practices, they can learn CLIL management, activities, and language use. Finally, they will discuss differences between ELT and CLIL.

CLIL-CPD(40 h in total)	CLIL classroom research (15 h)CLIL lesson study (5 h)CLIL materials development (5 h)CLIL curriculum development (5 h)CLIL cognitive development (5 h)CLIL assessment (5 h)

Participants do not have any lectures but do research on CLIL with the support of tutors. Research focuses on CLIL practices, materials, curriculum, cognitions and assessment in integrated learning. Participants teach research lessons and observe each other, and have reflective discussion. They do teacher research.

CLIL-CKD(20 h in total)	Developing content knowledge and skills in English (10 h)Further studies on content knowledge in English (10 h)

This program helps participants develop content knowledge and skills, for which choose specific topics and study them with the support of tutors. They have lectures, read books, and watch videos in English. They finally discuss how they teach CLIL.

On-site CLIL (in Europe for 1 week)

Participants visit schools in Europe and experience CLIL classrooms for one week: classroom observation, CLIL on Japan, discussion and other collaborative activities with CLIL teachers in Europe.

called *Practical Language (English) Teacher Education Curriculum Development Based on Language for Specific Purposes (LSP)* (Sasajima, 2012).

J-CLIL can help support CLIL teacher networks not just in Japan but also between Japan and other countries. The teacher education programs can also be provided outside Japan. J-CLIL includes CLIL in other languages, especially in Japanese, Chinese and Korean. In the past two years, J-CLIL has contributed to building CLIL teacher networks in order to develop better CLIL pedagogy and promote the CLIL TE system. We have thus far realized that CLIL has the potential to change the current language learning situation in Japan, which is divided between Japanese as a national language and English as the foreign language. Japan has not considered other foreign languages or multilingual situations. However, the CLIL concept comprises plurilingualism and pluriculturalism in Europe (Council of Europe, 2001), so it is necessary that CLIL in Japan should consider languages other than English including Japanese. In this sense, CLIL teacher networks can add plurilingual and pluricultural dimensions to CLIL implementation and teacher education.

6   Conclusion

This chapter has discussed CLIL TE in the Japanese context. Its focus has been on pedagogy, as distinct from the methodology. Pedagogy has a variety of definitions. Learning and Teaching Scotland (2005, p. 9) defines that: 'Pedagogy is about learning, teaching and development influenced by the cultural, social and political values we have for children…in Scotland, and underpinned by a strong theoretical and practical base.' On the other hand, the methodology can be seen as the systematic methods or principles of teaching and learning. Compared to methodology, pedagogy can be more flexible and diverse. Developing CLIL pedagogy and providing teacher education are therefore the key aims of the current activities of J-CLIL.

In Japan, CLIL will not likely to be included in the national curriculum as in some EU countries. In addition, EMI can be used as a synonym of CLIL, focusing on ELT closely related to globalization in Japan as well as other Asian countries. In contrast to EMI, CLIL is aimed at helping learners improve English by focusing on practical English use combined with content knowledge and skills. However, there is still some confusion about what CLIL is and how it should be implemented in Japan. In this chapter, the contextualized CLIL framework is proposed as illustrated in Fig. 12.1. Based on this CLIL framework, the action-oriented CLIL TE and CLIL materials development were carried out, and it described how teachers could develop their CLIL pedagogy or CLIL PCK through these activities. In CLIL teacher education, it is important for teachers to exploit and cultivate CLIL competencies through a collaborative and reflective lesson study among themselves. As there are concerns about the disparity and diversity of CLIL concepts in Japan, it is necessary to provide CLIL TE programs in which CLIL teachers can share ideas and develop their CLIL pedagogical competencies. J-CLIL seeks to support the CLIL teacher networks and plans to offer further CLIL TE programs in the future.

CLIL pedagogy and teacher education have always been significant in CLIL implementation in any contexts. However, we should respect the characteristics of CLIL and should not just follow some standards or curricula that have been established by some CLIL experts or leading teacher educators that have experienced teaching in CLIL in their own contexts. Each CLIL context is unique even in Europe; For example, CLIL in Spain, in France, in the Netherlands, and in Finland are all different. Not only that, but each CLIL teacher in each context may teach their own version of CLIL. Diversity and flexibility can be important characteristics of CLIL and add its attraction as an approach to learning and teaching. However, CLIL teachers always need to be aware of the core pedagogical elements of CLIL and seek opportunities to have action-oriented CLIL TE. Moreover, they should develop their own professional knowledge and skills for future CLIL pedagogy in global contexts. Therefore, CLIL teacher networks, such as J-CLIL, will continue to play a significant role.

References

Ainley, J., & Carstens, R. (2018). *Teaching and Learning International Survey (TALIS) 2018 Conceptual Framework*. OECD Education Working Papers No. 187. Paris: OECD Publishing.

Byram, M. (1997). *Teaching and Assessing Intercultural Communicative Competence*. Clevedon: Multilingual Matters.

CLIL for Children. (2016). *Guidelines on How to Develop CLIL Materials and Lesson Plans in Primary Schools*. Retrieved from http://www.clil4children.eu/wp-content/uploads/2017/02/Guidelines-CLIL-materials_1A5_rel01.pdf

Council of Europe. (2001). *Common European Framework of Reference for Languages: Learning, Teaching, Assessment*. Cambridge, UK: Press Syndicate of the University of Cambridge.

Coyle, D. (1999). Theory and planning for effective classrooms: Supporting students in Content and Language Integrated Learning contexts. In J. Masih (Ed.), *Learning through a Foreign Language*. London: CILT. *Key Data on Teaching Languages at Schools in Europe*. (2008). Brussels: Eurydice Network.

Coyle, D. (2006). Content and language integrated learning: Motivating learners and teachers. *Scottish Languages Review, 13*, 1–18.

Coyle, D., Hood, P., & Marsh, D. (2010). *CLIL: Content and Language Integrated Learning*. Cambridge, UK: Cambridge University Press.

de Graaff, R., Koopman, G. J., & Westhoff, G. (2007). Identifying effective L2 pedagogy in content and language integrated learning (CLIL). *Vienna English Working Papers, 16*(3), 12–19.

Denman, C., & Al-Mahrooqi, R. (2018). *Handbook of Research on Curriculum Reform Initiatives in English Education*. Hershey: IGI Global.

European Parliament & Council. (2006). Annex: Key competences for lifelong learning—A European reference framework. *Official Journal of the European Union, L394*, 13–18.

Eurydice. (2006). *Content and Language Integrated Learning (CLIL) at School in Europe*. Retrieved from http://www.indire.it/lucabas/lkmw_file/eurydice/CLIL_EN.pdf

Farell, T. S. C., & Martin, S. (2009). To teach standard English or world Englishes? A balanced approach to instruction. *English Teaching Forum, 47*(2), 1–5.

Fernandez, C., & Yoshida, M. (2004). *Lesson Study: A Japanese Approach to Improving Mathematics Teaching and Learning*. Mahwah, NJ: Lawrence Erlbaum Associates.

García, O. (2009). *Bilingual Education in the 21st Century: A Global Perspective*. Malden, MA and Oxford: Blackwell and Wiley.

Holliday, A. (2006). Native-speakerism. *ELT Journal, 60*(4), 385–387.

Jackson, P. W. (1968). *Life in Classrooms*. New York: Holt, Rinehart & Winston.

Kolb, D. A. (1984). *Experiential Learning: Experience as the Source of Learning and Development*. Upper Saddle River, NJ: Prentice-Hall.

Learning & Teaching Scotland. (2005). *Let's Talk about Pedagogy: Towards a Shared Understanding for Early Years Education in Scotland*. Dundee: Learning and Teaching Scotland.

Lightbown, P. M. (2014). *Focus on Content-based Language Teaching*. Oxford: Oxford University Press.

Long, M. H. (2009). Methodological principles for language teaching. In M. H. Long & C. J. Doughty (Eds.), *The Handbook of Language Teaching* (pp. 373–394). Oxford: Wiley-Blackwell.

Lyster, R. (2007). *Learning and Teaching Languages Through Content: A Counterbalanced Approach*. Philadelphia: John Benjamins.

Marsh, D. (2002). *CLIL/EMILE—The European Dimension: Actions, Trends and Foresight Potential*. Jyväskylä: University of Jyväskylä.

McLagan, P. A. (1997). Competencies: The next generation. *Training & Development, 51*(5), 40–48.

MEXT. (2008). Section 9 foreign languages in the course of study. Retrieved from http://www.mext.go.jp/component/a_menu/education/micro_detail/__ icsFiles/afieldfile/2011/04/11/1298356_10.pdf

MEXT. (2014a). *English Education Reform Plan Corresponding to Globalization*. Retrieved from http://www.mext.go.jp/en/news/topics/detail/__icsFiles/ afieldfile/2014/01/23/1343591_1.pdf

MEXT. (2014b). *Eigo Kyoiku noarikatanikansuru Yushikisha Kaigi*. Retrieved from http://www.mext.go.jp/b_menu/shingi/chousa/shotou/102/index.htm

Nikula, T. (2016). CLIL: A European approach to bilingual education. In N. Van Deusen-Scholl & S. May (Eds.), *Second and Foreign Language Education. Encyclopedia of Language and Education* (3rd ed.). Cham: Springer.

Sasajima, S. (2011). *CLIL: Atarashii Hassoo no Jugyo (CLIL: A New Perspective on the Classroom)*. Tokyo: Sanshusha.

Sasajima, S. (2012). *Practical Language (English) Teacher Education Curriculum Development Based on LSP*. Report of Current Research Supported by Grant-in-Aid for Scientific Research in 2008–2011 (No. 20520515). Retrieved from http://lspteachereducation.blogspot.com

Sasajima, S. (2013). How CLIL can impact on EFL teachers' mindsets about teaching and learning: An exploratory study on teacher cognition. *International CLIL Research Journal, 2*(1), 56–66.

Sasajima, S. (2014a). *An Exploratory Study of Japanese EFL Teachers' Kokoro— Language Teacher Cognition at Secondary School in Japan*. Saarbrucken, Germany: Lambert Academic Publishing.

Sasajima, S. (2014b). *CLIL Theory and Practice* [Presentation Slides]. FD Seminar at Meio University.

Sasajima, S. (2017a). *CLIL can Vary in Each Teacher and Learner* [Presentation Slides]. Symposium Individual Factors in CLIL Teachers and Learners, The 18th World Congress of Applied Linguistics in Rio de Janeiro.

Sasajima, S. (2017b). *CLIL Theory and Practices* [Presentation Slides]. CLIL Workshop at Tohoku University.

Shulman, L. (1987). Knowledge and teaching: Foundations of new reform. *Harvard Educational Review, 57*(1), 1–22.

Swain, M. (2006). Languaging, agency and collaboration in advanced second language learning. In H. Byrnes (Ed.), *Advanced Language Learning: The Contribution of Halliday and Vygotsky* (pp. 95–108). London, UK: Continuum.

Wenger, E. (1998). *Communities of Practice: Learning, Meaning, and Identity.* Cambridge: Cambridge University Press.

13

CLIL Teacher Education in Spain

Magdalena Custodio Espinar

1 European and Spanish Educational Context for CLIL

The European Union (EU) has made a strong commitment to the development of educational and social policies that promote the teaching and learning of second and third languages at schools. Since the publication of the White Paper on Education and Training titled *Teaching and Learning: Towards the Learning Society* by the European Commission in 1995, a clear European aspiration has been "for everyone, irrespective of training and education routes chosen, to be able to acquire and keep up their ability to communicate in at least two community languages in addition to their mother tongue" (Commission of the European Communities, 1995, p. 47). This has led to the widespread adoption of the teaching of two foreign languages in the curriculum for primary and/ or general secondary education.

But how are these languages taught? At the beginning of the 1990s, abundant research was conducted in Europe in order to find new

M. Custodio Espinar (✉)
Faculty of Education, Universidad Pontificia Comillas, Madrid, Spain

© The Author(s) 2019
K. Tsuchiya, M. D. Pérez Murillo (eds.), *Content and Language Integrated Learning in Spanish and Japanese Contexts*, https://doi.org/10.1007/978-3-030-27443-6_13

approaches and methods to teach and learn foreign languages likely to meet the challenges of these EU policies. The institution responsible for promoting quality language education in Europe, called European Centre for Modern Languages[1] (ECML), organized a programme of international projects on language education. In its Action Plan 2004–2006 Promoting Language Learning and Linguistic Diversity, it was clearly stated that "Content and Language Integrated Learning (CLIL), in which pupils learn a subject through the medium of a foreign language, has a major contribution to make to the Union's language learning goals" (Commission of the European Communities, 2003, p. 8). Since then, there have been many initiatives, programmes and European projects that have been designed for the promotion and dissemination of models of language teaching and, particularly, of CLIL. An early initiative was the creation of the Common European Framework of Reference for Languages: Learning, Teaching, Assessment (CEFR), an instrument in which levels of language proficiency are defined to check progress and measure the level of students' proficiency in a foreign language. In 2006, Eurydice published a survey which provided the first overview of CLIL at School in Europe (Eurydice, 2006). In order to disseminate good practices in CLIL in different European countries, the Windows on CLIL project included the design of the CLIL Matrix to guarantee CLIL quality teaching and learning. The PROCLIL TEAM (2006–2009) and the CLIL Cascade Network (CCN) drew on the knowledge and experience gained over the years of the application and research on CLIL in different European countries and universities. Other actions aimed at the promotion of CLIL and the development of courses for the initial training of language and content teachers through the theoretical and practical update on CLIL and the creation of resources for teachers and students. For example, the TIE-CLIL 1998–2014 project (Translanguage in Europe—Content and Language Integrated Learning) aimed to promote plurilingualism through the introduction of CLIL in five different EU languages (English, French, German, Italian and Spanish). Another

---

[1] Links to this and other institutions, regulations, programmes and projects mentioned in this chapter have been listed in the appendix in alphabetical order.

example is the Clil4U project, focused on producing materials and resources to support the implementation of CLIL in primary schools and vocational colleges. As a result of these and many other actions, CLIL provision has been widespread throughout the European education system (European Commission/EACEA/Eurydice, 2017).

However, as pointed out in the Action Plan 2004–2006, "it is the authorities in Member States who bear the primary responsibility for implementing the new push for language learning in the light of local circumstances and policies, within overall European objectives" (Commission of the European Communities, 2003, p. 5). Hence, in the last 15 years, all the Autonomous Communities of Spain have regulated some kind of bilingual education based on CLIL at primary, secondary and, recently, infant education (three to six years of age). This has been possible because, in Spain, there is a decentralized education system. Education policy is devolved to each Autonomous Community on the basis of national legislation, which sets guidelines for the whole country. According to Frigols, in Megías Rosa (2012), this situation has enabled Spain to be a pioneer in CLIL, as its decentralized nature has allowed it to cover the entire spectrum of programmes developed in Europe (Megías Rosa, 2012). As Lasagabaster and Ruiz de Zarobe (2010) point out, Spain can thus be a context to inspire other countries wanting to foster foreign language learning through CLIL.

In spite of these differences due to the strongly regionalized implementation, as documented by Lasagabaster and Ruiz de Zarobe (2010), there are also common factors among these programmes (Ministerio de Educación Cultura y Deporte [MECD], 2013). The following common features can be highlighted:

- Their main goal is the development of communicative competence in a holistic way.
- The linguistic policy that underlines all these bilingual programmes is linked to the EU 2020 Strategy, which includes policies for the development of multilingual education promoted by the EU institutions.
- Specific regulations for the implementation of the bilingual programmes have been introduced. These cover foreign language learning,

the integrated treatment of languages and the possibility of teaching subjects in foreign languages without changing the official curricula.
– CLIL is identified as a key strategy for teaching non-language curricular contents in a foreign language. (MECD, 2013)

However, the language education context in Spain is not restricted only to a Spanish/English bilingual programme since some of the Autonomous Communities have two official languages. Thus, there is a wide and varied offer of languages learnt at school depending on the Community (Table 13.1)

In this complex educational context, Spain has become one of the leaders in Europe in the development of bilingual and multilingual education policies based on CLIL (Coyle, Hood, & Marsh, 2010, p. xxx;

Table 13.1 Languages of instruction in education in Spain

Status	Languages of instruction	Levels
State official language + Foreign language	Spanish + English, French, German, Italian, Portuguese	Primary (6–12) Secondary (12–16) Bachillerato (16–18)
State official language + Official language of the Autonomous Community	Spanish + Basque, Catalan, Galician, Occitan, Valencian	Primary (6–12) Secondary (12–16) Bachillerato (16–18)
State official language + Official language of the Autonomous Community + Foreign language	Spanish + Basque + English/French Spanish + Catalan + English/French Spanish + Galician + English/French/ Italian/Portuguese Spanish + Valencian + English/ French/Italian/Portuguese Spanish + Catalan + Portuguese	Primary (6–12) Secondary (12–16) Bachillerato (16–18) Secondary (12–16) Bachillerato (16–18)

Taken from Key Data on Teaching Languages at School in Europe—2017 Edition. Eurydice Report (European Commission/EACEA/Eurydice, 2017, p. 161)

Llinares & Dafouz, 2010). But how are teachers trained to face the challenge of CLIL? What is necessary for CLIL to be effective? Frigols, in Megías Rosa (2012), explains that it is necessary to train teachers and invest in teacher training because if this investment is not made, CLIL programmes will end up using the same pedagogy as before, but with the only change being that content is taught in a different language. This author states that in the long run, this produces just the opposite result of what was intended (cf. Megías Rosa, 2012, p. 5). It underestimates the fact that teaching in a foreign language is not the same as teaching in a mother tongue (Dafouz, 2015).

2 Pre-service CLIL Teacher Education

The Bologna Process is an intergovernmental cooperation of 48 European countries in the field of higher education. Spain is a member state of the Bologna Process and the European Higher Education Area, initiated with the Bologna Declaration 1999 (MECD, 2003). This process aims to introduce a more comparable, compatible and coherent system for European higher education. Among other repercussions, it has brought the three-cycle degree structure (bachelor/master/doctorate) and the introduction of a shared system of credits known as European Credit Transfer and Accumulation System (ECTS) into the European Higher Education Area.

According to the international study promoted by the Organization for Economic Cooperation and Development (OECD) called TALIS (OECD, 2014), there has been a qualitative and quantitative increase in initial training required by teachers after the Bologna Process (OECD, 2014). An example of this is the reform that initial education of primary and secondary teachers has undergone in Spain. Below is a summary of the new teacher education programmes introduced after the Bologna Process (MECD, 2003):

– Primary teachers study a degree in primary education (4 years/240 ECTS) and have teaching practice at schools every year (50 ECTS, including the practicum and the dissertation). There is the possibility to study *menciones*[2] (mentions), a type of specialization with a very low ECTS value (30–60 ECTS). One of these mentions can be in a foreign language. In addition, it is compulsory to obtain a B1 level in a foreign language to complete the degree (B2 for the mention in a foreign language). As pointed out by García Jiménez and Lorente García (2014), a generalist perspective has been chosen in this academic programme, with the mentions substituting the old elective subjects (*asignaturas optativas*) and relegating the specialization for postgraduate studies.

– Secondary teachers study a degree in specific content areas (4 years) after which they have to complete a master's degree in Teaching in Secondary Schools (60 ECTS; regulated by law), which involves a practicum of 16 ECTS (including the master's dissertation), an average of 360 hours of internship at schools, depending on the university, which represents 20% of the total of the master's degree. (MECD, 2013)

In spite of these improvements in initial teacher training in Spain, there is still a mismatch between teachers' qualifications and the demands of bilingual programmes because this system based on "mentions" has meant a significant reduction of the training a teacher receives to teach a foreign language. 30–60 ECTS is insufficient to meet the needs of bilingual schools (Jover, Fleta, & González, 2016). At primary level, Fernández Cézar, Aguirre Pérez, and Harris (2013) explain that future teachers in bilingual schools will find similar difficulties because the teacher training programmes offered by the faculties of education are not being designed to meet the demands of this kind of teaching. They point out that the

---

[2] The mentions were offered by universities in consonance with the Royal Decree 1594/2011, of November 4, which establishes the teaching specialties of infant and primary teachers. They are:

– Educación Infantil (Infant Education).
– Educación Primaria (Primary Education).
– Lengua extranjera: Inglés (Foreign Language: English).
– Lengua extranjera: Francés (Foreign Language: French).
– Lengua extranjera: Alemán (Foreign Language: German).
– Educación Física (Physical Education).
– Música (Music).
– Pedagogía Terapéutica (Therapeutic Pedagogy).
– Audición y Lenguaje (Hearing and Speech).

new academic programme does not provide all the graduates with the necessary tools to face challenges in bilingual education contexts. Actually, only students who study a mention in a foreign language, usually English, are trained for this (although they just have 30–60 ECTS), which makes it necessary to develop complementary training programmes for students of the other mentions to ensure that all trainee teachers will be able to teach at bilingual schools. Fernández Cézar et al. (2013) report having implemented these complementary courses at their faculty.

The increasing demand for teachers in bilingual education programmes has led to the emergence of masters in bilingual education and CLIL, fostering a model of palliative in-service training for CLIL. These programmes seem to be leading the current pedagogical change, which is necessary to develop bilingual education in Spain. In sum, there are many critical voices from universities, calling for a review of the academic programmes and a strategic plan for the higher education institutions themselves (Fernández Cézar et al., 2013; Jover et al., 2016).

This process of revising and renewing provision can be supported by the experience pre-service teachers gain during the practicum at bilingual schools implementing CLIL. These experiences and the relationships they build over a year during the practicum can provide feedback on the changes and demands generated in the CLIL classroom. If undergraduates are involved in research, this feedback could serve to inform the design of more realistic academic programmes, which are more likely to meet the needs of bilingual education. Besides, this will give them opportunities to explore contemporary issues related to bilingual education and CLIL (European Commission, 2017). Additionally, future teachers will be trained in research skills, which will help to overcome this important gap in initial teacher training (Perines, 2018).

Delicado and Pavón (2016) point out that bilingual teacher training initiatives at higher education should focus not only on linguistic skills but also on methodological competence of future CLIL teachers. They have demonstrated that a collaborative relationship between university professors and experienced teachers of bilingual schools benefits the training of future teachers for this type of education. Fernández and Johnson (2016) report another promising strategy to improve infant and primary education degrees by designing an academic programme based on current teaching profiles required at bilingual schools. Buckingham, Custodio Espinar, and López Hernández (2018) describe an experience of collaborative teaching in the context of a one-semester course on CLIL taught to fourth-year teacher trainees. This course aims to reduce the gap between theory and practice, to improve reflective practice in the classroom and to further develop teachers' pedagogical content knowledge (Murphy & Martin, 2015).

As Fernández Díaz (2017) explains, the increasing demand for teachers to work in the wide network of bilingual schools in the Community of Madrid should be accompanied by the reinforcement of these programmes. They should aim to develop in trainee teachers both the knowledge of the foreign language and the CLIL methodology necessary to effectively teach their subjects in a foreign language in bilingual schools.

3   In-service Teacher Training for CLIL

To become part of the bilingual education programmes implemented throughout Spain, each Autonomous Community has established specific requirements for teachers to teach curricular contents in a foreign language. In general, teacher training for CLIL is not mandatory to teach in a bilingual programme. Only a few Autonomous Communities require mandatory initial training for CLIL. Thus, training to teach through CLIL is voluntary in the majority of the Autonomous Communities in Spain, and language proficiency is the sole selection criterion (B2 or C1 level in CEFR depending on the Community). In many cases, if the level of proficiency can be accredited by means of official certificates, it guarantees direct access to the programme. This produces the unwanted effect that teachers relate their competence in CLIL with their own level of English and curricular content knowledge rather than to their actual knowledge of CLIL (Banegas, 2012).

As a result of this regulatory situation, it is possible to find, working together in bilingual schools, teachers with a high linguistic and methodological training for CLIL and teachers who lack formal training on bilingual education methodologies (Herrero Rámila, 2015; Pena Díaz and Porto Requejo, 2008). According to Herrero Rámila (2015), in the Community of Madrid, the teachers on the bilingual programme find that colleagues lack training and consider it highly advisable to adequately train a greater number of professionals since the current number of CLIL qualified teachers is insufficient to cover all the available positions.

Salaberri Ramiro (2010) points out the training needs of the different profiles of teachers involved in the teaching of CLIL in Spain:

- Language teachers need training both in their levels of linguistic competence and in the learning approaches they promote in the classroom, so that they ensure a real communicative context.
- Content teachers need training in their levels of linguistic competence but also training on how to use the foreign language as a vehicle for learning the content they teach through it. These teachers are often able to observe and reflect on their own CLIL teaching practice, even to describe it, but lack metalinguistic concepts to do so (Martín del Pozo, 2011). Besides, as Rubio Mostacero (2009) has shown, these teachers lack information about CLIL methodology and often do not have the economic and material resources and adequate training to use the foreign language effectively in classroom instruction.
- Teachers of Spanish language need training to develop a methodology which is compatible with the principles for foreign language and content teachers described above and to ensure that the curriculum is coordinated both in the objectives and in the contents. (adapted from Salaberri Ramiro, 2010, pp. 151–152)

Salaberri Ramiro also points out that all teachers need training in the linguistic and cultural repercussions involved in the learning of content in a foreign language and the development of communicative learning strategies (2010). That is, they should be trained to use flexible and student-centred pedagogies, including the use of the CEFR, as a means to assess content and language in an integrated manner.[3]

---

[3] In CLIL content is assessed with reference to an official curriculum, but there is no language curriculum in CLIL. This situation makes it necessary to train teachers to use scales such as the CEFR to be able to assess the progression of the language learnt in the CLIL lessons because the language should not be an invisible component of CLIL (Custodio Espinar, 2017).

Calle Casado (2015) refers to two types of courses. On the one hand, training courses for language teachers on how to integrate content. On the other hand, training courses for content teachers on how to integrate the learning of a foreign language in the teaching of curricular contents. He points out that CLIL training programmes must be designed to develop the competencies that this approach requires and promote not only the improvement of linguistic competence but also the integration of language with content.

In general, in-service training actions for bilingual education programmes in Spain can be summarized as below (MECD, 2013):

– Lifelong training programmes to improve the linguistic and methodological competence as a resource for the bilingual or plurilingual programme.
– Mobility programmes, exchanges and stays abroad including training in prestigious universities and institutions.
– Periods of linguistic immersion and intensive courses to improve the linguistic competence in the foreign language organized in the Official Language Schools.
– Courses, working groups, conferences, seminars and workshops about CLIL and other aspects of bilingual education.
– Online linguistic and methodological training through the regional teacher training centres.
– Specific training plans for teachers who teach certain programmes such as the double programme Spanish *Bachillerato* and French *Bacalauréat* called Bachibac or the national bilingual programme developed by agreement between the Spanish Ministry of Education and the British Council called MEC–British Council.
– Coordination and preparation of didactic materials. (ibid.)

However, these training actions do not always have the expected impact on teachers' expertise (Pérez-Cañado, 2016). Thus, the lack of pedagogical content knowledge of bilingual methodology perceived by teachers (Herrero Rámila, 2015) is one of the most important challenges to meet in all types of content-based instruction (Morton, 2016).

To address this situation, the Ministry of Education has implemented an integral programme to support the teaching and learning of foreign languages in Spain called the PALE programme 2010–2020 (*Programa Integral de Aprendizaje de Lenguas Extranjeras*). PALE was presented at an Education Conference in 2011 by the Ministry of Education as a strategy to meet the needs of students, teachers, schools and families, in relation to the improvement of their linguistic competence. For teachers, PALE aims to promote their in-service and pre-service training to improve both their linguistic and methodological competence in order to enable them to teach a foreign language and curricular content in an integrated manner. PALE is currently in the third phase of implementation, and Communities such as Valencia, Aragón, Asturias or Cantabria include it in their teacher training programmes.

At the regional level, each Community offers a wide variety of courses and training programmes. In the Community of Madrid, for example, to be part of the Bilingual Programme, teachers have to obtain a linguistic accreditation, which is regulated by law, to impart CLIL in bilingual public schools or private schools partly maintained with public funds. This *habilitación lingüísitca* (linguistic qualification required by teachers to teach CLIL in the Bilingual Programme) can be obtained in two different ways: Having a C1 or higher level according to the CEFR in the foreign language or through a knowledge test that consists of two phases (Phase 1: Reading, listening comprehension, written expression, grammar and vocabulary; Phase 2: Oral expression). In addition, it is necessary to have the university degree corresponding to the stage of education for which the accreditation is requested (infant, primary or secondary), and there must be a working relationship with a school implementing the Bilingual Programme. There is also a linguistic training programme called *Plan de Formación en Lenguas Extranjeras* (PFLE) that caters for the training of these CLIL teachers in the Community of Madrid. This plan has been designed and implemented by the Directorate General of Innovation, Scholarships and Grants at the Regional Ministry of Education. It includes courses in English, French, German or Spanish, which cover language skills, methodological training and leadership and management. These courses are offered at B2 or C1 levels according to the CEFR and are delivered in different formats: face-to-face, online and blended.

The training mainly takes place in Madrid, but there are courses abroad in the United Kingdom, United States, Canada, Ireland, France, and so on. The courses can last from one to more than three weeks, and they are always offered outside of teaching hours. It should be noted that the training that takes place abroad includes air travel, training expenses and accommodation, although local maintenance and transportation expenses are borne by the participant. All courses are recognized with teacher training credits.

However, none of these courses is mandatory nor are any of them linked to the accreditation process to teach through CLIL. This is also the case in many other Autonomous Communities, and it is an issue that must be addressed in order to balance the training levels of CLIL teachers and to reduce the heterogeneity in their CLIL competence profile. In sum, we can no longer rely solely on teachers' effort, involvement and enthusiasm, and there is a clear need for more extensive pre-service and in-service training for CLIL teachers (Fernández & Halbach, 2011).

4   Current Profile of the CLIL Teacher in Spain

Spain has been the focus of recent research on CLIL teachers' training needs. Here is a summary of the most relevant research activity in this field included in Pérez-Cañado (2016):

- CLIL meets some teachers' demands, such as new technologies, access to mobility and global communication (Pérez-Vidal, 2013).
- Foreign language proficiency levels of teachers are too low, and there is a lack of adequate training in language skills (Ruiz Gómez & Nieto García, 2009). However, Olivares Leyva and Pena Díaz (2013) show that the stakeholders involved in the language training of bilingual teachers felt that the courses were satisfactory.
- The lack of adequate materials has been pointed out by Ruiz Gómez and Nieto García (2009), Halbach (2010), and Fernández and Halbach (2011).

- Content teachers need training in interpersonal social language, more awareness of cognitive academic language, pronunciation and improvisation (Martín del Pozo, 2011).
- Teachers' knowledge of CLIL, the use of student-centred methodologies and gaps in knowledge of CLIL methodology are areas to improve (Fernández & Halbach, 2011; Pena Díaz & Porto Requejo, 2008; Rubio Mostacero, 2009).
- Collaboration, coordination and teamwork must be addressed in teacher training programmes (Lorenzo, 2010; Pena Díaz & Porto Requejo, 2008; Ruiz Gómez & Nieto García, 2009). (ibid.)

Pérez-Cañado (2016) also explains that the challenge of CLIL is seen as a source of professional satisfaction because it impacts on the methodological innovation and the level of reflection but "the picture which transpires is one of extremely motivated teachers with serious training deficits" (p. 3). She concludes that teachers perceive they have a higher level of linguistic competence than of CLIL competence, which suggests that the time has come to strengthen methodological training for CLIL. Pérez-Cañado's survey also shows that Spanish CLIL teachers are aware of their limitations and demand greater training in linguistic competence, as well as materials and resources and continuous professional development. Content teachers seem to be especially lacking in knowledge of metalinguistic terminology, intercultural competence and access to materials and resources. The study also revealed a direct relationship between language proficiency and the mastery on theoretical aspects of CLIL (Pérez-Cañado, 2016). This partly supports the commitment of the educational authorities to focus on language training. However, it needs to be borne in mind, as Ioannou-Georgiou and Pavlou (2011) point out that there is no CLIL unless language and content teaching methodologies are integrated, and this requires formal and specific training.

All these issues are fundamental in the description of CLIL teachers' profile in Spain and their training needs. Over the last decade, in light of these and other results, the universities and educational administrations have designed a series of strategies and have boosted their pre-service and in-service teacher training programmes, some of which have been described above. But what is the real impact of these policies on CLIL teachers' linguistic and CLIL competences? How can we measure the outcomes of these purported improvements in CLIL teacher training programmes?

From the perspective of educational research, there is an urgent need to verify that these actions which aim at improving the teaching competence for CLIL are having the expected impact, and that they are indeed the best training options, in comparison to other possible options. Lancaster (2016a) points out that teachers are not taking advantage of methodological upgrade courses and study licences. An important question arises from this situation: Are there other alternative training actions more likely to impact on CLIL teachers' training? Are these alternatives being explored and studied?

From the point of view of alternative in-service training, Banegas, Pavese, Velázquez, and Vélez (2013) implemented and evaluated the integration of content and language learning in Argentinean secondary classrooms through teachers developing their own materials in a collaborative action research project. The experience revealed a growth in professional development and an influence on their motivation and autonomy, which, in turn, influenced their students' motivation and language skills. The project embodied a democratic perspective in education, in which decisions respond to the real problems that CLIL teachers face in their classrooms.

Alternative approaches have also been tried in initial teacher education. For example, Cabrera and Leggott (2014) implemented a new model in which trainees became more actively involved in their own professional development process through being engaged in action research. This made their trainee teachers more aware of the fact that learning to teach is a lifelong process, and they also became more aware of the importance of developing the competencies required to support learners' language learning.

Some advantages of these alternative training actions are as follows: First, there is a strong contextualization of the training. Second, this contextualization reduces the time and economic resources needed. Third, collaborative participation in the training allows the interaction and feedback among trainee teachers and/or in-service CLIL teachers with different profiles and training backgrounds, all collaborating in the same team. These reasons make this training model based on collaborative action research an effective alternative to traditional training courses. It is one that is well worth being considered by teacher education curriculum designers, and it could well be promoted by the educational authorities in their in-service training programmes for CLIL teachers in Spain.

5   Future Perspectives for CLIL Teacher Education in Spain

The paradigm shift in teaching and, more specifically, in language teaching has not yet been completed, and this is due, among other reasons, to deficient planning of initial and lifelong teacher training programmes to face the challenges of new emerging educational models (Banegas, 2012; Coyle et al., 2010; Escobar, 2011; Jover et al., 2016; Lancaster, 2016a; Madrid & Pérez-Cañado, 2012; Marsh & Langé, 2000; Navés & Victori, 2010; Pérez-Cañado, 2016). This teacher training deficit has repercussions for CLIL teachers. It is important to point out that CLIL teachers have to cope with a range of demands that can put pressure on them. They are expected to be confident in the foreign language, have good knowledge of curricular content, be skilled in the methodological strategies demanded by CLIL and up to date with the use of ICT for educational purposes in a constructivist and learner-centred approach to teaching and learning. Deficiencies in any of these areas may cause teachers to have a confidence crisis or low self-esteem about their teaching (Deller, 2005; Lancaster, 2016b; Pena Díaz & Porto Requejo, 2008). CLIL can be very rewarding from the point of view of improving students' linguistic competence (Shepherd & Ainsworth, 2017), but, at the same time, it is very demanding from the point of view of the teaching skills it demands from CLIL teachers (Pérez-Cañado, 2015).

It is clear, therefore, that despite the wide implementation of bilingual programmes throughout the Spanish territory, and, after more than two decades since the introduction of CLIL in the European education systems, there is still the need for improving in-service and pre-service training for CLIL. In this complicated task, determining CLIL teachers' competencies is a prerequisite for the diagnosis of training needs and the design of courses and plans likely to satisfy them (Halbach, 2009; Mehisto, Marsh, and Frigols, 2008).

There are many frameworks available which propose competence profiles for bilingual teachers. At the international level, there is the "CLIL Teacher's Competence Grid" by Bertaux, Coonan, Frigols, and Mehisto (2010) and the "European Framework for CLIL Teacher Education" by Marsh, Mehisto, Wolff, and Frigols (2010). At the Spanish level, we have the core CLIL teacher competencies defined by Pavón Vázquez and Ellison (2013), Madrid Manrique and Madrid Fernández (2014) and Pérez-Cañado (2015). However, as this chapter has argued, training programmes for CLIL teachers are not as effective as might be expected, and they do not satisfy these teachers' training needs. We have seen that this is connected with two main factors: the fact that CLIL training is not well integrated into university teacher education programmes, and the emphasis placed by educational authorities on language proficiency at the expense of methodological expertise. Pérez-Cañado (2018) describes the current needs in relation to seven core CLIL teacher competences (Pérez-Cañado, 2015): linguistic competence (mainly for content teachers and pre-primary and primary teachers), pedagogical and organizational competence (attention to diversity and CLIL methodological training, particularly, for pre-service teachers), scientific knowledge (lack of knowledge in theory of language and learning underlying this approach and main features of these types of programmes), interpersonal and collaborative competencies (dealing with insufficient time and mixed-ability groups), and reflective and developmental competence (poor impact of in-service training for CLIL; also discussed Chap. 2 in this volume).

Many authors have argued that, if initial training plans were more connected to these competencies, investment in in-service teacher training could be substantially reduced (Banegas, 2015; Delicado and Pavón, 2016; Hüttner, Dalton-Puffer & Smit, 2013; Madrid Manrique & Madrid Fernández, 2014). This would have the advantage of making it possible to increase the quality and quantity of the training on offer. Perhaps more importantly, it would help to guide providers towards new research agendas more likely to ensure a greater impact of teacher education on the whole CLIL teaching community.

Banegas (2012) claims that in the design of policies to implement CLIL, there must be a tripartite negotiation among administrators, curriculum planners and those responsible for the success of CLIL, the teachers. He highlights the importance of educational policies such as the introduction of bilingual programmes addressing teacher development first and not last, as is often the case.

In conclusion, the challenge for the development of an efficient and effective bilingual teacher training strategy requires the training of CLIL teachers with a preparatory, non-palliative character (Banegas, 2012; Pavón Vázquez & Ellison, 2013). These training actions need to be linked to the training process at university, in contact with the teaching practice in CLIL classrooms, as in the project described by Fernández Díaz, Gutiérrez Esteban, and Fernández-Olaskoaga (2015), which is aimed at strengthening the university-school relationship. Evaluate studies to assess the extent to which the adopted pedagogical options to train CLIL teachers produce the desired results should be carried out not only by the educational authorities but also by those responsible for the curriculum design for initial CLIL teacher education at university level (Pérez-Cañado, 2016).

There is also a need for the adoption of alternative training models, such as collaborative action research, oriented to the homogenization of in-service CLIL teachers' competence profile. Moreover, external evaluations of a more formative nature and independent studies, such as the one carried out by Dobson, Pérez Murillo, and Johnstone (2010) in the MEC-British Council schools, are necessary and urgent in these programmes. These studies should not focus exclusively on the measurement of students' academic performance but should be open to a critical and reflective analysis by all the stakeholders that make up bilingual education in Spain, particularly the CLIL teachers.

In short, it seems reasonable, at this stage in the development of bilingual and multilingual education policies in Spain, to put the emphasis on the evaluation and diagnosis of CLIL teachers' training needs. These evaluations should be done in both pre-service and in-service teacher training contexts, making sure that they identify the needs of the teachers themselves, based on empirical evidence gathered in CLIL classrooms (European Commission, 2017). Additionally, it should lead the processes of curriculum review at the university level and the design of training programmes at the administrative level. Pre- and in-service teacher training should be seen as the key to any future vision for improvement of bilingual education and the development of CLIL (Coyle, 2011; Pérez-Cañado, (2016).

Appendix

Bilingual Programme Community of Madrid
https://comunidadbilingue.educa2.madrid.org/

Bologna Process
https://ec.europa.eu/education/policy/higher-education/bologna-process_en

CLIL Matrix
http://archive.ecml.at/mtp2/clilmatrix/EN/qMain.html

Clil4U
http://languages.dk/clil4u/#Project_background
Common European Framework of Reference for Languages: Learning, Teaching, Assessment (CEFR)
https://www.coe.int/en/web/common-european-framework-reference-languages/home
Double programme Spanish Bachillerato and French Bacalauréat called Bachibac
http://w3.recursostic.edu.es/bachillerato/bachibac/web/es/

European Centre for Modern Languages (ECML)
https://www.ecml.at/

European Credit Transfer and Accumulation System (ECTS)
https://ec.europa.eu/education/resources/european-credit-transfer-accumulation-system_en

Example of training courses for content teachers
https://www.britishcouncil.es/en/teach/teacher-training/clil-essentials-online

Linguistic accreditation in the Bilingual Programme Community of Madrid
http://w3.bocm.es/boletin/CM_Orden_BOCM/2015/04/21/BOCM-20150421-8.PDF

Master's degree in Teaching in Secondary Schools
https://www.boe.es/diario_boe/txt.php?id=BOE-A-2011-20181

MEC-British Council programme
https://www.mecd.gob.es/educacion/mc/bilinguismo/convenio-mecd-bc.html

PALE programme 2010–2020 (*Programa Integral de Aprendizaje de Lenguas Extranjeras*)
https://www.campuseducacion.com/files/programa-integral-aprendizaje-lenguas-ce-23-03-11.pdf

PFLE programme (*Plan de Formación en Lenguas Extranjeras*) Community of Madrid
http://innovacion.educa.madrid.org/plan2018/index.php/index/seccion/0

TALIS (International Survey of Teaching and Learning)
https://www.mecd.gob.es/inee/evaluaciones-internacionales/talis/talis-2013.html

TIE-CLIL 1998–2014
http://www.tieclil.org/index.htm

References

Banegas, D. L. (2012). CLIL teacher development: Challenges and experiences. *Latin American Journal of Content & Language Integrated Learning, 5*(1), 46–56. https://doi.org/10.5294/laclil.2012.5.1.4

Banegas, D. L. (2015). Sharing views of CLIL lesson planning in language teacher education. *Latin American Journal of Content and Language Integrated Learning, 8*(2), 104–130. https://doi.org/10.5294/laclil.2015.8.2.3

Banegas, D., Pavese, A., Velázquez, A., & Vélez, S. M. (2013). Teacher professional development through collaborative action research: Impact on foreign English-language teaching and learning. *Educational Action Research, 21*(2), 185–201. https://doi.org/10.1080/09650792.2013.789717

Bertaux, P., Coonan, C. M., Frigols, M. J., & Mehisto, P. (2010). *The CLIL Teacher's Competence Grid*. Retrieved from http://lendtrento.eu/convegno/files/mehisto.pdf

Buckingham, L. R., Custodio Espinar M., & López Hernández, A. (2018). *Collaborative Competence in Pre-service Teacher Training: A Team-Teaching Experience*. Presented at IV Congreso internacional sobre educación bilingüe en un mundo globalizado. Enfoques contemporáneos de enseñanza y aprendizaje, Comunidad de Madrid and Franklin Institute, Alcalá de Henares, Madrid.

Cabrera, M. P. M., & Leggott, D. (2014). Action research in English as a foreign language teacher training in Spain: Trainees' perception of their development of competencies for effective teaching and a comparison with language teacher competency development in the UK. *Utrecht Studies in Language and Communication, 27*, 59.

Calle Casado, J. J. (2015). *Teacher Training for CLIL: Lessons Learned and Ways Forward*. tesis de grado, Universidad de Jaen, Jaen.

Commission of the European Communities. Directorate-General for Education, Training, and Youth. (1995). *Teaching and Learning: Towards the Learning Society*. White Paper on Education and Training. Brussels: ERIC Clearinghouse.

Commission of the European Communities. (2003). *Promoting Language Learning and Linguistic Diversity: An Action Plan 2004–2006*. Brussels: European Commission.

Coyle, D. (2011). *Teacher Education and CLIL Methods and Tools*. Retrieved from http://www.cremit.it/public/documenti/seminar.pdf

Coyle, D., Hood, P., & Marsh, D. (2010). *CLIL—Content and Language Integrated Learning*. Cambridge: Cambridge University Press.

Custodio Espinar, M. (2017). The Role of Language Teaching in the CLIL Classroom. *Pearson English Blog*. Retrieved from https://www.english.com/blog/author/custodio/

Dafouz, E. (2015). Más allá del inglés: la competencia lingüística multidimensional como estrategia para la enseñanza en la universidad internacional. *Educación y Futuro, 32*, 15–34.

Delicado, G., & Pavón, V. (2016). Training primary student teachers for CLIL: Innovation through collaboration. *Pulso: Revista de Educación, 39*, 35–57.

Deller, S. (2005). Teaching other subjects in English (CLIL). *English! Spring*, 29–31.

Dobson, A., Pérez Murillo, M. D., & Johnstone, R. M. (2010). *Bilingual Education Project Spain: Evaluation Report: Findings of the Independent Evaluation of the Bilingual Education Project of the Ministry of Education (Spain) and the British Council (Spain)*. Madrid: Ministry of Education (Spain) and British Council.

Escobar, C. (2011). Colaboración interdisciplinar, partenariado y centros de formación docente: tres ejes para sustentar la colaboración del profesorado AICLE 1. In C. Escobar Urmeneta & L. Nussbaum (Eds.), *Learning Through Another Language*. Bellaterra: Servei de Publicacions de la Universitat Autònoma de Barcelona.

European Commission. (2017). *On a Renewed EU Agenda for Higher Education*. Brussels: European Commission.

European Commission/EACEA/Eurydice. (2017). *Key Data on Teaching Languages at School in Europe—2017 Edition*. Eurydice Report. Luxembourg: Publications Office of the European Union.

Eurydice. (2006). *Content and Language Integrated Learning (CLIL) at School in Europe*. Brussels: Eurydice European Unit.

Fernández, R., & Halbach, A. (2011). Analysing the situation of teachers in the Madrid Bilingual Project after four years of implementation. In Y. Ruiz de Zarobe, J. M. Sierra, & F. Gallardo del Puerto (Eds.), *Content and Foreign Language Integrated Learning. Contributions to Multilingualism in European Contexts* (pp. 241–270). Frankfurt-am-Main: Peter Lang.

Fernández, R., & Johnson, M. (2016). *Enseñanza bilingüe en la educación universitaria. El enfoque CLIL del Centro Universitario Cardenal Cisneros*. Alcalá de Henares: CUCC.

Fernández Cézar, R., Aguirre Pérez, C., & Harris, C. (2013). La formación de maestros en Aprendizaje Integrado de Contenidos en Lengua Extranjera

(AICLE): Un estudio en Castilla La Mancha. *Revista de Formación e Innovación Educativa Universitaria, 6*(1), 33–44.

Fernández Díaz, E. M., Gutiérrez Esteban, P., & Fernández-Olaskoaga, L. (2015). Una investigación colaborativa interuniversitaria para repensar un modelo docente comprometido con el cambio educativo. *Revista Interuniversitaria de Formación del Profesorado, 29*(1), 143–155.

Fernández Díaz, M. J. (2017). Entrevistas. Formación inicial de maestros. M.ª José Fernández Díez. Decana de la Facultad de Educación UCM. *Revista Digital EducaMadrid*. Retrieved from https://www.educa2.madrid.org/web/revista-digital/entrevistas/-/visor/m-jose-fernandez-diez-decana-de-la-facultad-de-educacion-ucm

García Jiménez, E., & Lorente García, R. (2014). Grado en Maestro de Educación Primaria: Motivaciones y preferencias en la elección de mención. *Aula de Encuentro, 1*(16), 103–119.

Halbach, A. (2009). The primary school teacher and the challenges of bilingual education. In E. Dafouz & M. C. Guerrini (Eds.), *CLIL Across Educational Levels: Experiences from Primary, Secondary and Tertiary Contexts* (pp. 19–26). Madrid: Richmond Publishing.

Halbach, A. (2010). From the classroom to university and back: Teacher training for CLIL in Spain at the Universidad de Alcalá. In Y. Ruiz de Zarobe & D. Lasagabaster (Eds.), *CLIL in Spain: Implementation, results and teacher training* (pp. 243–256). Newcastle upon Tyne: Cambridge Scholars Publishing.

Herrero Rámila, C. (2015). *El Programa de Colegios Bilingües de la Comunidad de Madrid. Un análisis del proceso de cambio ocurrido a través de sus profesores.* tesis doctoral, Universidad Autónoma de Madrid, Madrid.

Hüttner, J., Dalton-Puffer, C., & Smit, U. (2013). The power of beliefs: Lay theories and their influence on the implementation of CLIL programmes. *International Journal of Bilingual Education and Bilingualism, 16*(3), 267–284.

Ioannou-Georgiou, S., & Pavlou, P. (2011). *Guidelines for CLIL Implementation in Primary and Pre-primary Education*. PROCLIL, European Commission.

Jover, G., Fleta, T., & González, R. (2016). La Formación Inicial de los Maestros de Educación Primaria en el Contexto de la Enseñanza Bilingüe en Lengua Extranjera. *Bordón, Revista de Pedagogía, 68*(2), 121–135.

Lancaster, N. K. (2016a). Stakeholder perspectives on CLIL in a monolingual context. *English Language Teaching, 9*(2), 148–177.

Lancaster, N. K. (2016b). *The Effects of Content and Language Integrated Learning on the Oral Skills of Compulsory Secondary Education Students: A Longitudinal Study.* tesis doctoral, Universidad de Jaén, Jaén.

Lasagabaster, D., & Ruiz de Zarobe, Y. (Eds.). (2010). *CLIL in Spain: Implementation, Results and Teacher Training*. Newcastle upon Tyne: Cambridge Scholars Publishing.

Llinares, A., & Dafouz, E. (2010). Content and language integrated programs in the Madrid region: Overview and research findings. In D. Lasagabaster & Y. Ruiz de Zarobe (Eds.), *CLIL in Spain: Implementation, Results and Teacher Training* (pp. 95–114). Newcastle, UK: Cambridge Scholars.

Lorenzo, F. (2010). CLIL in Andalusia. In D. Lasagabaster & Y. Ruiz de Zarobe (Eds.), *CLIL in Spain: Implementation, results and teacher training* (pp. 2–11). Newcastle upon Tyne: Cambridge Scholars Publishing.

Madrid, D., & Pérez-Cañado, M. L. (2012). CLIL teacher training. In J. d. D. M. Agudo (Ed.), *Teaching and Learning English through Bilingual Education*. Newcastle upon Tyne: Cambridge Scholars.

Madrid Manrique, M., & Madrid Fernández, D. (2014). *La formación inicial del profesorado para la educación bilingüe*. Granada: Universidad de Granada.

Marsh, D., & Langé, G. (2000). *Using Languages to Learn and Learning to Use Languages*. Jyväskylä: UniCOM, University of Jyväskyläyväskylaty of Jyvä Jy.

Marsh, D., Mehisto, P., Wolff, D., & Frigols, M. J. (2010). *European Framework for CLIL Teacher Education: A Framework for the Professional Development of CLIL Teachers*. Graz: European Centre for Modern Languages.

Martín del Pozo, M. A. (2011). *Teacher Training for CLIL in Higher Education: A Needs Analysis from a Language Awareness Perspective*. Paper presented at the II Congreso Internacional de Enseñanza Bilingüe en Centros Educativos. Madrid: Universidad Rey Juan Carlos.

MECD. (2003). *La integración del sistema universitario español en el espacio europeo de enseñanza superior*. Documento-Marco. Madrid: Ministerio de Educación, Cultura y Deporte.

MECD. (2013). La enseñanza de las lenguas extranjeras en el sistema educativo español Curso Escolar 2012/13. *Colección Eurydice España-REDIE*. Madrid: Ministerio de Educación, Cultura y Deporte.

Megías Rosa, M. (2012). Formación, Integración y Colaboración: Palabras clave de CLIL. Una Charla con María Jesús Frigols. *Encuentro, 21*, 3–14.

Mehisto, P., Marsh, D., & Frigols, M. J. (2008). *Uncovering CLIL: Content and Language Integrated Learning in Bilingual and Multilingual Education*. Oxford: Macmillan Education.

Morton, T. (2016). Conceptualizing and investigating teachers' knowledge for integrating content and language in content-based instruction. *Journal of Immersion and Content-Based Language Education, 4*(2), 144–167. https://doi.org/10.1075/jicb.4.2.01mor

Murphy, C., & Martin, S. N. (2015). Coteaching in teacher education: Research and practice. *Asia-Pacific Journal of Teacher Education, 43*(4), 277–280. https://doi.org/10.1080/1359866X.2015.1060927

Navés, T., & Victori, M. (2010). CLIL in Catalonia: An overview of research studies. In D. Lasagabaster & Y. Ruiz de Zarobe (Eds.), *CLIL in Spain: Implementation, Results and Teacher Training* (pp. 30–55). Newcastle: Cambridge Scholars Publishing.

OECD. (2014). *TALIS 2013 Results: An International Perspective on Teaching and Learning*. OECD Publishing. https://doi.org/10.1787/9789264196261-en

Olivares Leyva, M., & Pena Díaz, C. (2013). How do we teach our CLIL teachers? *Porta Linguarum, 19*, 87–99.

Pavón Vázquez, V., & Ellison, M. (2013). *Examining Teacher Roles and Competences in Content and Language Integrated Learning (CLIL)* (Vol. 4, pp. 65–78). Linguarum Arena.

Pena Díaz, C., & Porto Requejo, M. D. (2008). Teacher beliefs in a CLIL education project. *Porta Linguarum, 10*, 151–161.

Pérez-Cañado, M. L. (2012). CLIL research in Europe: Past, present, and future. *International Journal of Bilingual Education and Bilingualism, 15*(3), 315–341. https://doi.org/10.1080/13670050.2011.630064

Pérez-Cañado, M. L. (2015). Training teachers for plurilingual education: A Spanish case study. In D. Marsh, M. L. Pérez-Cañado, & J. Ráez Padilla (Eds.), *CLIL in Action: Voices from the Classroom* (pp. 165–187). Newcastle upon Tyne: Cambridge Scholars Publishing.

Pérez-Cañado, M. L. (2016). Teacher training needs for bilingual education: In-service teacher perceptions. *International Journal of Bilingual Education and Bilingualism, 19*(3), 266–295. https://doi.org/10.1080/13670050.2014.980778

Pérez-Cañado, M. L. (2018). Innovations and challenges in CLIL teacher training. *Theory into Practice, 57*(3), 1–10. https://doi.org/10.1080/00405841.2018.1492238

Pérez-Vidal, C. (2013). Perspectives and lessons from the challenge of CLIL experiences. In C. Abello-Contesse, P. M. Chandler, M. D. López-Jiménez, & R. Chacón-Beltrán (Eds.), *Bilingual and Multilingual Education in the 21st Century. Building on Experience* (pp. 59–82). Bristol: Multilingual Matters.

Perines, H. (2018). ¿Por qué la investigación educativa no impacta en la práctica docente? *Estudios sobre Educación, 34*, 9–27. https://doi.org/10.15581/004.34.9-27

Rubio Mostacero, M. D. (2009). *Language Teacher Training for Non-language Teachers: Meeting the Needs of Andalusian Teachers for School Plurilingualism Projects. Design of a Targeted Training Course.* Jaén: Universidad de Jaén.

Ruiz Gómez, D. A., & Nieto García, J. M. (2009). Las secciones bilingües en Secundaria y Bachillerato. Marco organizativo. Dificultades y propuestas [Bilingual sections in secondary education and Baccalaureate. Organizational framework. Difficulties and proposals]. In *Atención a la diversidad en la enseñanza plurilingüe. I, II y III Jornadas Regionales de Formación del Profesorado* (CD-ROM).

Salaberri Ramiro, S. (2010). Teacher training programmes for CLIL in Andalusia. In D. Lasagabaster & Y. Ruiz de Zarobe (Eds.), *CLIL in Spain: Implementation, Results and Teacher Training* (pp. 140–161). Newcastle upon Tyne: Cambridge Scholars Publishing.

Shepherd, E., & Ainsworth, V. (2017). *English Impact. An Evaluation of English Language Capability.* Madrid: British Council. Retrieved from https://www.britishcouncil.org/sites/default/files/g303_03_english_impact_report_madrid_web1.pdf

14

The Internationalization of Spanish Higher Education: An Interdisciplinary Approach to Initial Teacher Education for CLIL

María Dolores Pérez Murillo

1 Introduction

Spanish universities are undergoing a process of internationalization and reform in accordance with the Bologna Process, which called for a unified European Higher Education Area (EHEA) by 2010 (Doiz, Lasagabaster, & Sierra, 2013; Fortanet-Gómez, 2013; Pavón & Gaustad, 2013). As Lagasabaster (2015) puts it:

> European governments regard the internationalization of higher education as one of the key elements to improve, develop, modernize and strengthen their respective university systems, the Bologna Process playing a key role in their endeavours to boost internationalization in the European Higher Education Arena (EHEA) (p. 260).

Internationalization in higher education is defined by Knight (2003) as "the process of integrating an international, intercultural, or global

M. D. Pérez Murillo (✉)
School of Education, Complutense University in Madrid, Madrid, Spain
e-mail: perezmur@edu.ucm.es

© The Author(s) 2019   **339**
K. Tsuchiya, M. D. Pérez Murillo (eds.), *Content and Language Integrated Learning in Spanish and Japanese Contexts*, https://doi.org/10.1007/978-3-030-27443-6_14

dimension into the purpose, functions or delivery of postsecondary education" (p. 2). In the Spanish context, it is associated with the value attached to English as an international language. Dearden (2014) reports that public opinion in Spain considers teaching through English essential for Spanish universities in order to compete with international students. Furthermore, "English is considered a fundamental skill for mobility and employability and not simply a foreign language" (ibid., p. 21).

Internationalization is closely linked to the prevalence of language teaching where an additional language is used, "for the learning and teaching of both content and language" (Coyle, Hood, & Marsh, 2010, p. 1). This educational initiative is referred to as CLIL (Content and Language Integrated Learning) at primary and secondary education levels and ICLHE (Integrating Content and Language in Higher Education) in tertiary education (Pérez-Vidal, 2015; Smit & Dafouz-Milne, 2012; Wilkinson & Zegers, 2007). In both CLIL and ICLHE contexts, English is the preferred language of instruction in Spain and other European countries, at the expense of other additional languages like French or German (Dalton-Puffer, 2011; Nikula, 2017; Pérez-Vidal, 2015). For the sake of clarity, no distinction will be made between two approaches that are used for teaching through English in Spanish universities (Aguilar & Muñoz, 2014; Ramos-García & Pavón Vázquez, 2018; Smit & Dafouz-Milne, 2012): ICLHE, where both content and language are integrated, and English Medium Instruction (EMI), which focuses on content learning only.

This chapter focuses on initial teacher education for primary CLIL at the School of Education, University Complutense of Madrid (UCM), from the perspective provided by a Teaching Innovation Project (TIP), which has been set up in response to the university's drive for internationalization (see Custodio Espinar, this volume, for pre-service and in-service training in Spain). The widespread implementation of bilingual programmes nationwide at infant, primary and secondary levels demands high-quality initial teacher education and continuous professional development for CLIL (Escobar Urmeneta, 2011; Lagasabaster & Ruiz de Zarobe, 2010; Madrid & Pérez Cañado, 2012; Navés, 2009). However, Spanish universities' curricular reform, in accordance with the Bologna Process, has reduced the training of prospective pre-primary and primary teachers in Foreign Language and Didactics, in the new Undergraduate Teaching Degrees.

However, the recent trend towards implementing English-medium courses at Schools of Education in different disciplines may provide the opportunity for complementing future primary teacher development. Bearing all this in mind, our TIP addresses issues of interdisciplinary teaching and learning in English-medium subjects and teacher collaboration. Interdisciplinarity in teaching and learning is defined by Jacobs (1989) as "a knowledge view and curriculum approach that consciously applies methodology and language from more than one discipline to examine a central theme, issue, problem, topic, or experience" (p. 8). An interdisciplinary approach seems appropriate for CLIL contexts, in which cross-curricular links among the different disciplines are encouraged (Dobson, Johnstone, & Pérez Murillo, 2010; Mehisto, Marsh, & Frigols, 2008; Segovia et al., 2010). Furthermore, interdisciplinarity is at the heart of CLIL where language and content are integrated. Therefore, it should play an important role in the training of future CLIL teachers, "interdisciplinarity has become more central to knowledge. It should be not peripheral to teacher education" (Klein, 2002, p. 201).

The chapter is divided into three parts. First, the characteristics of CLIL/ICLHE implementation in the Spanish context will be explored. Then the impact of internationalization and reform in Spanish universities will be described. This is followed by a case study of the impact of unified EHEA on the bachelor's degree in Primary Education at UCM. The chapter moves on to a description of innovation introduced in the degree that fosters faculty collaboration through interdisciplinary initiatives. Finally, some conclusions will be drawn about initial teacher education for CLIL in the context of the Bologna Process and the EHEA, and some implications of an interdisciplinary collaborative approach to professors' professional development will be outlined.

2 CLIL in the Spanish Context

The Spanish education system is decentralized, and the responsibility for education policy and research is divided between the central government (Ministry of Education, Culture and Sport, MECD) and the local authorities of the 17 autonomous communities (Delgado, 2014). Multilingualism is promoted in Spain, in accordance with the Spanish

Constitution of 1978, since more than one language is spoken in some of the autonomous regions. These regional languages (Catalan/Valencian, Galician and Basque) have co-official status with Spanish with the result that "40% of the population live in bilingual areas" (Lasagabaster & Huguet, 2007, p. 2). Furthermore, as a member state of the European Union (EU) since 1986, Spain has adopted EU language education policy, which is also plurilingual in nature, "individual plurilingualism and societal multilingualism are the principles which underpin the language policies of both the European Union and the Council of Europe, albeit accompanied by different emphases on European identity" (Coleman, 2006, p. 1).

Spaniards, just as all EU citizens, are encouraged to learn two additional languages, apart from their mother tongue, following the European Commission Action Plan 2004–2006 (European Commission, 2004). However, in reality, according to a European Commission Survey (Eurobarometer, 2012), only a quarter of Europeans can speak at least two additional languages. Therefore, increasing the numbers of speakers of additional languages at school can help meet this plurilingual goal. In this context, "Content and Language Integrated Learning (CLIL), in which pupils learn a subject through the medium of a foreign language, has a major contribution to make to the Union's language learning goals" (European Commission Action Plan 2004–2006, p. 8). As Llinares (2015) states, the interest of the European Union for CLIL programmes was "to improve students' foreign language proficiency, together with a long tradition of poor results in foreign languages in some member states" (p. 60).

There is no doubt that this bilingual approach to language teaching was introduced in Spain to adhere to the European Union's (EU) multilingual policies (Smit & Dafouz-Milne, 2012; Tsuchiya & Pérez Murillo, 2015), but there was already "a growing awareness of the need to learn foreign languages" (Lagasabaster & Ruiz de Zarobe, 2010, p. ix). Many were the reasons for this interest in learning foreign languages, particularly English, as Reichelt (2006) puts it:

Spain faces unique challenges in the area of English-language teaching (ELT). The current enthusiasm for learning the language, the thriving private market for ELT, and curricular reforms in public schooling, along with initiatives for earlier and earlier English-language education, indicate strong determination to improve levels of English-language proficiency (p. 8).

In recent years, CLIL schools have sprung up all over Spanish territory at the pre-university level where English is largely used in an attempt to improve pupils' competence in an additional language (Pérez-Vidal, 2011; Ruiz de Zarobe & Lasagabaster, 2010). In 2016, nearly all primary school pupils in Spain learnt English as a foreign language. The percentage is very similar in upper secondary with 99.7% of pupils learning English, whereas only 24.5% chose to learn French or 2.3% chose German (EUROSTAT, 2018). In this multilingual country, the implementation of CLIL/ICLHE has resulted in a great diversity of models at all educational levels with bilingual (mainly Spanish/English) in monolingual regions or trilingual in those autonomous communities with two official languages, the minority language and Spanish as the official language in the whole territory (Cenoz, 2017; Fernández-Fontecha, 2009; Frigols, 2008; González Gándara, 2015; Lagasabaster & Ruiz de Zarobe, 2010; Muñoz & Navés, 2007).

3 Teaching Through English in Higher Education in Spain

Academic internationalization in higher education is considered paramount for the EU's economic and political integration (Altbach & Knight, 2007). For this reason, "the Bologna process harmonizes entire academic systems to ensure compatible degree structures, transferable credits, and equal academic qualifications throughout the EU" (p. 293). This has led to Spanish universities undertaking an internationalization process where undergraduate and postgraduate programmes are offered, very often in English, acknowledging its role as an international language: "reality indicates that it is English which is preeminent and has become the language that is used as a means of instruction at universities in Europe and worldwide" (Doiz et al., 2013, p. xvii).

3.1 Role of English in Spanish Higher Education After EHEA

According to a large-scale survey in 28 European countries conducted by Wächter and Maiworm (2014), the provision of English-taught programmes (ETPs) at higher education in Europe has increased dramatically over the past decade, due to the Bologna Process. However, the authors observed that there are major regional differences related to the spread of ETPs and the size of enrolment. Northern European countries have been very active in implementing ETPs, whereas Southern Europe, including countries like Spain with 84 universities (50 public and 34 private), is well behind, the only exception being Cyprus. As Kelly (2017) puts it: "Spain, where language learning has long been the Cinderella of the education system, has been a relative latecomer to this trend, but has slowly embraced it and the number of ETPs continues to rise" (p. 48). Many are the reasons why language learning in Spain has lagged behind. As Fortanet-Gómez (2008) points out, "Spanish is one of the languages most widely spoken in the world, the preference given in recent years to the teaching and learning of regional languages in bilingual areas, or the late internationalization of economy and politics, among others" (p. 22). In the same vein, Dafouz, Camacho, and Urquía (2014) state that "for decades the country's national level of English has remained one of the lowest in the European Union (EUROSTAT 2010), and, as a result, only a small percentage of higher education students can actually study and work in this language" (p. 224).

Nevertheless, ICLHE is gaining momentum at the tertiary education level, and there are increasing numbers of courses at both undergraduate and postgraduate levels taught in English. According to a recent publication by the Board of Rectors of Spanish Universities (CRUE, 2018), in the 2016–2017 academic year, programmes with over 50% of the curriculum taught in English accounted for 7.5% of the bachelor's degrees and 10.4% of the master's programmes in state universities. The number of bilingual courses increases in private universities to 17.8% in undergraduate and 14.3% in postgraduate programmes. Spain was one of 47 countries that signed the Bologna Declaration, "a major move towards English as medium of instruction (EMI) in Europe" (Kirkpatrick, 2014, p. 4). Following the 2007 university reform law (MECD, 2007a), the Bologna Declaration of a European Space for Higher Education had to be implemented in all Spanish universities in the academic year 2010/2011. Moreover, the EU is expanding its international programmes worldwide, mainly in Latin America and the Asia–Pacific regions. Spain is not an exception to this process, as can be seen by the fact that all official degrees awarded by Spanish universities are recognized for academic and professional purposes in a total of 53 countries worldwide, including some Latin American countries (Spanish Service for Education Internationalization, SEPIE).

3.2 Challenges Facing the Implementation of ICLHE in Spain

Implementing courses in English (as a global language) poses many challenges for Spanish universities (Gardner, 2012). These include the language requirements for students and professors involved in the bilingual courses or the training needed to teach through English, among others. Some of these issues will be discussed in the following sections.

3.2.1 Choice of English-Medium Instruction in the Context of Multilingual Spain

According to Pérez-Vidal (2015), "The Bologna declaration has not prioritized the language of instruction" but rather "the need for harmonization and transparency of higher education qualifications" (p. 36). This has resulted in English-taught courses being offered at higher education institutions outside English-speaking countries. In the Spanish context, the growing role of English in higher education involves not only neglecting other additional languages like French or German but is also seen as a threat to Spanish minority languages (Cots, Llurda, & Peter Garrett, 2014; Lagasabaster, 2015; Vila Moreno & Bretxa, 2014). In the European

Commission Action Plan 2004–2006 (European Commission, 2004), higher education institutions are encouraged to promote language learning and linguistic diversity, since teaching in English may become a threat to the national language. However, there is concern in Europe about English being the main language of instruction in European universities (Kirkpatrick, 2014; Phillipson, 2006; Wilkinson, 2013), and this issue has to be taken into account when planning courses since the national perception could be that "the first language (L1) is losing prestigious domains to English" (Wilkinson, 2013, p. 19).

In the same vein, Delgado (2017) advocates a more important role of the Spanish language in the internationalization of Higher Education (HE), as he puts it: "more work must be done to develop the potential of Spanish as a higher education language by exploring possibilities not only in the Spanish-speaking world, but also in other countries and regions with a growing interest in our language and culture" (p. 21). Similarly, Kelly (2017) encourages Spanish universities to take advantage of the asset of instructing in Spanish, a language which is widely spoken. This is also explicitly stated in "the Strategy for the Internationalization of Spanish Universities" (*Ministerio de Educación, Cultura y Deporte, MECD*, 2014b), which provides guidelines to develop and implement Spanish internationalization and mobility strategies.

Furthermore, in countries with more widely spoken languages such as Spain, Germany or France, "the perception is often that there is no need to introduce programmes fully taught in English since foreign students already speak or want to learn the domestic language" (Wächter & Maiworm, 2014, p. 61). In a preliminary study on undergraduate courses provided by Spanish universities in the early years of the implementation, Ramos-García (2013) found that there were three main types of programmes offered in an additional language: bilingual degrees (Spanish-English), degrees fully conducted in a foreign language and even some course modules in the foreign language in non-bilingual degrees. The language of instruction was often English, though an exceptionally small number of courses were taught in French, German and/or Italian, and this trend seems to be continuing. In a more recent study (Ramos-García & Pavón Vázquez, 2018), the number of undergraduate degrees had increased, and there was a clear preference for bilingual programmes in English. They identified 292 bilingual (Spanish-English) degrees and only 39 delivered fully in English, with one each in French and Italian.

3.2.2 Language Requirements for Students and Teachers

Accrediting levels of competence in an additional language is essential for university students. They need to certify their language skills for enrolment on courses taught in an additional language, including master's programmes as well as for graduation or international mobility. Halbach, Lázaro, and Pérez (2013) survey in Spanish universities found great disparity in their English-language entry requirements for students as well as in their systems for assessing and accrediting language skills, and this was due to the differences in language policies among the institutions. Five years later, in a follow-up study, Halbach and Lázaro (2015) acknowledged that the situation had changed considerably in relation to the ways in which learning English was promoted at university, and how the levels achieved were accredited. They argue that it was mainly the collaboration of two higher education institutions that helped to unify criteria to certify the level of command of the language: the CRUE Linguistic groups that were set up in 2011 and Association of Higher Education Language Centres (ACLES). However, still much work needs to be done, and Halbach and Lázaro (2015) highlight the important role that the CRUE can play in this process.

In an attempt to establish a common language policy in Spain, the CRUE published a document (Bazo et al., 2017) with recommendations on different aspects of university internationalization, including the accreditation of students, faculty members and administrative staff. They suggest a B1 Common European Framework of Reference for Languages (CEFR) level or above (depending on the university) for students to obtain an undergraduate degree certificate, CEFR level of C1 for professors to teach in an additional language and CEFR B1 to C1 for administrative staff in charge of duties related to internationalization of the university.

3.2.3   Training to Teach Through English

As for the accreditation and training of professors who teach through English, in a recent survey of European universities, O'Dowd (2018) notices that there is "a need for universities to pay greater attention to the whole issue of training teaching staff before and while they engage in EMI" (p. 561). This is also true about the ICLHE implementation in Spain, as Dafouz (2011) points out "(it) is still lacking appropriate teacher training programmes that can actually enhance teachers' current FL (Foreign Language) skills and methodology as well as maximize students' achievement in the target language" (p. 205). In the same vein, Halbach and Lázaro (2015) assert that to improve the quality of their programmes taught in an additional language, Spanish universities must provide linguistic and methodological training for their teaching staff.

However, some professors may feel reluctant to teach in the additional language, as was shown in Aguilar's (2015) study with engineering professors in Spain who followed an EMI approach in their lessons, prioritizing the content and refusing to teach English. This resonates with Airey's (2012) study with Swedish Physics professors, since in both cases the professors did not consider language learning relevant. Aguilar concludes that "it seems reasonable to claim that EMI lecturers should be trained and made aware about minimal necessary pedagogic adaptations that even a good EMI requires" (ibid., p. 12). She also acknowledges the important role that language teaching specialists can play in the internationalization process of universities.

Some initiatives involving teacher collaboration have been shown to help university professors to cope with the demands of course modules taught through an additional language. Tandem teaching between content and language teaching specialists can provide the necessary methodological tools for content specialists to adapt materials and teaching style for course modules in which English is the medium of instruction (Cots, 2013). On the other hand, the INTE-R-LICA research project brings together content specialists from the field of economics and business and applied linguists to support higher education institutions, professors and students with courses delivered in English. The project initially originated from the collaboration of applied linguists from the English Studies Department and business Faculty at the School of Economics and Business Administration, UCM, but acquired an international dimension by incorporating members from other European universities.

4 Impact of Internationalization at UCM School of Education

UCM is the largest university in Spain with over 75,000 students and around 7000 professors. After the implementation of the aforementioned 2007 university reform law (MECD, 2007a), the university offers course modules in English at both undergraduate and postgraduate level. According to Ramos-García (2013), the courses offered at the undergraduate level are related to the areas of Business Administration, Economics and Engineering, with a clear preference for bilingual groups (English-Spanish). In the 2018–2019 academic year, the following bachelor's degrees are partially taught in English: Business Administration and Management, Economics, Primary Education, Psychology and Computer Science Engineering. The university set up a Plan for Curricular Internationalization in 2016, "a cutting-edge initiative in Spain" (Martín del Pozo, 2016, p. 75). The plan aims to promote internationalization both at home and abroad, the use of English and the gradual implementation of other languages, without neglecting Spanish. Some actions of the plan involve the organization of teacher training courses for faculty members teaching in bilingual groups and one-day seminars, to share experiences of best practices in internationalization of higher education within the UCM, offer guidelines to implement courses in an additional language and present research findings, among other objectives.

The School of Education has over 4000 students enrolled in the different undergraduate and postgraduate courses that are offered, which are taught by over 300 professors. Jover, Fleta, and González (2016) identified approximately 30 bachelor's degrees in Primary and Pre-Primary Education either partially or fully conducted in English in Spain, with

45% in state universities and 55% offered in private institutions (p. 128). One of these bilingual degrees is offered at the UCM, accounting for one of the five groups into which the cohorts for bachelor's degree in Primary Education are divided. This programme started in response to the widespread implementation of CLIL in schools in the Madrid region (Llinares & Dafouz, 2010).

The main objective of the Bilingual Primary Education Degree Programme (initiated in 2011–2012) at the UCM School of Education is to promote the future job placement of students who graduate, within the network of bilingual schools in the Madrid Autonomous Community (see Fleta, this volume for bilingual schools in the Madrid region). At least 50% of the university courses in this degree programme are taught in English by language teaching and content specialists, starting from the first year of this four-year degree. Therefore, the aim is for students to gain linguistic and professional teaching competences, in the holistic integrated context of an ICLHE approach. One year later, in the 2012–2013 academic year, a specialization module for Foreign Language Major (*Mención de inglés*) started. Unlike the bilingual programme, instruction in English is carried out by language specialists and accounts for approximately 20% of the total course modules. Like the bilingual group, it aims to meet the demand for professional CLIL training in the Madrid region.

The maximum number of students enrolled in these two strands is 40 in each group. In line with the Plan for Curricular Internationalization at UCM, the entry requirement for both programmes is CFER B2. Professors involved in modules in which English has been introduced as a medium of instruction need at least CFER C1. Students in those two strands obtain the qualification of Primary Degree-Foreign Language Major, and most of them will take up a career in teaching in the Madrid region.

However, since the implementation of the Bologna Process, initial teacher education for CLIL constitutes a challenge for Schools of Education in Spain, where the number of bilingual schools in the different autonomous communities, including Madrid, has increased dramatically in the last decade (De la Maya Retamar & Luengo González, 2015; Llinares & Dafouz, 2010). One of the duties of CLIL Initial Teacher

Education is to provide the skills and competences that prospective primary teachers will need, which according to Haataja, Kruczinna, Àrkossy, and Costa (2011), are the following:

- Knowledge of the psychological aspects of bi- and plurilingualism
- Subject-related second language skills
- Knowledge of a wide range of methodologies for the teaching of subject content and the second language
- The ability to find teaching materials in the second language and adapt them for use in the CLIL classroom
- Readiness to plan and undertake a training placement (ibid., p. 16)

However, the number of credit hours designated to Language Teacher Education in the various aspects of Foreign Language and Didactics has been considerably reduced in the new Teaching Degrees, following the Bologna Declaration (1999) that called for a unified EHEA with a common structure of university studies. As De la Maya Retamar and Luengo González (2015) point out, there is insufficient training in foreign languages or CLIL methodology in current Primary Education Degrees, with the result that "graduates will have serious difficulties to participate in plurilingual development programs" (p. 127).

Different initiatives have been carried out in the bachelor's degree in Primary Education at different Schools of Education in Spain. Thus, Romero and Zayas (2017) report a bottom-up project in which university professors introduced innovation by implementing plurilingualism (including other additional languages, apart from English). Following the recommendations provided by Marsh, Pavón, and Frigols (2013) on higher education degree programmes taught in English, Barrios-Espinosa, López-Gutiérrez, and Lechuga-Jiménez (2016) carried out an innovation project where teacher collaboration was encouraged. As they put it, university professors should "share, work together and collaborate in group discussions, needs identification and collective solutions" (p. 213). Delicado and Pavón (2016) describe an initiative involving collaboration between university professors who teach through the medium of English and experienced bilingual teachers working in local bilingual schools, who bring their classroom experiences into university seminars. In the next section, another initiative, involving interdisciplinary faculty collaboration and primary classroom teachers who participate in bilingual teacher education will be described.

5   Interdisciplinary Teaching for Initial Teacher Education Innovation Project

The importance of interdisciplinary teaching and learning in higher education cannot be underestimated. As Pozuelos, Rodríguez, and Travé (2017) point out, there is a need to combine the disciplinary approach with other interdisciplinary initiatives so that knowledge is constructed from different and complementary perspectives. In initial teacher education, there are some early interdisciplinary initiatives (Altava, Pérez, & Ríos, 1999; Feixas, Codó, & Espinet, 2009). However, interdisciplinarity in Spanish higher education is increasing "as a result of the European convergence and the means for fostering innovation in teaching" (Segovia et al., 2010, p. 155). In addition, students enrolled in the Primary Education Degree are supposed to acquire adequate knowledge, not only of the primary curriculum areas but also of the interdisciplinary connections that exist among them (MECD, 2007b). Therefore, interdisciplinary teacher faculty collaboration across academic disciplines through joint planning, decision-making and goal-setting becomes essential in Spanish Schools of Education.

Furthermore, the importance of teamwork between language teaching and content specialist teachers has been greatly emphasized in CLIL contexts. As Genesse and Hamayan (2016) put it, "A CLIL approach requires that language and content teachers at the same grade level take into account how each is building on the other's lessons and how each can help the other expand learning" (p. 166). This has implications for initial teacher education because as opposed to traditional approaches:

> CLIL involves a new focus on curricular integration and interdisciplinarity. It also means assuming a methodology based on cooperative, interactive learning and on the use of materials and technological resources and

reimagining the activity of the teachers who need to work in a multidisciplinary way (Segovia et al., 2010, p. 163).

Wilkinson (2013) provides ways to make this faculty collaboration effective at higher education. He distinguishes between "highly integrated team-teaching" or tandem teaching (Cots, 2013), where language teachers work together and "parallel or adjunct teaching" where the language support to students is provided separately from content courses, although after discussions with content staff.

In the light of all this, following the implementation of the Bilingual Group and the English Language Major in the Undergraduate Degree in Primary Education at our university, an interdisciplinary five-stage TIP has been developed since the 2013–2014 academic year at the UCM School of Education, with the last stage of the project still ongoing at the time of writing. The project entitled "Initial Teacher Education for CLIL: Interdisciplinary Innovation Project" has been funded by the UCM and focuses on teacher collaboration in content areas that are taught through English in the Primary Education Degree. An interdisciplinary approach called the "shared model" (Cone, Werner, & Cone, 2009) is chosen in which two or more subject areas are integrated into the same topic, which in turn, make up part of the curricular contents and competences to be developed in the university courses. Students, in turn, work in groups and are supported by their professors' construct knowledge and understanding of the subject matter.

5.1 Aims of the Project

The project encourages teacher collaboration to enhance the students' linguistic and methodological skills, necessary to teach in CLIL primary schools. An important component of the project is a two-day workshop which takes place every year in which bilingual Primary Education classroom teachers in the Madrid region are invited to come to the School of Education to share their classroom experiences with the prospective teachers. The project pursues the following objectives:

1. To develop collaboration among university professors who instruct in English, providing a forum for the exchange of ideas and experiences from different perspectives and disciplines.
2. To familiarize prospective teachers with cross-curricular teaching/learning within an Integrating Content and Language in Higher Education (ICLHE) context.
3. To promote collaborative work among teaching staff in the different departments of our School of Education.
4. To build a basis to enable future teachers to collaborate on interdisciplinary tasks, in order to introduce innovation in their classrooms.
5. To bring the university closer to real classroom situations and develop an awareness of the reality of bilingual primary schools by inviting classroom teachers to participate in teacher education.

5.2   Participants

The number of group members has increased from 5 in the first year of implementation to 15 in the current project, and it is now a consolidated and stable group. To the initial three disciplines involved in the project (Foundations of Art Education, Teaching Primary Physical Education and Training for Bilingual Education), two more academic subjects were added (Educational Psychology and Music in Primary Education), making a total of five.

The members of this interdisciplinary team are the five professors of the different subject areas, in-service CLIL teacher trainers (who are former Primary Education Degree students), language and content specialists and the university librarian in charge of enhancing students' research skills. From last year, our project has an international dimension, with the addition of a member from Yokohama City University, a Japanese partner university and an Art Educator from The Museum of Modern Art in New York. The number of students involved in the first year of the project was 75, increasing to over 100 in the following years. Students from Year 1 to 4 of the degree participate in the project, including students from different EU countries in the ERASMUS

(European Community Action Scheme for the Mobility of University Students) exchange programme.

5.3 Project Stages

At the initial stage of the project, the team members meet to organize the two-day workshop on good practices in bilingual teaching and learning and to plan and design the activities that are going to be carried out in the different disciplines, as well as the specific roles of the classroom professor and other team members.

Afterwards, an implementation stage follows. First, the "Cross-curricular activities for the Bilingual Primary Classroom" workshop takes place at the beginning of the first semester. Both content and language bilingual teachers from bilingual primary schools present the interdisciplinary work that they have carried out in their CLIL primary classrooms. Then, cross-curricular activities in the different subjects are implemented by the professors in the different courses of the degree (Years 1 to 4), involving more collaborative planning and analysis of the materials to be used for interdisciplinary work. Finally, the evaluation of the project, which serves as a basis for reflection on how well the different components worked, is carried out and future actions discussed and included in the final project report.

5.4 Project Themes and Activities

Barnes (2018) points out the importance of cross-curricular pedagogies to help develop children's creativity in the primary classroom. In his view, our experience of the world is cross-curricular and everything can be understood from multiple perspectives. As he puts it, interdisciplinary or "cross-curricular teaching and learning relies on making links between two or more traditional curriculum subjects in response to an authentic experience, problem, theme or question so that new learning occurs in each subject" (p. xv). In line with Barnes (ibid.), the interdisciplinary activities in our project revolve around a different theme every year.

Following the recommendation of the European Parliament and of the Council on key competences for lifelong learning (European Parliament, 2006), a competency-based approach has been adopted in the Spanish primary curriculum since 2006. This policy mandates that all curricular areas must contribute to students' acquisition of the basic competences. According to García Sánchez and Rodríguez Collado (2015), "competences describe the students' ability to apply basic and specific skills in everyday life situations" (p. 132). However, as Granados Sánchez, Pamies, Romero, and Villanueva (2015) claim, there is a need to train future teachers in the basic competences. The current competences for Primary Education curriculum (MECD, 2014a) are listed below:

1. Linguistic communication (communication in the mother tongue and in foreign languages)
2. Mathematical competence and basic competences in science and technology
3. Digital competence
4. Learning to learn
5. Social and civic competences
6. Sense of initiative and entrepreneurship
7. Cultural awareness and expression

Bearing in mind the interdisciplinary nature of the basic competences in the Spanish primary curriculum, it seemed the appropriate framework for the cross-curricular activities of our work with prospective teachers. In the five years of the project implementation, four basic competences have been studied through the perspective provided by the different disciplines. The first competence, improving communication in a foreign language, has been a priority throughout the project. Multiple Intelligences Theory (Gardner, 1993) gave us the opportunity to introduce learning to learn, which is the "ability to improve learning in an autonomous way, to cope with uncertainty and to find different responses and solutions to problems" (Granados Sánchez et al., 2015, p. 67). ICT was also studied from a cross-curricular perspective to facilitate CLIL learning (Vlachos, 2009), that is, digital competence. Finally, in the last two years, the social and civic competences have been explored to raise the awareness of future teachers in areas such as gender equality, ethnic and cultural diversity, and social inequalities, so that they may educate their students to be tolerant and respectful of human rights and social justice.

Throughout the five years of the project, students have carried out different interdisciplinary activities that have been adapted to their students' levels and needs. For instance, for the Social Justice theme, Year 4 students developed CLIL lesson plans for different subject areas (Literacy, Physical Education, Music, Arts and Crafts, and Science) by using picture books that teach civic education, under the supervision of the experienced teacher educators and experts in these subjects.

5.5 Methods and Results

The methodology used to evaluate the project included mixed methods, ranging from the undergraduate student surveys (to investigate their perception and learning related to interdisciplinarity) to field observations and written reflections by professors. As for the surveys, a pre-and-post questionnaire was administered at the beginning and end of the different courses and served as a basis for reflection on the development of the project by the team. Both questionnaires were semi-structured. Open-ended questions were used to obtain a deep understanding of the respondents' views on cross-curricular lessons, such as the undergraduate students' perceptions about their knowledge on the topic at the beginning and end of the innovation project and details about interdisciplinary training at any level of their education. A Likert-type scale was used for the closed-ended questions, with a 5-point response scale (1 being the lowest and 5 the highest). They covered different topics regarding the role of interdisciplinarity in pre-service teacher education, such as the importance of participating in real cross-curricular teaching experiences, the role of collaboration among professors from different subjects or their views on the importance of these types of activities in their future teaching practices (the post-project questionnaire used in one of the disciplines is provided in Appendix 1). The Annual Project Reports are published every year on the project's website.

In the Project 2018–2019 Annual Report, most first-time participants reported that they had not had previous interdisciplinary experience. However, in the final questionnaire, they agreed with the rest of the groups that the interdisciplinary approach followed in the different course modules taught in English had been useful for them. Figure 14.1 shows the students' perceptions on the impact of interdisciplinary teaching/learning in the disciplines involved in the project during the 2018–2019 academic year and the corresponding year of the degree of the students: Educational Psychology (Year 1); Teaching Primary Physical Education (Year 2); Art Education (Year 3) and Training for Bilingual Education (Year 4, two groups): Bilingual Group (MBL) and the English Language Major (Group A).

The results obtained from the final questionnaires showed that the students had a positive attitude towards interdisciplinary teaching and learning and they were able to make cross-curricular links among the different subject areas.

In addition, they expressed satisfaction with the methodology used in these disciplines and the different interdisciplinary activities that they carried out for university course work. They also acknowledged the positive peer relationships that they had developed through collaborative work in the project. Finally, they stated their intention to implement an interdisciplinary approach in teaching Primary Education in their future teaching practice.

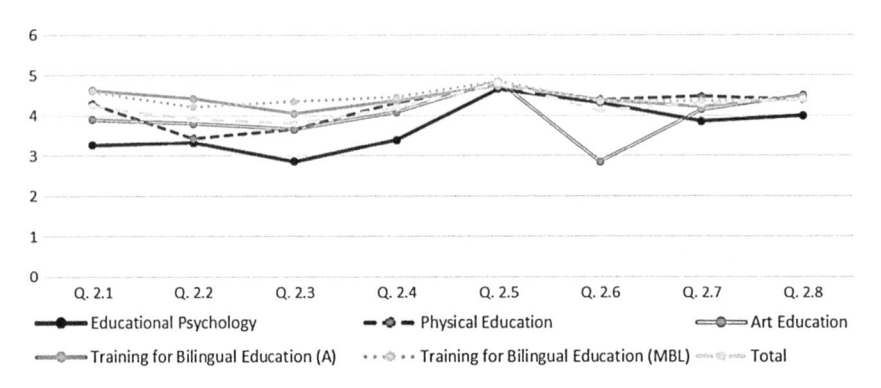

Fig. 14.1 Combined results of the students' perceptions on the impact of interdisciplinary teaching/learning of four subjects (academic year 2018–2019)

During the five-year project, the professors have learnt how to work together as a team. However, interdisciplinary university faculty collaboration requires time and effort so that our students, prospective teachers, obtain a global perspective of education in these subjects, making their learning more meaningful and relevant. As Vangrieken, Dochy, Raes, and Kyndt (2015) put it, "a large array of obstacles needs to be overcome and pitfalls need to be avoided, but at the same time there is an ample amount of points of action and a diverse array of reasons for teachers to collaborate because all parties involved in education benefit" (p. 36). This leads us to conclude that teacher collaboration between language teaching specialists and content teachers is needed at all educational levels, and teacher educators should not be an exception.

6 Conclusions

In this chapter, I have attempted to shed light on the impact of the EU's academic internationalization policy in Spain and, in particular, on the UCM School of Education bachelor's degree in Primary Education that trains students to teach children aged 5–12 years.

The Bologna Process called for a unified EHEA. Spanish public and private universities are increasing their offer of Undergraduate and Postgraduate programmes conducted in an additional language, very often English, acknowledging its role as an international language. The term Englishization "has been used to refer to the spread of English as medium of instruction in institutions of higher education in non-Anglophone countries" (Piller, 2016, p. 179). This raises challenges related to the use of English as a language of instruction in a multilingual country. In Spain, there is a clear preference for bilingual programmes (English-Spanish) since Spanish is a widely spoken language, in line with "the Strategy for the Internationalization of Spanish Universities" guidelines provided by the MECD (2014b). In this context, the growing role of English in higher education involves neglecting other additional languages like French or German.

The internationalization of Spanish universities also poses challenges involving assessing and accrediting of students' command of English because of the different universities' language policies, or the recommended level of English required for faculty members who teach through English and Administrative staff in charge of duties related to internationalization of the university. Another important challenge refers to the linguistic and methodological training of the teaching staff involved in bilingual programmes and the debate about the choice of teaching approaches: EMI (focus on content only) or ICLHE (integrating language and content).

On the other hand, the implementation of the Bologna reform process in Spain has reduced the curricular time for the training of prospective primary teachers in Foreign Language and Didactics in the new undergraduate Teaching Degree. This is unfortunate in a context where the widespread implementation of nationwide bilingual programmes at pre-university level demands high quality initial teacher education and continuous professional development for CLIL. Therefore, after the Bologna Process, initial teacher education for CLIL constitutes a challenge for Colleges of Education in Spain, where the number of bilingual schools in the different regions, including Madrid, has increased dramatically in the last decade. The increasing number of courses that use English in instruction in different disciplines of the Teaching Degrees may provide an opportunity to complement the initial teacher education provision. Bearing this in mind and following the implementation of the Bilingual Group and the English Language Major in the Undergraduate Degree in Primary Education, an interdisciplinary five-stage TIP has been carried out since the 2013–2014 academic year at the UCM School of Education.

The project is framed against the backdrop of the CLIL/ICLHE bilingual teaching approach. Professors in the different disciplines who teach through the medium of English work collaboratively to introduce students to subject content knowledge through studying the curriculum in English. It is a wide-ranging team of professors from different fields of knowledge (Educational Psychology, Art Education, Language Teaching, Physical Education and Music) who employ a common framework (the seven basic competences of the Spanish Primary Education curriculum) to implement interdisciplinary activities and introduce innovation in their classrooms. Such initiatives can help to cope with challenges posed by the new scenario after the EHEA, in which language teaching specialists work in collaboration with content specialists, and an ICLHE approach is used for the training of prospective primary teachers, and in which content and language are fully integrated. In this respect, other types of teamwork, such as collaboration between university faculty and classroom teachers, in which they participate in teacher education initiatives together, seem to point in the right direction.

Furthermore, more research studies need to be carried out to explore the nature of faculty collaboration and the benefits of an interdisciplinary approach in ICLHE settings, particularly after the growth of CLIL programmes at pre-university level. As Dafouz et al. (2014) rightly put it, "Nonetheless, in spite of the dimension and fast implementation of CLIL programmes across Europe, at the tertiary level there is still an urgent need for interdisciplinary research that will help to provide empirical evidence and, ultimately, reinforce content teacher and language specialist collaboration" (p. 224).

To conclude, Spanish universities are confronted by numerous challenges, not least those related to "renewed work organization" (Vangrieken et al., 2015, p. 37). We believe that an interdisciplinary collaborative approach to teaching/learning is a quality model for good practice in teacher education.

This five-year teaching innovation project was supported by the University Complutense of Madrid: PIMCD 2014/166 (2014–2015); PIMCD 2015/124 (2015–2016); and Innova Docencia no. 10 (2016–2017), Innova Docencia no.13 (2017–2018) and Innova Docencia no. 32) (2018–2019).

Appendix

POST-PROJECT QUESTIONNAIRE

As you know, you have participated in an educational innovation experience with the aim of enabling you to acquire the necessary competences to make interdisciplinary teaching proposals as future primary teachers. In "Training for Bilingual Education" we have used picturebooks to design cross-curricular teaching units to develop gender awareness in the CLIL classroom.

It would be very helpful for us to have your feedback on the experience, so we would appreciate your honesty in answering the following questions.

Personal Information

- Are you male or female?

- Age:

- Nationality:

Part 1:

1.- Once we have finished the cross-curricular task above, what do you understand by "interdisciplinary teaching"?

2.- Please indicate your level of agreement with each of the following statements, giving each a number (**1 being the lowest and 5 the highest**).

1) The training that I have received throughout this educational experience has been a good opportunity to understand the existing connection between the different subjects	1	2	3	4	5
2) Collaboration between professors from different subjects in the Degree has improved our training to be future teachers	1	2	3	4	5
3) My participation in this bilingual experience is enabling me to better understand the curriculum of other subjects	1	2	3	4	5
4) My participation in this real interdisciplinary teaching experience has improved my training to be a future teacher	1	2	3	4	5
5) As a teacher, I intend to carry out interdisciplinary proposals in the future.	1	2	3	4	5

6) I am satisfied with what I have learnt during this course about interdisciplinary work	1	2	3	4	5
7) I believe that we have achieved the competences planned in the teaching guide of the course	1	2	3	4	5
8) The development of the course followed what is stated in the teaching guide	1	2	3	4	5
9) My degree of satisfaction towards each of the activities done (a, b, c,d and e) has been:					
a) Session 1: Picturebooks and gender equality	1	2	3	4	5
b) Session 2: Unit plan template and samples with picturebooks	1	2	3	4	5
c) Interdisciplinary group work	1	2	3	4	5
d) Feedback provided	1	2	3	4	5
e) Teaching unit presentation	1	2	3	4	5

Part 2:

3.- State below those aspects that you would highlight as the most positive of the cross-curricular experience in this subject.

4.- Is there any aspect of the experience that you think needs improving? Please, state which.

5.- Other suggestions and comments.

THANK YOU FOR TAKING THE TIME TO FILL IN THIS QUESTIONNAIRE!

References

Aguilar, M. (2015). Engineering lecturers' views on CLIL and EMI. *International Journal of Bilingual Education and Bilingualism, 20*(6), 722–735. https://doi.org/10.1080/13670050.2015

Aguilar, M., & Muñoz, C. (2014). The effect of proficiency on CLIL benefits in engineering students in Spain. *International Journal of Applied Linguistics, 24*, 1–18.

Airey, J. (2012). I don't teach language. The linguistic attitudes of Physics lecturers in Sweden. *AILA Review, 25*, 64–79. https://doi.org/10.1075/aila.25.05air

Altava, V., Pérez, I. C., & Ríos, I. M. (1999). La interdisciplinariedad como instrumento de formación del profesorado. *Revista electrónica interuniversitaria de formación del profesorado, 2*(1), 241–250.

Altbach, P. G., & Knight, J. (2007). The internationalization of higher education: Motivations and realities. *Journal of Studies in International Education, 11*(3–4), 290–305.

Barnes, J. (2018). *Applying Cross-curricular Approaches Creatively* (Learning to Teach in the Primary School Series). London: Routledge.

Barrios-Espinosa, E., López-Gutiérrez, A., & Lechuga-Jiménez, C. (2016). Facing challenges in English medium instruction through engaging in an innovation project. *Procedia—Social and Behavioral Sciences, 228*, 209–214. https://doi.org/10.1016/j.sbspro.2016.07.031

Bazo, P., Centellas, A., Dafouz, E., Fernández, A., González, D., & Pavón, V. (2017). *Documento marco de política lingüística para la internacionalización del sistema universitario español*. Madrid: Conferencia de Rectores de Universidades Españolas (CRUE).

Cenoz, J. (2017). The target language, the sociolinguistic and the educational context in CLIL programs. In A. Llinares & T. Morton (Eds.), *Applied Linguistics Perspectives on CLIL* (pp. 247–257). Amsterdam: John Benjamins.

Coleman, J. (2006). English-medium teaching in European higher education. *Language Teaching, 39*(1), 1–14. https://doi.org/10.1017/S0261444 80600320X

Cone, T. P., Werner, P., & Cone, S. (2009). *Interdisciplinary Elementary Physical Education*. Champaign, IL: Human Kinetics.

Cots, J. M. (2013). Introducing English-medium instruction at the University of Lleida, Spain: Interventions, beliefs and practices. In A. Doiz, D. Lasagabaster, & J. M. Sierra (Eds.), *English-Medium Instruction at University. Global Challenges* (pp. 106–128). Bristol: Multilingual Matters.

Cots, J. M., Llurda, E., & Peter Garrett, P. (2014). Language policies and practices in the internationalisation of higher education on the European margins: An introduction. *Journal of Multilingual and Multicultural Development, 35*(4), 311–317. https://doi.org/10.1080/01434632.2013.874430

Coyle, D., Hood, P., & Marsh, D. (2010). *CLIL: Content and Language Integrated Learning.* Cambridge: Cambridge University Press.

CRUE. (2018). *La Universidad Española en Cifras, 2016/2017.* Retrieved from http://www.crue.org/SitePages/La-Universidad-Espa%C3%B1ola-en-Cifras.aspx

Dafouz, E. (2011). English as the medium of instruction in Spanish contexts: A look at teacher discourses. In Y. Ruiz de Zarobe, J. M. Sierra, & F. Gallardo del Puerto (Eds.), *Content and Foreign Language Integrated Learning* (pp. 189–209). Bern, Switzerland: Peter Lang.

Dafouz, E., Camacho, M., & Urquía, E. (2014). 'Surely they can't do as well': A comparison of business students' academic performance in English-medium and Spanish-as-first-language-medium programmes. *Language and Education, 28*(3), 223–236.

Dalton-Puffer, C. (2011). Content-and-language integrated learning: From practice to principles? *Annual Review of Applied Linguistics, 31*, 182–204.

De la Maya Retamar, G., & Luengo González, R. (2015). Teacher training programs and development of plurilingual competence. In D. Marsh, M. L. Pérez Cañado, & J. R. Padilla (Eds.), *CLIL in Action: Voices from the Classroom* (pp. 114–129). Newcastle upon Tyne: Cambridge Scholars Publishing.

Dearden, J. (2014). *English as a Medium of Instruction—A Growing Global Phenomenon: Phase 1.* London: British Council.

Delgado, L. (2014). Governance of higher education in Spain. In S. Bergan (Ed.), *Leadership and Governance in Higher Education* (pp. 120–146). Berlin: Raabe Academic Publishers.

Delgado, L. (2017). Higher education systems and institutions, Spain. In J. C. Shin & P. Teixeira (Eds.), *Encyclopedia of International Higher Education Systems and Institutions* (pp. 1–11). Dordrecht: Springer.

Delicado, G., & Pavón, V. (2016). Training primary pre-service teachers for CLIL: Innovation through collaboration. *Pulso, 39*, 35–57.

Dobson, A., Johnstone, R., & Pérez Murillo, M. D. (2010). *Evaluation Report of the Bilingual Education Project.* Madrid: Spanish Ministry of Education, Culture and Sport & British Council, Spain.

Doiz, A., Lasagabaster, D., & Sierra, J. M. (Eds.). (2013). *English-Medium Instruction at University. Global Challenges.* Bristol: Multilingual Matters.

Escobar Urmeneta, C. (2011). Colaboración interdisciplinar, partenariado y centros de formación docente: tres ejes para sustentar la colaboración del profesorado AICLE. In C. Escobar Urmeneta & L. Nussbaum (Eds.), *Learning through Another Language* (pp. 203–230). Bellaterra: Servei de Publicacions de la Universitat Autònoma de Barcelona.

European Commission. (2004). *Promoting Language Learning and Linguistic Diversity: An Action Plan 2004–2006*. Brussels, Belgium: European Commission. Retrieved from https://eur-lex.europa.eu/LexUriServ/LexUriServ.do?uri=COM:2003:0449:FIN:en:PDF

European Commission. (2012). *Special Eurobarometer 386, "Europeans and their Languages Report"*. Brussels, Belgium: European Commission. Retrieved from http://ec.europa.eu/commfrontoffice/publicopinion/archives/ebs/ebs_386_en.pdf

European Parliament, Council of the European Union. (2006, December 30). *Recommendation of the European Parliament and of the Council of 18 December 2006 on Key Competences for Lifelong Learning*. Brussels, Belgium: Official Journal of the European Union (2006/962/EC), OJ L 394, 10–18. Retrieved from https://eur-lex.europa.eu/legal-content/EN/TXT/PDF/?uri=CELEX:3 2006H0962&from=CS

EUROSTAT. (2018). *Foreign Language Skills Statistics. Statistics Explained*. Retrieved from https://ec.europa.eu/eurostat/statistics-explained/index.php/Foreign_language_skills_statistics

Feixas, M., Codó, E., & Espinet, M. (2009). Enseñar en inglés en la universidad: Reflexiones del alumnado y el profesorado entorno a las experiencias AICLE. In R. Roig (Ed.), *Investigar desde un contexto educativo innovador* (pp. 137–154). Alcoy, Alicante: Marfil.

Fernández-Fontecha, A. (2009). Spanish CLIL: Research and official actions. In Y. Ruiz de Zarobe & R. M. Jiménez Catalán (Eds.), *Content and Language Integrated Learning. Evidence from Research in Europe* (pp. 3–21). Bristol: Multilingual Matters.

Fortanet-Gómez, I. (2008). Questions for debate in English medium lecturing in Spain. In R. Wilkinson & V. Zegers (Eds.), *Realizing Content and Language Integration in Higher Education* (pp. 21–31). Maastricht: Maastricht University.

Fortanet-Gómez, I. (2013). *CLIL in Higher Education: Towards a Multilingual Language Policy*. Bristol: Multilingual Matters.

Frigols, M. J. (2008). CLIL implementation in Spain: An approach to different models. In C. M. Coonan (Ed.), *CLIL e l'apprendimento delle lingue. Le sfide del nuovo ambiente di apprendimento* (pp. 221–232). Venice, Italy: Libreria Editrice Cafoscarina.

García Sánchez, M. L., & Rodríguez Collado, M. M. (2015). The impact of competence-based education on bilingual programs in Andalusian Secondary Schools. In D. Marsh, M. L. Pérez Cañado, & J. Ráez Padilla (Eds.), *CLIL in Action: Voices from the Classroom* (pp. 130–149). Newcastle upon Tyne: Cambridge Scholars Publishing.

Gardner, H. (1993). *Frames of Mind: The Theory of Multiple Intelligences*. New York: Basic Books.

Gardner, S. (2012). Global English and bilingual education. In M. Martin-Jones, A. Blackledge, & A. Creese (Eds.), *The Routledge Handbook of Multilingualism* (pp. 247–263). London: Routledge.

Genesse, F., & Hamayan, E. E. (2016). *CLIL in Context: Practical Guidance for Educators*. Cambridge: Cambridge University Press.

González Gándara, D. (2015). CLIL in Galicia: Repercussions on academic performance. *Latin American Journal of Content and Language Integrated Learning, 8*(1), 13–24.

Granados Sánchez, J., Pamies, J., Romero, A., & Villanueva, M. (2015). The introduction of a competence-based Curriculum in Spain: From the primary school to the training of teachers. *E-Pedagogium, 2*, 62–74.

Haataja, K., Kruczinna, R., Àrkossy, K., & Costa, C. (2011). *CLIL-LOTE-START. CLIL-LOTE-START—Content and Language Integrated Learning for Languages Other than English—Getting Started!* Graz, Austria: European Centre for Modern Languages of the Council of Europe, UCML. Retrieved from https://www.ecml.at/Portals/1/documents/ECML-resources/CLIL-LOTE-START-EN.pdf?ver=2018-03-21-093109-230

Halbach, A., & Lázaro, A. (2015). *La acreditación del nivel de lengua inglesa en las universidades españolas: Actualización 2015*. Retrieved from https://www.britishcouncil.es/sites/default/files/british-council-la-acreditacion-del-nivel-de-lengua-inglesa.pdf

Halbach, A., Lázaro, A., & Pérez, J. (2013). La lengua inglesa en la nueva universidad del EEES. *Revista de Educación, 362*, 105–132. Retrieved from http://www.mecd.gob.es/revista-de-educacion/

Initial Teacher Education for CLIL: Interdisciplinary Innovation Project. (n.d.). Retrieved April 3, 2019, from https://www.ucm.es/admin/apps/?apn=web&ope=grupos

Jacobs, H. H. (1989). *Interdisciplinary Curriculum: Design and Implementation*. Alexandria, VA: Association for Supervision and Curriculum Development, ASCD.

Jover, G., Fleta, T., & González, R. (2016). La Formación Inicial de los Maestros de Educación Primaria en el contexto de la Enseñanza Bilingüe en Lengua Extranjera/Pre-Service Education of Primary School Teachers in the Context of Foreign Language Bilingual Teaching. *Bordón, 68*(2), 121–135.

Kelly, D. (2017). Language policy for internationalisation: Spanish as an asset. In A. Pérez-Encinas, L. Rumbley, L. Howard, & H. de Wit (Eds.), *The Internationalisation of Higher Education in Spain: Reflections and Perspectives.* Madrid: Spanish Service for the Internationalisation of Education (SEPIE). Retrieved from http://sepie.es/doc/comunicacion/publicaciones/SEPIE-ENG_internacionalizacion.pdf

Kirkpatrick, A. (2014). ELF and/or multilingualism? *The Asian Journal of Applied Linguistics, 1*(1), 4–15.

Klein, G. (2002). Interdisciplinarity in study abroad. In C. Haynes (Ed.), *Innovations in Interdisciplinary Teaching* (pp. 201–220). Westport, CT: Oryx Press.

Knight, J. (2003). Updated definition of internationalization. *International Higher Education, 33*, 2–3.

Lagasabaster, D. (2015). Language policy and language choice at European Universities: Is there really a 'choice'? *European Journal of Applied Linguistics, 3*, 255–276.

Lasagabaster, D., & Huguet, A. (Eds.). (2007). *Multilingualism in European Bilingual Contexts.* Clevedon: Multilingual Matters.

Lagasabaster, D., & Ruiz de Zarobe, Y. (Eds.). (2010). *CLIL in Spain: Implementation, Results and Teacher Training.* Newcastle upon Tyne: Cambridge Scholars Publishers.

Llinares, A. (2015). Integration in CLIL: A proposal to inform research and successful pedagogy. *Language, Culture and Curriculum, 28*(1), 58–73. https://doi.org/10.1080/07908318.2014.1000925

Llinares, A., & Dafouz, E. (2010). Content and language integrated programmes in the Madrid region: Overview and research findings. In D. Lagasabaster & Y. R. de Zarobe (Eds.), *CLIL in Spain: Implementation, Results and Teacher Training* (pp. 99–114). Newcastle upon Tyne: Cambridge Scholars Publishers.

Madrid, D., & Pérez Cañado, M. L. (2012). CLIL teacher training. In J. d. D. M. Agudo (Ed.), *Teaching and Learning English through Bilingual Education* (pp. 181–212). Newcastle upon Tyne: Cambridge Scholars Publishers.

Marsh, D., Pavón, V., & Frigols, M. J. (2013). *The Higher Education Languages Landscape: Ensuring Quality in English Language Degree Programmes.* Valencia: Valencian International University.

Martín del Pozo, M. A. (2016). The internalization of universities and the English Language. In M. Geat & V. A. Piccione (Eds.), *The Reasons of Erasmus: Scientific Research and Intersections. For Education in Present Days: Humanities, Internationalization, Networking, Innovation* (pp. 67–81). Rome: RomaTrE-Press.

MECD. (2007a, April 13). *Ley Orgánica 4/2007, de 12 de abril, por la que se modifica la Ley Orgánica 6/2001, de 21 de diciembre, de Universidades.* «*BOE*» 89. Retrieved from https://www.boe.es/buscar/doc.php?id=BOE-A-2007-7786

MECD. (2007b, December 29). *ORDEN ECI/3857/2007, de 27 de diciembre, por la que se establecen los requisitos para la verificación de los títulos universitarios oficiales que habiliten para el ejercicio de la profesión de Maestro en Educación Primaria.* «*BOE*» 312. Retrieved from https://www.boe.es/boe/dias/2007/12/29/pdfs/A53747-53750.pdf

MECD. (2014a, March 01). *Real Decreto 126/2014, de 28 de febrero, por el que se establece el currículo básico de la Educación Primaria.* «*BOE*» 52. Retrieved from https://www.boe.es/buscar/pdf/2014/BOE-A-2014-2222-consolidado.pdf

MECD. (2014b). *Estrategia para la Internacionalización de las Universidades Españolas.* Madrid: Ministerio de Educación, Cultura y Deporte.

Mehisto, P., Marsh, D., & Frigols, M. J. (2008). *Uncovering CLIL: Content and Language Integrated Learning in Bilingual and Multilingual Education.* Oxford: Palgrave Macmillan.

Muñoz, C., & Navés, T. (2007). CLIL in Spain. In A. Maljers, D. Marsh, & D. Wolff (Eds.), *Windows on CLIL: Content and Language Integrated Learning in the European Spotlight* (pp. 160–165). The Hague: European Platform for Dutch Education, and Graz: European Centre for Modern Languages.

Navés, T. (2009). Effective content and language integrated learning programmes. In Y. R. de Zarobe & R. J. Catalán (Eds.), *Content and Language Integrated Learning: Evidence from Research in Europe.* Bristol: Multilingual Matters.

Nikula, T. (2017). CLIL: A European approach to bilingual education. In N. Van Deusen-Scholl & S. May (Eds.), *Second and Foreign Language Education. Encyclopedia of Language and Education* (3rd ed.). Cham, Switzerland: Springer.

O'Dowd, R. (2018). The training and accreditation of teachers for English medium instruction: An overview of practice in European Universities. *International Journal of Bilingual Education and Bilingualism, 5,* 553–563. https://doi.org/10.1080/13670050.2018.1491945

Pavón, V., & Gaustad, M. (2013). Designing bilingual programmes for higher education in Spain: Organisational, curricular and methodological decisions. *International CLIL Research Journal, 2*(1), 82–94.

Pérez-Vidal, C. (2011). Language acquisition in three different contexts of learning: Formal instruction, stay abroad, and semi-immersion (CLIL). In Y. Ruiz de Zarobe, J. M. Sierra, & F. Gallardo del Puerto (Eds.), *Content and Foreign Language Integrated Learning. Contributions to Multilingualism in European Context* (pp. 103–127). Bern: Peter Lang.

Pérez-Vidal, C. (2015). Languages for all in education: CLIL and ICLHE at the crossroads of multilingualism, mobility and internationalisation. In M. Juan-Garau & J. Salazar-Noguera (Eds.), *Content-Based Language Learning in Multilingual Educational Environments* (pp. 31–50). Clevedon: Multilingual Matters.

Phillipson, R. (2006). English, a Cuckoo in the European higher education nest of languages? *European Journal of English Studies, 10*, 13–32. https://doi.org/10.1080/13825570600590846

Piller, I. (2016). *Linguistic Diversity and Social Justice: An Introduction to Applied Sociolinguistics*. Oxford: Oxford University Press.

Pozuelos, F. J., Rodríguez, F., & Travé, G. (2017). El enfoque interdisciplinar en la enseñanza universitaria y aprendizaje basado en la investigación. Un estudio de caso en el marco de la formación. *Revista de Educación, 357*, 213–214.

Ramos-García, A. M. (2013). Higher education bilingual programmes in Spain. *Porta Linguarum, 19*, 101–111.

Ramos-García, A. M., & Pavón Vázquez, V. (2018). The linguistic internationalization of higher education: A study on the presence of language policies and bilingual studies in Spanish Universities. *Porta-Linguarum, 2018*(III), 31–46.

Reichelt, M. (2006). English in a multilingual Spain. *English Today, 22*(3), 3–9. https://doi.org/10.1017/S0266078406003026

Research and Development Project INTERLICA. (n.d.). Retrieved April 3, 2019, from https://www.ucm.es/interlica

Romero, E., & Zayas, F. (2017). Challenges and opportunities of training teachers for plurilingual education. In J. Valcke & R. Wilkinson (Eds.), *Integrating Content and Language in Higher Education: Perspectives on Professional Practice* (pp. 205–225). New York: Peter Lang Publishing Group.

Ruiz de Zarobe, Y., & Lasagabaster, D. (2010). *CLIL in Spain. Implementation, Results and Teacher Training*. Newcastle upon Tyne: Cambridge Scholars Publishing.

Segovia, I., Lupiáñez, J., Molina, M., González-García, F., Miñán, A., & Real, I. (2010). The conception and role of interdisciplinarity in the Spanish education system. *Issues in Integrative Studies, 28*, 138–169.

Smit, U., & Dafouz-Milne, E. (2012). Integrating content and language in higher education: An introduction to English-medium policies, conceptual issues and research practices across Europe. *Special Issue of AILA Review, 25*, 1–12.

Spanish Service for Education Internalisation, SEPIE. (n.d.). What to study in Spain? Retrieved April 3, 2019, from http://sepie.es/internacionalizacion/what-to-study-in-spain.html

Tsuchiya, K., & Pérez Murillo, M. D. (2015). Comparing the language policies and the students' perceptions of CLIL in tertiary education in Spain and Japan. *Latin American Journal of Content and Language Integrated Learning, 8*, 25–35.

Vangrieken, K., Dochy, F., Raes, E., & Kyndt, E. (2015). Teacher collaboration: A systematic review. *Educational Research Review, 15*, 17–40. https://doi.org/10.1016/j.edurev.2015.04.002

Vila Moreno, F. X., & Bretxa, V. (2014). *Language Policy in Higher Education: The Case of Medium-Sized Languages*. Bristol: Multilingual Matters.

Vlachos, K. (2009). The potential of information communication technologies (ICT) in content and language integrated learning (CLIL): The case of English as a second/foreign language. In D. Marsh, P. Mehisto, D. Wolff, R. Aliaga, T. Asikainen, M. J. Frigols-Martin, S. Hughes, & G. Lange (Eds.), *CLIL Practice: Perspectives from the Field* (pp. 189–198). Finland: CCN, University of Syvaskyla.

Wächter, B., & Maiworm, F. (Eds.). (2014). *English-Taught Programmes in European Higher Education*. Bonn: Lemmens Medien. Retrieved from http://www.aca-secretariat.be/fileadmin/aca_docs/images/members/ACA-2015_English_Taught_01.pdf

Wilkinson, R. (2013). English-medium instruction at a Dutch University: Challenges and pitfalls. In A. Doiz, D. Lasagabaster, & J. M. Sierra (Eds.), *English-Medium Instruction at University. Global Challenges* (pp. 3–24). Bristol: Multilingual Matters.

Wilkinson, R., & Zegers, V. (2007). *Researching Content and Language Integration in Higher Education*. Nijmegen: Valkhof Pers.

15

Prospective Teachers' Perceptions of CLIL in Spain and Japan: Translingual Social Formation through EMI-CLIL Lectures

Keiko Tsuchiya and María Dolores Pérez Murillo

1 Introduction

Globalisation has transformed individuals' lives in many aspects, and language education is not an exception. In the field of Applied Linguistics, this process has caused *a multilingual turn* (May, 2014), a paradigm shift from monolingual norms to "the existing bi/multilingual repertoires of learners" (p. 8). Multi/plurilingual practice in various contexts has been depicted by a number of applied linguists (Blackledge & Creese, 2010; Canagarajah, 2013; Duff, 2015; García & Li Wei, 2014; Martin-Jones, 2015; May, 2014). According to Duff (2015), "[m]ultilingualism and transnationalism are intimately tied to globalization, which affects poli-

K. Tsuchiya (✉)
International College of Arts and Sciences, Yokohama City University, Yokohama, Japan
e-mail: ktsuchiy@yokohama-cu.ac.jp

M. D. Pérez Murillo
School of Education, Complutense University in Madrid, Madrid, Spain
e-mail: perezmur@edu.ucm.es

© The Author(s) 2019   **373**
K. Tsuchiya, M. D. Pérez Murillo (eds.), *Content and Language Integrated Learning in Spanish and Japanese Contexts*, https://doi.org/10.1007/978-3-030-27443-6_15

cies related to citizenship, education, language assessment, and many other areas of 21st-century applied linguistics and society" (Duff, 2015, p. 61). In the European context, multi/plurilingual education policies have been introduced since the late 1990s in EU nations. Romero and Zayas (2017) argue that this has been perceived positively. As they put it, "[a]t the turn of the twenty-first century, the social and political context in Europe has been favourable [to plurilingual education]" (Romero & Zayas, 2017, p. 206). In the globalised society where people migrate between nations, English has been perceived as a social and cultural capital, and English language education has been prioritised by governments as Gardner (2012) states:

> Linked to the demand for [global] English is the rise of English in education internationally as governments introduce English in schools earlier and earlier, as content areas are increasingly being taught in English, as universities teach more courses through English, and as the demand for an education in a language with such valuable and portable global capital increases with migration and transnational lifestyles. (Gardner, 2012, p. 250)

To capture the *education-based social transformation* (cf. Duff, 2015; Vertovec, 2009) in Europe and Asia, this chapter compares language policies and prospective teachers' perceptions of EMI-CLIL (Content and Language Integrated Learning in English as a Medium of Instruction) at universities in Madrid, Spain and Kanagawa, Japan. The following section reviews the rationales behind the introduction of EMI-CLIL in higher education in both countries.

2   Introduction of EMI-CLIL in Spain and Japan

To enhance the mobility of citizens in the EU, in 1982, the Council of Europe established a set of principles to improve multilingual education through the learning of modern European languages in 1982 (Council of Europe, 1982). The Bologna Declaration (European Commission, 1999) encouraged mobility by implementing the framework for undergraduate and postgraduate degrees across the EU countries. This framework allowed higher education institutions to transfer credits and promote student mobility through the ERASMUS programme (also see Smit & Dafouz, 2012). Thus, higher education has played an important role in improving multi/plurilingual practices through exchanging programmes which allow many students to stay in other countries at least for a term, during which they can obtain language qualifications.

The ERASMUS programme has drastically increased the mobility of university students from 3244 students in 1987–1988 to 267,547 in 2012–2013 (EU, 2015). Also, the number of EMI programmes in higher education institutions in the EU has been boosted from 725 in 2001 to 8089 in 2014 (Wächter & Maiworm, 2014). In the case of Spanish universities, "[t]hirty-three of them include bilingual (or plurilingual) programmes in their undergraduate courses" (Ramos, 2013, p. 103). Bilingual education was also introduced to pre-university education in Madrid in the late 1990s with the Spanish Ministry of Education, Culture and Sports "Bilingual and Bicultural Project" in partnership with the British Council (Dobson, Pérez Murillo, & Johnstone, 2010; MECD, 2017). The practice of CLIL has been widely implemented (Llinares & Dafouz-Milne, 2017) to an extent that in the 2015–2016 school year, 40.2% of primary students and 25.7% of secondary students were taking subject classes in a foreign language (MECD, 2017). Two years later, in the 2007–2018 school year, over 45% of primary schools and more than half of the secondary schools in Madrid were bilingual (Pérez Murillo, 2018).

In Japan, English became a required subject in secondary schools in the late 1990s (MEXT, 1998). Ten years later, there was another reform of the Course of Study in 2008 which encouraged the use of the target language in upper secondary education: "teaching English through English". At the same time, *foreign language activities* were introduced to the fifth and sixth grades in primary education, and this became a formal subject in the latest curriculum reform. At tertiary level, EMI has been promoted in line with the government language policies since the early 2000s (MEXT, 2012). The *Strategic Plan to Cultivate Japanese with English abilities* was presented in 2002, and the Action Plan was issued in the following year to meet the demand for a workforce with English proficiency to enable the growth of the Japanese economy in the globalised society (MEXT, 2003). In 2008, the Top Global University Project was launched, which aims to increase the number of international students in Japanese universities to 300,000 by 2020 (MEXT, 2009). The plan initially provided funding to 13 universities selected as centres for internationalisation in 2009, and this rose to 37 universities in 2014 (MEXT, 2014). The policy document *Higher Education in Japan* published in 2012 describes the internationalisation of universities as follows:

> Amid ongoing globalization, in order to develop an educational environment where Japanese people can acquire the necessary *English skills* and also *international students* can feel at ease to study in Japan, it is very important for Japanese universities *to conduct lessons in English for a certain extent*, or to develop courses where students can obtain academic degrees by taking lessons conducted entirely in English. [...] Of course, such universities still also provide *substantial Japanese-language education courses*. (MEXT, 2012, our emphases)

To cope with the globalised society, EMI has been introduced to universities in Japan to provide Japanese with necessary English skills and to attract international students. Following these language policies, 41% of universities in Japan provided subject classes in English in undergraduate courses in the fiscal year 2015 (MEXT, 2017). However, it is worth noting that only two languages, English and Japanese, are mentioned as a medium of instruction, and the concept of multilingualism is never mentioned in the document. As Tsuchiya and Pérez Murillo (2015) indicated, there are different rationales behind the implantation of EMI in Japan and European countries: in the former, the policy is *reactive* to provide the workforce with English proficiency for economic purposes, whereas, in the latter, it is a *proactive* strategy to realise the EU's multilingual policy (Commission of the European Communities, 2003). That said, there are critics who see the Bologna Process as promoting *linguistic imperialism* as discussed in Kirkpatrick (2014a).

Considering the context of the introduction of EMI-CLIL in Spain and Japan, the current study examines how prospective teachers in both sites perceive EMI-CLIL. Stakeholders' perceptions of CLIL have been investigated in various aspects: Spanish students' perceptions of CLIL in relation to their foreign language proficiency and motivation have been examined at the secondary level (Lasagabaster, 2011; Lasagabaster & Doiz, 2016) and at the tertiary level (Dafouz, Núñez, Sancho, & Foran, 2007; Maíz-Arévalo & Domínguez-Romero, 2013). In Austria, Hüttner, Dalton-Puffer, and Smit (2012) looked at vocational school students and teachers' belief about CLIL as a language education policy. Ikeda (2013) carried out a study of CLIL course evaluations by students and teachers in a state secondary school in Japan. However, how future teachers perceive EMI-CLIL as a social practice in the two respective contexts (Japan and Spain) has not hitherto been studied. To fill this gap, two research objectives are addressed in this study: (1) to examine future teachers' use of languages in daily life and (2) their perceptions of EMI lectures at the tertiary level. A questionnaire survey and focus group interviews were conducted to obtain their views. The results are discussed in reference to the concept of *imagined community* (Norton, 2001), which is reviewed in the following section.

3   Language Learning and Imagined Community

Researchers in second language acquisition used to see language learners as individuals in a language classroom, examining their psychological and personal characters rather than their sociocultural backgrounds, communities they belong to and people they interact with outside the classroom. Around the mid-1990s, a shift in how language learners were perceived began to take place. Norton Pierce (1995) reconceptualised language learners as *social beings* in the framework of sociocultural theories developed by poststructuralists. This new concept emphasised learners' multiple and changing *identities* and posited the concept of *investment* in language learning rather than *motivation* to "capture the complex relationship of language learners to the target language and their sometimes ambivalent desire to speak it" (p. 9).

Based on the seminal work of Andersen (1983), the notion of *imagined communities* was used in Norton's (2001) study of immigrant learners in Canada. Imagined communities are defined as "groups of people, not immediately tangible and accessible, with whom we connect through the power of the imagination" (Kanno & Norton, 2003, p. 241). Thus, the community where the target language is spoken is an *imagined community* for language learners, which is for them "a desired community that offers possibilities for an enhanced range of identity options in the future" (Norton & Toohey, 2011, p. 415).

The focus of this study is prospective teachers' perceptions of EMI-CLIL in higher education in Spain and Japan. The situations of these students are different from those of informants in Norton's research. In the context of her studies, the learners were immigrants who had gone (or were going) through the process of *transnational social formation*, moving from their home countries to a host country for various reasons (Duff, 2015; Vertovec, 2009). In contrast, the experiences of the Spanish and Japanese prospective teachers are not *transnational* but rather *translingual* practices through the EMI-CLIL they have experienced. In this context, how they perceive the EMI-CLIL classes and what *imagined communities* they are associated with through language learning are of our central interest.

4 Research Data and Method

A questionnaire survey was conducted to investigate students' perceptions of EMI-CLIL in the two sites, Madrid, Spain, and in Kanagawa, Japan, from 2013 to 2015. In total, 500 respondents contributed to the study (408 in Spain and 92 in Japan). Spanish informants were undergraduate students who majored in the Primary Education Degree Programme at a university in Madrid, Spain. Some of them (149 students) were enrolled in the bilingual strand, which was launched in 2011. The entry level of the strand is B2 level in the Common European Framework of Reference for Languages (CEFR), and nearly 65% of the curriculum was conducted in English. The others (259 students) were in the Mainstream course mainly taught in Spanish, and they had different levels of English proficiency (ranging from CEFR levels A2 to B2). The Japanese informants (92 students) were undergraduate students in the Department of Arts and Sciences at a university in Kanagawa, Japan. All the students attended an undergraduate course of English Language Teaching (ELT), which was an EMI module and compulsory to the students who wish to receive the certificate to become secondary school English teachers in Japan. They are required to obtain a TOEFL PBT score of over 500 before by the end of the second year.

The survey was conducted in both sites from 2013 to 2015. Furthermore, three audio-recorded focus group interviews were conducted in Japan in 2015 to probe deeper into these students' views. The questionnaire survey was developed based on that of Fortanet-Gómez (2013). Background information collected focused on students' personal backgrounds (course they were enrolled on and countries they had lived in) and their language repertoires (their first, second and other languages, and the use of those languages in everyday life). In terms of their perceptions of EMI-CLIL, they were asked if they thought lessons should be conducted both in their first language (L1) and English in primary, secondary and tertiary levels, and what they saw as the advantages and disadvantages of EMI-CLIL (see Appendix 1).

In addition to the questionnaire survey, ten Japanese undergraduate students (three males and four females) agreed to take part in the focus group interviews (see Table 15.1). Most of them majored in Human

Table 15.1 Participants of the focus group interviews

	Names	Male/ Female	Grade	Department	Study Abroad
Group 1	Ken	Male	2nd	Human Science	
	Sawa	Female	2nd	Human Science	
	Yuri	Female	2nd	Human Science	
Group 2	Aki	Female	2nd	Sociology	Short Study Abroad
	Sora	Male	2nd	Environmental Studies	
	Mako	Female	3rd	Human Science	
Group 3	Haru	Female	2nd	Liberal Arts	Thailand (1year)
	Kota	Male	3rd	Human Science	
	Yayoi	Female	3rd	Social Relations	
	Mai	Female	4th	Human Science	Short Study Abroad

Note: All names are pseudonyms

Sciences and some studied Sociology, Environmental Studies, Arts and Culture and Social Relations. One student had spent a year in Thailand when she was in secondary school, and two others claimed they had been on short study abroad programmes although they did not provide the information about the countries they stayed in and the precise durations. All of them were enrolled in the ELT course mentioned above. Three group interviews were arranged: two groups of three and one group of four members. In the interviews, the participants were first asked to talk about their experiences of learning English, and then the following topics were discussed, which were adapted from Hornberger (1988) and Pérez Murillo (2001):

Discussion Topic: What do you think of those statements?

- All subjects should be taught in English.
- Some subjects should be taught in English and others in Japanese.
- The same subject should be taught in both languages.
- Both languages should always be used during lectures.

The discussions were audio-recorded and transcribed for analysis. The annotation system of the Cambridge and Nottingham Corpus of Discourse in English (CANCODE) (Adolphs, 2006) was applied to the transcripts.[1] A thematic analysis (Guest, MacQueen, & Namey, 2012) with Nvivo (QSR, 2014) was applied to the survey data, and a conversation analytic approach was also used for the qualitative analysis of the interview data. To find out how they position themselves as language learners in social interaction, for example, the students' use of the *membership categorisation device* (Sacks, 1992; Schegloff, 2007) was investigated, which is defined as "cultural conventions in terms of which categories are grouped in relation to other categories" (Hutchby & Wooffitt, 2008, p. 36).

---

[1] The plus symbol + indicates a continuous sentence, and the equal symbol = signals an unfinished sentence. <$G?> indicates inaudible sounds, and <$E>...</$E> shows extralinguistic information.

5 Quantitative Analysis

Figure 15.1 illustrates the results of Q5 in the questionnaire survey: languages that the prospective teachers use in family/friend gatherings and on TV/Internet. In family situations, 90% of the students in all the groups communicate in their first language (L1). When they meet their friends, 42.3% of the students in the bilingual strand use the two languages (English and Spanish), and 12.1% of the students claim that they use more than two languages in this context. As for students in the Spanish mainstream strand and the Japanese students, about three quarters communicate only in their L1, with remaining 25% using both English and L1. In both settings, the use of other languages in addition to Japanese and English is limited. The students seem to engage in bi/multilingual practices more in the use of media: more than 80% of

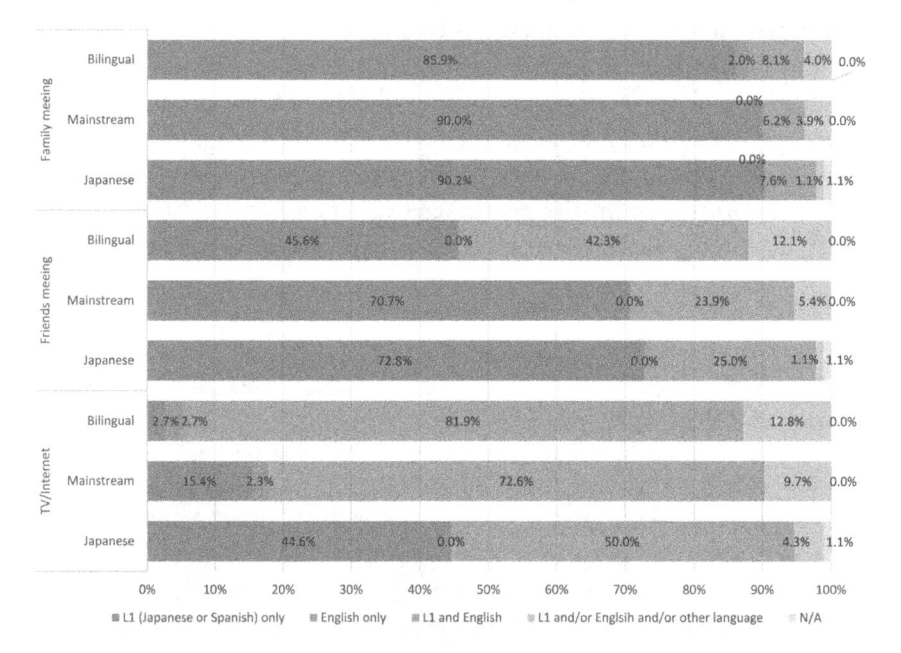

Fig. 15.1 Languages used in daily life. In the figures, Spanish students in the bilingual strand in Madrid are indicated as *Bilingual* (*n* = 149), Spanish students in the mainstream strand in Madrid as *Mainstream* (*n* = 259) and Japanese students in the ELT course in Kanagawa as *Japanese* (*n* = 92)

students in the bilingual strand watch TV and use the Internet in two languages, L1 and English, and 12.8% of them do so in three languages or more. A similar tendency is observed in students in the mainstream: more than 70% of the students use L1 and English when using broadcast and social media, and 9.7% use more than two languages for those purposes. Although the percentage is lower than the other two groups, about half of the Japanese students use both L1 and English when they watch TV or use the Internet, and the percentage is slightly larger than that of those who only use Japanese for these purposes (the former is 50% and the latter 44.6%). There are also few Japanese students who watch TV and use the Internet in English, Japanese plus other languages (4.3%).

Figure 15.2 shows the results of Q6: the degree to which the students agree with the introduction of the bilingual classes taught in primary, secondary and tertiary education. About 80% of the students in the bilingual strand agree or completely agree with EMI-CLIL in secondary and tertiary levels, and this increases to more than 85% when it comes to the introduction of EMI-CLIL in primary education. The percentage of the students in the mainstream strand who favour the use of two languages as a medium of instruction (agree or completely agree) in secondary education is similar to that of the students in the bilingual strand (about 80%). However, the percentages decline to about 70% in EMI-CLIL in primary and tertiary levels. Most Japanese students also agree or

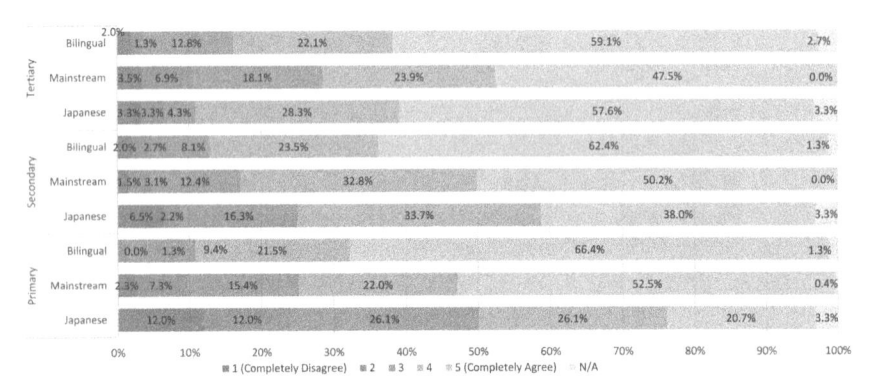

Fig. 15.2 Dis/agreement of CLIL in primary, secondary and tertiary education

completely agree with EMI-CLIL lectures at universities (about 85%) and secondary education (about 70%), but the percentage of the students who agree or completely agree with subject classes both in L1 and English in primary education is considerably lower at less than 50%. As reviewed in the previous section, *foreign language activities* were introduced to primary education in 2011, following the reform of the *Course of Study* in 2008, which seems to affect the students' perceptions of EMI-CLIL in primary education in Japan.

6 Qualitative Analysis

In the next two sections, we will focus on Spanish and Japanese students' responses to Q7 in the questionnaire survey. They were asked to write their opinions about EMI-CLIL in higher education, answering the question: what do you think are the advantages and disadvantages of the subject classes taught in English at university? In both cases, the students' comments were stored and annotated with NVivo, and a thematic analysis was conducted.

6.1 Spanish Prospective Teachers' Perceptions of CLIL: Thematic Analysis

Figures 15.3 and 15.4 illustrate the structures of the coding schemes added to the data of the students' comments in the bilingual strand and the mainstream strand, respectively (see Appendix 2 for the code descriptions). Each code was first annotated to a distinct theme in the texts (e.g., *Future Career*), and then those codes were classified into hierarchical categories (e.g., *Future Career* is placed under the supra-category *Positive*) (see Fig. 15.3).

There are similarities and differences in the themes extracted from comments in the two strands. Similarities are students in both groups raised five codes (*Become Plurilingual, Learn English and Content, Improve English Skills, Future Career and International Students* as sub-codes of *POSITIVE*) and another four codes (*English Ability, Difficult to*

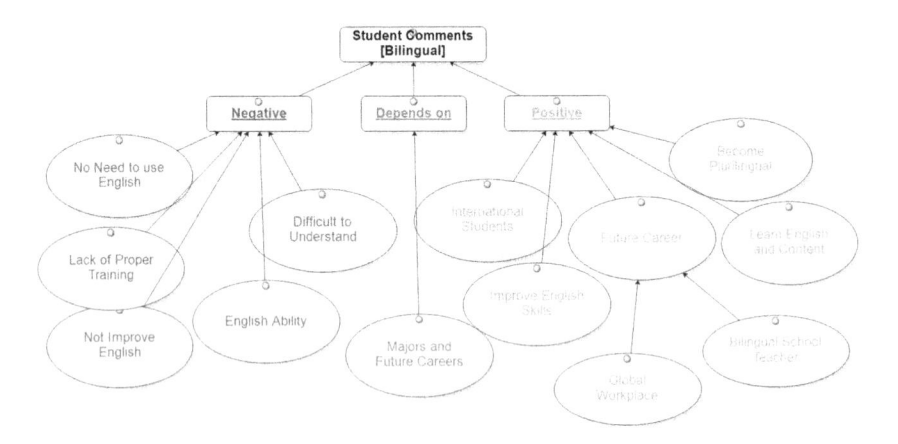

Fig. 15.3 Spanish students' (bilingual strand) perceptions of EMI-CLIL

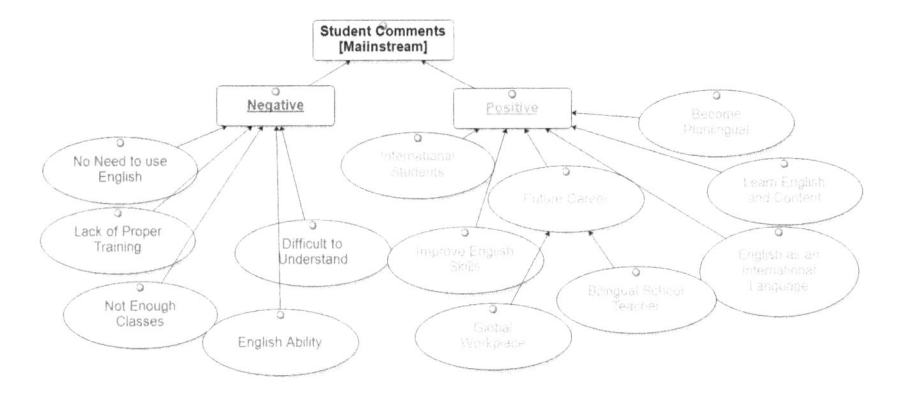

Fig. 15.4 Spanish prospective teachers' (mainstream strand) perceptions of EMI-CLIL

Understand, No Need to Use English and Lack of Proper Training) under the supra-code *Negative*. The difference between the two strands is that an additional code was added: *depends on*, in the comments from the students in the bilingual strand, which has a sub-code *Majors and Future Careers*. There are a few codes which appear in only one of the groups: the theme *Negative-Not Improve English* is only observed in the comments from the bilingual strand group and two themes *Negative-Not Enough Classes* and *Positive-English as an International Language* are found only in the mainstream group.

Comments 15.1 and 15.2 are instances of the code *Positive-Future Careers*: prospective teachers in Madrid have a positive attitude towards EMI-CLIL classes since they are useful to prepare themselves to become a worker in an international environment and a teacher in a bilingual school.

Comment 15.1 (Positive—Future Career-Global Workplace)
The main advantage is that if you want *to work in other country* [sic] you will be able to understand concepts and *to communicate with your workmates*. (SB2014-1-5)

Comment 15.2 (Positive—Future Career-Bilingual School Teacher)
It also helps us for our future as teachers *if we work in a bilingual school* we must perfectly control the language. (SB2015-6-18)

Some students, however, claim that whether to choose the EMI-CLIL classes or not depends on their academic majors and future careers as shown in Comment 15.3.

Comment 15.3 (Depends on—Majors and Future Career)
I think that decision [sic] of studying Spanish and English specially at university depends on *the degree you are studying and what you want in the future*. (SB2014-1-20)

Spanish prospective teachers also value the importance of becoming plurilingual through EMI-CLIL (see Comment 15.4), and they also acknowledge that English as an international language (EIL), or English as a Lingua Franca (Seidlhofer, 2011), is used to communicate among people with different lingua-cultural background (see Comments 15.5).

Comment 15.4 (Positive—Become Plurilingual)
Advantages: We learn to *express ourselves in a diferent* [sic] *language*. (SM2015-7-9)

Comment 15.5 (Positive—English as an International Language)
Is [sic] important to know languages *for comunicate [sic] to someone from other country [sic]*. (SM2016-1-21)

In relation to the theme of EIL, some students commented that EMI-CLIL lectures are necessary to accept international students who come to their university through the ERASMUS programme as shown below.

> Comment 15.6 (Positive—International Students)
> The advantages are the relation [sic] with *other people (erasmus, tourist) at the university*. (SM2015-8-6)

Spanish future teachers also raised some negative factors in EMI-CLIL in higher education. Some of them criticised lecturers for not receiving enough training to teach EMI-CLIL classes (see Comment 15.7). Others, especially students in the mainstream strand, claimed that they did not use English in their daily lives (see Comment 15.8).

> Comment 15.7 (Negative—Lack of Proper Training)
> You can know the subject with different languages, but most of *the teachers don't know how to do it*. (SM2015-9-6)

> Comment 15.8 (Negative—No Need to Use English)
> The disadvantages are that *in general we don't speak English*. (SM2014-3-2)

A few students in the mainstream strand also complained that there were not enough EMI-CLIL classes for them to take as shown in Comment 15.9.

> Comment 15.9 (Negative—Not Enough Classes)
> The first advantage is that we can feel more confident about learning English but, I think *only one subject isn't enough*. (SM2015-1-52)

Two students in the bilingual strand criticised the EMI-CLIL classes for not being effective to improve their English skills as they just learned English vocabulary and expressions specific to the subject matter and English presentation skills.

> Comment 15.10 (Negative—Not Improve English)
> *We do not improve our English* as such we only increase formulaic language, vocabulary, presentation skills. (SB2016-4-52)

Similar concerns were observed in comments from the Japanese prospective teachers although there are some differences in their attitudes towards EMI-CLIL between Spanish students and the Japanese counterparts, which are examined in the following section.

6.2 Japanese Prospective Teachers' Perceptions of CLIL: Thematic Analysis

Figure 15.5 illustrates the structure of the coding schemes added to the data of the Japanese students' comments.

The code *Positive* includes three sub-codes: *Learn English and Content, Improve English Skills* and *Future Career*. Comment 15.11, for example, is categorised into *Positive—Learn English and Content* since it shows the student's positive attitude towards EMI-CLIL classes, where they can learn both English and subject contents.

Comment 15.11 (Positive—Learn English and Content)
Learners can learn English words and knowledge of the subject at the same time if they have skill to understand. (JS2015-34)

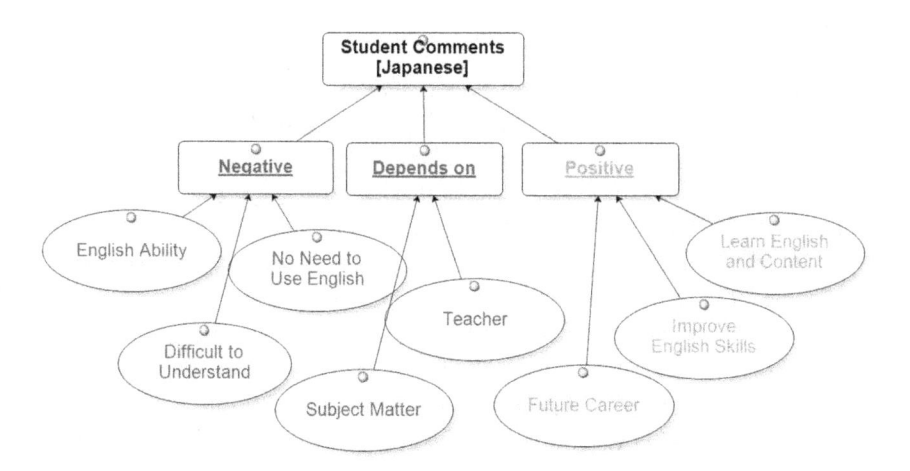

Fig. 15.5 Japanese students' perceptions of EMI-CLIL

Comment 15.12 is an instance of *Positive—Future Career*, which expresses the student's desire to work abroad in the future and the expectation that EMI-CLIL classes will enhance this possibility.

> Comment 15.12 (Positive—Future Career)
> I think that it is advantage, because *I could work abroad.* (JS2014-6)

While these codes are also found in the Spanish students' data, the themes such as *Bilingual School Teacher, Become Plurilingual and International Students* did not appear in the Japanese data because of the sociocultural factors in the Japanese context: There are neither bilingual schools nor a multi/plurilingual policy, and there are fewer international students in Japan than in Spain.

Another supra-code *Negative* is also divided into three branches, *English Ability, Difficult to Understand* and *No Need to Use English*, all of which were also observed in the Spanish students' comments. Some Japanese students express concern about the lack of their English ability (see Comment 15.13) and the difference in English proficiency among students. Comment 15.14 is categorised in *Negative-Difficult to Understand*, which reflects concerns that some students cannot fully understand subject contents through EMI-CLIL classes although it will benefit the improvement of their English skills.

> Comment 15.13 (Negative—English Ability)
> I prefer classes in Japanese. *I don't have so much vocabulary,* so it's hard for me. (JS2013-1)

> Comment 15.14 (Negative—Difficult to Understand)
> Disadvantages: Some students *can't understand importanct [sic] informa-tion.* (JS2015-28)

Similarly, other students commented that they can only learn relatively easy contents through EMI-CLIL classes since their English proficiency is not good enough and it takes more time to understand content knowledge in English.

The other sub-code of *Negative* is *No Need to Use English*. Comment 15.15 is an example which includes both aspects: the lack of need for EMI and the concern about the *domain loss* of the local language (also see Kirkpatrick, 2014a):

Comment 15.15 (Negative—No Need to Use English)
If not necessary, *we don't need to use English*.
Pros: chances to listen and speak.
Cons: *where will Japanese go?*
(JS2014-15)

The theme was also found in the Spanish data, with some Spanish students also showing concern about the domain loss for Spanish.

Some other students pointed out that the effectiveness of EMI-CLIL depends on the subject matter and teachers, which are categorised into the third supra-code *Depends* on with two sub-codes, *Teacher* and *Subject Matter*.

Comment 15.16 (Depends on—Teacher)
Depends on teacher. Native class [sic] makes me confused. (JS2013-20)

Comment 15.17 (Depends on—Subject Matter)
It depends on the contents of the class. Technical subjects should be taught in Japanese. (JS2013-24)

In Comment 15.16, the student expressed the difficulty she/he faced in the EMI-CLIL taught by a professor who is a native speaker of English, although further information about the nature of difficulty was not provided. Comment 15.17 is one of *Depends on—Subject Matter*, which highlights the importance of the choice of subjects which are taught in EMI-CLIL. These two codes are unique to the Japanese student data although a similar consideration was raised in the Spanish data, which was labelled with a different sub-code as *Depends on—Majors and Future Careers*. The next section describes the results from the focus group interviews with the Japanese students, investigating *multiple imagined communities* they belong to.

6.3   Japanese Prospective Teachers' Perceptions of CLIL: Focus Group Interview

From the analysis of the students' use of the *membership categorisation devices* (MCD) (Sacks, 1992) in the focus group interviews, two social memberships with which the Japanese students are associated were identified: as a member of *the imagined local Japanese community* and *the imagined global community* where English is used.

In Extract 15.1 from Group 1, Ken was talking about one of his friends who graduated from an International Baccalaureate (IB) school. Ken told the group that the friend learned subjects in English, even science subjects, that is, physics and chemistry. At the same time, he differentiated himself from IB graduates, saying in line 80, "*for them*, it is easier to have subject classes in English" than in Japanese, categorising himself as an "ordinary" Japanese university student who only had English language classes in a secondary school and did not find it easy to take EMI-CLIL classes at university.

76	Ken	なんか友達に あのIBっていって あの英語をしゃべるのに 特化した教育プログラムって 今なんか 外国から入ってきた やつを取り入れている学校の人がいて その人はなんか ほとんど授業英語＋
		(a friend of mine was in an IB [International Baccalaureate], where [the immersion programme] in foreign countries was applied, and most classes were taught in English)
77	Yuri	うん
		(mhm)
78	Ken	＋高校までずっと英語だったらしくて＋
		([he learned subjects] in English till high school)
79	Sawa	うんうん
		(mhm mhm)
80 →	Ken	＋そういう人たちにとっては なんか 英語の授業の方が 英語でやってもらった方が分かり易いっとかっていうのが あるらしくて＋
		(for them, it is easier to have subject classes in English)
81 Yuri&Sawa		うーん
		(mhm)
82	Ken	＋なんか人によるっぽいんですけど なんか化学とか物理 とかも英語でやっていたらしくて＝
		(it depends on students, but chemistry and physics were also taught in English)
83 →	Yuri	<$E> laugh </$E> でも その人たちは じゃあ外国人なんですね 日本人じゃなくって.
		(But then they are foreigners, not Japanese, aren't they.)

Extract 15.1   from Focus Group 1: People outside the imagined community

After listening to Ken's story, Yuri laughs in line 83 and continues her turn with: "then they are foreigners, not Japanese, aren't they". She positions herself as a Japanese in *the imagined local community* where only Japanese language is used as a medium of instruction in school, and positions IB graduates as not belonging to this community.

A similar instance was observed in Group 3's discussion. In line 55 in Extract 15.2, Kota initiated the discussion topic, "Subjects should be taught in English". The other members, Mai and Haru, immediately expressed their disagreement with the statement in lines 56 and 57, which was followed by the confirmation by Kota in line 58, "Yeah".

55	Kota	次はあれ Subjects should be taught in English. (.) いや=
		(The next [the topic] is Subjects should be taught in English. er)
56	Mai	ぜんぶ 全部じゃない
		([It does] not [mean] all [subjects])
57	Haru	これは全部じゃなくても＋
		(This [EMI-CLIL] does not have to [be applied to] all [subjects])
58	Kota	ねえ
		(Yeah)
59	→ Haru	＋ やっぱり うん 私たち日本人だから <$E> laugh </$E>
		(Yeah because we are Japanese)
60	All	<$E> laugh </$E>
61	Haru	母国語でやった方が やっぱり一番理解＝
		([we] understand best [when we learn] in our mother tongue)
62	Mari	たしかに<$G?>
		(True)

Extract 15.2 from Focus Group 3: Japanese as an imagined identity

In line 59, Haru provided an account of her disagreement with the statement, saying, "Yeah because we are Japanese", to which the others respond with laughter. She then adds in line 61, "[we] understand best [when we learn] in our mother tongue", to which Mai agrees in line 62 with "True". Thus, Haru also positioned herself as a member of *the imagined local community* where Japanese people learn subjects in Japanese, which seemed to be shared with the other group members.

Extract 15.3 from Group 2, on the other hand, includes a discussion where another *imagined community* the Japanese students wish to belong to was recognised. From line 183 to line 185, Aki shares a story she had heard about the experience of study abroad, starting with the utterance in line 183, "but have you heard the story that you will understand [English] three months after you started study abroad".

183	Aki	でも留学とか海外にいって、なんか3か月目で意味がわかる みたいな きいたことある？ (but have you heard the story that you will understand [English] three months after you started study abroad?)
184	Mako	うんうん (mhm mhm)
185	Aki	なんか「はっ！理解できた！」みたいな (It was like, 'oh! I can understand [English]!')
186	Sora	へー (really)
187	Mako	ふーん (mhm)
188	Aki	それと似てて 全部英語で ばあーとやって 最初は苦痛だけど どんどん耳が慣れてきて「あれ、なんかわかる」みたいな状況に させたいのかな これはって思うんですけど ([EMI-CLIL classes] are similar [to the study abroad programme], it is hard at first, but your ears will be familiar with [English] and [you will feel] 'oh I can [understand English]'. That's the situation [teachers tried to let students' experience in EMI classes] I think)
189 →	Sora	なりたいなそんな状況に <\$E> laugh </\$E> (I want to be like that)
190	Aki	<\$E> laugh </\$E>
191 →	Mako	なりたい <\$E> laugh </\$E> (I want to be [like that])

Extract 15.3 from Focus Group 2: Desire to improve English skills

Aki goes on to relate the story to EMI-CLIL classes at university, concluding in line 188 that, "[EMI-CLIL classes] are similar [to the study abroad programme]" and that these classes will be enable students to understand English. Sora and Mako listen to Aki and provide acknowledgements in lines 184, 186 and 187. In lines 189 and 191, Sora and Mako express their desire to become a member of *the imagined global community* where English is used like students who study abroad. The analysis of these focus group discussions, then, shows *the dual imagined communities* in relation to which these Japanese students position themselves.

7 Translingual Transformation Through CLIL

CLIL is a bilingual approach to language education, but it can also be viewed as an education-based process of social and cultural (re)production (Bourdieu & Passeron, 1977, p. 10), which involves "uses of multi-linguistic and semiotic resources", "different social actors" and "language-in-education practice and policies" (Martin-Jones, 2015, pp. 446–447). In this section, we illustrate the current situations of CLIL in Spain and in Japan, respectively, which were obtained from the percep-tions of prospective teachers, in reference to the concept of *transnational transformations* (Vertovec, 2009).

In his view, globalisation has brought the phenomenon of *transnation-alism*, where "certain kinds of relationships have been globally intensified and now take place paradoxically in a planet-spanning yet common—however virtual—arena of activity" although there are "great distances and notwithstanding the presence of international borders (and all the laws, regulations and national narratives they represent)" (p. 3). In migrant *transnationalism*, migrants have connection with both the send-ing countries and receiving, or host, countries, and in the process of transnationalism, *transformations* occur in three levels, namely, *socio-cultural transformations, political and economic transformations* and *religious transformations*, which affect *national, regional and local contexts* as illustrated in Fig. 15.6 (Vertovec, 2009).

Through the process, migrants acquire *transnational habitus* (Bourdieu & Passeron, 1977); in other words, *transnational competence* is con-structed and acted upon, which features "dual orientations" and "a per-sonal repertoire comprising varied values and potential action-sets drawn from diverse cultural configurations" (p. 69).

In the case of CLIL in Madrid, the future teachers are aware of the social changes which have been happening in the local community. These include the implementation of bilingual programmes in schools in local areas and the presence of international students on the ERASMUS programme in local classrooms. They are also aware of a wider global community which is accessible through the promotion of

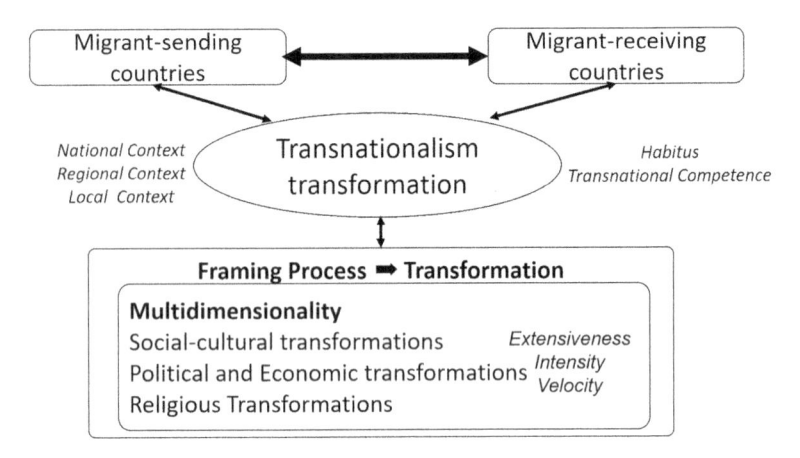

Fig. 15.6   The transnational transformation (Adapted from Vertovec, 2009)

the mobility among EU countries. Thus, they relate their experience in EMI-CLIL classes with not only their local community but also the global communities where the ERASMUS students are from and where they might work in future. Although the Spanish prospective teachers do not cross the borders of countries like migrants, EMI-CLIL classes in bilingual schools and at university allow them to experience a process of *education-based translingual transformation* in the social-cultural domain, which can be seen in their desire to be plurilingual (see Fig. 15.7).

The Japanese prospective teachers, on the other hand, seem to perceive EMI-CLIL classes as a beneficial pedagogical practice to improve their English skills for a future career in an international workplace, which is *their imagined global community*. There seems to be an assumption that the experience of EMI-CLIL classes is similar to that of study abroad programmes (see Fig. 15.8). They do not seem to link the practice in EMI-CLIL with their local community since Japanese people use Japanese in schools and in their daily lives in their *imagined local community*. Hence, the translingual transformation seems to be limited in the Japanese context to the area of economic policy, and there is resistance to translingual transformation in the social-cultural domain.

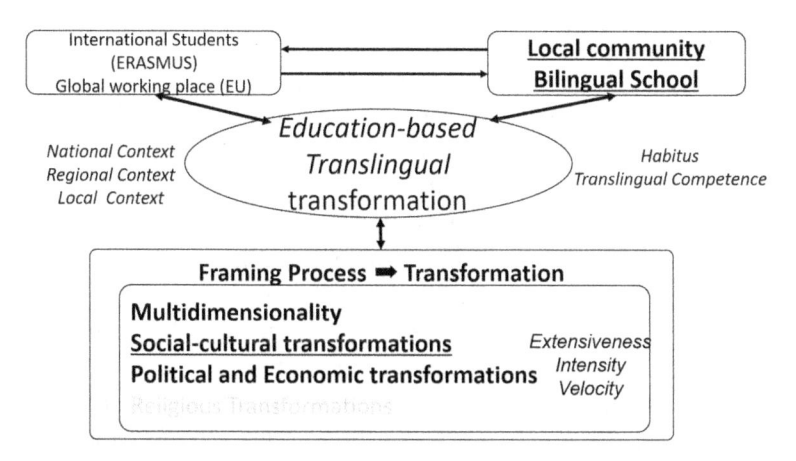

Fig. 15.7 Education-based translingual transformation in Madrid

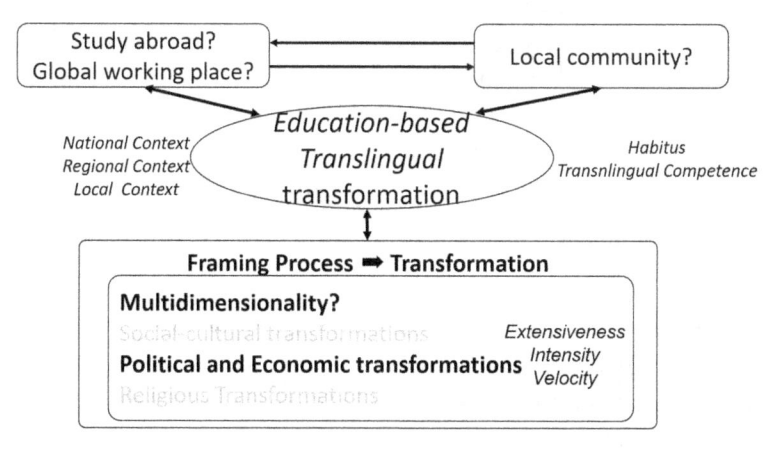

Fig. 15.8 Education-based translingual transformation in Kanagawa

8 Conclusion

This chapter started with a review of the language policies in the modern history of Spain and Japan and the rationales behind the implementation of EMI-CLIL in their education systems. EMI-CLIL has been introduced in different social and economic contexts in Europe and in Japan (also see Tsuchiya & Pérez Murillo, 2015). In the former, it is a proactive strategy in line with the EU's multilingual policy, whereas, in the latter, it is a more reactive approach to equip the workforce with English proficiency for economic purposes. The Spanish students, for whom local bilingual schools and ERASMUS students have been part of their common daily lives, perceive the practice of EMI-CLIL in association with communities in their local area and beyond, that is, the mobility among EU countries, and show a positive attitude to being plurilingual.

In the Japanese context, however, ambivalence towards EMI-CLIL was more visible in Japanese prospective teachers' voices. This can be seen in the fact that although they desired to acquire English skills through EMI-CLL classes, at the same time they resisted the transformation of the medium of instruction from Japanese to English in subject classes. In the case of the immigrants in Canada in Norton (2001), their resistance to language learning was caused by the lack of teachers or colleagues' understanding of the learners' imagined identities and communities. For the Japanese students, their ambivalence towards EMI lectures seems to derive from the duality of *their imagined communities: the imagined global community* where the target language is used and the *imagined local community* where only Japanese is used, and their awareness of the *cultural and linguistic capital* (Bourdieu & Passeron, 1977) the two communities offer.

Although this study has investigated the perceptions of prospective teachers in only two sites in Europe and Asia, it sheds light on one of the crucial areas for future CLIL research: what Asian countries including Japan can learn from the success of CLIL in European countries (Dalton-Puffer, 2008). Future research needs to focus on how to localise and appropriate CLIL in these contexts, protecting dual or multiple identities of language learners (Kirkpatrick, 2014b) and avoiding the risk of domain *loss* of local languages due to EMI (Kirkpatrick, 2014a).

Acknowledgement This study was supported in part by JSPS Grant-in-Aid for Young Scientists (B) No. 26870599.

Appendix 1: The Questionnaire Survey

Personal backgrounds:

Q1. Programme you are enrolled in and your grade.
Q2. Countries you have lived.
Q3. Are you an international student?

Language repertoire:

Q4. Your first language (L1), second language (L2) and other languages.
Q5. Your use of languages in family meetings, friends' meetings, and TV/Internet.

Subject classes in English:

Q6. Do you agree with the following statements? (Likert-scale: "1" means you do not agree and "5" means you completely agree.)
- 6-1: L1 and English should be used as languages of instruction at primary school.
- 6-2: L1 and English should be used as languages of instruction at secondary school.
- 6-3: L1 and English should be used as languages of instruction at university.

Q7. What do you think are advantages and disadvantages of the subject classes taught in English at university?

Appendix 2: Code Descriptions

Codes	Descriptions
Students' Comments	
Positive	Positive perceptions of EMI-CLIL in students
Improve English Skills	EMI-CLIL classes improve students' English skills
Learn English and Content	Students can learn both English and contents in EMI-CLIL classes
Future Career	EMI-CLIL classes benefit students' future careers
Global Workplace	Students can work abroad in the future
Academic Research	English is used in academic research
Negative	Negative perceptions of EMI-CLIL in students
Different English Proficiency	There are differences in English proficiency among students
Should Learn in their first language	Students should learn subjects in their first language
Not Necessary	EMI classes are not necessary
Lose Culture	Their own cultures will be lost due to EMI-CLIL
Contents Suffer	Students do not learn contents well in EMI-CLIL
Difficult to Understand	Students have difficulties to understand contents in EMI-CLIL
Easy Content	Students can learn only easy contents in EMI-CLIL
Depends	It depends on the situations
on Teacher	It depends on teachers of EMI-CLIL courses
on Contents	It depends on subject contents

References

Adolphs, S. (2006). *Introducing Electronic Text Analysis: A Practical Guide for Language and Literary Studies*. London: Routledge.

Andersen, B. (1983). *Imagined Communities*. New York: Verso.

Blackledge, A., & Creese, A. (2010). *Multilingualism: A Critical Perspective*. London: Continuum.

Bourdieu, P., & Passeron, J.-C. (1977). *Reproduction in Education, Society and Culture*. London: Sage Publications.

British Council, Spain. Retrieved from http://www.mecd.gob.es/educacion-mecd/dms/mecd/educacion-mecd/areas-educacion/sistema-educativo/ensenanzas/ensenanzas-idiomas/centros-bilingues/bepevaluationreport-pdf.pdf

Canagarajah, S. A. (2013). *Translingual Practice: Global Englishes and Cosmopolitan Relations*. London: Routledge.

Commission of the European Communities. (2003). Promoting Language Learning and Linguistic Diversity: An Action Plan 2004–2006. Retrieved from http://ec.europa.eu/education/doc/official/keydoc/actlang/act_lang_en.pdf

Council of Europe. (1982). Recommendation No, R (82): 18. Council of Europe, Committee of Ministers. Retrieved from https://wcd.coe.int

Dafouz, E., Núñez, B., Sancho, C., & Foran, D. (2007). Integrating CLIL at the tertiary level: Teachers' and students' reactions. In *Diverse Contexts-converging Goals. CLIL in Europe* (pp. 91–101). Frankfurt: Peter Lang.

Dalton-Puffer, C. (2008). Outcomes and processes in content and language integrated learning (CLIL): Current research from Europe. In W. Delanoy & L. Volkmann (Eds.), *Future Perspectives for English Language Teaching* (pp. 1–19). Heidelberg: Carl Winter.

Dobson, A., Pérez Murillo, M. D., & Johnstone, R. (2010). *Bilingual Education Project Spain Evaluation Report*. Madrid: Spanish Ministry of Education/British Council.

Duff, P. A. (2015). Transnationalism, multilingualism, and identity. *Annual Review of Applied Linguistics, 35*, 57–80.

European Commission. (1999). The Bologna Declaration on the European Space for Higher Education. Retrieved from http://ec.europa.eu/education/policies/educ/bologna/bologna.pdf

European Union. (2015). *The EU and the Bologna Process: Working Together for Change*. Luxembourg: Publications Office of the European Union. Retrieved from http://ec.europa.eu/dgs/education_culture/repository/education/library/publications/2015/bologna-process-brochure_en.pdf

Fortanet-Gómez, I. (2013). *CLIL in Higher Education: Toward a Multilingual Language Policy.* Bristol: Multilingual Matters.

García, O., & Li Wei (2014). *Translanguaging.* London: Palgrave Macmillan.

Gardner, S. (2012). Global English and bilingual education. In M. Martin-Jones & A. Blackledge (Eds.), *The Routledge Handbook of Multilingualism* (pp. 247–264). Oxon: Routledge.

Guest, G., MacQueen, K. M., & Namey, E. E. (2012). *Applied Thematic Analysis.* Thousand Oaks: Sage Publications.

Hornberger, N. H. (1988). *Bilingual Education and Language Maintenance. (Topics in Sociolinguistics).* Holland: Foris Publications.

Hutchby, I., & Wooffitt, R. (2008). *Conversation Analysis.* Cambridge: Polity Press.

Hüttner, J., Dalton-Puffer, C., & Smit, U. (2012). The power of beliefs: Lay theories and their influence on the implementation of CLIL programmes. *Journal of Bilingual Education and Bilingualism, 16*(3), 267–284.

Ikeda, M. (2013). Does CLIL work for Japanese secondary school students?: Potential for the 'weak' version of CLIL. *International CLIL Research Journal, 2*(1), 31–43.

Kanno, Y., & Norton, B. (2003). Imagined communities and educational possibilities: Introduction. *Journal of Language Identity & Education, 2*(4), 241–249.

Kirkpatrick, A. (2014a). English as a medium of instruction in East and Southeast Asian Universities. In N. Murray & A. Scarino (Eds.), *Dynamic Ecologies: A Relationship Perspective on Languages Education in the Asian-Pacific Region* (pp. 15–29). Dordrecht: Springer.

Kirkpatrick, A. (2014b). Internationalization or Englishization: Medium of instruction in Today's Universities. *The Asian Journal of Applied Linguistics, 1*(1), 4–15.

Lasagabaster, D. (2011). English achievement and student motivation in CLIL and EFL settings. *Innovation in Language Learning and Teaching, 5*(1), 3–18.

Lasagabaster, D., & Doiz, A. (2016). CLIL students' perceptions of their language learning process: Delving into self-perceived improvement and instructional preferences. *Language Awareness, 25*(1–2), 110–126.

Llinares, A., & Dafouz-Milne, E. (2017). Content and language integrated programmes in the Madrid region: Overview and research findings. In Y. R. de Zarobe & D. Lasagabaster (Eds.), *CLIL in Spain: Implementation, Results and Teacher Training* (pp. 95–114). Newcastle upon Tyne: Cambridge Scholars Publishing.

Maíz-Arévalo, C., & Domínguez-Romero, E. (2013). Student's response to CLIL in tertiary education: The case of business administration and economics at Complutense University. *Revista de Lingüística y Lenguas Aplicadas, 8*, 1–12.

Martin-Jones, M. (2015). Multilingual classroom discourse as a window on wider social, political and ideological processes. In N. Markee (Ed.), *The Handbook of Classroom Discourse and Interaction* (pp. 446–460). Chichester: Wiley Blackwell.

May, S. (Ed.). (2014). *The Multilingual Turn: Implications for SLA, TESOL and Bilingual Education*. London: Routledge.

MECD. (2017). *Facts and Figures: 2016/2017 School Year*. Madrid: Ministry of Education, Culture and Sports, Spain. Retrieved from https://www.mecd. gob.es/servicios-al-ciudadano-mecd/dms/mecd/servicios-al-ciudadano-mecd/estadisticas/educacion/indicadores-publicaciones-sintesis/datos-cifras/Datosycifras1617ing.pdf

MEXT. (1998). *Gakushu Shido Yoryou (in Japanese, The Course of Study for Upper Secondary School)*. Tokyo: MEXT (Ministry of Education, Culture, Sports, Science & Technology. Retrieved from http://www.mext.go.jp/b_menu/shuppan/sonota/990301/03122603/009.htm

MEXT. (2003). *The Action Plan to Cultivate 'Japanese with English Abilities' (in Japanese, 「英語が使える日本人」の育成のための行動計画)*. Tokyo. Retrieved from http://www.mext.go.jp/b_menu/shingi/chukyo/chukyo3/004/siryo/04031601/005.pdf

MEXT. (2009). *Global 30*. Tokyo: Ministry of Education, Culture, Sports, Science and Technology Japan. Retrieved from http://www.uni.international.mext.go.jp/

MEXT. (2012). *Higher Education in Japan*. Higher Education Bureau, Ministry of Education, Culture, Sports, Science and Technology Japan. Retrieved from http://www.mext.go.jp/english/highered/__icsFiles/afieldfile/2012/06/19/1302653_1.pdf

MEXT. (2014). *Selection for the FY 2014 Top Global University Project*. Ministry of Education, Culture, Sports, Science and Technology Japan. Retrieved from http://www.mext.go.jp/b_menu/houdou/26/09/__icsFiles/afieldfile/2014/10/07/1352218_02.pdf

MEXT. (2017). Current status of higher education reform in FY2015 [in Japanese, 大学における教育内容等の改革状況について (平成27年度)]. Retrieved from http://www.mext.go.jp/a_menu/koutou/daigaku/04052801/__icsFiles/afieldfile/2017/12/13/1398426_1.pdf

Norton, B. (2001). Non-participation, imagined communities, and the language classroom. In M. P. Breen (Ed.), *Learner Contributions to Language Learning: New Directions in Research* (pp. 159–171). London: Pearson Education Limited.

Norton, B., & Toohey, K. (2011). Identity, language learning, and social change. *Language Teaching, 44*(4), 412–446.

Norton Pierce, B. (1995). Social identity, investment, and language learning. *TESOL Quarterly, 29*(1), 9–31.

Pérez Murillo, M. D. (2001). *Talk and Texts in Bilingual Classrooms: A Case Study of the Spanish School in London.* Unpublished doctoral dissertation, Lancaster University, Lancaster, UK.

Pérez Murillo, M. D. (2018). Factores de Calidad en los Programas AICLE de la Comunidad de Madrid. In J. L. Ortega-Martín, S. P. Hughes, & D. Madrid (Eds.), *Influencia de la política educativa de centro en la enseñanza bilingüe en España* (pp. 105–113). Madrid: Spanish Ministry of Education/ British Council.

QSR. (2014). *NVivo10.* London: QSR International.

Ramos, A. (2013). Higher education bilingual programmes in Spain. *Porta Linguarum, 19*, 101–111.

Romero, E., & Zayas, F. (2017). Challenges and opportunities of training teachers for plurilingual education. In J. Valcke & R. Wilkinson (Eds.), *Integrating Content and Language in Higher Education* (pp. 205–226). Frankfurt: Peter Lang.

Sacks, H. (1992). *Lectures on Conversation* (Vols. 1 and 2). Malden, MA: Blackwell Publishers.

Schegloff, E., A. (2007). A tutorial on membership categorization. *Journal of Pragmatics, 39*, 462-482.

Seidlhofer, B. (2011). *Understanding English as a Lingua Franca.* Oxford: Oxford University Press.

Smit, U., & Dafouz, E. (2012). Integrating content and language in higher education: An introduction to English-medium policies, conceptual issues and research practices across Europe. *AILA Review, 25*, 1–12.

Tsuchiya, K., & Pérez Murillo, M. D. (2015). Comparing the language policies and the students' perceptions of CLIL in tertiary education in Spain and Japan. *LACLIL, 8*(1), 25–35.

Vertovec, S. (2009). *Transnationalism.* London: Routledge.

Wächter, B., & Maiworm, F. (2014). *English-Taught Programmes in European Higher Education. The State of Play in 2014.* Bonn: Lemmens.

16

Conclusion: CLIL—Reflection and Transmission

Keiko Tsuchiya and María Dolores Pérez Murillo

1 CLIL: Transgressing Borders

New knowledge spreads like sunlight, which travels from space, where it was generated, to the atmosphere and reaches the earth, where it is reflected on the surface. Reacting to the texture and material of the surface, the light then behaves in a distinctive manner by emitting different colours and tremors. Content and language integrated learning (CLIL) crosses many borders: the pedagogical approach of CLIL first travelled within European countries and has now reached non-European countries, evolving in the education systems of each region as described in Part I of this volume. CLIL practices transgress the boundaries between sub-

K. Tsuchiya (✉)
International College of Arts and Sciences, Yokohama City University, Yokohama, Japan
e-mail: ktsuchiy@yokohama-cu.ac.jp

M. D. Pérez Murillo
School of Education, Complutense University in Madrid, Madrid, Spain
e-mail: perezmur@edu.ucm.es

© The Author(s) 2019
K. Tsuchiya, M. D. Pérez Murillo (eds.), *Content and Language Integrated Learning in Spanish and Japanese Contexts*, https://doi.org/10.1007/978-3-030-27443-6_16

ject content classrooms and language classrooms, integrating content and language learning, as shown in the chapters in Part II. CLIL studies encompass a range of fields, from the interaction in CLIL classrooms from perspectives of linguistics and applied linguistics, which includes systemic functional linguistics and discourse studies as addressed in Part III to sociolinguistic and pedagogical issues as focused on in Part IV (also see Llinares, 2015 and Llinares & Morton, 2017).

Lasagabaster (2015) proposed four levels of the internationalisation of language policies on the basis of Spolsky's (2004) three components, *language planning, language practices* and *language ideology*: (1) *macro level*, that is, EU policies; (2) *meso level*, that is, national guidelines for language education; (3) *micro level*, that is, internal guidelines in an individual institution; and (4) *nano level*, that is, language choices of stakeholders (ibid., p. 259). Utilising the framework, the features in CLIL in Spain and Japan explored in this book are compared and summarised as below.

	Spain	Japan
The macro/meso levels: the introduction of CLIL	Top-down, proactive	Bottom-up, reactive
The micro level: The diffusion of CLIL	Primary – Secondary – Tertiary – Pre-Primary	Tertiary – Primary – Secondary
CLIL teacher training	Interdisciplinary education degree courses in higher education	Workshops provided by teachers' associations, local educational authorities and some ELT courses in higher education organised by individual teacher educators
The nano level: CLIL and multilingualism	Societal and individual multilingualism	Individual multilingualism

In the macro/meso levels, as reported in Chap. 2, the concept of CLIL was developed to promote the European Union's multilingual policy, and it has been implemented in several member states including Spain. As Sylvén (2013) states, "CLIL in Spain has virtually exploded during the last decade. Having a history of bilingualism in some of its autonomous regions, the teaching of content through another language than Spanish is fairly uncontroversial" (p. 303). However, as explained in Chap. 3, in Japan, there is no supra-national organisation equivalent to the EU to plan language policies across Asian countries. In Japan, CLIL is not implemented in subject lessons taught in an additional language but in English lessons as part of the official syllabus. However, the Japanese national curriculum, the *Course of Study*, which was recently updated, encourages cross-curricular teaching and learning in foreign language classrooms in secondary schools. Also, CLIL in English has been adapted in tertiary education to meet the demands of the global economy. Thus, CLIL in Spain could be said to be "proactive (creating situations)", while in Japan it can be seen as "reactive (responding to situations)" (Coyle, Hood, & Marsh, 2010, p. 6) (also see Tsuchiya & Pérez Murillo, 2015).

At the micro level in the context of Spain (see Chap. 2), the diffusion of CLIL in formal education started from some subject classes in primary and secondary bilingual schools but has now expanded to tertiary and pre-primary education.[1] The order is slightly different in Japan (see Chap. 3): some universities first adapted CLIL pedagogy in their foreign language courses (mainly English classes) first, and more recently a few local education authorities have introduced CLIL in primary and secondary schools in the self-governing regions. In Spain, university education departments offer well-developed interdisciplinary CLIL teacher education programmes within degree courses. This is not the case in Japan where a teacher association, such as J-CLIL, or local education authorities provide workshops for teachers who are interested in the pedagogy, and some pre-service CLIL teacher education programmes are implemented as part of English Language Teaching (ELT) courses by individual teacher educators at universities (see Chaps. 12, 13, 14 and 15).

To summarise the nano-level practices on both sides, the concepts of *societal multilingualism* and *individual multilingualism* could be employed. In reference to Beardsmore's (1986) theory, Fortanet-Gómez (2013) lists the elements of societal and individual multilingualism: the former features *social status, geographic bilingualism* and *language practice and plan-*

---

[1] Except for the Spanish Ministry of Education and British Council (MECD/BC) joint Bilingual Education Project (BEP), which started in 1996 and it has been implemented in pre-primary education as well as primary and secondary education in different Spanish autonomous communities.

ning, while the latter relates to *language acquisition and competence*, *cognitive organisation* and *social cultural identities* (adapted from Fortanet-Gómez, 2013, pp. 7 and 13). As examined in Chap. 15, CLIL in the Spanish context affects and is affected by both societal and individual multilingualism, whereas CLIL in Japan seems to focus mainly on individual learners' competence with little attention to societal aspects.

2   Transformation Through CLIL

As the notions of the multilingual turn (May, 2014) and alternative approaches to second language acquisition (Atkinson, 2011) indicate, language education in the globalised society is taking on an increasingly reflexive and performative perspective. CLIL aligns with this trend, and it can be seen as a transformer of the current educational system. In the theory of *critical pedagogy*, Pennycook (2001, p. 117) categories three perspectives on schools and classrooms as social phenomena: (1) a *standard view* regards classrooms as not social but purely "educational space", (2) from a *reproductive standpoint*, classrooms reflect "dominant social interests", which are reproduced through the social system, and (3) a resistance standpoint treats "all knowledge as political" and sees classrooms as "social cultural struggle". To this he adds a more positive prospect for classrooms as a social practice:

> What is needed […] is a way of understanding resistance and change. This is important not only because we need better understanding of what actually goes on in classrooms but also because as educators, we need a sense that we can *actually do something*. (Pennycook, 2001, p. 127, our emphasis)

This perspective can be termed as a *transformative view*, and this is where CLIL can fit in. In other words, CLIL can be recognised as *a transformative pedagogy* for better education as evidenced through this volume. It is hoped that this volume can be a useful resource for teachers and researchers to understand the different shapes CLIL takes on in distinct contexts and to *actually do CLIL* teaching and research in their own ways and according to their own needs.

References

Atkinson, D. (Ed.). (2011). *Alternative Approaches to Second Language Acquisition*. London: Routledge.

Beardsmore, B. H. (1986). *Bilingualism: Basic Principles*. Boston, MA: College-Hill Press.

Coyle, D., Hood, P., & Marsh, D. (2010). *Content and Language Integrated Learning*. Cambridge: Cambridge University Press.

Fortanet-Gómez, I. (2013). *CLIL in Higher Education: Toward a Multilingual Language Policy*. Bristol: Multilingual Matters.

Lasagabaster, D. (2015). Language policy and language choice at European Universities: Is there really a 'choice'? *International Journal of Applied Linguistics, 3*(2), 255–276.

Llinares, A. (2015). Integration in CLIL: A proposal to inform research and successful pedagogy. *Language, Culture and Curriculum, 28*(1), 58–73.

Llinares, A., & Morton, T. (2017). *Applied Linguistics Perspectives on CLIL*. Amsterdam: John Benjamins Publications.

May, S. (Ed.). (2014). *The Multilingual Turn: Implications for SLA, TESOL and Bilingual Education*. London: Routledge.

Pennycook, A. (2001). *Critical Applied Linguistics: A Critical Introduction*. Mahwah, NJ: Lawrence Erlbaum Associates.

Spolsky, B. (2004). *Language Policy*. Cambridge: Cambridge University Press.

Sylvén, L. K. (2013). CLIL in Sweden—Why does it not work? A metaperspective on CLIL across contexts in Europe. *International Journal of Bilingual Education and Bilingualism, 16*(3), 301–320.

Tsuchiya, K., & Pérez Murillo, M. D. (2015). Comparing the language policies and the students' perceptions of CLIL in tertiary education in Spain and Japan. *LACLIL, 8*(1), 25–35.

Afterword: CLIL in Spain and Japan: Synergies, Specificities and New Horizons

Since the term Content and Language Integrated Learning (CLIL) was conceived in the 1990s as a venture for promoting European multilingualism and multiculturalism, many attempts have been made to enhance its uniqueness in contrast with other similar programmes in other parts of the world (such as Immersion and Content-Based Instruction). The geographical expansion of CLIL in the last couple of decades, and the complexity of its implementation in Europe and other parts of the world, has meant that even within the so-called CLIL programmes, the variety is substantial and growing. This new scenario necessarily requires a reconceptualisation of what is meant by CLIL. Its expansion in different geographical contexts with different educational and cultural specificities has meant that "a CLIL programme" can actually mean different things in different parts of the world (Llinares, 2015). In order to understand this variety, terms such as "soft" and "hard" CLIL (Ball, Kelly, & Clegg, 2015) have been used to distinguish between language-led programmes, where language is taught with a content-oriented approach (soft CLIL), and content-led programmes, where language is attended to in content classes taught through an additional language (hard CLIL). Two of the geographical contexts that can probably best synthesise the variety of CLIL programmes and approaches are Japan and Spain. This

© The Author(s) 2019
K. Tsuchiya, M. D. Pérez Murillo (eds.), *Content and Language Integrated Learning in Spanish and Japanese Contexts*, https://doi.org/10.1007/978-3-030-27443-6

volume is unique as it provides a picture of CLIL in both contexts from a range of perspectives (policy, practices, interaction and pedagogy/ teacher education). It contributes, then, to the call for more studies comparing contexts (Cenoz, 2015; Nikula, Dafouz, Moore, & Smit, 2016) in order to identify synergies but also cultural/educational specificities, which necessarily have an impact on the success of CLIL programmes. This volume shows similarities across Spain and Japan, for example, in that one of the forces driving CLIL implementation is the perceived lack of success in the tradition of teaching foreign languages, which explains the enthusiasm for the implementation of CLIL programmes in both settings by different stakeholders (educational authorities, teachers, families, etc.). Another similarity is the pervasive dominance of English in both contexts as the main language of instruction. Drawing on Dalton-Puffer, Nikula, and Smit's (2010) concept of Content and English Integrated Learning (CEIL), the focus on CEIL (English) rather than CLIL (any language) contrasts with the initial European aim of enhancing multilingualism but clearly responds to internationalisation interests in both contexts, where English is clearly perceived as the world's major lingua franca. In contrast, interesting divergences across the two contexts also emerge in the volume. These include the different motivational interests towards CLIL and English language learning, which seem to be more integrative in Spain than in Japan, and the more frequent implementation of "hard" CLIL in Spain and "soft" CLIL in Japan.

From a *policy* perspective, the first two chapters (by Madrid et al. and Tsuchiya) give a thorough overview of the development of foreign language teaching leading to CLIL in the respective contexts. Madrid et al.'s chapter provides evidence of the variety of CLIL programmes in Spain and the substantial amount of research that shows the positive effects of CLIL on language learning, but calls for more studies that focus on the effect of CLIL on content learning. In parallel, Tsuchiya describes the recent change in language education at primary and secondary levels in Japan, which has offered space for CLIL teaching.

The five chapters on *practices* illustrate the different contextual, pedagogic and research needs across the two contexts at different educational levels. For example, the attention to CLIL at the pre-school level in Fleta's chapter is particularly relevant for Spain, where CLIL has started to be implemented widely at the pre-primary level. In turn, the research interest in the implementation of content-led activities in the language class is more relevant in Japan, where soft CLIL is the most common approach. This is exemplified in Yamano's chapter, which illustrates the role of the 4Cs and functions of language using a CLIL approach in the language class. These two chapters also illustrate another difference across the two contexts, which is the degree of exposure to the target language. While five-year-olds in Spanish pre-primary bilingual programmes have five sessions of CLIL per week, in the Japanese context, students in grades 5 and 6 have one session of CLIL per week. At the secondary school level, del Pozo and Yamazaki focus on the role of collaborative learning in CLIL in Spain and Japan, respectively. Del Pozo's contribution is an example of hard CLIL. From the perspective of a content specialist, she sees CLIL as a way to innovate in content teaching and pay attention to ways in which students can be scaffolded into learning content in a more engaging way. Similarly, Yamazaki sees collaborative learning in CLIL as a way to innovate in the English class. Finally, at the tertiary level, Uemura et al. highlight the role of the teaching-learning cycle in CLIL as a part of Systemic Functional Linguistics (SFL) applications to education, and in line with Yamano and Yamazaki, they refer to the need for more collaboration between content and language teachers, a pending issue in CLIL programmes around the world. All in all, in the two different contexts, at different educational levels (pre-primary, primary, secondary and tertiary) and with different approaches to CLIL (soft or hard), the chapters in this section seem to conclude that CLIL goes beyond improving L2 competencies. Interestingly, it is presented as a catalyst to improve pedagogical practices in general.

The section on *interaction* shows the important role of interactional practices in CLIL (Nikula, Dalton-Puffer, & Llinares, 2013). In line with Yamazaki and del Pozo, Pastrana focuses on group work activities, this time observing the role of students' interactional practices in content and language integrated learning, using SFL as a model for the analysis (in line with Uemura). In her study, she shows how primary CLIL students are able to participate in group discussions, not only paying attention to how they co-construct content in the L2 but also taking into account the interacting roles of the children participating in the activity. Similarly, using an approach that sees language as inseparable from content, Evnitskaya shows the role of Cognitive Discourse Functions (CDFs) (Dalton-Puffer, 2013) in content and language integrated learning and highlights the need to offer linguistic tools for learners to be able to convey these functions in the L2 in their expression of academic content. Tsuchiya's study identifies the functions of translanguaging in tertiary education in Japan and calls for more studies that highlight the role of translanguaging across tasks and different cultural backgrounds.

Finally, in the section on *pedagogy and teacher education*, Sasajima highlights that CLIL methodology in Japan requires a specific approach. Both Sasajima and Custodio refer to the need for CLIL teacher training. This is in line with Pérez Murillo's claim for the Spanish context, which shows that this is a pending issue and a clear area of improvement in both contexts. Specific initial CLIL teacher education programmes together with continuing professional development programmes are key for an effective implementation of CLIL. This is a major future challenge in both the Japanese and the Spanish contexts.

In the final chapter, Tsuchiya and Pérez Murillo compare the two contexts by highlighting the more proactive approach of CLIL in Spain (drawing on EU policy) versus the more reactive approach in Japan, with the need to produce competent speakers (Japan). Spain can also be seen as an example of the harmony between both approaches as one key driving force in the success of CLIL programmes in Spain was also reactive, drawing on parental interest in their children's improvement in learning foreign languages (particularly English). The idea of the translingual transformation in Japan being more related to economic gains than to the sociocultural domain is extremely interesting and perhaps Spain is not that different in that respect. The willingness to be truly multilingual is probably more a European dream than a real aspiration for students and their families. The multilingual advantage is still not sufficiently present in the Spanish society, where the instrumental advantages of being proficient in English are still more powerful than being multilingual and multicultural. In fact, Somers and Llinares (2018) showed that CLIL secondary school students in Spain had slightly more instrumental than integrative motivation towards CLIL, although they were both integratively and instrumentally motivated. In other words, in line with Japan, the economic gains and future prospects related to English seem to be an important driving force for the interest in CLIL in Spain as well.

All in all, this volume has represented two different CLIL contexts, which share the view of CLIL as key in improving second language learning and making it more authentic. In spite of the differences in starting age, levels of exposure or type of CLIL (hard or soft), interestingly, both contexts highlight the positive role of collaborative work, interaction and applying models like SFL or CDFs, which see language as inseparable from content and, thus, help understand how content and language can be best taught and learnt in integration. In other words, CLIL is also seen as a window of opportunities to improve language and content pedagogy in general. Another point of synergy is the need to pay attention to initial teacher training, which is also surprisingly scarce in a context like Spain, with more than 20 years of CLIL implementation. Finally, both contexts share the tension between CLIL as a springboard to better economic opportunities (through English) or as an opportunity for multilingual/multicultural/international citizenship. This volume should not only appeal to educators, researchers and policy-makers in the two contexts at hand but also be highly relevant for other CLIL/multilingual education contexts.

Autonomous University of Madrid, Spain   Ana Llinares

References

Ball, P., Kelly, K., & Clegg, J. (2015). *Putting CLIL into Practice*. Oxford, UK: Oxford University Press.

Cenoz, J. (2015). Content-based instruction and Content and Language Integrated Learning: The same or different? *Language, Culture and Curriculum, 28*(1), 8–24.

Dalton-Puffer, C. (2013). A construct of cognitive discourse functions for conceptualising content-language integration in CLIL and multilingual education. *European Journal of Applied Linguistics, 1*(2), 216–253.

Dalton-Puffer, C., Nikula, T., & Smit, U. (2010). Charting policies, premises and research on Content and Language Integrated Learning. In C. Dalton-Puffer, T. Nikula, & U. Smit (Eds.), *Language Use and Language Learning in CLIL Classrooms* (pp. 1–19). Amsterdam: John Benjamins.

Llinares, A. (2015). Integration in CLIL: A proposal to inform research and successful pedagogy. *Language, Culture and Curriculum, 28*(1), 58–73.

Nikula, T., Dafouz, E., Moore, P., & Smit, U. (Eds.). (2016). *Conceptualising Integration in CLIL and Multilingual Education*. Bristol: Multilingual Matters.

Nikula, T., Dalton-Puffer, C., & Llinares, A. (2013). CLIL classroom discourse: Research from Europe. *Journal of Immersion and Content-Based Language Education, 1*(1), 70–100.

Somers, T., & Llinares, A. (2018). Students' motivation for Content and Language Integrated Learning and the role of programme intensity. *International Journal of Bilingual Education and Bilingualism*, 1–16. https://doi.org/10.1080/13670050.2018.1517722

Index[1]

---

[1] Note: Page numbers followed by 'n' refer to notes.

9 783030 274450